太 玄 經

THE ELEMENTAL CHANGES

THE ANCIENT CHINESE COMPANION TO THE *I CHING*

The T'AI HSÜAN CHING
of Master Yang Hsiung

Text and Commentaries
Translated by Michael Nylan

STATE UNIVERSITY OF NEW YORK PRESS

Published by
State University of New York Press, Albany

For information, address State University of New York Press,
State University Plaza, Albany, N.Y. 12246

Production by Cathleen Collins
Marketing by Nancy Farrell

Library of Congress Cataloging in Publication Data

Yang, Hsiung, 53 B.C.–18 A.D.
    [T'ai hsüan ching. English]
    The elemental changes :   The ancient Chinese companion to the *I
ching* / text and commentaries translated by Michael Nylan.
        p.   cm. — (SUNY series in Chinese philosophy and culture)
    Includes index.
    ISBN 0-7914-1628-3 (alk. paper)
    1. Divination—China. 2. Cosmology, Chinese. I. Nylan, Michael.
II. Title. III. Series.
BF1770.C5Y3613   1994
299'.51282—dc20   93-15594
                                                            CIP

10   9   8   7   6   5   4   3   2   1

To the memory of Lily P'eng Ch'en.

Contents

Contents

Introduction

For millennia Chinese readers have seen the *T'ai hsüan ching* (here entitled *The Elemental Changes* and called the *Mystery* by its devotees) as a true guide for those seeking the Way of the sages. Today, in the West, readers will find the *Mystery* an essential tool for understanding the Tao as it operates in the cosmos, in the psyche, or in sacred texts like the *I ching*. Written in 2 B.C., the *Mystery* represents the first grand synthesis of the dominant strands of Chinese thought. As it weaves together elements of Confucianism, Taoism, Yin/yang Five Phases theory, alchemy, and astrology into a systematic, organic whole, all the fundamental components of early Chinese belief appear within its pages.

As a book of divination, the *Mystery* provides a method for weighing alternative courses of action. As a book of philosophy, it conveys a sense of the elemental changes in life. Intricately structured in eighty-one tetragrams (four-line graphs), the *Mystery* accounts for the movements of the sun, moon, and stars, the shifting rhythms of the seasons, the alternations of night and day, and the ebb and flow of cosmic energy—in short, all the dynamic relations of the realms of Heaven, Earth, and Man. It addresses questions of Fate, assessing the degree of control that individuals have over their destinies. It suggests the fabric that binds families, communities, and states together.

As a book of poetry, the *Mystery* unfolds a literary vision of seeming simplicity but surpassing depth. The long poem divides into short sections of rhyming couplets that focus upon a single mundane event or familiar phenomenon. An ancient Chinese proverb says, "If you don't know what is far away, look for it near by." It is through the concrete and the obvious that the *Mystery* approaches the intangible and the abstruse. At the same time, Yang Hsiung drew upon his vast knowledge of archaic texts to construct imagery that is allusive, multilayered, and complex—a fit paradigm for the mysterious Tao threading its way through the ever-changing whole of human and cosmic existence.

1

In the title *T'ai hsüan ching*, the word *t'ai* (pronounced "tie") simply means "great" or "supreme." *Ching* (pronounced "jing" as in "jingle") is an honorific title bestowed on a work to indicate its status as a sacred classic in the Chinese canon. The term *hsüan* (which rhymes with "tan") carries an enormous range of meaning from "black" to "darkness" to "hidden" to "mystery." Its overtones are stillness, isolation, nondifferentiation, and inaccessibility by purely rational processes. In early Chinese thought, such ideas bear no unpleasant connotations. They express that aspect of experience which can be known only by quiet and deep contemplation, or by special illumination. Yang Hsiung uses *hsüan* in his title to indicate the profound state of darkness, silence, ambiguity, and indefiniteness out of which creation springs. In the cosmogonic scheme, it is the undifferentiated state out of which first yin and yang, then the Five Phases, and ultimately the myriad phenomena of the experiential world develop. In Nature as humans perceive it, *hsüan* is the latency out of which individual things are born and out of which events shape themselves. In the sage—that is, the ideal human being, the perfect student of the *Mystery*—*hsüan* is the spiritual inwardness that precedes conscious decision and action, insuring that they will be in harmony with the divine process known as "the Way." *Hsüan*, in other words, signifies the creative aspect of the Tao wherever it is manifested. In Yang's *Mystery*, the ineffable Tao, although without visible form, contains unseen all the myriad forms, patterns, and categories that underlie process and interaction.

In divination, a person seeks association, re-creation, and reintegration with the Tao. That is why the divination begins with a seemingly random event, the turn of the coin, by which the inquirer signals his or her acceptance of Time and change. To welcome, rather than resist, these unsettling aspects of human existence becomes the indispensable first step in the kind of creative thinking needed to respond flexibly and appropriately to ever-changing, complex situations.

SOURCES OF THE *MYSTERY*

The *Mystery* was composed in response to three important philosophical texts: the *Tao te ching* of Lao tzu, the *I ching* book of divination, and the *Analects* of Confucius. From the *Tao te ching*, the *Mystery* draws its characterization of the mysterious, even paradoxical, Tao as the basis for all existence in the cosmic order. From the *I ching*, the *Mystery* borrows the notion of the crucial importance of timing with regard to cosmic operations in general, and to individual fate in particular. From the *Analects* of Confucius, the *Mystery* takes the idea that humanity is sacred only insofar as it creates true community.

The philosophical classic, the *Tao te ching* (often called the *Lao tzu* after its author), begins its description of the divine Tao with the following poem:

> The way that can be told is not the common way.
> The name that can be named is not the common name.
> What has no name is the beginning of Heaven and Earth.
> What has a name is the mother of the myriad creatures.
> Those without desires contemplate its secrets.
> Those who have desires contemplate its periphery.
> These two emerge together, but differ in name.
> Together, they are called "Mystery."
> Mystery of mysteries,
> Gateway to the myriad secrets.

Although there is some disgreement about the exact meaning of this poem, most who take it seriously believe that it presents the mystic Tao in two different aspects: the Tao as the ineffable fountainhead outside of and prior to phenomenal experience and as the immanent process that actualizes things and events from their potentiality. Joining these two mysteries is the never-broken connection between the changes we see and the unchanging ground of all process.

The *Lao tzu* passage finds its echo in the *Mystery*:

> The Mystery of which we speak in hidden places unfolds the myriad
> species, without revealing a form of its own. It fashions the stuff of
> Emptiness and Formlessness, giving birth to the regulations. Tied to the
> gods in Heaven and the spirits on Earth, it fixes the models. It pervades
> and assimilates past and present, originating all categories. It evolves
> and segregates yin and yang, generating the *ch'i*. Now severed, now
> conjoined, [through the interaction of yin and yang, the various aspects
> of] Heaven-and-Earth are fully provided indeed!

Like that of Lao tzu, Yang Hsiung's vision of the Mystery bridges the gap between cosmos and consciousness, between the inexpressible and the concrete.

The *Mystery* draws its emphasis on the importance of timely action from the *I ching*, or *Book of Changes*. An emphasis on the choice of an auspicious time for initiating activity is noticeable in most, if not all divination texts. The *I ching* goes beyond vague generalities, however, to explain timeliness as a learned response to the dynamic, but unitary Tao that engenders the multiplicity of changes. Therefore, the *Changes* text makes a critical distinction between "what is within form" (i.e., existing in the phenomenal world of change) and "what is beyond form" (the eternal patterns embedded in a ultimate state that gives rise to and determines form).

The dynamic basis for change lies in the complementary opposition between two different modes of the "stuff" (*ch'i*) of all things: an activating mode called yang (associated with light, activity, and heat) and a responsive mode called yin (associated with dark, rest, and cold). In operation, each of these two in turn gains strength until it is dominant, at which point it yields to the advance of the other. Since the waxing of one is in exact proportion to the waning of its partner, a perpetual cycle of birth, death, and rebirth can occur without any permanent imbalance. This alternation of the two modes spawns all change. But since both the quality (i.e., the degree of refinement) and the proportion of yin and yang vary in individual things, each thing in the universe comes to possess a unique combination of properties. This accounts for all the variation that we see in the world around us. Therefore, yin and yang *ch'i* as both universal "life-stuff" and dynamic process integrate things by making them subject to common forces and regular phases, while generating endless changes.

The *I ching* specifically tries to locate the "gate of change"—that phase of transition where things and events first come out of formlessness into an intermediate state of bare perceptibility (often identified with the image or symbol). After passing through this gate, things eventually develop concrete form and fully individuated characteristics. There are two distinct benefits to be gained from locating this gate of change. First, only during an early stage can human beings hope to have some degree of control over natural process; once things have "passed the gate" (i.e., become fully individuated), they are less amenable to outside control. Second, by understanding the process of individuation out of primordial chaos, the seeker can hope to recapture the unitary reality that lies behind the world as we know it. In this way, he or she may align the self with the divine aspects of creation in a process called "centering." As the *I ching* says, "To know the incipient stirrings of change: Therein lies the divine!" Two early poems in the *Mystery* point to a similar truth:

> From small defects he can return.
> He can then be taken as model.
> That minor defects can be turned
> Means: He need not go far to set things right.

> Failing in small things,
> Attack them yourself
> At the source.
> Attacking minor failings oneself
> Means: As yet, others do not know of them.

The *I ching* suggests that the wise person, perceiving the patterns "beyond form," is able roughly to predict when trends are about to arise. Then, in a timely fashion, that person may adjust to changing external circumstances. The first hexagram in the *I ching* provides a good example of this in successive images. The dragon (symbol of the perfected human being) is at first hidden. Next it "appears in the field." Then it flies high. Only at the end does it have "cause to repent." The essence of the dragon does not change, but the creature adapts its conduct as it travels through the life-cycle of birth, maturity, and decay. Like the marvelous dragon, the would-be sage modifies her own conduct in anticipation of the cyclical changes wrought by time. In that way, at the very least, physical danger can be avoided; and at best, the wise can "ride on" (i.e., take advantage) of coming trends to secure good fortune. Since the divination responses in the *Mystery* are keyed directly to the calendar, the close relationship between Time and individual fate is more clearly identified in Yang Hsiung's text than in the *I ching*.

Just as the *Mystery* draws upon Lao Tzu's *Tao te ching* for its characterization of the single, undifferentiated primordial chaos, and upon the *I ching* (the *Book of Changes*) for its description of the gate between the formless Tao and the multiplicity of things, so Yang Hsiung's masterwork reflects early Confucian tradition in its consideration of human virtue. Yang Hsiung stresses an important truth found in the Confucian *Analects*: the individual can only realize his innate human potential if he learns how to join with other human beings in creative and harmonious union. For Confucius and his early followers, the proper end of life is a scrupulous attention to human relations, whose success requires the mediating "language" of ritual practice. Harmony can prevail, Yang Hsiung assumes, only when "natural" distinctions of age, gender, and experience are upheld so that conflicts are minimized. At the same time, true union (defined by Yang Hsiung as a "meeting of the minds") can exist only when an individual understands others through a process of "likening to oneself" (*shu*, usually translated as "consideration" or "reciprocity"). Perfect human interaction, then, must come from a delicate balance of hierarchy and equality, just as perfect ritual depends equally upon external forms and an inner commitment to Goodness. Not surprisingly, the exact method of maintaining such balance in human relations, like the Tao itself, is inherently a Way "that cannot be told." In other words, no set rules can be given for it. The would-be sage can only be advised as to which course of action lies in the "right direction."

Yang expected people to consult books of divination to learn about fate. He knew that "ordinary folk" (not necessarily the unlettered) tend to consult such books in hopes of being told which course of action will benefit them most. He also knew that the sophisticated thinker would find much more in the divination process: divination may establish a close identification between the inquirer and the ancient author(s) of the divination text. As the questioner "immerses the self" ever more deeply in the sages, an intuition arises that allows the cryptic words on the page to apply to the particular situation at hand.[1] The quality of this intuition is the only proof that the questioner has fully "internalized the model." Then, as Yang writes, "What is divine is not outside any longer." In discovering the mind of the sages, then, the inquirer reverently engaged in the divination procedure learns to see into the recesses of his or her own heart. The enlightened reader perceives the sacred act of divination as the perfect paradigm for all moral acts, then, for all seek to "reanimate the old" through a complex process of identification and re-creation. In this way, the *Mystery* provides illumination for audiences at all levels of awareness. While the ordinary reader finds in it a series of examples outlining the decided advantages of moral behavior, the truly sympathetic reader engaged in a continuous dialogue with the text gradually uncovers a far more complicated analysis of the influence of personal morality and Time on individual fate.

THE PATH TO GOOD FORTUNE

The *Mystery* posits four major factors affecting the length and quality of a person's life: Virtue, Tools, Position, and Time.

Virtue refers mainly to a roster of traditional virtues, including filial piety, honesty, loyalty, and modesty. In general, Yang believes that inner Goodness conveyed to other human beings through the language of ritual forms is what allows humans to reach their full creative potential: "the Way of humanity is to make contact." Virtue is the single mode of behavior capable of fostering necessary social order while satisfying our most basic human needs to communicate. As a committed follower of Confucius, Yang Hsiung believes that perfect Virtue lies within the grasp of each and every human being, even if lamentably few choose to pursue its course.

By *Tools,* Yang Hsiung means not only material artifacts (like jars, stoves, and carts) but also the arts and institutions that civilize society. This single rubric covers such disparate items as compass and carpenter's square, the Confucian Classics, the ritual system, supportive friendships, and the family, since all are tools for civilization. Thanks to the legacy of the ancient sages, all the proper Tools needed for civilization already exist. However, the individual can take full advantage of these available tools only if he or she has been trained in their proper use. By this training he or she acquires "practical wisdom" (*chih*). Without such training, the individual either ruins good Tools or chooses Tools that are inadequate or inappropriate to the task. Yang Hsiung provides many fine examples to illustrate his point. In one, a benighted soul lugs a boat overland, then rides a cart into water. By analogy, those who employ the teachings of the sages solely to acquire wealth, rank, or long life misapply the Tool designed to further self-cultivation and social harmony.

Position refers to both social rank and the physical location that the individual occupies at the precise moment when action is required. The stock example of good position is that of the ruler, who by his position (regardless of his character) has greater access to resources and opportunities (at least while he remains on the throne). By virtue of his Position, then, he has what we might call a "strategic advantage" over others. Being in the right place at the right time, tradition suggests, is at least partly a matter of luck, since even the great sage-master Confucius failed to secure a government position commensurate with his talents. But Confucius lived in troubled times. In well-ordered states Virtue helps to secure Position.

Time refers not only to the interlocking cycles of yin/yang and the Five Phases, it also covers the individual cycle of each phenomenon in the cosmos. Each unit of Time carries its own constraints and benefits. For example, at the age of ninety, women do not bear children, although they may be singularly honored for their accumulated wisdom and experience. For this reason, we can think of Time as synonymous with present (or timely) "opportunity." Yet Time, insofar as it is produced by Heaven, lies essentially outside human control.

Yang Hsiung's central arguments about the moral life all follow directly from his single statement that Time lies outside human control. Since individual human fate depends upon the interaction among four variables, one of which is Time, fate itself by definition lies largely beyond human control. Virtue, however, lies within the grasp of each and every dedicated individual. Tools and Position also depend, to a certain extent, upon human endeavor. Therefore, we can help to shape (if not absolutely determine) our destiny if we use the time we have to master Virtue, Tools, and Position, the three aspects of human existence that we *can* control.

Given the manifest advantages associated with the path of Goodness, the perceptive person, even if not yet perfectly good, should realize the inherent wisdom of becoming one with the eternal Tao. Since the Tao refuses to draw attention to its unseen cosmic operations, human beings must likewise learn to shun all self-promotion. Once a person is truly moral, he comes to "delight in the Way," which is the goal of the sage and the best reward for a moral life. Only those who approach the Mystery through the three paths of Confucius, Lao tzu, and the *I ching* can appreciate both the fundamental unity of the Way and the multiplicity of its manifestations. Only then are they ready to become full partners in the miraculous triad of Heaven-Earth-Man.

STRUCTURAL COMPARISONS: THE *I CHING* AND THE *MYSTERY*

The structure of the *Mystery* is based on that of the *Changes*. By the first century B.C., the *I ching* consisted of a set of sixty-four texts, each associated with a six-line graph (or "hexagram"), in which component lines could be either solid or broken (signifying yang if solid, yin if broken). Under each hexagram, there are six assigned texts, each of which corresponds to one line of the graphic symbol (hence, the "Line Texts"). The core text of the *Mystery*, like that of its prototype, the *Changes*, presents a series of linear complexes. For the hexagram of the *Changes*, however, the *Mystery* substitutes a four-line tetragram whose component parts read from top to bottom (i.e., in the opposite order from the *Changes*). Also in contrast to the *Changes*, where lines are categorized as either yin (broken) or yang (unbroken), the divination procedure prescribed in Yang's instructions involves three possibilities for each line of the graph: (1) an unbroken line (correlated with Heaven), (2) a line broken once (representing Earth), or (3) a line broken twice (symbolizing Man as one of the triadic realms, living between Heaven and Earth). Four lines, each with three possibilities, mean that there are eighty-one (3^4) possible tetragrams in *Mystery*, rather than the sixty-four (2^6) hexagrams of the *Changes*. Each tetragram begins with a Head text in three parts: a title (which names one aspect of the comprehensive Mystery, such as "Measure" or "Diminishment"), an image that refers to the cycles of yin/yang, and a second image that chronicles the birth, growth, and decay of the myriad things of the universe. To each tetragram is appended nine separate Appraisal texts, which convey a sense of evolution over time, on the model of the Line Texts of the *Changes*.

In addition to the core text of eighty-one Heads with their 729 Appraisals, Yang Hsiung provides ten autocommentaries—on an analogy with the famous "Ten Wings" appended to the *I ching*. Generally speaking, the "Wings" commentaries relate the Line Texts to the moral, cosmological, and epistemological concerns of their authors, who were shaping a new Confucian orthodoxy in the closing centuries B.C. The *Mystery*'s autocommentaries, which reflect the same theoretical interests, can be divided roughly into four kinds of essays: (1) treatises on cosmology; (2) lists of the standard correlations proposed by Yin/yang Five Phases theorists; (3) texts that explain the eighty-one tetragrams by reference to a microcosm, either a single tetragram or a pair of tetragrams; and (4) one text whose sole purpose is to reiterate the Appraisal themes.

There are four theoretical treatises on cosmology: the "Evolution," the "Illumination," the "Representations," and the "Diagram." The long autocommentary entitled "Numbers" lists the various Yin/yang Five Phases associations, so that questioner may deduce more specialized lessons from the generalized message presented by images in the text. Two autocommentaries (the "Polar Oppositions" and the "Interplay of Opposites") treat smaller units of two tetragrams as microcosms of the binary oppositions at work in the larger cosmic Tao. The "Elaboration" commentary discusses Yang's opening tetragram as a microcosm of the whole book. The "Revelation" essay, on the cosmic repercussions of human conduct, acts as summary for the whole *Mystery*.

A final autocommentary, the "Fathomings," is perhaps the most important for the modern reader. The "Fathomings" offers valuable interpretive

Table 1.

Commentary	Correspondent Ten Wings commentary
Hsüan ts'e Fathomings	Hsiang Images
Hsüan ch'ung Polar Oppositions	Hsü kua Sequence of the Hexagrams
Hsüan ts'o Interplay of Opposites	Tsa kua Interplay of Opposites
Hsüan li Evolutions	Hsi tz'u Appended Judgments (also called "Great Commentary")
Hsüan ying Illumination	Hsi tz'u
Hsüan shu Numbers	Shuo kua Discussion of the Trigrams
Hsüan wen Elaboration	Wen yen Elaborated Teachings
Hsüan yi Representations	Hsi tz'u
Hsüan t'u Diagram	Hsi tz'u
Hsüan kao Revelation	Shuo kua

clues to the questioner, for it restates the significance of each Appraisal text. In this edition, following early Chinese usage, the appropriate "Fathomings" text is printed immediately after each related "Appraisal" text, so that their relationship can be seen at a glance.

(For reference, Table 1 lists the ten autcommentaries to the *Mystery* with their corresponding *Changes* "Wings.")

ON THE AUTHOR

Master Yang Hsiung was born in 53 B.C., in Cheng-tu (modern Chengdu), in the province of Szechwan. By his early thirties, he had come to Ch'ang-an (modern Xi'an), then the capital of the Western Han dynasty (206 B.C.–A.D.

8). After winning fame as the foremost poet of his age, Yang Hsiung was appointed poet laureate to the court in 10 B.C.

In middle age, shortly after the death of his beloved son, Yang Hsiung experienced a sense of profound revulsion for his earlier poetic efforts. Condemning court poetry as frivolous, he turned to composing works of philosophy. Following a draft of the *Mystery* in 2 B.C. came two lengthy philosophical poems. In A.D. 12, Yang finished the *Fa yen* (*Model Sayings*), which employs the same dialogue form found in the Confucian *Analects* to evaluate the conflicting drives for immortality, fame, power, and Goodness. When Yang died in A.D. 18, his genius was still being made the butt of cruel jokes by envious contemporaries.

Though one of Yang's detractors had snidely predicted that the *Mystery* text would soon be relegated to the scrap-heap, its pages used "to cover soy-sauce pots," Yang Hsiung's philosophical contributions were recognized by the very next generation of thinkers to succeed him. That generation, then, hailed Yang Hsiung as a Master of Confucian philosophy, and designated his masterwork, the *Mystery*, a classic (*ching*), securing its place in Chinese tradition.

KEY TERMS

The Five Classics of Confucianism

The Five Classics of Confucianism are the *Book of Odes,* the *Documents,* the *Chronicles* (usually called the *Spring and Autumn Annals*), the *Book of Changes,* and the *Rituals.* (A sixth classic, devoted to music, is thought to have been lost or incorporated into one of the ritual texts.) The Classics are "Confucian" in two senses; Confucius (551–479 B.C.) and his followers used some of them as texts for moral instruction, much as the Greek pedagogues once used Homer. Also, tradition ascribed to Confucius the tasks of compiling, editing, and in some few cases composing the works in this repository of wisdom, although modern scholarship disputes the pious legend that Confucius had a hand in forming the collection. The interpretive problem shared by both early disciples and modern scholars alike is that the Five Classics contain extremely heterogeneous material of different subjects, styles, dates, and points of view. The *Odes* is a collection of songs and hymns that reflect everyday life in court and countryside during the period 800–600 B.C. The *Documents* purports to be a collection of archival materials that preserves important edicts and memorials outlining the responsibilities of the ruling elite. The *Chronicles* reads like a court diary for the rulers of the small state of Lu during the years 722–484 B.C. A divination manual eventually converted for use as a philosophical treatise, the *Changes* attempts to reproduce through graphic symbols and attached texts the multiplicity of changing phenomena produced by the single cosmic Tao. And the three separate volumes of ritual texts are said to include some three thousands discrete rules of conduct, as well as a description of ideal government structure.

Confucian orthodoxy presumed that a single message underlay all Five Classics, despite the variety of materials included therein. But it should come as no surprise that scholars have often been frustrated in their attempts to find in this corpus a unified vision of the world. In the Han dynasty (206 B.C.–A.D. 220), an ongoing literary debate focused on inconsistencies in the Five Classics. Nevertheless, during the two millennia from 134 B.C. to A.D. 1905, the Five Classics provided the basic curriculum for training in proper literary styles and served as the core material tested in civil service exams. From China, the influence of this collection eventually expanded into Japan, Korea, and Vietnam, so that it came to occupy for all East Asia a position roughly analogous to that of the Bible in the West.

On Ch'i

The origin of the term is unknown. No Shang or early Chou graphs can be conclusively identified with the concept. The character we now use for *ch'i* shows clouds of stream rising over cooked rice. The graphic form suggests what bubbles or boils over, what fumes, what is agitated; it may also imply some kind of nourishment. In fact, the root meaning of *ch'i* appears to be "vapor" or "breath." Like early Greek, Indian, Latin, and Hebrew philosophy, early Chinese belief presumes a "life breath" that vitalizes as it circulates through bodies or the air. Undifferentiated *ch'i* is the dynamic universal stuff out of which all the disparate things of the cosmos condense (at birth) and into which they dissolve (at death). Like breath, *ch'i* typically operates in rhythmic, floodlike pulses, as it alternates between inhalation (expansion) and exhalation (contraction) in regular cycles. Only bad *ch'i* is blocked or stagnant.

Perhaps the closest English equivalent to *ch'i* is "vitality." As latent energy stored in the Tao, *ch'i* is undifferentiated, but as vital energy operating in the universe, *ch'i* is definable in quality and characteristic in its configurations. By some mysterious process the originally undifferentiated *ch'i* makes for distinctive entities. *Ch'i* can be congealed or compacted in liquid and solid forms. *Ch'i* comes in different grades. The lowest grade of *ch'i* (called "muddy") leads to various malfunctions, including physical deformity, muddled thinking, and excessive desire. The purest refined *ch'i* (the "quintessential" or *ching*) is reserved for two kinds of light-giving entities: the luminous heavenly bodies and the enlightened minds of the sages. Very important, then, is the notion that *ch'i,* as the basic stuff that informs the entire cosmos and binds all humans to the rest of phenomenal existence in Heaven-and-Earth, precludes an absolute dividing line between humans and things. Understandably, the notion of *ch'i* has also worked against the development of the transcendent/immanent dichotomy presumed by many Western thinkers. At the same time, *ch'i* functions as the physical medium that allows sympathetic "mutual response" to take place between categorically related entities. Therefore, *ch'i* theory from earliest times has been preoccupied with the nature and significance of macrocosmic influences on microcosmic processes.

In Master Yang Hsiung's time, the single term *ch'i* signified both the "material stuff" in continual process on Heaven-and-Earth and the underlying dynamism predisposing that stuff to assume specific form, though Sung neo-Confucianists a millennium later were to draw a neater conceptual line between *li* ("internal principle") and *ch'i* ("material stuff"). We must remember that for the early Chinese, human *ch'i,* despite its obvious physicality, had a definite moral dimension as well. In the properly functioning heart/mind, for example, *ch'i* is said to gather at "the spirit abode." What's more, the will to do good is said to be "commander over the *ch'i.*"

In the case of humans, a finite store of *ch'i* endowed at birth is somehow passed down from parents to the child. The birth of a human being, in effect, represents an accumulation of *ch'i.* Over the course of an individual lifespan, the *ch'i* tends to become less active. Physical overexertion may cause it to "block." Tension and stress equally frustrate it. Immoral acts also are said to "abuse the *ch'i*" to the degree that they engender shame, anxiety, and restlessness, for these emotional states produce certain physical symptoms, such as constricted breathing and palpitations of the heart. Human beings, then, have some measure of control over the rate at which their original *ch'i* stagnates or is depleted. Balance in the mental and emotional spheres can be induced by the process dubbed "self-cultivation." Various techniques designed to retain (and ideally augment) the *ch'i*'s activity include both moral and physical "arts": moderation in daily habits, adjustment of posture, meditation as "inward training," habituation to goodness, and a calm acceptance of fate. The philosopher Mencius (?371–?289), for example, tells his disciples simply that "the way to make *ch'i*" is to "nourish it with integrity."

Master Han Fei (d. 233 B.C.) links the conservation of *chi*'s vitality with the acquisition of political power and material wealth. Extending his imagery, I think of *ch'i* as operating like money in the bank: An individual can deposit or withdraw *ch'i* from his fund. What's more, he can inherit a sum or bequeath it to his descendants. Like great reserves of wealth, a great reserve of vital *ch'i* represents the potential to influence others. *Ch'i* thus provides the basis for the charismatic power of the virtuous man. All Confucians insist that each newborn is credited with sufficient *ch'i* to realize the full human potential for sagehood, even though few are wise enough to exercise their innate capacities.

In summation, early Chinese thinkers view all cosmic change in terms of the dynamic process inherent in vital *ch'i*. *Ch'i* is substance, activity, and vitality.

Yin/Yang Five Phases Theory: Correlative Thought

The Chinese cosmological system, which assumed its definite shape in China no later than the third century B.C., envisioned the world in terms of two interlocking systems: yin/yang and the Five Phases (often translated, less accurately, as the Five Agents or the Five Elements). This is sometimes known as correlative thought, or categorical thinking.

According to the theory, there evolved out of primordial chaos one cosmic pattern with dual aspects known as yin and yang. All of phenomenal existence reflects this pattern. The myriad things can be categorized as either male or female, light or dark, day or night, hot or cold, superior or inferior, and so on. This duality is one of the constant norms of the universe, as illustrated by the regular alternation of day and night, of summer and winter. Yin and yang, though opposing, are also complementary in that one can never act independently of the other; the waxing of one invariably entails the waning of the other. Taking an example from nature, the summer solstice is the longest day of the year but, in another sense, it also marks the onset of winter; subsequently, the days grow ever shorter and colder until the winter solstice. The familiar figural representation of yin/yang emphasizes this fluid symbiotic relation. The curvilinear areas of dark and light enfold each other within a perfect circle that knows no beginning or end; the tiny seeds of each are discovered in the swelling contours of its opposite. At the culmination of one, its opposite is born, and on and on, in a constant process of advance and retreat, making and unmaking. In this way, "movement back" becomes "the Way of the Tao." Men of virtue in studying the cosmic patterns infer from this that in victory lies defeat, and in humility, greatness.

Yin/yang may not seem so alien to us, since our language predisposes us to think in terms of positive/negative. But it is far more difficult for us to conceptualize cosmic process in terms of the Five Phases. The list of the Five Phases invariably includes Water, Fire, Wood, Metal, and Earth, though different orders of enumeration are preferred by various classical authorities. The Phases are essentially five different types of process. According to one early authority, "water goes down, fire goes up, wood is pliable," and so on. Each Phase is said to "rule" (i.e. to predominate) a certain period of time (a dynasty, a season, a set of hours), before it gives way to the next phase. This connection with time resulted in conceptual overlays between systems of yin/yang and the Five Phases, as in the following chart (Table 2).

Table 2.

Rising Yang		yields to	Rising Yin	
Wood	Fire	Earth	Metal	Water
Spring	Summer	transition	Autumn	Winter
East	South	Center	West	North
Green	Red	Yellow	White	Black

The Chinese soon set about classifying all known entities into groups of fives, constructing exhaustive lists which they hoped would elicit order from the seeming chaos of the world. Yang Hsiung lists all the major correlations in his autocommentary chapter entitled "Numbers of the *Mystery*." By laws of sympathy and repulsion, things accounted as categorically alike (i.e., correlated with the same Phase) were said to be drawn to one another while things which were categorically different purportedly repelled each other. Again, according to the same theory, careful "inference by analogy from objects of the same kind" (*t'ui lei*) could facilitate the intuitive apprehension of all parts of the ineffable Tao by some form of indirect communication that is simply not possible through logical argument.

The initial difficulty, of course, lay in determining the exact boundaries of each logical category, so that inferences were not mistakenly drawn. Generations of Chinese scholars, first the early Logicians and later the Han scholastics, devoted a great deal of time and energy to this problem. Due to the occasional rift between logic and language, their first task was to establish formal rules of logic by which to discover the defining characteristics of each entity in the universe, so that essential attributes could be clearly distinguished from accidental attributes. For example, the Logicians determined that a horse must have one head, four legs, and the propensity to run, though it need not be red or black. The color of a horse, then, is a nonessential attribute, something that only accidentally subsists in a particular horse, but does not define the species. While it was relatively simple to agree upon fundamental definitions for animals, shapes, and inanimate objects, the true definition of human nature was a thornier problem, as it touched upon a host of problems which stubbornly resisted solution by the logical method:

> What is the proper definition of human nature?
> What is the proper sphere and existential significance of human activity?
> What can humans reasonably hope to accomplish in this life?

In the Han Confucian synthesis, then, the protoscientist's impulse towards categorization and the logician's search for orderly expression joined forces with the ethical concerns of the traditional scholar. Categorical thinking, inherently preoccupied with the relation of macrocosm to microcosm, came to be applied to many areas of inquiry, most significantly (1) portent theory; (2) the rectification of names; and (3) point-by-point analogies between the human body, the body politic, and the universe. We are familiar enough with body analogies; we often talk of "heads of state," for example. Portent theory and the rectification of names, however, may need some explanation for the modern reader.

Early Chinese portent theory assumed that the king as focus for his state exerts an influence for good or for ill upon those entities that are accounted his categorical analogues: Heaven, because it is high; the Big Dipper, as pivot for the sky; the father, as head of the household; and so on. More specifically, evildoing on the part of man—especially the "One Man," the ruler—provokes dislocations in his counterparts in the natural world. The good ruler, far from decrying these omens, welcomes them as reproofs of his erroneous ways sent by a caring Heaven, compelling him to reform.

To successfully apply categorical thought to happenings in the external world, it was incumbent upon the individual not only to locate himself in a parallel scheme of ethical categories (such as "ruler," "mother," "son," or "court advisor") but also to understand the ethical requirements of the assigned role he currently plays. This led many early Chinese thinkers, including Yang Hsiung, to conflate the earlier Confucian call for a "rectification of names" with the naturalists' talk of Five Phases theory. According to Confucius, greater linguistic precision was required for logical thought and effective action:

> If words are not correct, then speech does not conform [with what was intended]. And if speech does not conform with what was intended, then affairs cannot be completed [properly]. . . . Therefore, let a ruler be a ruler and a father be a father.

For early Confucians, a person failing to fulfill his or her proper societal roles was accounted a "human portent" no less significant than a baleful prodigy in the skies above or earthquakes, floods, and droughts on earth.

The early Chinese assumed that the transition from primordial chaos to civilized order represented successive stages of increasing differentiation. In effect, the Chinese argued that the world as they knew it had evolved by a process analogous to human attempts to identify, demarcate, and name significant geographical, political, social, and religious boundaries. From this they concluded that there existed in the primordial Tao a divine basis for the development of the various human orders. Some Han thinkers even argued that humans engaged in the search for intrinsic categories can further or complete the cosmic processes through their continual ordering and reordering of categories. This helps to explain why categorical thinking and correlative thought figure so largely in Chinese philosophical writings.

Self-Cultivation

"Self-cultivation" refers to the arduous process by which the individual intent on virtue fulfills his own innate potential. This process consists in making second nature the traditional virtues (filial piety, good faith, consideration for others, and so on). For early Confucians, including Yang Hsiung, humans at birth have in their original endowment a host of contradictory impulses and desires, including those for food, sex, and community. Just as the artisan works jade to release its true beauty from rough-hewn pieces, any moral deficiency in the person is polished and carved away until an "elegant and accomplished gentleman" emerges. Time and precision are needed for the process, but complete dedication to the Good is the chief requirement if human nature is to be refined. There are many paths leading to self-cultivation, but the most important is emulation of worthy models past and present, followed by the study of the Five Confucian Classics. Once the noble lessons of various masters, living and dead, have been internalized, the perfectly civilized man emerges.

We can think of moral development as taking place in three successive stages, with self-cultivation the culmination. Stage 1 corresponds to the individual's first awareness of the mix of good and evil impulses, moral and physical desires, inherent in human nature at birth. In Stage 2, the good impulses begin to predominate as a result of moral messages received from a variety of sources: the models presented by family members, oral teachings, and so on. Confucius implied that those who reached this stage of development might be accounted "educated":

> A young man's duty is to behave well to his parents at home and to his elders abroad, to be cautious in giving promises and punctual in keeping them, to have kindly feelings toward everyone, but seek the intimacy of the Good. . . . [As to one who acts thus,] others may say of him that he still lacks education, but I for my part should certainly call him an educated man.

But Confucius also advised his disciples to go on to study the "polite arts" (poetry, archery, and music, for example) when they had energy to spare. In stage 3, then, the polite arts become tools by which members of the moral elite can hope to gain an exquisite sensitivity to the moral patterns embodied in ritual conduct. In effect, the acquisition of new skills reconfigures each individual's perception of structures, values, and imperatives. As the philosopher Hsün tzu remarked, "Once the proper arts are mastered, the mind will follow them."

This notion may sound somewhat familiar to us, for it corresponds to our own complex definitions of nobility. Still, the Chinese idea of nobility is not entirely equivalent to our own. The European tradition, embracing a more individualistic vision, tends to emphasize noble conduct as a laudable end in itself, while the early Chinese never tired of reminding us that personal self-cultivation is merely the first step in a process of forming harmonious communities in family, town, state, and empire. As Yang Hsiung writes, "Cultivate oneself so that one can later contact others."[34]

"Center Heart" (Chung Hsin)

The phrase *chung hsin* dates back at least as early as the *Odes* (compiled sixth century B.C. from earlier materials). In the *Odes,* the verb-object unit signifies "what centers the heart"; it compares in meaning with the adjective-noun syntactical unit *hsin chung* ("the center of the heart"), though it is strikingly more emphatic.

Since the truest emotions presumably reside at the deepest core of one's being, by a slight extension *chung hsin* came to be equated with the feelings that "are not put on for others to see," feelings that are completely genuine. After the heart was identified as the seat of the inborn conscience by Mencius, the same expression came to be loosely identified with the evaluating mind. The *Mystery,* for this reason, insists that "inside there is a ruler." At the same time, the characteristic activity of the evaluating mind is to center the self, in the sense of reestablishing an equilibrium free from emotional bias. Only then can the mind's perceptions hope to "hit the mark," and so prompt the moral self unerringly. For Yang Hsiung, the way of the sage lies in paying attention to the center heart, in centering the self, and in "hitting the mark" by the correct identification with Confucian tradition. Thus the *Mystery* employs all these associations for the phrase *chung hsin.*

Ritual

A daughter bows low and eschews the use of her father's personal name. In solemn state ceremonies the emperor periodically offers sacrifices to various protective deities. Imperial ministers wear caps with seven silk pendants but junior officers are allowed only three. The aged and the pious are honored at annual feasts sponsored by the local magistrate. A professional spirit medium on the ridge of the roof calls out "Ho! come back!" to a departing soul, urging it to return to the world of light and life. At the marriage feast, fish are presented to the newly married couple as tokens of fertility. And the rich harmonies of bell and drum exert a powerful effect upon the worlds of Man and nature so that "the common people, the gods, beasts, and birds" happily join in the refrain.

The Han Chinese would consider all these examples of the Confucian ritual system. Though Confucius seems to signify by the term ritual a narrow code of conduct expected of the gentleman, by Han times, the concept embraces many popular religious practices as well. In the Han, ritual meant exhaustive lists of detailed prescriptions governing all aspects of behavior (including physical gestures), as well as an unwritten code of good manners. Sumptuary regulations and taboos, and all manner of ceremonies, formal and informal, at every level of society, were included. At the heart of Han Confucianism lay this body of ritual practice, rather than a logical system. For ritual, as significant pattern, could work to clarify and cohere reality in at least four related ways: First, ritual patterns imitate the character of the unseen sacred Tao, upon which they are modeled. Second, ritual tradition represents the distilled—and therefore, supremely potent—wisdom of the sages throughout history. Third, ritual performance leads the individual to a new understanding about the place of the authentic self in society. Fourth, as if by magic, the correct performance of ritual so pleases observers and co-participants that they devote their best efforts to forging communities, the quintessential human activity. At the heart of effective ritual lies the will to understand others by a process of "likening [others] to oneself," then allowing each his due.

For ritual to prove effective, it was believed, its conventions have to become second nature so that inner disposition combines with outer form in a fitting manner that is understandable to all. This characterization of ritual contrasts sharply with the modern tendency to equate the term with mechanical or repetitive conventions as opposed to the authentic. We can learn much from Han society, where ritual performed a variety of functions: The ritual act could teach even the unlettered the prevailing notions of social hierarchy and intimacy. By "securing men in their position," ritual also habituated men to the social virtues associated with their station. In effect, it became the glue binding the human community together, mitigating base desires and transmuting them into mutual consideration. At the same time, ritual presupposed the possibility for most, if not all, social acts to become emblematic of the divine cosmic order, thereby closing the gap between the sacred and the mundane.

TRANSLATOR'S NOTE

Citations in the text refer to four standard translations currently available in print:

The Analects of Confucius, trans. by Arthur Waley (London, Allen & Unwin, Ltd., 1938; rpt. New York, Vintage House, n.d.).
Lao tzu: Tao te ching, trans. by D. C. Lau (Harmondsworth, Penguin, 1985).
Mencius, trans. by D. C. Lau (Harmondsworth, Penguin, 1984).
The I ching, or Book of Changes, trans. by Richard Wilhelm (Princeton, Princeton University Press, 1967).

Citations to the Wilhelm translation list the relevant page number(s); citations to the other standard translations refer to chapter and verse. The present translation has modified these translations in some cases where it is appropriate.

Method of Divination

The early Chinese used yarrow stalks (*Achillea millefolium*) for divination, probably because the Chinese word for "yarrow" is written with the graph for "old" under the graph meaning "plant." Apparently this visual pun led the Chinese to the idea that the yarrow stalk could serve as an excellent medium to facilitate communication between the living and the ancestors, who collectively represent the sum of wisdom and experience available to all who learn the means to draw on it.

Coins have come to be used as a convenient substitute for yarrow stalks. With coins, two different methods will simulate the original method of divination using yarrow stalks. If the questioner comes to the divination with a clear and untroubled mind, the first method of divination will prove adequate. However, most of us approach the oracle in a troubled state of mind. In that case, the second method of divination is recommended, since the very length of the divination process will help the questioner focus attention on the problem to be solved. That should insure that the proper answer comes from the *Mystery*.

FIRST METHOD

You will need four coins altogether. Put two of them aside, holding them in reserve. Toss the remaining two coins at the same time. If both come up tails, toss them again. Continue tossing both until at least one coin comes up heads. (The probability of two heads will be $^1/_3$; the probability of one, $^2/_3$.) If, of the two coins, only one comes up heads, it is designated as yin. If both coins come up heads, the result is yang. The first trial, then, will result in either yin or yang.

Next, take up the two coins you have held in reserve. Follow the same procedure, tossing both coins until either one or two heads comes up. Having completed the tosses of all four coins, you will have one of three configurations: yang-yang (4 heads), yin-yin (2 heads total), or the mixture yin/yang (3 heads total). Yang-yang will correspond to 9; yin-yin to 7; and yin-yang to 8. The number 9 is equivalent to the twice-broken line of Man; 8, to the divided line of Earth; and 7, to the solid line of Heaven. Now the first line of the tetragram can be drawn.

To arrive at a complete tetragram of four lines, three more applications of the entire procedure are needed. Remember: the tetragram in the *Mystery,* unlike the hexagram in the *Changes,* is constructed *from the top down.* When the questioner has a four-line graph, the graph will direct the user to the appropriate Head text.

SECOND METHOD

Sit facing south. Take thirty-six coins. Set one reverently aside to the left (east) as a way of honoring the cosmic unity we call the Tao. Set three more coins aside to the right (west) as a way of honoring the sacred triad of Heaven-Earth-Man. Toss the remaining thirty-two coins one at a time. Place all those coins that come up heads in one pile in the southwest. Place those coins that come up tails in a second pile to the southeast. From the southwest pile of heads remove the coins by threes until a remainder of one, two, or three is left. Keep the removed coins separate. Next, turn to the southeast pile of tails. Now, from that pile, remove coins by threes until a remainder of one, two, or three is left. Again, keep the removed coins separate.

Next, gather together the remainders from both piles on the table (they will add up to either 2 or 5) directly in front of you. It is now time to reaffirm your desire to reintegrate the Tao in your own individual destiny. Therefore, take the one coin that you have segregated to the left and the three coins initially set aside to the right and add them to the pile directly in front of you. Now move this pile directly away from you to the extreme south.

Next, turn your attention back to the coins in the southwest pile of heads. Once more remove the coins by threes until a remainder of one, two, or three is left. Add these remaining coins to the pile in the extreme south. Then turn your attention to the coins in the southeast pile of tails. Remove the coins in sets of threes until a remainder of one, two, or three is left. Add these remaining coins to the pile in the extreme south.

At this point, the total number of coins left in the combined southwest and southeast piles will add up to 27, 24, or 21. Divide the 27, 24, or 21 by three to honor to sacred triad of Heaven-Earth-Man. The results will be 9 (equivalent to the twice-broken line of Man), 8 (the divided line of Earth), or 7 (the solid line of Heaven). When you have 9, 8, or 7, you have derived the first line (i.e., the top line) of the four-line tetragram.

Gather all thirty-six coins together, and repeat the entire procedure three more times to arrive at a complete tetragram. Remember to begin at the top and build down, though the *Changes* builds from the bottom up.

The point of these instructions becomes clear if we apply them to a specific example. Say that the results of your four trials give you the following lines:

yang/yang (9)
yin/yin (7)
yang/yin (8)
yin/yang (8)

The resultant graphic symbols looks like this:

twice-broken line [corresponding to Man]	— — —
unbroken line [corresponding to Heaven]	———
once-broken line [corresponding to Earth]	—— —
once-broken line [corresponding to Earth]	—— —

To arrive at the Tetragram number from the graphic symbol, the inquirer uses the following formula provided by Yang Hsiung in one of his autocommentaries:

If the bottom line of the four-line graphic symbol is unbroken, count 1. If it is broken once, count 2. If it is broken twice, count 3.

If the second line from the bottom is unbroken, do not add anything. If it is broken once, add 3. If it is broken twice, add 6.

If the third line from the bottom is unbroken, do not add anything. If it is broken once, add 9. If it is broken twice, add 18.

If the top line of the tetragram is unbroken, do not add anything. If it is broken once, add 27. If it is broken twice, add 54.

In the four-line symbol we are using for this example, the bottom line is 2. Working upward, we would add 3, zero, and 54 to arrive at a total of 59. The coherent beauty of Master Yang's mathematical system inspires confidence in the sacred truth of his divination pronouncements.

You are now ready for the final step before reading the appropriate texts of our example, Tetragram 59. Each tetragram is assigned 4 and ¹/₂ days of the calendar year. In this final step, compare the calendar dates assigned to the tetragram arrived at through the divination process (See Table 2) with the date on which the divination is performed (i.e., the current date). If the days assigned to the tetragram are later than the date on which divination is performed in the calendar year, this is inherently auspicious. If the days assigned to the tetragram are earlier than the date on which divination is performed, this is inherently inauspicious. Yang Hsiung tells us why in his autocommentaries: whatever lies in the future can still be changed by the creative applications of precepts outlined in the *Mystery*. There is still time, in other words, to "approach the Mystery" by applying its message to our lives. In our example, Tetragram 59 corresponds to a date in early September. A divination that produced Tetragram 59 in late December would tend to be inauspicious, since whatever lies in the past can no longer be changed. If the date of the divination coincides with the date assigned to the tetragram produced, the *Mystery* offers us a special reminder about the importance of timely response.

Once the questioner has derived a four-line graph by using one of these two methods above, she should turn to the appropriate tetragram indicated by the divination. The nine Appraisals assigned to each tetragram appear to treat a simple proposition about life through a depiction of a specific object or event found in daily life.

The Appraisals at the same time should be seen as a progression; together they map the main stages in the questioner's developing response to the situation faced. Appraisals 1–3 are categorized as Thought (*ssu*), the initial period of inner reflection that precedes outer-directed action. Appraisals 4–6 detail Good Fortune (*fu*), the period of fruitful activity. Appraisals 7–9 talk of Calamity (*huo*), the potential failure that may result from immoral or untimely action. Table 3 should help to clarify the significance of each of the nine Appraisals associated with a single tetragram under its Head text.

Table 3.

Response		Significance of Appraisal
Thought		
1 = interior thought	2 = middle thought	3 = exterior thought
Good Fortune		
4 = small good fortune	5 = medium fortune	6 = great good fortune
Calamity		
7 = nascent calamity	8 = median calamity	9 = maximum calamity

Although there are nine Appraisals associated with each Head text, the questioner should focus on only three, for the Appraisals (unlike the Line texts of the *Changes*) are to be read according to the time of day when the divination is carried out. This emphasizes the necessary interaction between cosmic Time and human choice in the production of an individual fate. If the act of divination is carried out in the morning, Appraisals 1, 5, and 7 of the given tetragram are read and considered; if in the evening, Appraisals 3, 4, and 8; if at the "median" times, Appraisals 2, 6, and 9. (Since Yang Hsiung did not specify these periods of time more definitely, it is impossible to be certain whether he meant by "median" the afternoon or the periods centered around noon and midnight. In any case, these periods may be determined with some latitude by users of the book.)

Three Appraisals are assigned, in short, so that the inquirer can learn the short, middle, and long-term prospects for the situation in question. Let us say, for the sake of example, that the divination that produced Tetragram 59 was carried out in the evening. After reading the so-called Head text, the inquirer should focus on Appraisals 3, 4, and 8. Appraisal 3 envisions the family elders as "gateway" to a host of ancestors beyond the grave. Appraisal 4 implicitly contrasts the ideal of genuine reverence with two clumsy acts of ritual obeisance and sacrifice. Appraisal 8 depicts a flock of small birds fleeing from birds of prey. Here, when the initial flash of insight fails to inform later conduct, disaster ensues.

What if, after serious reflection, none of these images appears to have much to do with the question posed in your divination? By consulting the *Mystery*'s "Numbers" autocommentary, the inquirer will find a range of significant associations for key symbols in the Appraisals texts. In our example (using Tetragram 59), some of the key symbols in Appraisals 3, 4, and 8 are gates, sacrifices, and birds. The "Numbers" autocommentary links sacrifices, for example, with a long list of correlations, including long trips, hunting, robbery, and deafness. By contemplating such correlations, the inquirer expands the scope of the divination, fostering an intuitive, creative reading of the situation. Only then will the *Mystery* text function as a Polestar for an entire universe of explanatory discourse. As an ever greater variety of experience and perception is packed into the seemingly simple words of the text, the individual ideally apprehends the fundamental unity and order of the cosmos. The circle that is the cosmos begins to close, and time is seen rightly as an integral part of the eternal evolving order, rather than as a despotic force whose demands are arbitrary.

Because the creative process requires a journey into the unknown, the *Mystery* insists that the divination procedure should not be used for trivialities, but for only the most serious questions. As the *Mystery* stipulates,

> If the issue is not in doubt, do not divine. If your plan is improper, do
> not divine. If you do not intend to act in accordance with the outcome of
> the divination, it is exactly as if you had not divined.

If the divination procedure is to "succeed" (i.e., establish communion with the cosmic Tao), the individual must demonstrate a genuine will to approach the Mystery and dedicate the self to embodying its attributes. The inquirer's mind must always be correctly oriented (*chen*) to the Right. Essentially, the would-be sage achieves identity with the cosmic Way by single-minded concentration on virtue—a discipline as much spiritual as intellectual. Yang Hsiung promises that

> When one divines with single-minded concentration, the spiritual forces
> bring about changes [that reveal an answer to the inquiry]. When one has
> deliberated [on this response] with single-minded concentration, one's
> plans are appropriate. When one has established what is right with
> single-minded concentration, no one can snatch it away.

However, the sacred efficacy of the divination tool is easily impaired if the user's mind lacks moral integrity (*ch'eng*), since integrity is the single quality that unites the individual with the cosmic order. In consequence, the *Mystery,* like other famous Chinese divination texts, makes no promises about the accuracy of its predictions unless the divination is carried out when the inquirer is in a correct spiritual state. After all, divination represents a true communication between Man and the divine impulses operating in Heaven-and-Earth, which the coins or yarrow stalks only facilitate.

The importance of the will in this process cannot be overestimated for, as Yang Hsiung writes, "Whoever wants to draw near to the Mystery, the Mystery for its part will draw near to him." Having once experienced a revelation of the Tao, one is free to join the rank of the sages, whom Yang Hsiung describes in the following terms:

> Contemplating Heaven, they become Heaven. Contemplating Earth, they become Earth. Contemplating the divine, they become divine. Contemplating Time, they become timely.

The *Mystery,* if properly employed, can lead to an experience of the divine as it operates within the universe and within the self. A "mystery" is something dark in itself that sheds light on what is around it. One Chinese master said of the *Mystery,* "To one who is incapable of examining it, it seems as if it contains nothing. To one who is capable of examining it, there is nothing that it does not contain." The *Mystery,* comprehensive yet profound, enjoins the reader to take up the supreme challenge: Can we learn to adjust our behavior in such a way that we promote, even complete the operation of the cosmic Way?

Translation of the *Mystery*

LIST OF TETRAGRAMS

No. 1. Center / Chung

中 ☰

Dec. 22–Dec. 26 (A.M.)

No. 2. Full Circle / Chou

周 ☷

Dec. 26. (P.M.)–Dec. 30

No. 3. Mired / Hsien

礥 ☷

Dec. 31–Jan. 4 (A.M.)

No. 4. Barrier / Hsien

閑 ☱

Jan. 4 (P.M.)–Jan. 8

No. 5. Keeping Small / Shao

少 ☶

Jan. 9–Jan. 13 (A.M.)

No. 6. Contrariety / Li

戾 ☳

Jan. 13 (P.M.)–Jan. 17

No. 7. Ascent / Shang

上 ☴

Jan. 18–Jan. 22 (A.M.)

No. 8. Opposition / Kan

干 ☴

Jan. 22 (P.M.)–Jan. 26

No. 9. Branching Out / Shu

狩 ☷

Jan. 27–Jan. 31 (A.M.)

No. 10. Defectiveness / Distortion / Hsien

羨 ☰

Jan. 31 (P.M.)–Feb. 4

No. 11. Divergence / Ch'a

差 ☱

Feb. 5–Feb. 9 (A.M.)

No. 12. Youthfulness / T'ung

童 ☷

Feb. 9 (P.M.)–Feb. 13

No. 13. Increase / Tseng

增 ☴

Feb. 14–Feb. 18 (A.M.)

No. 14. Penetration / Jui

銳 ☴

Feb. 18 (P.M.)–Feb. 22

No. 15. Reach / Ta

達 ☴

Feb. 23–Feb. 27 (A.M.)

No. 16. Contact / Chiao

交 ☲

Feb. 27 (P.M.)–Mar. 3

No. 17. Holding Back / Juan

耎 ☲

Mar. 4-Mar. 8 (A.M.)

No. 18. Waiting / Hsi

傒 ☳

Mar. 8 (P.M.)–Mar. 12

No. 19. Following / Ts'ung

從 ☶

Mar. 13–Mar. 17 (A.M.)

No. 20. Advance / Chin

進 ☶

Mar. 17 (P.M.)–Mar. 21

No. 21. Release / Shih

釋 ☶

Mar. 22–Mar. 26 (A.M.)

No. 22. Resistance / Ke

格 ☶

Mar. 26 (P.M.)–Mar. 30

No. 23. Ease / Yi

夷 ☶

Mar. 31–Apr. 4 (A.M.)

No. 24. Joy / Le

樂 ☶

Apr. 4 (P.M.)–Apr. 8

No. 25. Contention / Cheng

爭 ☶

Apr. 9–Apr. 13 (A.M.)

No. 26. Endeavor / Wu

務 ☶

Apr. 13 (P.M.)–Apr 17

No. 27. Duties / Shih

事 ☶

Apr. 18–Apr. 22 (A.M.)

No. 28. Change / Keng

更 ☶

Apr. 22 (P.M.)–Apr. 26

No. 29. Decisiveness / Tuan

斷 ☶

Apr. 27–May 1 (A.M.)

No. 30. Bold Resolution / Yi

毅 ☶

May 1 (P.M.)–May 5

No. 31. Packing / Chuang

裝 ☶

May 6–May 10 (A.M.)

No. 32. Legion / Chung

衆 ☶

May 10 (P.M.)–May 14

No. 33. Closeness / Mi

密 ☶

May 15–May 19 (A.M.)

No. 34. Kinship / Ch'in

親 ☶

May 19 (P.M.)–May 23

No. 35. Gathering / Lien

斂 ☶

May 24–May 28 (A.M.)

No. 36. Strength / Ch'iang

彊 ☶

May 28 (P.M.)–June 1

No. 37. Purity / Ts'ui

睟 ☶

June 2–June 6 (A.M.)

No. 38. Fullness / Sheng

盛 ☶

June 6 (P.M.)–June 10

No. 39. Residence / Chü

居 ☶

June 11–June 15 (A.M.)

No. 40. Law/Model / Fa

法 ☶

June 15 (P.M.)–June 19

No. 41. Response / Ying

應 ☶

June 20–June 24 (A.M.)

No. 42. Going to Meet / Ying

迎 ☶

June 24 (P.M.)–June 28

No. 43. Encounters / Yü

遇 ☶

June 29–July 3 (A.M.)

No. 44. Stove / Tsao

竈 ☶

July 3 (P.M.)–July 7

No. 45. Greatness / Ta

大 ☶

July 8–July 12 (A.M.)

No. 46. Enlargement / K'uo

廓 ䷀

July 12 (P.M.)–July 16

No. 47. Pattern / Wen

文 ䷀

July 17–July 21 (A.M.)

No. 48. Ritual / Li

禮 ䷀

July 21 (P.M.)–July 25

No. 49. Flight / T'ao

逃 ䷀

July 26–July 30 (A.M.)

No. 50. Vastness/Wasting / T'ang

唐 ䷀

July 30 (P.M.)–Aug. 3

No. 51. Constancy / Ch'ang

常 ䷀

Aug. 4–Aug. 8 (A.M.)

No. 52. Measure / Tu

度 ䷀

Aug. 8 (P.M.)–Aug. 12

No. 53. Eternity / Yung

永 ䷀

Aug. 13–Aug 17 (A.M.)

No. 54. Unity / K'un

昆 ䷀

Aug. 17 (P.M.)–Aug. 21

No. 55. Diminishment / Chien

減 ䷀

Aug. 22–Aug. 26 (A.M.)

No. 56. Closed Mouth / Chin

唫 ䷀

Aug. 26 (P.M.)–Aug. 30

No. 57. Guardedness / Shou

守 ䷀

Aug. 31–Sept. 4 (A.M.)

No. 58. Closing In / Hsi

翕 ䷀

Sept. 4 (P.M.)–Sept. 8

No. 59. Massing / Chü

聚 ䷀

Sept. 9–Sept. 13 (A.M.)

No. 60. Accumulation / Chi

積 ䷀

Sept. 13 (P.M.)–Sept. 17

No. 61. Embellishment / Shih

餝 ䷀

Sept. 18–Sept. 22 (A.M.)

No. 62. Doubt / Yi

疑 ䷀

Sept. 22 (P.M.)–Sept. 26

No. 63. Watch / Shih

視 ䷀

Sept. 27–Oct. 1 (A.M.)

No. 64. Sinking / Ch'en

沈 ䷀

Oct. 1 (P.M.)–Oct. 5

No. 65. Inner / Nei

内 ䷀

Oct. 6–Oct. 10 (A.M.)

No. 66. Departure / Ch'ü

去 ䷀

Oct. 10 (P.M.)–Oct. 14

No. 67. Darkening / Hui

晦 ䷀

Oct. 15–Oct. 19 (A.M.)

No. 68. Dimming / Meng

瞢 ䷀

Oct. 19 (P.M.)–Oct. 23

No. 69. Exhaustion / Ch'iung

窮 ䷀

Oct. 24–Oct. 28 (A.M.)

No. 70. Severance / Ke

割 ䷀

Oct. 28 (P.M.)–Nov. 1

No. 71. Stoppage / Chih

止 ䷀

Nov. 2–Nov. 6 (A.M.)

No. 72. Hardness / Chien

堅 ䷀

Nov. 6 (P.M.)–Nov. 10

No. 73. Completion / Ch'eng	No. 76. Aggravation / Chü	No. 79. Difficulties / Nan
成	劇	難
Nov. 11–Nov. 15 (A.M.)	Nov. 24 (P.M.)–Nov. 28	Dec. 8–Dec. 12 (A.M.)
No. 74. Closure / Chih	No. 77. Compliance / Hsün	No. 80. Laboring / Ch'in
閟	馴	勤
Nov. 15 (P.M.)–Nov. 19	Nov. 29–Dec. 3 (A.M.)	Dec. 12 (P.M.)–Dec. 16
No. 75. Failure / Shih	No. 78. On the Verge / Chiang	No. 81. Fostering / Yang
失	將	養
Nov. 20–Nov. 24 (A.M.)	Dec. 3 (P.M.)–Dec. 7	Dec. 17–Dec. 21 (A.M.)

Intercalary Heads

踦 嬴

Dec. 21 (P.M.) and
Leap Year Feb. 29

Chung
No. 1. Center
December 22–December 26 (a.m.)

Correlates with Heaven's Mystery;
Yang, the phase Water; and the I
ching Hexagram no. 61, Good
Faith at Center; the sun enters the
Drawn Ox constellation, 1st degree

HEAD: Yang *ch'i*, unseen, germinates in the Yellow Palace. Good faith in every case resides at the center.

Although this tetragram is correlated with the Water phase, the Yellow Palace, apparently a term for the shadowy underground realm, is associated in the cycle of Five Phases with Earth. Earth symbolizes what is strong and stable; water, what exerts power through ceaseless movement. This tetragram represents the balance point between opposing impulses from which creative activity emanates. The second line, with its reference to "good faith" at "center," alludes to the title of the corresponding *I ching* Hexagram no. 61. By a pun, however, the last sentence of the Head text can also read, "Expansion in every case resides at center." In that case, the Head also refers to the mysterious process by which future events become present phenomena, displacing phenomena into the past and providing the momentum for cyclic processes.

Yang Hsiung summarizes the dominant meaning of the Head entitled Center in the aphorism: "Integrity, when it occupies the inner part, is preserved in the center." The first Head and its Appraisals, read in the light of Yang's own commentaries, lead the reader to recognize integrity as the central virtue precisely because of its all-encompassing nature. Integrity not only establishes the unity of Man with the visible world of Heaven-and-Earth, but it also puts him in touch with the primal Mystery hidden at the cosmic origin (Appraisal 1). The individual may easily fail to attain this integrity if he relies on specious absolutes—the polarization of yin/yang, for example. He will also fail if he is mired in the moral ambiguity (Appraisal 2) that results when an individual disregards his sacred duty to make names (conceptual categories) correspond to realities (Appraisal 8). Because the petty man ignores the Mystery within him, he is obstructed in both his private desires and public ambitions (Appraisals 4, 6). In contrast, the aspirant to sagehood devotedly imitates the universal, unchanging patterns, and so is led to decisions that make his activities effective (Appraisals 3, 5, 7).

The first nine Appraisals of Tetragram 1 refer to a time immediately following the winter solstice, approximately $4^1/_2$ days in length. Within that brief period, yang begins to emerge from the domination of yin. Patterns set in these first nine Appraisals recapitulate the entire annual cycle covered by all eighty-one tetragrams. At the same time, this "nested" cycle of nine

Appraisals stands not only for cosmic process but also for the cycle of human action from initial contemplation to final outcome.

Appraisal 1: Primal oneness encompasses all.
It is profound.

Fathoming 1: Primal oneness, all-encompassing
Means: This is the correct state of contemplation.

"Primal oneness" is a set phrase describing the initial cosmic state of nondifferentiation prior to the appearance of forms. In moral psychology, this is analogous to the initial centering of human inwardness that leads to conscious, responsible action. The term "all-encompassing" is used to describe that power of the Way acting through the sage which enables him to see beyond differentiation, so that he can "merge the myriad things and make them one." "Profound," of course, is synonymous with "mystery" and signifies the creative, yet indeterminate origins of Heaven and Earth, as well as the psychic center within which the sage finds the germs of his future actions.

In the Fathoming, the "correct state" describes the faithful adherence of the sage to the Way of the ancients. By virtue of this orientation, the sage participates in the integrity of the Tao.

Appraisal 2: Spiritual forces war in darkness,
Deploying yin and yang for battle.

Fathoming 2: Spirits warring in the dark
Mean: There good and evil are juxtaposed.

The earliest texts in China depict the cosmos in terms of binary phases symbolized by yellow (the light of day) and black (the dark). This helps us to understand the *Changes* imagery, "Dragons battle in the wilds, their blood black and yellow" (W, 395). This oddly anthropomorphic sentiment reflects a strong imbalance in the forces of yin and yang *ch'i*, associated with dark and light respectively. In the Center tetragram we see solid lines occupying every position in the graphic symbol. Yin and yang, challenging each other at this point in the cycle, are in extreme imbalance. As the forces for good and evil confront one another in the darkness of primal origin, of midwinter, and of the hidden recesses of the heart and mind, the separation of polarities out of the indeterminate Mystery is bound to be premature and inauspicious.

Appraisal 3: The dragon emerges at the center,
Its head and tail stretch forth,
Fit for use.

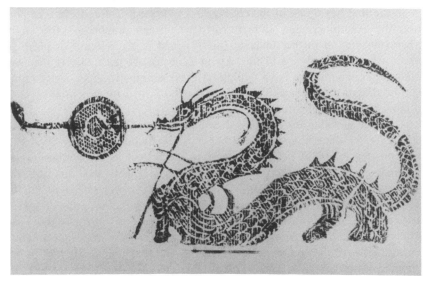

Figure 1. A dragon with a ceremonial jade pi *circlet.*

Fathoming 3: Dragon emerging at center
Means: It reveals its creativity.

Few Chinese images are as rich in association as that of the dragon. The first Chinese dictionary describes the dragon as "chief among the scaly creatures. It can be dark or brilliant, small or large, short or long. At the vernal equinox, it ascends to the sky; at the autumnal equinox, it hides in the deeps." The dragon is protean and timely; it marks two critical points in the annual cycle by its ascent and descent. Thus it is associated with virile yang *ch'i*, with the East and spring, and with the growth of the myriad things on earth.

In the first hexagram of the *Changes*, a sequence of dragon images portrays the exemplary man in reclusion (the unseen dragon in Line 1), in office (the dragon in the fields in Line 2), and at the summit of political power (the dragon flying in the sky in Line 5). At least this is the way orthodox commentators have explained these enigmatic texts. They argue that the dragon symbolizes the noble man who fulfills his potential by conforming to the present situation.

The dragon found in Appraisal 3, when compared with these pictures of the dragon in the *Changes*, is neither entirely hidden nor fully· apparent. With the separation of nascent yang from the primal darkness, the dragon has emerged from the waters barely enough to reveal its head and tail. Yet even before the dragon appears in its full glory, it is recognized as "fit for use." Why? Another Chinese classic defines "usefulness" in terms of adherence to ritual. Through ritual, Yang's exemplar keeps his integrity (his "exact center"), despite the ups and downs of fortune. Yang draws an obvious contrast between the dragon in this Appraisal and the "hidden dragon" in the Changes, which is said to be "of no use" (W, 7).

In cosmogony, Appraisal 3 of this tetragram corresponds to a third stage following primal chaos (stage 1) and the separation of yin and yang *ch'i* (stage 2). Here, the first emergence of forms (stage 3) also foreshadows the proliferation of phenomena in the world as we know it (stage 4).

> Appraisal 4: Lowliness, emptiness, nothingness, compliance —
> Despite a full portion of nature and Decree,
> He is still blocked.

> Fathoming 4: Blocked into the lowly and empty
> Means: He cannot receive in full.

Yang's own "Elaboration" autocommentary tells us how to interpret this difficult Appraisal. The passage reads:

> The petty man cannot find it in his heart to embrace emptiness. . . .
> Although he is debased, he cannot be approached. Although he is empty,
> he cannot be filled. When doing without would be appropriate, he is
> capable of possessing. When compliance would be appropriate, he is
> capable of striking out in an untried direction. Therefore, "despite a full
> portion of nature and Decree," he lacks [the humility] to avoid [inappropriate action]. That is why "he is blocked."

This Appraisal, of course, presents a contrast to the previous Appraisal. Here the *Mystery* shows, not the timeliness of the noble man, but the small man's inability to adapt to time and circumstances. His moves, in consequence, are "blocked."

Appraisal 5: When the sun is centered in the sky,
  Use this time to become a master.

Fathoming 5: Sun centered in the sky,
  Means: The noble man merits his place.

The center represents the mediating balance point between oppositions. In this central Appraisal among the nine, we find a triple coincidence of auspicious "centrality": the name of the Head; the correlation of the Appraisal with Earth, representing the center in the cycle of the Five Phases; and the image of the sun at high noon. Since the good man, like the sun, uses his light to illumine the entire realm, the imagery employed here suggests a cosmic analogue of ideal government, which seeks to mediate fairly between opposing needs and opinions.

Appraisal 6: The moon losing its fullness
  Is not as good as new light in the west.

Fathoming 6: The waning moon
  Means: Ignoble men are the first to retreat.

Like the previous text, this Appraisal is concerned with light (and therefore, enlightenment). However, by the sixth Appraisal, we have passed the point of balance already. For this reason, as Yang writes, "We contemplate waxing and waning." The degree of remaining light is measured through moon imagery, because even-numbered Appraisals in this tetragram are aligned with yin. Since a bright light would correspond to Appraisal 5, we see the moon moving into its third quarter, no longer quite round. Yang himself defines the moral significance of this image as, "The small man in the fullness of his powers brings needless ruin upon himself."

Neither the sun nor the moon actually rises in the west. But by roughly the second or third night of each lunar month, the moon has fallen far enough behind the sun to be reborn as the first crescent, just above the western horizon at sunset when the sky is dark enough to make it visible. This configuration is "better" in the sense that the first crescent signals a half-cycle of uninterrupted growth. Half a month later we have only a half-cycle of decay.

Appraisal 7: Fully matured:
  Fire stores what nurtures.
  Water embraces rectitude.

Fathoming 7: Embracing the fully ripe
  Means: This is the rule for employing subjects.

If the first Head is a microcosm of the eighty-one Heads correlated with the round of the seasons, this Appraisal, speaking of maturity and storage, represents autumn as the balance between Fire and Water, the cosmic phases correlated with summer and winter respectively. To the early Chinese, Fire suggests the nourishing and fructifying activity associated with summer and, by extension, the use of rewards. Water implies purification, rectitude, and reliance upon punishment for correction. Both rewards and punishments are needed if order is to be established.

> Appraisal 8: When yellow is not yellow,
> It overturns the norms of autumn.

> Fathoming 8: That the yellow is not yellow
> Means: He lacks the virtue of the center.

The point of this Appraisal is spelled out in Yang's "Elaboration" autocommentary: "The petty man fails to model himself on the center." That is, he fails to model himself on the Supreme Mystery, on the proper yin/yang relation, and on the Mean in human relations. When the nine Appraisals are grouped by threes, Appraisal 8 becomes the center of the final triad. Its centrality associates it with the phase Earth and the color yellow, both emblems of balance between yin and yang. But in the sequence of nine Appraisals, it is correlated with Wood (which signifies yang's increase), with the color green, and with night. As these two sets of correspondences are at war, what should be yellow in this autumnal Appraisal is not.

> Appraisal 9: When souls are overturned,
> Ch'i and form revert.

> Fathoming 9: Overturned souls reverting
> Mean: Time is not overcome.

Death is the separation of *ch'i* and form. What had emerged from undifferentiated *ch'i* now returns to it as the soul breaks down into its constituent parts, which eventually revert to the shadowy bournes of the spirit world. The cycle within Tetragram 1 has now come full circle. At the same time, the image of death prefigures the evolution of successive tetragrams from Tetragram 1, as unbroken lines give way to broken ones. Note also that the correlation of Appraisal 9 with the end of the life cycle is so strong that it apparently negates the general rule by which odd-numbered Appraisals in odd-numbered tetragrams are connected with auspicious yang *ch'i*.

Within the larger cycle of nine Appraisals, smaller cycles operate. The Appraisals abound, for example, in correlates to yin/yang and in echoes of the *Book of Changes*. Images of darkness and the moon (associated with

Water in Appraisals 1 and 6), of the dragon (Wood, 3) of centering (Earth, 5), and of Fire (Appraisal 7) reflect the significance of each Appraisal in the cosmogonic succession of the Five Phases. Each group of three Appraisals within the nine is also a world in miniature that reflects a continuum from incipience to maturation to decline, each with its assigned place in the ninefold scheme. The first three Appraisals, representing the phase of commencement, move from the dark language of nondifferentiation (Appraisal 1) through the polarization of yin/yang within the darkness (Appraisal 2) to the precisely and positively described image of the emergent dragon (Appraisal 3). An image of decline is not yet germane. The second set of three Appraisals, concerned with culmination, begins with a temporally vague, abstract picture of responsiveness and obstruction (Appraisal 4), moves through the noonday emblem on which the larger series of nine Appraisals pivots (Appraisal 5), and ends with a concrete lunar image of decline played off against renewal (Appraisal 6). The final triplet is entirely related to decline; there is no room for new growth. At first, ripeness and nurture are still pertinent to what is nevertheless static (Appraisal 7). The central Appraisal 8 provides a picture of decay in which ambiguity gives way to inversion. The last situation (Appraisal 9) dramatically evokes dissolution. Although this dissolution ends the larger cycle, various associations imply the beginning of a new one.

The Appraisals work, then, like a Chinese puzzle. Not only do we find cycle fitted within cycle, but one clue after another ties the series of Appraisals to every microcosm important to Man. The Fathoming of the first Appraisal asserts Man's participation, alongside that of Heaven and Earth, in the cosmic Tao. There are also several reminders of the ages of Man. The first Appraisal recalls the womb; the third, the young adult's entry into an official career; the fifth, culminating accomplishment; the seventh, mature stability; and the ninth, natural death in old age. The symbology of administration appears in the apposition of punishment and virtue, and in allusions to attributes of the exemplary ruler (in the fifth position) and to his vassals (surrounding him in the fourth and sixth positions correlated with yin *ch'i*).

Chou

No. 2. Full Circle
December 26 (p.m.)–December 30

Correlates with Heaven's Mystery;
Yin; *the phase Fire; and the* I
ching *Hexagram no. 24, Return;*
the sun enters the Drawn Ox
constellation, 5th degree

HEAD: Yang *ch'i*: comes full circle. Divine, it returns to the beginning. Things go on to become their kinds.

Just as the center supplemented by a circumference describes a complete form, Tetragram 2 expands upon the themes of the first tetragram. Not surprisingly, the Tao as the totality of Being is drawn as a circle, because all the myriad things seamlessly derive from and return to it. Also, the circle, as in Greek philosophy, is regarded as the embodiment of perfection in that nothing can be added to it. Seeking the Tao is seen as a circular process insofar as any series of correct propositions made about it ultimately leads back to the same solution. In addition, the circle often signifies equitable treatment since all points on the circumference of a circle stand equidistant from its center.

Despite these auspicious associations, the notion of coming full circle also spells danger. If there is incomplete closure at the critical juncture where one circuit ends and another begins, the necessary cyclical patterns of the cosmos will be interrupted or derailed. This tetragram corresponds to the time right after the winter solstice, a period when special caution is required because of the fragile nature of nascent yang overwhelmed by yin. At this time, as the *Book of Changes* states,

> The kings of antiquity closed the passes at the time of the solstice.
> Merchants and strangers did not go about, and the ruler did not travel
> through the provinces (W, 505).

The Head text shows yang *ch'i* in circuit. While there is no clear demarcation of boundaries with regard to yang's action (a state reminiscent of primal chaos), mysteriously yang *ch'i* prompts each of the myriad things to begin the process of individuation. Humans participate in this process, of course, and can even help to guide it, when they conform with the natural processes as exemplified by ritual. Ritual, like the Tao, establishes the balance between community and individuation, thereby insuring the continuity of all life cycles.

> Appraisal 1: Returning to the heart of Heaven,
>   In what virtue does he err?
>   The Way is blocked.

> Fathoming 1: That the heart's return is blocked
>   Means: The center does not reciprocate.

The *Changes* hexagram Return claims to embody the mind of Heaven and Earth in urging a turn away from error (W, 505). Clearly, no task is more fundamental to the individual than intelligent conformity with the patterns of Heaven, but the real difficulty lies in ascertaining Heaven's will. The *Mystery* presumes that it can be discerned in three ways: (1) in decisions made by the individual who has "self-knowledge" (W, 504); (2) in the patterns of civilization transmitted by sage-rulers; and (3) in the expressed will of the people, on the assumption that "Heaven sees as the people see." The ultimate test of a particular course of action is whether it promotes the virtue of reciprocity. In most cases, evil at the center (i.e., in the heart/mind) stems from the individual's failure to accord to others the same consideration he himself demands. As a result, community is broken.

> Appraisal 2: A pivot set directly center
> Sweeps full circle, not in angles.

> Fathoming 2: A pivot placed directly center
> Means: Set your thoughts on the Mean.

In the heavens, the Dipper functions as a pivot around which the various starry configurations revolve. Aligned with the *axis mundi*, it insures the seamless alternation of night and day. The charismatic virtue of the superior individual is like the "pivot" or "pole" of All-under-Heaven insofar as it steadies and defines the movement of all lesser aspects of creation; according to Confucius, "He who rules by moral force is like the Polestar, which remains in its place while all the lesser stars do homage to it." Moral force is built by adherence to the Mean.

> Appraisal 3: What I give out and what I take in
> Are chief factors in good luck or ill.

> Fathoming 3: What comes from me, what enters me
> Means: We cannot but take care.

One commentator assumes that these lines refer to the effect of external situations ("what enters me") upon motivation ("what proceeds from me"). But the compound "exit/enter" usually refers to effort or funds expended, compared with the return received (in either the material or spiritual sense). This, then, is the Chinese version of "As a man sows, so shall he reap."

> Appraisal 4: He is girded by hook and belt,
> On which is tied a ring of jade.

> Fathoming 4: Girded by hook and belt
> Means: He shows self-constraint.

Circling comes up no fewer than four times in this brief passage: once as a belt encircling the waist, once as a belt looping around its hook, again in the jade ring, and finally, as a man returning to his best self by accepting necessary constraints.

Jade is highly prized by the Chinese for many reasons. First, human nature is likened to jade in discussions about self-cultivation, since the inherent beauty of both is only enhanced through polishing. In particular, jade ornaments suspended from the belt symbolize the well-regulated life, for their rhythmic tinkling sounds remind the wearer to measure his steps. Second, jade exemplifies the constancy of the superior man because jade is cool to the touch in any weather. Third, since Neolithic times jade has been thought to have unique life-giving properties. For this reason, jade was used for many funeral goods, including the famous jade suits excavated at Man-ch'eng. The jade ring specifically stands for the eternal nature of the life process. All of these associations come neatly into play here, as ritual conduct strengthens the good person in conformity with the eternal Tao.

> Appraisal 5: He dwells at the center of the land,
>   And there sets his golden carriage.
>   Heaven's warnings increase.

> Fathoming 5: The dwelling, the gold, the increased warnings
>   Mean: The petty man does not triumph.

Since Position 5 corresponds to the Son of Heaven, it is likely that a member of the ruling elite is at fault. There are other indications as well. The dwelling is located in the center of the country, that is, the capital. The carriage is synonymous with administration or management since it conveys persons in a style and comfort far above that accorded common men. But here, as in the *Changes*, the rider is "troubled by the golden carriage" (W, 184). Despite his elevated position, those in power are petty individuals whose fondness for luxury and display eventually comes back to haunt them.

> Appraisal 6: Good faith encircles his integrity
>   And penetrates to Heaven above.

> Fathoming 6: Good faith sustaining his integrity
>   Means: It communicates on high.

Heaven appears to be a reliable model, since the seasons alternate in a set pattern without fail and the fixed stars do not depart from their courses. As the good person develops her capacity for good faith and integrity on Heaven's model, Heaven is sure to reward her. "Good faith" refers to social relations, to keeping promises and fulfilling one's duties within the family and in office. The term "integrity," by contrast, usually embraces realms (both inner and cosmic) beyond social relations. It refers to that perfect conformity of the inner mind of Man with Heaven's will, which insures the integration of the human spirit with the cosmic realm. As one commentator to the *Mystery* put it, "Good faith is the Way of Man; . . . integrity, the Way of Heaven."

>Appraisal 7: Greatly immoral men, seeing their peers,
>   Return to cover.

>Fathoming 7: Great excess, seeing friends,
>   Means: Association is impossible.

In the *Mystery*, Goodness by definition produces community. While Fathoming 6 attests to the power of virtue to forge strong ties between Heaven and Man, here we find its opposite, vice, destroying any possibility of true friendship.

>Appraisal 8: Turning out faults from the self,
>   Misfortunes will not be great.

>Fathoming 8: Ridding himself of faults
>   Means: Calamity will not strike.

An initial failure, if truly repented, need not end in disaster. It is as if the good person "returns from no great distance" (W, 98–99).

>Appraisal 9: As he returns to ruin,
>   Some reject him and walk away.

>Fathoming 9: Returning to ruin
>   Means: His way is at an end.

Once again, the final Appraisal of this tetragram pictures complete dissolution. He who persists in evil finds that his associates desert him in droves.

Hsien
No. 3. Mired
December 31–January 4 (a.m.)

Correlates with Heaven's Mystery; Yang; the phase Wood; and the I ching Hexagram no. 3, Difficulty at the Beginning; the sun enters the Woman constellation, 2d degree

HEAD: Yang *ch'i* stirs slightly. Although stirred, it is mired in yin. "Mired" means: the difficulty attending the birth of things.

This tetragram explores the difficulty experienced at the start of any initiative. The character used for the title of this tetragram is made up of two components: the first means "stone," the second means "firm" or "solid." Clearly, movement is sluggish and weighted down at the beginning. The Head text, then, pictures yang *ch'i* like a child struggling to escape the dark hold of the cosmic womb. (Note the tetragram's correlation with the Woman constellation.)

The early Appraisals depict the disadvantages of inadequate development, which prevents clean extraction (of the hair from the head, of the worthy man from obscurity, of the world from its benighted customs). Therefore, the wise person awaits the proper time in the cycle so that trends are favorable, just as yang *ch'i* patiently waits until spring before manifesting itself.

Appraisals 5–7 skillfully use the metaphor of the journey to suggest the course of potential development from moral ignorance to full appreciation of the Tao. Like the traveler, the person set upon self-cultivation meets various obstacles and detours, but so long as she never swerves from the right path, she will eventually arrive safely at her destination.

> Appraisal 1: Yellow, pure, and immersed,
> Its boundaries are unseen,
> Stored away, pent-up in the Springs.

> Fathoming 1: Yellow, pure, and hidden,
> Means: Transformations take place in secret.

Since this tetragram corresponds to the second week after the winter solstice, yang *ch'i* remains confined to the watery netherworld of the Yellow Springs. Although its outline is unclear, its potency is signified by the adjectives "yellow" and "pure." Yang *ch'i* is yellow in two senses: it is essential to future development and nourishing like yellow Earth. It is pure in that it is both unadulterated and concentrated. Here it is poised to feed the roots of future action.

Position 1 is aligned with the Beginning of Thought, as well as with the Water phase. The watery depths symbolize the mind whose unseen operations precede action and may also suggest the suasive potential of the superior man.

> Appraisal 2: The yellow is impure,
> Bent at the root.

> Fathoming 2: That yellow is impure
> Means: What is central and suitable is lost.

One commentator attributes stunted development to the antagonistic relation between the agent Fire (assigned to Appraisal 2) and the agent Wood (assigned to the full tetragram and to Appraisal 3). But a second commentator is much closer to the mark: if the base is weak in any way, future growth is sure to be stunted. Our attention is drawn to the petty person whose weak conscience impedes his moral growth.

Appraisal 3: The rosy babe is lifted up
So that original purity
Will have its rightful end.

Fathoming 3: Newborn child, lifted and lifted,
Means: Father and mother attend to it.

The baby is naked, alerting us to Man's original likeness to the beasts. The newborn babe is rosy, with red signifying virile yang *ch'i,* and by extension, perfect potentiality, auspicious coherence, and the concentration of one's vital powers. However, the *Mystery* is careful to distinguish the potential for virtue from its eventual actualization in the noble man. Just as the naked child in its highly vulnerable state requires the support of both loving parents, so does full moral development depend upon careful training received from moral superiors.

Appraisal 4: Pulling out our faults
Is not possible by force.

Fathoming 4: Uprooting our faults
Means: This goes beyond physical strength.

The Appraisal's correlation with the phase Metal may account for its references to physical force. In any case, by referring to the difficulties of reform, these lines balance Yang's reference to original purity in Appraisal 3. The *Mystery* is careful not to promote an idealistic vision of Man in the state of nature. At birth the inborn nature is a mixture of good and evil; only those who weed out their evil tendencies can become truly good. But the application of physical force alone cannot produce improvement. The best way to correct bad habits is to follow the example of moral superiors, either in person or through the study of their teachings.

Appraisal 5: To pull the chariot
Out of mountain or abyss
Is a task befitting the great man.

Fathoming 5: Pulling chariots from mountain and abyss
Means: This is the strength of the highly placed.

As in the West, the abyss symbolizes desperate situations; the mountain, dangerous heights to be scaled. The term "great man" can refer either to a giant or to the worthy individual fit to govern others. If the chariot represents the ruler's political role, then we know that it takes a great man to rescue the stranded state from its precarious position. If the chariot signifies the pursuit of pleasure or power, it takes a great man to save us from our own obsessions.

> Appraisal 6: Leading his chariot,
>   He enters the ruins.

> Fathoming 6: Leading his chariot into the ruins
>   Means: He has not found the Way.

Here the chariot, so recently plucked from disaster, is driven in a direction that leads to ultimate destruction.

> Appraisal 7: Escaping perilous terrain,
>   He ascends the hill.
>   There he is brought an ox.

> Fathoming 7: To escape the defile, go up the hill
>   Means: There is no substitute for timely aid.

Although the carriage has not yet reached the safe ground of the level plain, imminent danger has been avoided by escaping to the hills. This move has two advantages: first, from the top of the hill, the driver can see the Way more clearly; second, the top of the hill is more defensible. Since someone brings an ox, suitable help from outside has been secured.

> Appraisal 8: Failing to pull the chariot free,
>   He cracks his ribs.

> Fathoming 8: Failing to pull the chariot free
>   Means: He harms his own person.

The petty individual who fails to measure his own strength will not be able to pluck himself from danger. Instead, his misguided efforts will simply compound his problems.

> Appraisal 9: High mountains tower.
>   Below, the river breaks in waves.
>   That man has an oar-drawn ferry.
>   With him, you can cross.

> Fathoming 9: High mountains, great rivers
>   Mean: Without the boat, impossible to cross.

Position 9 always represents an extreme situation. Here danger lies in alternative courses of action. Extreme caution must be exercised if death (physical or moral) is to be avoided. The wise individual keeps on the alert for outside help in order to survive.

Hsien
No. 4. Barrier
January 4 (p.m.)–January 8

Correlates with Heaven's Mystery;
Yin; *the phase Metal; and the* I
ching *Hexagram no. 3, Difficulty at
the Beginning; the sun enters the
Woman constellation, 6th degree;
the Dipper points NNE*

HEAD: Yang *ch'i* is barred by yin. Mired fast, all things are barred.

As the Winter Solstice solar period gives way to the Lesser Cold with Appraisal 4 of this tetragram, the power of yin *ch'i* grows progressively weaker. Still, yin is sufficiently strong to impede the emergence of yang, at least for now. Since the growth of the myriad things depends upon yang ch'i, they feel its predicament keenly.

Like Tetragram 3, this tetragram is correlated with the *Changes* hexagram entitled Difficulty Starting. All three texts illustrate human reliance upon a variety of aids, including tools and specialists, in building the civilized order. However, the *Changes* focuses upon carting, wooing, and hunting while Yang Hsiung considers many different barriers in his examination of human response to the outside world.

The single character in the tetragram title refers either to a crossbar at an entrance or to a horse corral. From these root meanings there evolved more abstract ideas of "defense," "obstacle," and "interception." Barriers are good if they prevent outside influences from harming the inner core. Habituation to goodness, for example, obstructs evil impulses. However, certain barriers have a negative impact since they prevent good influences from penetrating.

> Appraisal 1: Snakes lurk in the mud.
> All are female. None are male.
> None finally receive the gift.

> Fathoming 1: The snake in the mud is no hidden dragon.
> Meaning: The ruler on the dragon throne is no ruler.

Position 1 appropriately mentions the low ground of mud and mire. The hidden dragon in the *Changes* tradition signifies the superior man (especially the ruler) prior to action (W, 379). Because the dragon is thought to bring the rain needed by the agricultural community, it brings to mind many forms of grace that rain down from on high, including the ruler's benefactions to his subjects. Here, however, there is only a poor imitation of the dragon: a snake coiled in the mud. Although the dragon and snake were commonly classified as members of a single genus, crucial differences were said to exist. First, the dragon can by magic transform itself into various forms but the snake only molts its skin in a superficial change. Second, the dragon mates normally (and indeed, symbolizes fertility), but the snake is assumed to be hermaphroditic, and therefore self-generating; this violation of the "constant norm" of sexual reproduction is regarded as highly inauspicious. Third, the dragon brings fructifying rain while the snake merely brings harm to Man by its bite. Where the dragon is welcomed, the snake is feared.

This baleful imagery is intensified by the image of a snake that waits in mud. A contrasting *Changes* passage labels a similar wait auspicious (W, 26), but here, apparently, the snake lies in wait to ambush its victims. This is quite different from the "hidden" dragon (where "hidden" connotes "marvelous" and "mysterious"). Evil is compounded when all males are absent, because this points to an excess of yin *ch'i*. Since social bonds and self-interest are both secured when gifts are exchanged, the statement "None receive the gift" suggests profound social disorder. No wonder that "the ruler is no ruler."

> Appraisal 2: Barring his storehouse door,
> He secures the precious treasure.

> Fathoming 2: Locking his storehouse
> Means: The center heart is a deep, deep pool.

The innermost self (the center heart) is like a deep pool in at least five respects. First, its source, the Tao, is inexhaustible. Second, its source is unseen. Third, water reflects well only if it is clean and still; by analogy, the mind works well only if it is unmoved and clean as a result of daily self-examination. Fourth, water's flow is gradual and cumulative, like progress in self-cultivation. Finally, water's purity insures that, in the words of the *Lao tzu*, "it excels in benefiting without contending" (ch. 8).

Man's integrity is his precious treasure. To retain his integrity, the superior man bent on moral reform must keep himself from destructive outside influences, such as bad companions. Since Position 2 represents low position, the subject of these lines must patiently prepare for some future employment of his talents.

> Appraisal 3: The gate is shut but not bolted.
> The golden key is thrown away.

> Fathoming 3: Shut but not locked
> Means: Thieves steal through the gate.

In contrast to Appraisal 2, the individual refuses to take proper precautions to safeguard herself from harm. As the *Changes* states, "To be careless in guarding things only tempts thieves to steal" (W, 308).

Appraisal 4: Lifting our yoke or collar-bar,
    The gain is slight. It benefits
    Minor expeditions only.

Fathoming 4: Unharnessed from our yoke or collar-bar
    Means: The good man values keeping his word.

The yoke and collar-bar secure draft animals to a vehicle: the yoke is used for larger vehicles; the collar-bar, for smaller ones. But what have they to do with "keeping one's word"? Apparently, Yang Hsiung alludes to *Analects* 2/22:

> I do not see what use a man can be put to if his word cannot be trusted.
> How can a wagon be made to go if it has no yoke, or a carriage if it has
> no collar-bar?

Just as restraint must be applied before the draft animal can be harnessed for use, the individual must be willing to abide by his word before he can be of service to himself or others. Admittedly, a cart may be pulled for a short distance without yoke or collar-bar, but this soon proves a great (and unsustainable) waste of effort. By analogy, when an individual refuses to be bound by his promises, he is like a dangerous animal run amok. In the long run, only good faith can sustain societal relations.

Appraisal 5: Mired in evil, barred from good,
    He tries to pry us from our villainy
    Which is hard as rock, though not a rock.
    Danger.

Fathoming 5: Stuck and blocked, like a stone,
    Means: The enemy holds firm.

Position 5 is aligned with Earth; stones are the hardest parts of earth. Here Position 5 is aligned with inauspicious yin, thought to be relatively weak. For that reason, the individual feels his strength is insufficient to root out evil influences (in himself or others). The "enemy" within, offering stubborn resistance to reform, remains firmly in control, like a rock.

Appraisal 6: Safe behind his yellow walls,
    He rests on golden mats.

Fathoming 6: Yellow walls for barricades
    Mean: He is fortified by virtue.

Physical and spiritual barriers here work together. The wise man bars the entrance to his house with high earthen walls. He then rests safely inside, perhaps meditating or reading in the texts of the ancients. The Confucian Classics advise Man to

> Embrace virtue, your safeguard.
> Let your heirs be your fortress.

The cultivation of virtue promotes the safety of one's home and person. Virtue provides the best "refuge" and most "peaceful abode."

Appraisal 7: Staggering,
He is barred from his sleeping mat,
While someone sleeps securely in his house.

Fathoming 7: The gates are locked to those who stumble.
Meaning: Evil lies at home.

The individual, unable to conduct himself properly, finds that ease and security are denied him. Sooner or later, someone else will usurp his place at home.

Appraisal 8: The Red Stench spreads to the passes.
If the Great King does not bar its way,
Contagion will sweep the kingdom
And drive his house.

Fathoming 8: The Red Stench reaching the passes
Means: He fears it may enter the palace.

Here barriers are clearly needed. Only by blocking the passes can the inner regions of China be protected from plague raging at the borders. A plague, of course, is an apt metaphor for evil persons or evil influences. The great ruler bars their entrance to the heart/mind.

Appraisal 9: Barring gates on an empty house,
He keeps it utterly empty.

Fathoming 9: Barring the gates to keep it empty
Means: Finally, nothing can fill it.

The term "emptiness" has both good and bad connotations. Emptiness is praiseworthy when it refers to the virtues of humility and receptivity, as in Appraisal 4 of Tetragram 1. Here, however, emptiness portends a poverty of mind and spirit. Perhaps the individual has waited too long to bar the gate (i.e., to apply self-restraint), so that none of his "precious treasure" (his integrity) remains. A person devoid of all principle has nothing left to defend.

Shao
No. 5. Keeping Small
January 9–January 13 (a.m.)

Correlates with Heaven's Mystery;
Yang; the phase Earth; and the I
ching Hexagram no. 15, Modesty;
the sun enters the Woman constel-
lation, 11th degree

HEAD: Yang *ch'i*, rippling, spreads through the deep pool. Things like ripplets in its wake can keep themselves very small.

This tetragram describes the initial stirrings of the myriad things within the earth in the wake of yang *ch'i's* first generative pulses. In terms of language this is one of the simplest tetragrams since it borrows almost all of its images directly from the correspondent *Changes* hexagram entitled Modesty. The "Judgment" to that hexagram says:

> It is the Way of Heaven to empty the full and increase the modest. It is the Way of Earth to cramp the full and augment the modest. The ghosts and spirits harm the full and enrich the modest. It is the Way of Man to abhor fullness and approve the modest (W, 462).

In similar language, the *Lao tzu* identifies the Tao with "Pressing down what is high / Lifting up what is low" (ch. 77). Humility or self-deprecation is one of the primary virtues expected of the superior man. Whether in humble circumstances or in power, the superior man continually downplays his own achievements for practical as well as moral benefit. In cosmic terms, "reversal is the [characteristic] movement of the Tao," so that each thing falls prey to swift decline immediately after reaching full development. Only "holding fast to the submissive" (keeping away from the apex of florescence) can forestall inexorable devolution within the cyclic process. In purely human terms, excessive brilliance of any type is best hidden, lest it awaken the jealousy and enmity of fellow men or the gods. In Yang Hsiung's day, as in our own, great wealth often prompted swaggering arrogance, while poverty could provoke cadging or a kind of perverse pride. As the *Mystery* demonstrates, humility proves far more useful in all stations of life.

Appraisal 1: In darkness, he makes himself small,
Becoming consummately humble.

Fathoming 1: In obscurity, self-deprecation
Means: He conceals his humility.

The gentleman in obscure circumstances does not congratulate himself on his own modesty; as the *Changes* says, he is "modest about his modesty"

(W, 65). Nor does he seek to have others recognize him. Confucius said in the *Analects,*

> The good man does not grieve that others do not recognize his merits. His only anxiety is lest he fail to recognize theirs. . . . He does not care about not being in office. All he cares about is having the qualities that entitle him to office. He does not mind failing to get recognition. He is too busy doing the things that entitle him to recognition (1/16; 4/14).

Appraisal 2: Self-deprecation, less than complete,
   He clutches his cares to his breast.

Fathoming 2: Self-deprecation failing
   Means: His humility is imperfect.

The petty man occasionally assumes a mask of humility but in reality he is far too self-absorbed to be self-forgetful. Not surprisingly, he tends to ignore the needs of others. The danger is that, once offended, those around him may turn against him.

Appraisal 3: Modestly done, his actions succeed.
   He is a model for masters of men.

Fathoming 3: To be modest in success
   Means: His humility is tried and true.

Position 3 marks the transition from thought to action. So long as the individual remains a model of humility, he can successfully marshal the talents of those around him. The good man demonstrates his modesty in at least three ways. First, he complies with the teachings of the ancients, acknowledging their superiority. Second, he downplays his own attainments while acknowledging his dependence upon friends and advisors. Third, he effects all major changes in minor increments to avoid unduly alarming others. By the gradual accumulation of such modest accomplishments the good man transforms the circle of his acquaintances until they unconsciously imitate his attitude of compliance in their dealings with one another.

Appraisal 4: Taking penury as poverty,
   Some recklessly relieve it.

Fathoming 4: Preoccupied with poverty
   Means: He cannot maintain the Right.

Position 4 among the Appraisals corresponds to "lower rank." It is also correlated with the phase Metal. Perhaps this accounts for its concern with wealth. In any case, the subject of these lines has made two distinct errors:

not only is he self-absorbed; he has also chosen profit over righteousness. In contrast, the superior man who "delights in Heaven and recognizes his fate" overcomes ordinary anxieties about low position and poverty. Confucius said:

> If any means of escaping poverty presented itself, so long as it did not involve doing wrong, I would adopt it, even if my employment were only that of the gentleman who holds the whip. But so long as it is a question of illegitimate means, I shall continue to pursue what I love more, [righteousness]. . . . A gentleman takes as much trouble to discover what is right as lesser men take to discover what will pay.

Appraisal 5: What the Earth empties
Runs down to valley streams.

Fathoming 5: The Earth emptying itself
Means: Men regard this as sagely.

Position 5 corresponds to auspicious Day. Earth, aligned with center, becomes the gathering place for the hundred streams, just as the noble man draws loyal adherents to him "by virtue of his emptiness" (W, 542). Paradoxically, Earth's willingness to allow itself to be eroded is a major factor in its endurance. The good man, then, does well to imitate Earth's condescension.

Appraisal 6: The small cup is filled to the brim.
Once full, it later topples.

Fathoming 6: The small cup kept full
Means: How can it be worth filling?

This Appraisal corresponds to a point just after the apex of development. Recognizing the cyclical nature of fortune, the wise man in prosperity keeps himself especially humble, ever "mindful of danger when at peace" (W, 341). Here, however, a vessel of small capacity (symbolizing a man of slight worth) has been filled to the brim (i.e., given a job that strains his abilities). When position does not correspond with ability, disaster soon results. As the *Lao tzu* advises,

> Rather than fill it to the brim . . .
> Better to have stopped in time (ch. 9).

Appraisal 7: To examine oneself when poor
Helps make riches appear.

Fathoming 7: Self-assessment in poverty
Means: This invites great wealth.

When a gentleman meets with bad luck, he searches his own conscience before blaming others. As Confucius says, "Attack the evil within oneself. . . . And if you have made a mistake, do not be afraid of admitting the fact and amending your ways." Such humility on the part of the noble man means other men delight in his company, which, in turn, helps to ease his circumstances. What's more, his mental balance allows him to take maximum advantage of future opportunities.

> Appraisal 8: Though poor, he pretends he is not
> And so no one offers him relief.

> Fathoming 8: Poor but not poor
> Means: How can this be worthy of respect?

The individual, although impoverished (in either moral or financial terms), refuses to acknowledge his poverty. In consequence, he is likely to offend others with his braggadocio, pretense, and arrogance. The wiser person works within the constraints of his present societal role.

> Appraisal 9: Fine rain and drizzle
> Moisten parched gullies.
> In three days, the valley is soaked.

> Fathoming 9: Fine rain soaking the valley
> Means: Humility works quietly.

Fine rain signifies the humanizing influences of the sage. In the sacred imagery of ancient China, the valley symbolizes whatever nourishes and is good. The use of the magic "completion number," three, hints at the miracle involved in producing a truly civilized man through repeated small acts of goodness. With steady application, even the smallest improvements can lead to major accomplishments, just as Aesop suggested in his fable of the tortoise and hare.

Correlates with Heaven's Mystery; Yin; *the phase Water; and the* I ching *Hexagram no. 38, Opposition; the sun enters the Barrens constellation, 4th degree*

Li

No. 6. Contrariety
January 13 (p.m.)–January 17

HEAD: Yang *ch'i*, newly hatched, is very small. Things, each diverging and separating, find their proper categories.

Although yang *ch'i* is still weak, under its impetus the growth of the myriad things continues, with specific forms separating from undifferentiated chaos. The phrase "finding their proper categories" alludes to the *Changes,* which describes the evolution of all phenomena from their single origin in the Tao by reference to symbolic number magic and divination procedure (W, 313). Two fundamental questions remain: How do the disparate things relate to one another? And how do the myriad things relate to the mysterious One that spawned them? Correlative thinking (see Key Terms, page 10) offered one possible answer to the first question, an answer subsequently employed in China by masters of the various arts of medicine, astrology, and omen prediction. The relation of the One to the many (as essence to existence, the unknowable to the knowable) was a question largely left to poets and philosophers.

To suggest the interconnectedness of disparate parts of the triadic realms of Heaven-Earth-Man, Yang Hsiung gives familiar examples in this tetragram of mutually dependent, but distinctly different entities: back and belly, husband and wife, physical mind and judgment, life and death, substance and application. In each case he concludes that "separate ways" contribute to creative action and civilizing order. In combination, separate functions with distinctive properties ultimately add to a sum greater than their individual parts. Distinction, then, is undeniably useful.

At the same time, any act of individuation threatens desirable unity. This potential for discord prompted the sages to invent ritual, which acknowledges and mediates certain inequalities while teaching people to prefer consistency, cohesiveness, and stability over more disruptive alternatives.

> Appraisal 1: Once the Void is deflected,
> The heart inclines as well.

> Fathoming 1: The Void astray and the heart turned
> Mean: He embraces what is not upright.

In Yang's schema, Position 1 corresponds to the Beginning of Thought. Appropriately, Yang begins this Appraisal with a reference to the Void, an epithet for the innermost heart/mind. In the sage, this core is characterized by a perfect receptivity to shifting events processed by the five senses. However, as soon as the mind turns aside from the true Way, thoughts and emotions grow confused. (This is symbolized by the deviation from the strictly vertical or "upright" line.) Inappropriate persons or courses of actions are unduly favored. Based on false assumptions, the individual's judgment will be skewed. When the heart "has inclinations" (in other words, is prejudiced), the heart "inclines" toward a faulty course. Misfortune will quickly follow.

Appraisal 2: Straightening his belly,
    Pulling up his back,
    He achieves proper alignment.

Fathoming 2: A straightened belly
    Means: The center heart is settled.

Appraisal 2, early in the tetragram, appropriately refers to preliminary training of the heart/mind. All commentators agree that the belly refers to what is inside (and so relatively prior and important); the back, to what is outside. The message of this Appraisal is: rectify the inner self and good behavior will follow. Once good behavior becomes a habit, inner resolve is so strengthened that upright acts become progressively easier to perform. And so "the center heart is settled." Only then is the gentleman ready to transform others. Inner orientation supports outer reforms of ever greater scope.

Appraisal 3: He twists his belly
    In straightening his back.

Fathoming 3: A twisted belly and straight back
    Mean: Inner and outer are at war.

Here is a person who appears to be "straight" (presumably because he self-righteously pretends to virtue), but is crooked at the core. Position 3 marks the initial transition from Thought to Action. When thought and behavior fail to correspond, harmful tensions arise within the individual. Also, a censorious attitude toward others is likely to elicit their anger. Ultimately, such deceit and artifice end in misfortune.

Appraisal 4: Husband and wife take separate ways.
    It is the family they mean to preserve.

Fathoming 4: The separate ways of husband and wife
    Mean: Each has a separate sphere.

As in the two preceding Appraisals, inner contrasts with outer. Moving from the site of the physical body, the theme now shifts to the fundamental distinctions underlying a civilized order. In early China, the husband tended to public matters outside the home while the wife managed the domestic sphere inside the family residence. Through this division of responsibilities the family maintained harmony and material welfare. The fruitful nature of male/female complementarity is one theme found in the *Changes*:

> Heaven and Earth are opposites, but their action is concerted. Man and Woman are opposites, but their wills conjoin. The myriad things stand in opposition to one another, but their actions are by type (W, 575).

Figure 2. In Chinese mythology, the ssu *and* hsi *are the female and male respectively of a one-horned species. The* hsi *shown here looks very much like the female* ssu *of popular depictions, except that the* ssu *is less hairy.*

Appraisal 5: South by east, he aims at the *ssu*,
 But north by west, his arrow flies.

Fathoming 5: Taking aim at the *ssu* in the southeast
 Means: He does not hit its head.

In ancient Chinese myth, the *ssu* is a marvelous beast (occasionally identified as a rhinoceros or wild ox) easily recognized by the luminescent horn atop its head that renders it visible even at night, or while it bathes in deep waters. A rare creature, the *ssu* is considered the sport of kings, and so it appears in Appraisal 5, which is assigned to the Son of Heaven. Southeast China is a land of marshes and river valleys—the natural habitat for such a water creature.

The arrow aimed southeast flies in the opposite direction. Since the shining horn of the *ssu* makes it an easy target, even for the untrained archer, this mistake is particularly egregious. Clearly, the individual has lost all sense of moral direction. Intending to go one way, he ends up going the opposite. If he desires to improve his aim, numerous guides, including the Five Classics and the suasive example of good men, exist to instruct him. They are designed to help him straighten his thoughts like an arrow.

The text also works as oblique criticism of the leader's failure to appoint the right men to the appropriate rank. Tradition says that the *ssu*'s horn points unerringly to the good, so kings looking for true merit among various candidates for office purportedly had drinking cups made from horns of the *ssu*. The merits of applicants for official posts in ancient times were assessed during ceremonial archery contests. Both the *ssu* and archery, then, are associated with bureaucratic selection.

> Appraisal 6: Level, line, compass, and square:
> Different are their applications.

> Fathoming 6: Level, line, compass, and square
> Mean: Divergent are their ways.

All "great instruments" were invented by the ancients to help lesser men "first rule the self and then rule others." Although all are needed in construction, by no means do all these tools work in the same way. Level and line determine straight horizontal and vertical lines, while compass and square are needed to form perfect circles and corners. By analogy, each of the social institutions, including ritual, has its own function in building civilization, with each addressing a separate human need. It is characteristic of the sage-ruler that he always knows which tool to apply to the specific problem at hand.

> Appraisal 7: An unwomanly woman
> Has only herself in mind.
> She overturns her husband's plans.

> Fathoming 7: An unwomanly woman
> Means: This is utterly abominable.

As yin elements, women should be receptive rather than active, and concerned with domestic, rather than public events. In contrast with that ideal, the "unwomanly woman" described here not only has a mind of her own, she even works to undermine her partner's endeavors.

> Appraisal 8: Killing and birthing, each opposes the other.
> Harmony and centrality he takes as his way.

> Fathoming 8: Killing and birthing, mutually opposed,
> Mean: Centrality defines the limits.

Killing and birthing seem unalterably opposed, although Heaven participates in both. By analogy, those in authority act both to punish (through the

Figure 3. Fu Hsi and Nu Wa (deities associated with yang and yin ch'i *respectively) holding the compass and square as symbols of divine order.*

penal code, for example) and to foster (by means of rewards). Each activity is somehow rooted in a single standard derived from cosmic norms. He who acts through ritual to maintain the Mean will know how to apply the norms in individual cases.

> Appraisal 9: The Green Sprite's wife lives apart
> > In a separate house of the sky.
> > If the pattern is broken,
> > The harvest's bounty fails.

> Fathoming 9: The female mate of Green Sprite
> > Means: Failure brings defeat.

Green Sprite (Ts'ang-ling) is the planet Jupiter (allied with Wood and east), whose mate is the planet Venus (allied with Metal and west). In the normal course of events, these planets do not reside in the same lunar lodge. The Chinese say that this is because their natures are fundamentally opposed: Metal harms Wood. (It is, after all, the metal ax that chops wood.) Therefore, a conjunction of the two planets portends evil, especially to vegetation. The conjunction of Venus and Jupiter also presages civil war or usurpation.

Shang
No. 7. Ascent
January 18–January 22 (a.m.)

Correlates with Heaven's Mystery;
Yang; *the phase Fire; and the* I
ching *Hexagram no. 46, Pushing
Upward; the sun enters the Barrens
constellation, 8th degree*

HEAD: Yang *ch'i* engenders things in a place below. All things shoot through the earth, climbing to a higher place.

This tetragram is aligned with Fire, whose nature is to rise up; hence, the image of ascent. In the natural world of Heaven-and-Earth, it is now the Lesser Cold solar period, when the shoots of living things first appear, like arrow tips pushing their way through the soil.

In the parallel realm of Man, individuals also begin their upward drive. This ascent may be auspicious or inauspicious, depending on the motive force that propels it. On the one hand, this tetragram decries the misplaced "pushiness" typical of the ambitious individual intent upon securing worldly position or fame at any price. On the other hand, the individual is to be applauded for assiduous attempts at self-cultivation that aim at a higher Good. The correspondent hexagram (W, 179) attributes upward advance to perseverance:

> The image of pushing upward.
> Thus the noble man by compliant virtue
> Heaps up the small things
> To achieve the high and great.

Appraisal 1: Elevating his pure mind,
　　　　He blunts its bit-like sharpness.

Fathoming 1: Elevating his pure mind
　　　　Means: He is harmonious and happy.

In Position 1, which corresponds to the Beginning of Thought, Yang Hsiung refers to the heart/mind's potential for Goodness. In learning to ignore the desire for fame and power, the individual develops his best instincts. As a result, a stable happiness born of compliance with the cosmic norms replaces the sharpness associated with the clever, restless mind. As the *Lao tzu* (ch. 56) advises:

> Blunt the sharpness....
> Let your wheels move only along old ruts.

Ambitions that are too sharp may well harm the individual, just as the sharp tips of weapons can prick and sting.

> Appraisal 2: Rising without roots,
> > His thoughts climb to Heaven.
> > Falling back, he's stuck in the abyss.

> Fathoming 2: Rising without roots
> > Means: He is unable to sustain himself.

Man's roots lie in the inborn Goodness that constitutes part of his original nature. These roots must be cultivated carefully if they are to survive the stress and strain of daily life. Man's roots are also to be found in family and friends. Here an individual aspires to—or worse—accepts high position without thought of self-cultivation or of the needs of those in his circle. The climb to Heaven is proverbially "beyond one's reach." This advance is particularly unjustified so the person, sooner or later, is likely to topple into the "abyss" (destruction or obscurity).

> Appraisal 3: Flying out from dark ravines,
> > He soars to lush trees,
> > Drawn by their rare fruit.

> Fathoming 3: Out from ravines, up to the trees,
> > Means: He knows the way to go.

Appraisal 3 refers to an ancient Chinese poem (Ode 165), in which a bird, disturbed by the sound of the woodcutter's blows, flies to safety in a stand of tall trees. To any reader trained in the Chinese classics, the image of a bird coming out of a dark ravine would also bring to mind the idea of enlightenment following study of the Classics. With the word for "timber" a pun for "talent," we see that a man's very security depends upon developing his inborn capacities by following the hallowed precepts of the ancients.

> Appraisal 4: Reaching ever higher, though unaligned,
> > Like a plant, full-flowered without roots,
> > He wraps himself in empty fame.

> Fathoming 4: Reaching higher though unaligned
> > Means: He rises recklessly.

Position 4 corresponds to official rank and the turn to action. As the individual considers possible career moves, he should remember that correct alignment with the Way (i.e., the determined pursuit of Goodness) is the root of all merit and glory. Although the unscrupulous individual may prosper temporarily, danger lies ahead. Lacking the proper foundation in virtue, his advance soon falters, just as flowers plucked from their roots inevitably wilt. Once his unstable character is unmasked, the disapprobation of others will only hasten his downfall.

> Appraisal 5: Rising from the deep marsh, a crane calls,
> Stepping up to Heaven, unashamed.

> Fathoming 5: A calling crane, unashamed,
> Means: He has what it takes at center.

In China, the crane is associated with longevity. It is also known to fly high. In ancient Chinese imagery, then, the figure of the calling crane symbolizes the superior man whose reputation is well known. This crane is unashamed, despite the bold daring of its initiative, because its pure heart deserves such swift advance. Its call is heard in all directions since virtue compels men to follow its suasive example.

> Appraisal 6: He ascends to the hall,
> His upper and lower garments reversed.
> Men at court are dismayed.

> Fathoming 6: Ascending to the hall in disarray
> Means: The great masses are lost.

An ancient Chinese poem (Ode 100) uses clothes in disarray as a stock metaphor to criticize disorder at court. In his haste, an official confuses jacket and skirt, top and bottom. This reversal indicates subversion of the proper hierarchical relations. Those who witness this breach in ritual recognize it as an evil omen. Not surprisingly, they try to distance themselves from the perpetrator. The fault is especially grave since it occurs in the hall, the public room where the community gathers for the celebration of solemn rites.

> Appraisal 7: He climbs the rickety tower.
> Some prop it with wood.

> Fathoming 7: Ascending the tower with the aid of props
> Means: His supports hold firm.

The tower points not only to high position but also to the elevated mind, as in the famous T'ang poem:

> As daylight fades along the hills
> The Yellow River joins the sea
> To gaze unto infinity
> Go mount another storey still.

Figure 4. A Han dynasty watchtower.

Despite such good associations, high towers are inherently dangerous structures. Like the Tower of Babel, they can represent overweening ambition. "In great winds" (turbulent eras), they are vulnerable to collapse. The wise individual, recognizing the risks involved in his ascent, makes sure that he is provided with sturdy wooden props to forestall possible disaster. The prop, of course, may be knowledge of the Classics, the support of excellent friends, or the auspicious *ch'i* accruing from virtuous action. The opposite case is presented below.

> Appraisal 8: Scaling the dangerous heights,
> Someone axes the ladder beneath him.

> Fathoming 8: Scaling the peak, his ladder axed,
> Means: He loses his knights and commonfolk.

Once the individual rises to high position, he must maintain the support of those below. Otherwise, his subordinates will work to undercut him.

> Appraisal 9: Perched on a rotten stump,
> First he faces ruin, then finds a firmer base.

> Fathoming 9: Perched on a stump, then on a firmer base,
> Means: He later secures good men.

The arrogant individual finally repents of his earlier errors, humbling himself in order to win the support of worthy followers.

Correlates with Heaven's Mystery; Yin; the phase Wood; and the I ching Hexagram no. 46, Pushing Upward; the sun enters the Roof constellation, 3d degree

Kan
No. 8. Opposition
January 22 (p.m.)–January 26

HEAD: Yang [*ch'i*] in its support of things seems to be drilling into solid matter. Thrusting forward like a spear, there is penetration.

The title of this tetragram means "to hit or knock against," "to offend," "to seek," and "to violate." The clearly negative associations are employed by Yang in the unlucky, odd-numbered Appraisals, but the tetragram also celebrates some positive aspects of opposition, especially loyal opposition by advisors, which in some sense mimics the bracing effect of yang *ch'i* upon the myriad living things. The calendar indicates the Great Cold, a fifteen-day solar period as harsh as a remonstrant's stern admonition. Still, thanks to yang *ch'i*, the myriad things will eventually break out of their hard shells to meet the light of day. Similarly, the individual is beholden to loyal critics for the liberation of his thoughts. The fledgling moral conscience, then, depends for its survival on the expert "drilling" of a wiser individual. Inexpert advice, however, only further weakens the conscience, just as clumsy probing with a drill damages the base material.

> Appraisal 1: He cranks the drill,
>> Boring toward internal cracks.
>> Danger.

> Fathoming 1: The bit boring inside
>> Means: Turning the bit is wrong.

The drill is a metaphor for critical speech that gets through to the listener. The intelligent advisor, like the good artisan, carefully calculates his moves. Just as the drill tip must be applied with extreme care, words of loyal remonstrance must be aimed cautiously, lest further damage result. This is especially true if there are weak spots in the base material (the conscience).

> Appraisal 2: At the first small signs,
>> Oppose and rectify.
>> Only apply the model decrees.

> Fathoming 2: At first small signs, to oppose and rectify
>> Means: He greatly protests small errors.

The most effective remonstrance is leveled at incipient evil for the simple reason that mistakes are far easier to correct before they have become habits. Early reproofs help one who is basically good "deal with the thing while it is still nothing." All parties then join in applying the model decrees transmitted from the sages.

> Appraisal 3: He gags his mouth with wood,
>> And bolts tight the lock.
>> This is counter to propriety.

> Fathoming 3: Gagged and bolted tightly
>> Means: "Seeking salary is perverse."

The "gag" and "bolt" are slang for the rhetorical devices practiced by unscrupulous advisors. In the gag, the speaker prevents his opponents from answering his arguments; in the bolt, the speaker cleverly takes advantage of his listener's prejudices to construct a seemingly airtight argument. In this way, petty men secure their own fortunes while tricking the unwary listener into embarking on disastrous policies. Such scheming overturns the injunction of the *Odes* to "seek good fortune by no evil ways."

> Appraisal 4: Critical words cut to the bone
> Because the time is right.

> Fathoming 4: The time for sharp criticism
> Means: To be forthright is his way.

The "bone" signifies the innermost being. If an admonition "cuts to the bone," it means that it is both incisive and taken to heart, because the advisor has chosen the right time to level his criticism.

> Appraisal 5: He stupidly seeks a heap of sweets.
> Someone hands him an unfired tile.

> Fathoming 5: The striving of an ignorant man
> Means: The gift is not good.

The heap symbolizes what is high and great; sweets, whatever is most desirable. If an individual hankers for high position despite his own lack of qualifications, he is likely to meet with misfortune and insult, instead of support. The potsherd symbolizes the stern necessity to perform menial tasks. The subject, reaching too soon for a life of luxury and ease, experiences a life of poverty and hard labor.

> Appraisal 6: The trunk reaches to heaven.
> With propriety comes prosperity.

> Fathoming 6: Properly aligned for the trunk's reach
> Means: Thus is prosperity preserved.

In a yin tetragram, Position 6 represents the apex of the cycle; hence, the image of a tree piercing the sky. The tree trunk symbolizes the staunch friend and advisor. If the tree trunk is tall enough to reach to Heaven, it is surely grand enough to support any endeavor on Earth. (Contrast Appraisal 2, Tetragram 7.)

> Appraisal 7: When shouldered spears are many,
> Confrontations follow.

> Fathoming 7: Shouldered spears in great numbers
> Mean: They do not give way.

Spears symbolize a quarrelsome nature. Soldiers tend to meet misfortune because of their warlike proclivities. The final Fathoming line (literally, "not admitted [on?] the Way") is intentionally ambiguous. It can either mean that the bellicose ignore the decided advantages of the deferential Confucian Way, or that the troops do not yield their ground. Both situations prove equally dangerous.

> Appraisal 8: Fiery tongues inflame the city.
> He sprays water from a jar.

> Fathoming 8: Fiery tongues and water spewed
> Mean: Thus the noble man exorcises evil.

"Fiery tongues" refer to slanderers, whose rumors can fire up an entire city. The significance of the sprayed water is less clear. It probably refers to the exorcist's spitting holy water in all directions from a jar, an apt symbol for the purifying words of the good man. It is also possible that the gentleman spits to express his complete disdain for the slanderer. Since the contents of a single jar of water are hardly enough to quench a raging fire, clearly we witness a miraculously efficacious force.

> Appraisal 9: Reaching for the floating clouds,
> He forthwith falls from Heaven.

> Fathoming 9: Reaching for the floating clouds
> Means: Only then does Heaven let him fall.

In a passage in the *Analects* (7/15), Confucius claims that the thought of accepting ill-gotten gains is as remote from him as clouds floating overhead. Overreaching ambitions end in the individual's downfall, especially when cosmic trends are unfavorable, as they are in Appraisal 9. As a Chinese proverb says, "The higher the climb, the harder the fall."

Shu
No. 9. Branching Out
January 27–January 31 (a.m.)

Correlates with Heaven's Mystery; Yang; the phase Metal; and the I ching Hexagram no. 19, Approach; the sun enters the Roof constellation, 7th degree

HEAD: Yang *ch'i* is strong within, but weak without. All things, branching out, increase in size.

Although yang *ch'i* appears weak outside, it grows strong within, providing a base for the continued growth, proliferation, and differentiation of the myriad things. This tetragram signifies the initial stage of advance for things; as one commentator writes, "[Things] advance, but still have not reached florescence." Like the branching and leafing out of vegetation in early spring, the myriad things under the beneficient influence of yang *ch'i* spread out to cover the face of the earth.

> Appraisal 1: From the time I crawled,
> I have loved this hidden virtue.

> Fathoming 1: Crawling toward hidden virtue
> Means: It is as if I had not walked.

These lines aptly suggest the frustration experienced by the individual who desires to "walk in the Way." Impatient to achieve self-cultivation, it seems virtually impossible to reach the stage where virtue becomes an easy path. Realistically, the newcomer to self-cultivation can at best hope to make slow progress. For this reason, she is likened to the small baby creeping toward an elusive ("hidden") goal. The phrase "from the time I crawled" emphasizes her consistent devotion to following the Way.

> Appraisal 2: Dazzled, his all-consuming greed
> Does not help him gain his goals.

> Fathoming 2: Deluded by ever-greater greed
> Means: With many desires, he proceeds.

Position 2 marks the Middle of Thought. This tetragram takes "slow advance" as its theme. Here, however, thoughts grow frenzied as the individual plunges forward in pursuit of his desires. We know those desires to be unworthy, for "dazzling" has bad connotations in classical Chinese; it brings to mind delusion and blindness. The individual's perceptions are clouded by cupidity. The only glint in his eye is that provoked by enticing and elusive objects of desire. Driven by an overwhelming urge to fulfill his desires, the greedy individual cannot progress in the Way or achieve its long-term benefits. Paradoxically, all satisfaction eludes him, for his attempts to satisfy his desires merely feed the creation of ever-greater needs. Only a consistent effort to dampen desires can bring true happiness.

> Appraisal 3: Warmed, the low grasses spread
> Up mounds and hills, as they should.

> Fathoming 3: Warm grasses on mounds and hills
> Mean: The short look down on the tall.

When short grasses cover the hills, their vantage point allows them to overlook the highest of trees. This simple fact underlines the manifest advantages attached to "standing on the shoulders" of the ancient sages. The ordinary individual can make use of what is great (ritual and the Confucian Classics) to outperform others who are naturally more talented.

Appraisal 4: Pouncing on wine and food,
He battens but gains no renown.

Fathoming 4: Coveting wine and food
Means: In serving, he lacks direction.

Appraisal 4 stands for the official or an authority. Here a highly placed person neglects the responsibilities of his position. Lacking sufficient cultivation to check impulses toward luxury and self-indulgence, he cares only for the perquisites of his rank. Overindulgence in food and drink is a particular offense against virtue since their consumption is tied to ritual.

Appraisal 5: For branching out there is enough
If he trusts his sturdy carriage.

Fathoming 5: That there's enough for branching out
Means: His position is just as it should be.

The phrase "there is enough" suggests that any individual is well equipped to proceed along the Way of Goodness. Here the individual is even more fortunate, for the chariot (a metaphor for the support of those in high position) is also at hand. With it, he can hope to extend his influence in every direction. Virtue, position, and ability combine to make this an auspicious situation.

Appraisal 6: Branching out alone by leaps and bounds
Is good for small things, but not for great.

Fathoming 6: Expanding alone by leaps and bounds
Means: This cannot be turned to something great.

"Alone" is the crucial word in these verses. While American tradition often celebrates the romantic loner, Chinese tradition is suspicious of the claims to be a self-made man. In contrast to the subject of Appraisal 5, who uses all available help to extend his influence, the subject of these verses acts independently. If a person intends to go far, he should seek like-minded companions of virtue, who will both further his cause and restrain his conduct. Without such help, who can hope to progress far?

Appraisal 7: In old age, the time comes
To bring to fruition what has been learned.

Fathoming 7: White-haired, to meet the time
Means: In old age, he gets his chance.

Position 7, being past the midpoint of the tetragram, symbolizes aging and decay. So does the color white, which is aligned with autumn and the west, the region where the sun declines. Still, the Appraisal is aligned with yang *ch'i,* making it on balance lucky. Although the man of virtue, like the sun, approaches the hour of his demise, his accomplishments appear most brilliantly in old age, just as the light of the sun is most dazzling in late afternoon. Once the good man finally succeeds to a position of considerable power, reform among the people will quickly follow, securing his reputation forever.

> Appraisal 8: He is overrun with fleas and lice.
> Danger.

> Fathoming 8: The spread of fleas and lice
> Means: Parasites are not worth trusting.

Lice do far more than make their host uncomfortable; as parasites, they sap his vitality. In this, they are like bad companions or backbiting officials at court. Such men depend for their livelihood upon the host, but it is certain that the host cannot depend on them in return. Once they have weakened him sufficiently, they move on. They fail to operate by reciprocity, a fundamental Confucian virtue. Good men avoid these vermin at all costs.

> Appraisal 9: Throughout, he proceeds as if
>   On the edge of an abyss,
>   Bound head and foot.

> Fathoming 9: Bound throughout the entire advance
> Means: He fears to meet with harm.

Position 9 completes the characteristic activity of the tetragram, in this case slow "spreading out." In some sense, the limited movement in Position 9 brings us full circle to the crawling of Position 1. That may account for the curious image of a man (or an animal?) bound head to tail. Here the bound figure conveys the idea of caution from beginning to end in the face of dangerous entanglements. The wise person follows the injunction to "Be as careful at the end as at the beginning" (LT, ch. 64), never forgetting that "Beneath good fortune disaster crouches" (LT, ch. 58). For this reason, good luck prevails throughout.

Hsien

No. 10. Defectiveness or Distortion

January 31 (p.m.)–February 4

Correlates with Heaven's Mystery;
Yin; *the phase Water; and the* I
ching Hexagram *no. 62, Minor*
Error; the sun enters the Roof
constellation, 12th degree

HEAD: Yang *ch'i*, assisting things that are still in obscurity, pushes against the wrapping [of yin *ch'i*], distorting the shapes of things, so that they are not yet able to walk perfectly upright.

The generative action of yang *ch'i*, usually considered good, initially has mixed results as it operates on the growth of the myriad things. Since yang *ch'i* is not quite strong enough to break yin's influence at a single stroke, yang must force the hard casing constructed by yin *ch'i* to free the germinating embryos. In the process, the shapes of things are somewhat distorted, both by the pressure exerted on them and by their own wriggling out of their narrow cells of confinement. The uneven quality of weather in early spring, which grows hot and cold by turns, is attributed to this departure from the perfection of the circle.

> Appraisal 1: Starting off wrong,
> The path winds thereafter.

> Fathoming 1: Defective at the beginning
> Means: Later it is hard to correct.

Yang Hsiung's language is reminiscent of the *Book of Changes* tradition:

> Rectify the base and the myriad things will be in good order. But if you are off by a hair's breadth [at the beginning], you will miss by a thousand miles [at the end]. . . . Thus to conduct his affairs the noble man carefully considers the beginning.

Like the *Changes*, the *Mystery* emphasizes the ease with which a minor deviation from the Way leads over time to ever greater errors. For this reason, as the proverb goes, "There is nothing better than preventing depravity at its inception."

The early Chinese equated illogic with a "turn off course." The same verses, then, warn of the dangers attendant upon illogical argument. Since Position 1 represents the Beginning of Thought, the reader is urged not to stray from the point. Of course, the same metaphor works in Appraisal 2, the pair to this position.

Appraisal 2: From small defects he can return.
He can be taken as model.

Fathoming 2: That minor defects can then be turned
Means: He need not go far to set things right.

The *Changes* equates the return with the recovery of the true self through the admission and correction of one's failings (W, 342). It also identifies the superior Way with "taking great care at the beginning" of any transaction (W, 417). Clearly, error can be corrected with relative ease in the early stages, before it has taken hold of the heart/mind.

Appraisal 3: Swerving from the path,
He cannot go straight.

Fathoming 3: On a crooked path
Means: A straight course is impossible.

The individual blindly proceeds farther down the path of error. With his faulty sense of direction, he may also choose the winding road over the shortest route, which by definition is straight and open. Like a lost traveler, he persists in the mistaken belief that the wrong way represents a "return."

Appraisal 4: The circumstance contrives; the faulty seems
correct.
Lucky men do not deem this "happy coincidence."

Fathoming 4: Wrong, but right by circumstance
Means: The good return to the constants.

In general, wickedness ends in calamity. While luck may follow wrong-doing in a few cases, not to act by the "constant" rule is to gamble with one's security, even with one's life. As one Chinese canon observes, "The noble man lives at his ease, awaiting his fate, while the petty man courts dangers, looking for luck. . . . The superior man does not mistake luck for something reliable."

Appraisal 5: The great Way is level,
But narrow byways
Distress the grand carriage.

Fathoming 5: That the great Way is level
Means: Why not follow it?

The same character is used for both the "great" highway and the sur-name of Confucius. Therefore, Yang uses the image of the journey to dem-onstrate the inferiority of other philosophical schools compared with the moral teachings of Confucius. Other thinkers may have their use, admittedly, but their vision is partial and inadequate. Only Confucian teachings are comprehensive enough to offer guidance in every circumstance to all persons, including the leader symbolized by the grand carriage.

> Appraisal 6: When the Great Void strays,
> Some right it, some help it
> Get back on course.
> He finds men straight as arrows.

> Fathoming 6: When the mind strays, arrowlike men
> Mean: He obtains worthy officials.

As in Appraisal 1 of Tetragram 6, the Great Void is an epithet for the heart/mind. Mistaken perceptions leading to faulty conduct can be corrected by a concerted effort under the direction of good men. The honest criticism of loyal supporters constrains the weak conscience to undertake much-needed reform.

> Appraisal 7: To bend old truths
> Is to wander the road,
> And to go along with danger.

> Fathoming 7: Bending the old
> Means: He only acts to initiate ideas.

Those who deviate from the "way of the ancients" manipulate hallowed texts to justify their own corrupt readings. In the *Analects* (7/1), the sage-master Confucius spoke of himself as "a transmitter, not a creator." How, then, can lesser minds at a later date arrogate to themselves the task of creating new philosophies? What is it in humans that leads them to prefer novelty over the tried and true ways of the past? Innovators often create, rather than dispel confusion on key ethical issues. As the philosopher Mencius (4th c. B.C.) wrote, "There has never been one who could straighten others by bending himself."

> Appraisal 8: Though twisting his foot,
> He saves himself
> From a fall in the ditch.
> Now he faces the proper way.

> Fathoming 8: Twisting his foot
> Means: He avoids unlucky events.

Appraisal 8 comes near the end of the cycle. Due to its situation, only partial success is possible even when the verse, as here, is aligned with auspicious Day. The ditch is made of dirt; therefore, it stands for filth and corruption in general. In ancient China, the ditch also symbolized ignominious poverty, sickness, and death, since in times of famine or plague, corpses were hurled into wayside ditches without benefit of formal funerals. To dodge ultimate disaster ("the ditch"), the individual leaps aside, risking injury to his foot (a mere appendage, after all). Although he is injured, at least he redirects his efforts to avoid future disasters. Henceforth, he constrains himself to conform to the Way.

> Appraisal 9: The carriage axle breaks,
>   The yoke snaps.
>   The team of four tangles in its traces.
>   Men in high places spit blood.

> Fathoming 9: The axle breaks, they spit blood.
>   Meaning: In the end, it's too late for regrets.

A dramatic scene of collapse and chaos ends the tetragram. In the middle of a journey or battle, the conveyance belonging to a great man (the ruler?) collapses. The four horses hitched to the vehicle, their traces hopelessly entangled, struggle in vain to free themselves from the wreckage. With his chariot destroyed, the critically wounded great man has no way to flee, and slowly bleeds to death.

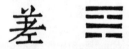

Ch'a
No. 11. Divergence
February 5–February 9 (a.m.)

Correlates with Heaven's Mystery; Yang; the phase Fire; and the I ching Hexagram no. 62, Minor Error; the sun enters the Roof constellation, 16th degree; the Dipper points ENE; the musical note is B

HEAD: Yang *ch'i*, wriggling, breaks open at the east. Lordly, it emerges from the multitude of obstructions.

This tetragram is aligned with the Spring Onset solar period. Accordingly, all images in the Head suggest the coming of the new season. With east as the direction of spring, it is only natural that yang *ch'i* should make its first appearance there. By a pun, even the particular wriggling form that yang takes (*ch'un* in Chinese) is synonymous with activity in the spring (also *ch'un*); like a young insect working its way out of its chrysalis, yang frees itself from the confinement of dark earth and yin *ch'i*. Yang *ch'i* is masterful, even godlike, in its promotion of the universal patterns that result in cosmic harmony. For that reason, it is called "lordly."

The tetragram title implies "divergence," "deviation," "variety," "discrepancy," "inequality," and "distinction." At this juncture, the myriad things diverge further in their characteristic appearances and activities, less threatened by the ill winds of winter. Divergence can lead to fault and error, no doubt, but distinction is to be applauded insofar as it underlies Man's ability to make ethical judgments.

> Appraisal 1: Failing in small things,
> Attack them yourself
> At the source.

> Fathoming 1: Attacking minor failings oneself
> Means: As yet, others do not know.

Continuing the argument of the previous tetragram, Appraisal 1 asserts the wisdom of correcting one's faults when they first appear so that error never grows obvious enough to become a source of shame.

> Appraisal 2: Being steeped in his desires,
> He brings about what he abhors.

> Fathoming 2: Steeped in his desires
> Means: He is gradually led to error.

The indiscriminate pursuit of pleasure usually ends in disaster. The wise person, then, moderates his desires lest he gradually become a slave to them, reducing his chances of future happiness.

> Appraisal 3: "Might there be ruin? Oh, might there be?"
> Thus he is led to the bright light.

> Fathoming 3: "Oh, ruin, such ruin!"
> Means: Shocked, he protects himself.

The worthy man weighs each action carefully, knowing full well that even minor mistakes may lead to his eventual downfall. In consequence, it is the prospect of ruin that prompts continued self-examination and speedy reform. Measuring his failings by the hard light of day (the "bright light"), the prudent individual goes on to win a reputation (a second "bright light"). That explains why, as the proverb goes, "In security the noble man is mindful of danger" (W, 341).

> Appraisal 4: Passing over small acts of goodness,
> He will not overcome.

> Fathoming 4: Foregoing small acts of goodness
> Means: He cannot reach greatness.

The *Changes* tells us that

> The petty man considers the small good to be of no advantage, so he
> makes no effort. He thinks the small sin does no harm, and so he does
> not give it up. . . . If good does not accumulate, it will not be enough to
> make a name for oneself (W, 340–1).

Another Chinese classic, the *Documents*, concurs:

> If you do not attend zealously to small acts, the result will affect your
> virtue in great ones.

Self-cultivation is a slow process of learning, whereby the individual becomes practiced in discerning and performing the good act. If the individual
is either too arrogant or too careless to make a habit of small acts of nobility, great virtue cannot be attained.

One commentator, however, reads "foregoing" as "going too far." This
Appraisal then critiques those who go too far in small acts of kindness
or conscience while ignoring the greater good. He offers examples from
Chinese tradition, including that of Wei Sheng. Wei Sheng had arranged to
meet his lady love under a bridge. The lady failed to show. When heavy
rains came, Wei Sheng refused to leave the spot, lest he break his word, and
so drowned under the bridge. The moral of the story is: those who are
overly concerned with small points lose sight of greater goals.

> Appraisal 5: Having passed the gate, he returns
> To enter, gaining that center court.

> Fathoming 5: Having missed the gate, turning to enter
> Means: Before going too far, he reverses his course.

The gate marks an easy access to the home. By extension, it symbolizes
whatever facilitates an easy entrance to understanding. For this reason, the
teachings of Confucius are frequently identified as gates to learning. The
center courtyard or lightwell is an integral part of the ancient Chinese house,
providing free access to the gods inhabiting the open air above, as well as
light and rainwater for the benefit of the inhabitants. As the inner sanctum
of the house, it also stands for the innermost thoughts of the individual and,
by a pun, for "conduct according to the Mean."

In these verses, then, the individual first awakens to the magnitude of his
error, then reforms his conduct in conformity with the Mean. His safe ar-
rival at the inner sanctum, despite initial confusion and physical barriers,
suggests that he has achieved moral perfection.

Appraisal 6: In a great hurry, he misses his gate,
And fails to enter his own house.

Fathoming 6: That in a rush, he does not enter
Means: Truly, this is cause for grief.

In contrast to the subject of the preceding Appraisal, this individual is so muddled that he fails to realize his error. Perhaps other enticements or heterodox teachings have overwhelmed plain good sense. Confucius said:

If a man finds he has made a mistake, then he must not be afraid of admitting the fact and amending his ways.... To have faults and make no effort to amend them is to have faults indeed!

Appraisal 7: As with a pile of eggs,
He acts with great caution.
From fear comes propriety, then safety.

Fathoming 7: Precarious as a pile of eggs
Means: From his own danger, he creates safety.

A pile of eggs is a popular metaphor in early China for critical danger. If one approaches any serious problem with due caution, it may be possible to save the situation. The greater the caution, the greater the likelihood of success.

Appraisal 8: He stumbles forth on fettered feet.
His jaw is branded, his eyebrows destroyed.

Fathoming 8: The fettered feet
Mean: From one step into calamity, no return.

A variety of punishments, each more dangerous than the last, is likely to befall the individual who does not mend his ways.

Appraisal 9: Passing decrepit city walls, he finds
Verdant shoots rising from stumps.

Fathoming 9: Passing the decrepit walls of the city
Means: Through self-reform, life is renewed.

Since neolithic times city walls in China have been constructed of wooden pillars packed with wattle-and-daub or tamped earth. Because the city wall encloses its inhabitants, defining the community and insuring physical safety, city walls in good repair signify security on the psychic, physical, and political levels. Accordingly, their upkeep is a top priority for stable administrations. Here the city walls are in utter disrepair. Either the city is deserted or its government mismanaged. Intruders can easily breach the city's defenses. Still, there are some signs of hope: from nearby fallen trees or the wooden supports in the wall itself, young shoots have begun to sprout. In the midst of death, renewal occurs. By analogy, even the most hardened of criminals can learn to recover his best self.

T'ung

No. 12. Youthfulness

February 9 (p.m.)–February 13

Correlates with Heaven's Mystery; Yin; the phase Wood; and the I ching *Hexagram no. 4, Youthful Folly; the sun enters the House constellation, 4th degree*

HEAD: Yang *ch'i* is first spied. Things like callow youths all still lack understanding.

This tetragram, like the previous one, is assigned to the Spring Onset solar period when plants and animals are expected to first emerge from their winter homes. The title character describes young animals whose horns have still not grown, the land still barren of vegetation, and youths of either sex who still lack the characteristic development of the heart/mind that makes people fully "human." The first signs of maturity start to appear now. So long as lack of development is primarily a function of time, we can anticipate the future happily. However, many promising trends may be nipped in the bud if they are not nurtured by trained caretakers.

For this reason, this tetragram advises the youth (or one who is new to any endeavor) to look for good teachers to guide the maturation process. Certain mistakes are particularly associated with youth (such as impetuosity, faulty judgment, and indecision due to lack of experience). Unless an appropriate master is found, such faults tend to multiply over time. As Yang Hsiung states categorically in his other "classic," the *Model Sayings*:

> To work at study is not as good as to work at finding a teacher. A teacher
> is a model for others. . . . Just as within a single noisy marketplace there
> are countless different ideas, within a book of a single chapter there are
> countless different theories. For the marketplace, a balance must be set
> up [to determine correct weight and value], so for each book, a teacher
> must be set up.

In contrast to the corresponding *Changes* hexagram, which praises certain childlike qualities, the *Mystery* censures the puerile.

> Appraisal 1: The fatuous youth is not awake.
> Meeting us, he is blind and dim.

Fathoming 1: A loutish youth who is unaware
Means: We fear he'll be "dark" 'til the end.

Appraisal 1 corresponds to the Beginning of Thought. The most important task for the immature youth is to find a good teacher to train his heart/
mind. A Chinese pun identifies the teacher as "the first-awakened one" who
leads others to the Way. Here, unfortunately, Position 1 corresponds to inauspicious Night, and so Yang Hsiung speaks of darkness: either the inane
youth selects a teacher who is equally ignorant ("He meets us, who are
[also] blind and dim") or the immature youth fails to heed his good teacher's
words ("[Even after] meeting us, he is blind and dim.") Under such conditions, no pupil can hope to gain enlightenment. Unless he changes his ways,
he is likely to remain in the dark—both unenlightened and in obscurity.

Appraisal 2: He casts the sacred milfoil.
He fires the turtle's shell.
Leaving the muck, he enters the anointed.

Fathoming 2: Casting milfoil, firing the turtle,
Means: He approaches the path of glory.

As Confucius tells us, the better part of wisdom is to recognize what you
do not know. For that reason, the youth in search of greater understanding
uses divination procedures to resolve cases of grave doubt. (Their sacred
character precludes casual use.) Divination by milfoil and by turtle are the
two ancient forms of prognostication hallowed by Chinese tradition. Significantly, each of these instruments for communication with the divine represents accumulated age and experience: the graph for "milfoil" contains the
character for "old" within it, while the marvelous capacities of the turtle are
attributed to its fabled longevity. By implication, if the ancients are con-
sulted in every doubtful case, a miracle will take place: the individual will
emerge from obscurity and muddleheadedness (the "muck") to gain honor
(an "anointment").

Appraisal 3: The Eastern Star already shines,
Yet he cannot proceed by its light.

Fathoming 3: The Eastern Star already shining
Means: Why not go?

Appraisal 3 marks the transition from Thought to Action. The necessary
preconditions for enlightenment are present since the Eastern Star already
shines. Good teachers are available, the Classics have been promulgated,
and all the various tools of civilization (including divination) have been
provided. For some reason, the individual fails to take advantage of the
opportunities for growth, assuming himself to be incapable of maturity. In

reality, he lacks sufficient will to follow in the Way. The *Analects* (7/3) condemns those who "hear of duty, yet do not move toward it."

Appraisal 4: Some follow those in front.
Those ahead light their way.

Fathoming 4: Following the ones in front
Means: Great is the light of those who lead.

In contrast to Appraisal 3, Appraisal 4 praises individuals who take full advantage of the illumination provided by moral exemplars of the past. Given the penetrating power of those exemplars, even those who follow at some distance in time and space can find their Way by the light. This contention implicitly refutes Chuang tzu's belief that the Classics represent only the "dregs" of the former sages' teachings.

Appraisal 5: If in thick brush, he seeks the *ssu*,
He finds a prize less valued.

Fathoming 5: Hunting the *ssu* in the brush
Means: The catch is not worth the praise.

The hunter lays a trap to catch a female *ssu*. (Probably a wild ox is indicated, although the prey may be a rhinoceros or some other marvelous beast.) The thick brush (that literally "covers" or "conceals") may function in several ways. Perhaps it keeps the hunter from finding his prey. Perhaps it conceals the hunter stalking his catch. Perhaps it hides a trap in the underbrush. In any case, there is no doubt that the hunter ignores important ritual rules that dictate that the female of the species is to be spared in the general slaughter. As one commentator remarks, the hunter "stops at nothing to get the game." (Hence, the pun for the second line in the Appraisal: "His [the hunter's] virtue is not admired."[1]) Such obsessive behavior not only diverts the hunter's attention from proper pursuits while weakening his sense of scruples; it also diminishes future stocks of game. Despite the "catch," the man himself may be "caught" short in the short term (if he is gored by his prey) or in the long term (when stocks are depleted). This is an excellent example of the Chinese propensity to address concerns from both moral and practical considerations.

This portrait of an evil hunter contrasts with stories told of the legendary sage-kings of antiquity. Good King T'ang, for example, purportedly constructed a special trap open on three sides so that beasts could easily escape it. In the same way, T'ang framed his laws in such a way that his subjects

---

1. Some editions read *te* ("virtue") instead of *te* ("what is caught").

found it easy to avoid being "framed" for criminal activities. The virtuous person displays a profound empathy for all living things.

> Appraisal 6: Open wide the tent,
> Inviting guests from every quarter.

> Fathoming 6: Throwing the tent open
> Means: He sees the many lights.

We tend to think of Chinese rulers as closeted in forbidden palaces, but early tradition made it incumbent upon every good ruler to conduct royal progresses throughout the land so that he could consult widely with candidates for public office. Here the ruler opens his private quarters to all comers, as a public sign of his avid desire for the moral enlightenment to be provided by the "leading lights" of his kingdom. With the tent flaps up, the night sky comes into view. The ruler is equally receptive to the constant norms illustrated by the starry firmament in its divine orbit (again, the "lights"). In consequence, the multitude of the ruler's subjects are transformed under his suasive example—yet a third instance of "many lights."

> Appraisal 7: Cultivating the puny
> He becomes a runt.

> Fathoming 7: Making the puny grow
> Means: There is nothing to be achieved.

If the individual lacks the acuity and commitment to greatness that properly define the mature adult, we compare his stunted intellectual and moral growth to the crippled form of a dwarf. Greatness is equated with strict adherence to the Confucian Way, since virtue represents the supreme human goal on practical as well as moral grounds. And development must be defined in terms of strengthening the discerning mind that knows greatness, rather than nurturing the lesser, even bestial parts of human nature. Physical development alone can hardly be considered an accomplishment.

> Appraisal 8: Some beat him, some prod him.
> He polishes the mysterious mirror of his mind
> And so changes.

> Fathoming 8: Beating and prodding him
> Means: In that way, his errors decline.

As the situation nears the end of its cycle, the individual finally responds to repeated and severe criticisms with a sincere attempt at moral reform. The wise individual is grateful for harsh criticism, since personal improvement usually depends on it. As the *Changes* writes, "To make immature fools develop, it helps to punish people" (W, 22).

The heart/mind is a mirror that reflects all sensory impressions, however fleeting. By clearing away all misguided notions and intellectual baggage, the individual restores the pristine clarity of that organ, "polishing his mysterious mirror" so that it functions properly. It is never too late to begin this process, although years of accumulated dust may complicate the task.

> Appraisal 9: The young buck butts the wild ox,
> Cracking its own skull.

> Fathoming 9: The buck butting the ox
> Means: In return, it harms itself.

The immature deer lacks the brute strength, the experience, and the skills necessary to defeat a dangerous opponent. In a serious miscalculation of its capacities, the fawn takes on the powerful wild ox (or possibly rhinoceros) known for its tough hide. It can neither fend off an attack by such a fearsome rival nor launch a counterattack. Inevitably, the fawn is gored or trampled by the ox. By analogy, the immature individual would do well to avoid all premature engagements with formidable adversaries. It is often pride that leads one foolishly into the fray.

Tseng
No. 13. Increase
February 14–February 18 (a.m.)

Correlates with Heaven's Mystery; Yang; the phase Metal; and the I ching Hexagram no. 42, Increase; the sun enters the House constellation, 8th degree

HEAD: Yang *ch'i* is burgeoning. Things accordingly pile up and increase. Daily manifesting [their energy], they grow.

As yang *ch'i* daily increases, under its protection all things prosper. This is a odd-numbered (i.e., yang) Head with an auspicious title, so the tetragram is lucky in its theme: an increase in moral acuity is based on a sound ethical foundation. This increase, of course, mimics yang *ch'i*, which productively expands only after building a solid inner base in Tetragram 9. Head 13 represents a major step forward from the immaturity discussed in the previous tetragram.

> Appraisal 1: Hearing aright, and increasingly silent,
> Outsiders fail to notice.

> Fathoming 1: Hearing aright, ever more silent,
> Means: He discerns what is inside.

Appraisal 1, signifying the Beginning of Thought, is here associated with auspicious Day. The first response of the gentleman to hearing the Way is to contemplate its miraculous patterns in awed silence. Temporarily distracted from mundane existence, the good man may even appear stupid to those of lesser understanding, as true virtue is recognized only by an inner circle of accomplished individuals. Having no desire to show off his knowledge of the Way, he applies what he has learned of the inner workings of the universe to the "inside," to the seeds of Goodness deep within himself. As the *Lao tzu* (ch. 33) says:

> He who knows others is clever
> He who knows himself has discernment.

> Appraisal 2: To increase his search for glory
> Without squaring his inner life
> Is benighted.

> Fathoming 2: Not increasing his "squareness"
> Means: He embellishes only the outside.

The contrast between internal and external continues. Squareness refers to "directional" behavior aimed at the Tao. It implies "squaring" thoughts and deeds, as well as acting within well-established bounds. The good person, then, takes it as a duty to make the outer life square with inner constraints (W, 393). A true increase in virtue works against artifice (W, 597) and pretension, but the petty person focuses on external adornment, hoping to fool others by superficial changes. Yang Hsiung puts a spin on the famous question posed by the *Lao tzu* (ch. 44): "Which is dearer, your name or your life?" Yang asks instead, "Which is dearer, the inner life or outer glory?"

> Appraisal 3: Trees stay put,
> And so steadily grow.

> Fathoming 3: Rooted trees, gradual increase,
> Means: They cannot be suppressed.

Wood comes up for two reasons. Appraisal 3 is assigned to agent Wood in the *Mystery*'s schema of correlations. At the same time, the Judgment attached to the correspondent *Changes* hexagram associates the "way of wood" with increase, success, and the promise of "daily advance without limit." However, trees can support extensive growth above only to the extent that they are firmly rooted below. They then become the model for acquiring virtue.

> Appraisal 4: His waist cannot bear the load
> Yet others add to the weight on top.

> Fathoming 4: That the center cannot hold
> Means: He can be defeated.

The poem depends upon a neat double entendre, with the same word meaning "waist" and "what is central" or "essential." As the fulcrum of the body, the waist bears the major portion of weight in any beast of burden, including man. With the physical center too weak to bear the initial burden, one can well imagine the damage that will result when additional weight is heaped on. By analogy, when the essential core of one's being is inadequate to deal with life's daily challenges, an extra crisis may send the person into complete collapse. The essential core, however, can be strengthened by various techniques of self-cultivation.

> Appraisal 5: In marshes, being low makes for capacity.
> Many waters converge there.

> Fathoming 5: That the low marsh holds much
> Means: From self-effacement springs greatness.

The *Lao tzu* (ch. 66) explains that, "the reason why the river and the sea are able to be kings of the Hundred Valleys is that they excel in taking the lower position." Modesty and self-effacement make for true greatness in that they compel the support of others. Appraisal 5 corresponds to the leader; clearly, the single most important attribute that qualifies the leader to head an enterprise is the ability to humble oneself, as demonstrated by the courteous treatment of subordinates and a willingness to accept harsh criticism.

> Appraisal 6: Like a torch, the Red Chariot spreads its light.
> One day increases our lists by three thousand.
> The noble man wins praise.
> The petty man takes wounds.

> Fathoming 6: By the Red Chariot, daily increasing,
> Means: The petty man is no match for the noble.

The Red Chariot probably refers to the sun in its daily round. The sun, in turn, suggests the good leader in two ways. First, the beneficent presence of the sage-ruler acts like the sun to enlighten, fostering peace and harmony wherever it goes. Second, the wise leader's favors are distributed fairly to all men of worth, just as the sun shines equally on every region of the earth. But what has this to do with the "increase of three thousand"? Literary convention associates the founding of the Chou dynasty (correlated with

Red and Fire in the Chinese schema) with just such an increase. After all, legend tells us that good King Wu in 1122 B.C. was able to muster three thousand troops in a few days' time to defeat the last evil tyrant of the Shang-Yin dynasty. As the philosopher Mencius (4th c. B.C.) asserts, "So long as the ruler of a state is drawn to benevolence, he will have *no match* in the empire."

Appraisal 7: With height increased,
　　　Cut back its peak
　　　To make the mountain stable.

Fathoming 7: Increased height and graded peak
　　　Mean: With loss, all is accomplished.

Paradoxically, the *Changes* associates final "expansion" with "decrease." The individual who trims her own desires for aggrandizement increases her chances of accomplishing her goals. Therefore, the wise person acts to curb herself in order to assure her own security, preferring to keep her growth in balance with a solid base of support. Nothing is more dangerous than unimpeded or unsupported increase, here symbolized by a mountain precipice. After all, the higher the position attained, the harder the fall.

Appraisal 8: Enslaved by a handful of cowries,
　　　Past profits shave future gain.

Fathoming 8: Enslaved for a handful of cash
　　　Means: First happiness, then ruin.

Cowries, one of the earliest forms of currency in China, signify wealth. The individual becomes a willing slave in return for material advancement. In his greed for cash, he accepts his own debasement, indicated here by the word "shaved," which refers to the tonsure of the indentured servant, the slave, or the convict. As in the New Testament story of Judas Iscariot, the paltry sums gained are contrasted with the magnitude of the moral loss.

Appraisal 9: Jagged peaks do not collapse
　　　When they lean on their foothills.

Fathoming 9: That rocky crags do not collapse
　　　Means: Many knights give firm support.

Appraisal 9 represents the extremities. In the case of mountains, the peak or precipice is the part most vulnerable to collapse. However, if the dizzying heights are supported by a firm base, they will not topple over even under the greatest stress. Likewise, if the leader is supported by many worthy subordinates, his rule cannot be overturned.

Jui
No. 14. Penetration
February 18 (p.m.)–February 22

Correlates with Heaven's Mystery;
Yin; the phase Earth; and the I
ching *Hexagram no. 53, Advance;*
the sun enters the House constella-
tion, 13th degree

HEAD: Yang *ch'i*, like a high hill, penetrates upward. That means the birth of things. All concentrate on oneness and avoid duality.

This tetragram witnesses the transition from the Spring Onset to the Rainfall solar period, usually sometime in late February. Things in their early stages typically show little differentiation. For example, the tips of vegetation just now pushing through the surface of the soil are so tightly furled that one plant is barely distinguishable from another. Perhaps from them Yang Hsiung takes his title, meaning "sharp tip" or "point" or "penetration." Succeeding Appraisals play out the full range of the title's meaning. Because a point or tip is sharp, the same term conveys mental or moral acuity; whatever is piercing, zealous, or focused; whatever is penetrating, or pointing in a particular direction. The same character also refers to what is comparatively trifling or insignificant, as in the English expression "the tip of the iceberg." Nearly all these meanings are employed below, requiring different translations for the same Chinese character. In many cases, the antonym for the title character is "duality" (associated with moral confusion), as the Head already suggests.

The tetragram presents oneness as its main theme, in the two senses of individual wholeness and social cohesion. But if those kinds of oneness are the proper goals of the individual, single-minded devotion—a third kind of oneness—is the means. As an earlier Confucian master wrote:

> If you pile up earth to make a mountain, wind and rain will rise up from
> it. If you pile up water to make a deep pool, dragons of all kinds will
> appear. If you pile up enough good deeds to make your charismatic
> virtue whole, a godlike understanding will come of itself and the sagely
> mind will be perfected. And so, unless you pile up little steps, you will
> never be able to journey a thousand *li*; unless you pile up tiny streams,
> you will have no way to fill a river or a sea. . . . Achievement consists in
> never giving up.

Only the focused mind can hope to discern the unifying principle behind the institutions and arts of civilization. For this reason, the Confucian Classics advise, "Carry forever the single mind." Accomplishment in all senses, then, is tied to the penetrating mind that depends on oneness.

Appraisal 1: The crab skitters side-to-side, lagging
Behind the worm in the Yellow Springs.

Fathoming 1: The crab skittering side-to-side
Means: His heart is not one.

The crab has six legs; the earthworm, none. Still, when the crab walks, it skitters from side to side; it is incapable of walking in a straight line, indicating that its mind moves in many directions at once. Because it is unable to concentrate, it never learns to make its own home; it must look for an empty hole dug by a snake or water serpent. Despite the apparent handicap of having no legs, the earthworm tunnels quickly to its destination by inserting the tip of its body. If a race were to be conducted in the Yellow Springs below ground, the earthworm would surely beat the crab. This Chinese version of the tortoise and hare fable conveys a different moral than that put forward by Aesop, however. The problem is not the crab's arrogance (although elsewhere Yang Hsiung inveighs against that attitude); instead, a superfluity of talents (i.e., too many legs) combines with aimless busywork to distract the crab from the most important task at hand.

Appraisal 2: Focus on the One,
Then nothing is unattainable.

Fathoming 2: Attainments from focus on the One
Mean: His grasp of the Way is sure.

The unlimited achievements that can be attained by anyone in single-minded pursuit of the Way present a direct contrast to the undirected activity of the crab. If the crab's progress is negligible, the advantages of "concentrating the mind, and unifying the will" are manifold. Unswerving devotion to learning finally enables the individual to "contact the spirits, becoming a partner in the triad with Heaven and Earth."

Appraisal 3: Agitated, his focus is erratic.

Fathoming 3: Pointing madly in his agitation
Means: He cannot dwell in the One.

The adverb "madly," as in our own language, denotes inconstancy, irregularity, the excessively emotional, and any deviation from what is proper. The individual certainly displays sufficient emotional intensity. Unfortunately, there is no particular commitment to steady advance along a single path of Goodness. Given the individual's frequent vacillations, no achievement is possible. The *Changes* aptly compares this haphazard course to the frenetic movements of the hamster (W, 562).

Appraisal 4: If acute in timing,
Nothing is not benefited.

Fathoming 4: To be sharp about time
Means: He gains what he can from the moment.

Development in any of the three triadic realms of Heaven-Earth-Man occurs only when it is timely. Even the sage-master Confucius could not overcome the limitations imposed by time to become ruler of the empire. How, then, can lesser men hope to prevail? The gentleman moves when an opportunity for advancement exists, but wisely retires when the time is not yet ripe, lest he endanger himself. Because he rides on prevailing trends to further his own goals, he is likely to benefit himself and others.

Appraisal 5: Penetrating East, he forgets the West.
Watching his back, he overlooks his heart.

Fathoming 5: Advancing East, ignoring the West
Means: Unable to reverse, he cannot escape.

As the center of the tetragram, Position 5 presents the main argument against one-sidedness, which holds for military strategists and philosophers alike: in becoming obsessed by a small corner of the truth, most men fail to comprehend general principles. In devising his strategy for living, the wise person considers all factors, just as the general preparing for battle considers all possible avenues of attack and retreat. It is the stupid person who concerns himself only with superficial, immediate gratification (the "back"), without weighing the fundamental risks (the "heart"). Having made no provision to extricate himself from difficulties, he now faces certain ruin; in effect, he has become his own worst enemy. The concentration applauded in Appraisal 3 here has turned into blind one-sidedness.

Appraisal 6: Acute in categories,
He holds within the Five Gauges
And Ten Thousand Measures.
He is tried and true.

Fathoming 6: Acute as to categories
Means: Riches and rank without measure.

The heart/mind of the sage has the capacity to embrace all within itself; it can "hold Ten Thousand Measures," as Yang Hsiung says. It also operates by strict standards (the Five Gauges) derived from cosmic norms. Because of his unfailing utility, the sage is employed in high office, where he is given "riches and rank without measure." Once in office he propagates moral standards and bestows material aid to all below.

Appraisal 7: Sharp for profit,
Dishonor and hatred set in.

Fathoming 7: Focused on profit
Means: Disgrace lies in being one-sided.

All early Chinese texts, whether Confucian or Taoist, warn against a preoccupation with getting rich. Excess in any one direction is likely to lead one astray. Profit-seeking in particular tends to blunt one's appreciation of moral distinctions. The good person devotes herself to cultivating the true Way and trusts Heaven for the rest.

Appraisal 8: Sharp when he ought to be sharp,
He saves himself from his own defeat.

Fathoming 8: Focused when he should be
Means: In fear, he turns the cause of calamity around.

Coming near the end of the tetragram, Appraisal 8 represents potential disaster. Still, the superior man can turn calamity to his own advantage if he applies his penetrating mind to the problem at hand. "He who is conscious of danger creates security for himself" (W, 353), snatching victory from the jaws of defeat.

Appraisal 9: High peak and steep bank
Come tumbling down.

Fathoming 9: High peaks, steep banks
Mean: With extreme sharpness, inevitable collapse.

High mountains, majestic in appearance, seem ultrastable and so eternal. Steep banks seem equally unassailable. Still, if "reversal is the movement of the Tao," any extreme situation is likely to revert to its opposite. The highest is made low.

Correlates with Heaven's Mystery;
Yang; the phase Water; and the I
ching Hexagram no. 11, Greatness;
the sun enters the Wall constella-
tion, 1st degree)

Ta
No. 15. Reach
February 23–February 27 (a.m.)

HEAD: Yang *ch'i* emerges, limb to branch to twig. There is nothing that does not reach its full extension.

The language used in this Head text is particularly beautiful. The luxuriant growth of trees suggests the burgeoning presence of yang *ch'i*. With its energy reaching out to ever smaller units, the web of yang's influence grows increasingly comprehensive until each aspect of the cosmos is profoundly affected. This progressive differentiation is analogous to the mind's ability to make ever finer distinctions, so that the tetragram Reach symbolizes mental perceptiveness and comprehension as well, which are two other possible translations for the title. Finally, the gracious condescension that yang *ch'i* displays toward phenomenal existence becomes the model for the good ruler in his dealings with the masses. These three kinds of reach (physical, mental, and political) are treated below, with most of the Appraisals operating on all three levels simultaneously.

> Appraisal 1: Though hidden, the center, on its own
> Comprehends, pushing through, undeterred.

> Fathoming 1: That the hidden center alone reaches
> Means: Inner clarity is boundless.

The innermost heart/mind of the superior man with its heightened powers of comprehension penetrates each problem in turn until it assimilates the daimonic powers of Heaven-and-Earth and the sages. If such marvelous powers are to be realized, great persistence is needed, as indicated by the repetition of images emphasizing the "push through." That process is hidden not only because of the depth of the individual's soul, but also because the mind's latent power is held in reserve prior to the decision to take action.

> Appraisal 2: Misleading the belly
> Affects the eye.

> Fathoming 2: That the belly's delusions reach the eye
> Means: It makes the Way unclear.

The theme is the interdependence of inner and outer. As in many early Chinese texts, the belly (the internal organ that stands for sensory desire and "gut" reactions) is contrasted with outer eye (the discriminating mind that makes contact with the outer world). If the belly is confused, the eye cannot hope to evaluate various courses of action properly. As one Chinese master cautions, "Do not let the senses confuse the mind."

> Appraisal 3: Only by sweeping down can the green wood's
> Excellence reach melons and gourds.

> Fathoming 3: Only by the green wood's condescension
> Means: Reciprocity within becomes the measure.

Gracious condescension is suggested in terms reminiscent of the Head text. To the Chinese reader, the downward sweep of verdant branches in spring inevitably recalls the flowing robes of the sage-kings of old. The great tree offers support and protection to lesser living things, just like the sage-king; here it allows the lowly but useful melons and gourds to wind their vines around its majestic form. Similarly, the person of great virtue does not avoid all contact with lesser individuals. Instead, she fosters others' development by a sympathetic understanding of their essential needs and natures. As a result, the lives of her subordinates are made secure. Consideration for others, in short, becomes the true measure of nobility.

> Appraisal 4: Petty wit has little reach.
> Greatly misled by the narrow and small,
> He will never be saved.

> Fathoming 4: Keen in small things, confused in great
> Means: He only knows one corner of the problem.

As teacher, Confucius looked for one attribute in his disciples: the ability, "given one corner of a problem," to correctly surmise the other three. A comprehensive view is desirable in every case. The sage, then, by definition is "all-seeing." A smattering of knowledge often leads to complacency, which in turn provokes disaster. For this reason, early Chinese texts typically castigate any form of one-sidedness.

> Appraisal 5: Having reached the Central Crossroad,
> Neither small nor great misleads him.

> Fathoming 5: Reaching the place where all paths converge
> Means: The Way is open in all four directions.

Appraisal 5 is the center of the tetragram. The lines are correlated with yang *ch'i* in a yang tetragram; hence, their auspicious character. The pursuit of Goodness is like a journey down a path. Once the individual fully assimilates the idea of the Mean, all roads lie open to him; regardless of which course is chosen, every action is consistent with morality. This imagery offers a direct contrast to that of Tetragram 31, Appraisal 6.

> Appraisal 6: A great reach has no bounds,
> It does not stop at center.
> Barriers create evil.

> Fathoming 6: A great reach, without bounds,
> Means: It should not continue on one side only.

Any reading of these lines depends upon the moral weight given the first phrase in the Appraisal and Fathoming: "great reach without bounds." Is this a description of morality or immorality? One commentator argues:

> The Great Way ought to reach every single place. It is not right to stop it in midcourse. If someone builds something confined by embankments [i.e., barriers between fields], that is to create a place where something does not get through. That is evil.

Unimpeded reach is a quality generally attributed to the moral superior in Han texts. At the same time, other commentators equate the phrase "no bounds" with dangerous license. In that case, the poem says,

> A great reach without bounds,
> [If] not stopped at center and regulated by ditches,
> Is evil.

> A great reach without bounds
> Means: Not right to let it continue on all sides.

In the rice fields, embankments are necessary if the fields are to be worked productively. In the human realm, various restraints are needed for the beneficial functioning of society. Otherwise, an unimpeded flow of emotions and ambitions will prove no less damaging to society than floodwaters are to new crops. The implied cultivation of the fields also suggests the cultivation of the mind, which depends upon the acceptance of a set of limits embodied in ritual. Without such constraints, the mind ranges so freely that its undeveloped powers fail to hit upon significant patterns in the triadic realms of Heaven-Earth-Man.

Appraisal 7: Reached by the flint probe's cut:
    With early loss comes later gain.

Fathoming 7: The scalpel reaching the affected spot
    Means: By this means, in the end, he is not disabled.

Early Chinese texts frequently compare the strictures of early training to unpleasant medicine or painful surgery forced upon the patient by the conscientious doctor. As the proverb says, "Good medicine is bitter to the tongue." Similarly, the harsh necessity of the penal code is likened to the flint probe employed in acupuncture. Early correction, however traumatic, results in future benefit. Once the old, diseased area has been cut away, new healthy growth can take its place.

Appraisal 8: Misleading the eye
    Affects the belly.

Fathoming 8: That the eye's delusions reach the belly
Means: The outer deceives the inner.

Following Appraisal 2 above, this verse reiterates the interdependence of mind and body, inner and outer. If the eye as the mind's receptor for outward impressions becomes confused for any reason, the resulting mistakes, sooner or later, are bound to affect the innermost self. For example, a half-starved man may reach for chalk to eat, rather than rice, or a well-dressed man may see himself as a gentleman. From such mistakes come physical and moral damage.

Appraisal 9: Perceiving his blame, he rights himself,
And in the end, he wins renown.

Fathoming 9: Comprehending blame, final renown,
Means: He's good at using the Way to retreat.

Alhough Appraisal 9 represents the final stage of calamity, here it is aligned with auspicious Day. The superior individual, in response to society's complaints about his conduct, amends his ways and retreats from evil, thereby securing a good name for himself.

Correlates with Heaven's Mystery; Yin; the phase Fire; and the I ching *Hexagram no. 11, Greatness; the sun enters the Wall constellation, 6th degree*

Chiao
No. 16. Contact
February 27 (p.m.)–March 3

HEAD: Yang makes contact with yin; and yin with yang. Things ascend to the Hall of Light, fully emergent and flourishing.

According to Chinese ways of thinking, the ideal human state is one of sustained, mutually beneficial contact between two or more parties. As Yang Hsiung says in his other philosophical classic, "It is the Way of Man to have social intercourse." Even more explicit is Confucius' emphasis on humaneness (*jen*), the virtue aligned with spring. In the "golden age" of the past, communities purportedly served the legitimate interests of all while maintaining the dignity of each. In the present, stable hierarchical relations weave elements of society together in a complex web of mutual obligation, but reciprocity (implying not only mutual obligation but also an empathetic "likening to oneself") is needed to temper the possible ill effects of

Figure 5. A scene of cosmic harmony, with birds, and animals, and humans in perfect accord.

unmediated power relations. The perfect community, therefore, is equally dependent upon hierarchy and reciprocity. In this, it is modeled upon the cosmos, where yang *ch'i* defines the patterns of growth, while yin responds appropriately. This tetragram celebrates such notions of ideal contact.

The Hall of Light, on the one hand, simply refers to the region above ground in the light of day. But the same term is used to describe the sacred site where the king makes ritual contact with the gods. Its use suggests that all things are sanctified by contact with the Mystery.

This tetragram is correlated with the Rainfall solar period. Rain symbolizes beneficent grace and germinating influence, whether the reference is to sexual contact or to political relations. Consequently, the general tone of this tetragram is lucky, except in those few cases where "stimulus and response" occurs between categorically dissimilar partners, prompting repulsion and disaster.

Appraisal 1: In the dark he contacts the gods.
He fasts but fails to use propriety.

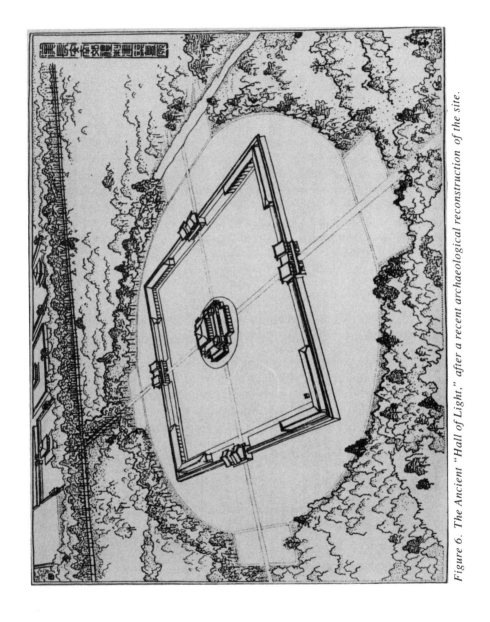

Figure 6. The Ancient "Hall of Light," after a recent archaeological reconstruction of the site.

Fathoming 1: Dark contact, improper,
Means: He harbors wrong, holding shame within.

Appraisal 1, corresponding to the Beginning of Thought, is aligned here with inauspicious Night. In approaching the unseen gods, an attitude of extreme reverence must be adopted. Fasting is a spiritual exercise designed to concentrate the spirit, focusing it upon an intimation of the divine implanted in our nature. The ordinary unthinking individual may perform this purification perfunctorily, assuming that the mere performance of ritual works like magic regardless of the intent behind it; in effect, this is operating on the mistaken notion that fasting alone, without a profound realignment of the self, is enough to please the gods. Conversely, the unreflective person may become overly preoccupied with the supernatural; in his anxiety to please the gods, he may neglect to maintain fundamental social relations, the root of all Goodness. Perhaps he assumes that the dark will provide sufficient cover for such "dark" errors. But sacred ritual, incorrectly practiced, is worse than useless; far from conferring blessings, it promotes evil and results in shame.

Appraisal 2: Dark contact, when based on trust,
Grows luminous.

Fathoming 2: Trust behind dark contact
Means: In good faith he meets the gods and spirits.

By definition, the divine is located wherever perceptible change is effected by an unseen cause. Although the Tao itself remains forever shrouded in mystery, the results of its operations are abundantly clear to all. In this set of verses, mutual trust prevails between gods and Man since a community of shared interests has been forged through correct ritual practice. The truly good person, whose charismatic virtue is luminous, even daemonically compelling, can hope to attract the blessings of the unseen world.

Appraisal 3: He contacts wood and stone.

Fathoming 3: Befriending wood and stone
Means: He cannot turn to other men.

Stone epitomizes whatever is hard; wood, that which is pliable. Things in different categories repel each other, creating a disastrous response, as in the antagonistic relation between wood (i.e., any kind of vegetation) and stone (i.e., axes or scythes). Knowing this, the wise person seeks alliances with those who are fully developed human beings. The benighted individual, in contrast, looks to make meaningful contact with those who are less than fully human—those who are no better than "wood and stone." The Confucian *Analects* cautions us, "Have no friends unequal to yourself."

> Appraisal 4: Contact, back and forth,
>> With fragrant smoke rising,
>> This is the gate of gain and ruin.

> Fathoming 4: Mutual contact, harmonious,
>> Means: He acts in concert with the gods.

Appraisal 4 represents the Beginning of Good Fortune; hence, this sketch of satisfactory relations between gods and Man. The fragrant fumes of burning sacrificial meats give the ritual participant intense satisfaction. The depth of his pleasure, as he well knows, derives from a fundamental correspondence between inner commitment to perfect integrity and its visible expression in solemn sacrifice. When inner and outer are in perfect accord, the individual joins the gods in the execution of the divine plan. Whether or not that plan will prevail among men is thus determined largely by individual choice.

> Appraisal 5: Contacting parrot and ape,
>> He fails to garner his glory.

> Fathoming 5: Befriending parrot and ape
>> Means: He goes the way of bird and beast.

In general, both parrots and apes exhibit a high degree of intelligence and curiosity, steady habits, and the capacity for speech. Yet despite their strong resemblance to human beings, neither parrot nor ape possesses the single most important characteristic of humans: the capacity for moral action framed by ritual. Unless a person observes the rules of propriety, her heart is no better than that of a bird or beast.

The parrot may also stand more specifically for flatterers and sycophants (since the bird only repeats its master's words); the ape traditionally stands for pompous blusterers (since it is given to dramatic beatings of its chest).

> Appraisal 6: How vast the great state!
>> With it small states seek contact.
>> "The sacred meats that we possess
>> We gladly share with you."

> Fathoming 6: Contact between great and small
>> Means: In treating worthies well, glory blazes forth.

Great states encourage minor states to enter into formal tributary relations; through ritual, the prestige of both parties is enhanced. Similarly, the wise leader encourages the support of strong allies by sharing profits with them; in the end, all benefit. As the *Changes* says, "I have a good goblet / Which I will share with you" (W, 237).

Appraisal 7: He befriends bird and rat,
Wasting his store of millet.

Fathoming 7: Contact with bird and rat
Means: Nothing but waste!

Echoing the images in Appraisal 5 above, this poem again exhorts the reader to learn to distinguish bestial men from the worthy. Clearly, the situation is now worse. Contact is made with animals that do not bear the slightest resemblance to human beings. In fact, bird and rat are two of the most notorious enemies of man, since their continual predations threaten the basic food stores of society. An individual has lost all ability to categorize properly when he befriends bird and rat.

Appraisal 8: Ax and lance fly back and forth.
Using his propriety, he will not rue the day.

Fathoming 8: Ax and lance, blow for blow,
Mean: In campaigns, he is invincible.

The use of force, properly employed in the defense of morality, is sanctioned here, and its ultimate success is guaranteed so long as the individual remains steadfast in his virtue. The succeeding Appraisal qualifies this celebration of war.

Appraisal 9: He unrightly joins in battle
And so is routed at the city wall.
Since he is cruel, he is devoured.

Fathoming 9: Cut down in the battle fray,
Means: How could he ever succeed?

In antiquity, the two great affairs of state were said to be sacrifice and war. Throughout this tetragram, the *Mystery* reminds us that no major project should be undertaken without the proper mental disposition. Even when an individual commands a force, its deployment will redound to his glory only if he acts for the Good and avoids unnecessary violence. Insatiable greed, ambition, or cruelty invariably backfires. The belligerent loses part, then all of his territory. Those in power should reserve their arms to punish recalcitrant evildoers on behalf of the entire society, rather than to seek private gain.

Juan
No. 17. Holding Back
March 4–March 8 (a.m.)

Correlates with Heaven's Mystery;
Yang; the phase Wood; and the I
ching Hexagram no. 5, Waiting; the
sun enters the Straddler constella-
tion, 1st degree; the Dipper points
due east; the musical note is E-flat

HEAD: Yang *ch'i* can be firm, can be pliant, can be active or at rest. Seeing difficulty, it shrinks back.

This tetragram begins the Startled from Hibernation solar period. Since yin still reigns, the myriad things continue to experience difficulties, but yang *ch'i* is by turns firm or flexible, at work or at ease. Avoiding direct confrontation with the stronger forces of yin, it handily survives to nourish all of Heaven-and-Earth. The overall pattern of increasing warmth in midspring testifies to its general effectiveness. This tetragram, then, celebrates acts of pliancy, tentativeness, timidity, reticence, and even weakness that ultimately lead to greater strength. Many technical arts and ritual acts are based on this principle.

This tetragram's alignment with Wood is significant since the primary characteristic of wood, according to the early Chinese, is its pliability. At the same time, wood is strong enough to support the weight of roofs and walls, even in the most munificent of palace structures. The *Mystery* applauds this combination of pliancy and strength.

> Appraisal 1: Ruddy shoots, with tips now sharp—
> Their advances profit by retreat.

> Fathoming 1: Ruddy tips now tightly furled
> Means: Retreat in order to move ahead.

In midspring, the tightly furled tips of various plants emerge tentatively from the soil. Although these points may appear extremely fragile, their compressed conelike shape works well to protect them while facilitating their steady upward thrust into the light. If the leaves were to unfurl too soon, before all danger of frost has passed, advance might well prove hazardous. By analogy, the wise individual is willing to yield to others, especially when the time is not yet right to advance her ideas. Her reticence gains her the friends and supporters necessary to win high rank and renown in the dangerous world outside.

> Appraisal 2: Shrinking his heart
> Makes for infirmity.

Fathoming 2: Holding back his mind
Means: The center lacks all courage.

Tactical retreat is required in certain situations, as the previous verse makes plain. However, due caution should not be confused with cowardice. The man of virtue must not waver when confronted with necessary moral decisions; neither should he shrink from proper commitments. Should his moral courage fail him, he is in danger of losing what distinguishes him. For this reason, one Chinese classic says, "The person who is humane but not armed has no ability to succeed."

Appraisal 3: Drawing in his knees,
He protects his joints.
Though not unconstrained,
There is no offense in the end.

Fathoming 3: Pulling back his knees
Means: It is improper for limbs to sprawl.

The poem hinges on a single pun: the word for "body joints" means "moderation" as well. The man of virtue at times may choose to draw back in order to protect his principles. At first glance, this decision seems to restrict his sphere of activity, but in the end the adoption of certain self-imposed limits saves him from moral or physical harm. This verse reminds us that there is no exact equivalent in early China to our notion of positive freedom.

Appraisal 4: Holding back his outbursts,
In three years, not a single peep.

Fathoming 4: Outbursts suppressed, with nary a peep
Mean: The right time is missed repeatedly.

Building on Appraisal 2, this poem chides the individual who hesitates to speak out against present evils. Because of his lack of courage, numerous opportunities for reform are missed. Confucius identifies this unwillingness to speak up when speech is appropriate as a typical bureaucratic failing.

Appraisal 5: The golden mushroom does not grow.
It awaits the propitious cloud.

Fathoming 5: That mushrooms of immortality do not grow
Means: They wait to be joined by their mates.

Golden fungi and felicitous clouds are auspicious omens that herald the rise of a sagely universal ruler. The golden fungus is also associated with immortality cults and the generative powers of spring. As in the *Book of Changes*, the very fact that portents—good or bad—exist demonstrates Heaven's continuing concern for Man, for Heaven-sent signs guide those in pursuit of the Way. The golden fungus, then, is eagerly awaited for many reasons. But to the Chinese, good things ideally come in pairs: official and ruler, husband and wife, and so on, with each partner joined in mutual reliance and benefit. Therefore, the golden fungus can appear only when its fitting match is found. That means, a true leader cannot arise without worthy supporters.

> Appraisal 6: Recoiling, he misses the time.
> Perhaps disaster follows him.

> Fathoming 6: Drawing back, missing the moment,
> Means: Jail then flight come later.

Having missed the opportunity to advance the cause of morality, the individual must seize the moment to draw back in the face of clear and present danger, or else risk offending those in power, who will then accuse him of various crimes. The moral coward, however, hesitates even now to act. As an autocommentary to the *Mystery* puts it,

> The noble man cultivating virtue, awaits the proper moment. He does not
> set out before the right moment, nor draw back after it has already
> passed. . . . Can this be said of anyone but the noble man?

> Appraisal 7: Tempering his moderation,
> Holding fast his principles,
> He offers his life for the cause.

> Fathoming 7: Less moderate, offering to die,
> Means: There is a ruler within him.

Appraisal 7, marking the Beginning of Calamity, depicts a brave man willing to offer his life, if need be, for the "cause." A wiser person, however, might have been able to avoid such dramatic self-sacrifice. Confucius labeled courage without canniness "mere foolhardiness."

> Appraisal 8: The crown of a hollow, dried-out tree
> Is struck by gusts that shake its limbs.
> The petty man has reason to hang back.
> Thrice he retreats before he is snagged.

> Fathoming 8: The quaking of hollow trees
> Means: The petty man suffers disgrace.

The hollow tree and the petty man are alike in not having a strong inner core. Without any inner resources, the petty man is also dry and lifeless. And finally, because he emphasizes secondary considerations over fundamental values, he resembles the crown of the tree, rather than its roots. Such an individual inevitably quails in the face of a stronger force. Unable to stand firm, he is seriously shaken. Knowing his own weaknesses, the clever (if immoral) individual refuses to take a stand on any issue, hoping thereby to elude danger. After all, such accommodation comes far more easily to him than undertaking the arduous task of self-reform. Still, his plan ultimately fails; in the end the petty man finds himself trapped by his own weaknesses.

> Appraisal 9: He regrets withdrawing.
> The past leaves, the future returns.

> Fathoming 9: Returns from regretted withdrawals
> Mean: Gain lies in the future.

In this last Appraisal, the individual comes to realize that his previous compromises and accommodations have been ill-timed, ill-advised, or immoral. He changes his course, returning to the Right, and in the end achieves his goal—so very great is the "return" for Virtue. Appraisal 9 marks the end of the cycle. Having gone as far in Holding Back as possible, the individual's moral sensibilities finally begin to reassert themselves.

Hsi
No. 18. Waiting
March 8 (p.m.)–March 12

Correlates with Heaven's Mystery; Yin; the phase Metal; and the I ching Hexagram no. 5, Waiting; the sun enters the Straddler constellation, 6th degree

HEAD: Yang *ch'i* has what it waits for. When it is permissible to advance, it advances, so that all things achieve their desires.

This tetragram is the twin of the previous one in two senses: both correlate with the same hexagram in the *Changes* and with the Startled from Hibernation solar period. For this reason, the Appraisals of Tetragram 18 generally reiterate the theme of Tetragram 17; once again, we are advised of the necessity of acquiescing in Heaven's patterns, waiting for the proper time to act. The propriety of this is proven by the natural world, where the myriad things patiently await warmer days to complete their separate destinies. The Head, however, registers a slight but significant change in terms of the wait.

In the previous tetragram, there was still a tendency to recoil in the face of danger. Now there is a sense of quiet strength that bides its time until the right time to act.

> Appraisal 1: Those whose villainy is hidden
> Await bad luck from Heaven.

> Fathoming 1: The wait by secret villains
> Means: No time is propitious.

By convention Heaven is omniscient; by definition, then, no evil can truly be hidden from it. Even if Heaven is understood simply as "the Way things are," the evildoer is inevitably unmasked by circumstances. It is true that a crime may well seem hidden if knowledge of it is kept from one's fellow men. Perhaps the intended crime has not yet been perpetrated, since Appraisal 1 corresponds to the Beginning of Thought. Still, cosmic operations invariably insure that nothing goes right for the criminal. That hidden villainy meets with Heaven's retribution is, in fact, one proof of the interconnectedness of Heaven-Earth-Man.

> Appraisal 2: Those whose virtue is hidden
> Await prosperity from Heaven.

> Fathoming 2: The wait by men of hidden virtue
> Means: Bright are the coming days.

In contrast to the previous Appraisal, the good person "piles up virtue in secret, then is showered with good fortune, plain as day," as one commentator writes. The hidden criminal waits uneasily, fearing Heaven's displeasure; secret virtue, in contrast, confidently anticipates Heaven's reward. Prospects are truly bright for such a person.

> Appraisal 3: He awaits a later date.

> Fathoming 3: Waiting until too late
> Means: He is remiss.

Since timely action is a key factor in success, the wise person is always on the lookout for opportune moments to further the Good. But here a person has overlooked the right time to act.

> Appraisal 4: Retracting his horn, righting his foot;
> Only by this he awaits the good.

> Fathoming 4: The horn retracted and the straightened foot
> Mean: He is not contrary or perverse.

The horn symbolizes aggressiveness. Because it is hard, it also signifies stubbornness. To retract the horn, then, means to withdraw from quarrels and competitiveness. The straightened foot walks in the right direction following the one true Way. Peaceable and reliable, the individual quietly lives out his days, trusting to his reward.

Appraisal 5: Great ranks flock to serve the palace,
    Meanly the petty men wait in vain.

Fathoming 5: Ranks in palace employ
    Mean: Rank cannot be got for nothing.

The palace of the Son of Heaven, the seat of central government, ideally functions as a kind of *axis mundi*, around which matters of state revolve. When a just society exists, men of virtue are induced by their leader's charismatic virtue to enter his service. Meanwhile, "petty men" of inferior virtue wait in vain for posts.

Appraisal 6: Awaiting good fortune, properly aligned,
    He will partake of gold.

Fathoming 6: Awaiting good fortune with utmost propriety
    Means: Rectitude can be taken like tonic.

The good person trusts to Heaven and awaits his fate, knowing that he has made every effort to cultivate the seeds of virtue within himself. Virtue enlivens him like a tonic. It may well win him fortune and fame. It can even secure him a kind of immortality. In this, virtue far excels the concoctions of potable gold advertised by quacks.

Appraisal 7: He recklessly awaits misfortune.
    This is the station of ill-omened men.

Fathoming 7: Awaiting misfortune recklessly
    Means: He makes a date with calamity.

Evildoers know that they will probably be punished for their crimes. In their hearts, they cannot help but be somewhat apprehensive about future retribution. But they feign complete unconcern and invite calamity by their reckless disregard for the Good. Their own deeds condemn them to perpetual unhappiness.

Appraisal 8: Discounting the calamitous in present calamity,
    We wait for Heaven to keep us alive.

Fathoming 8: Calamity is no calamity unless seen as such,
    Meaning: It is not Heaven that faults us.

When her luck is down, the superior person trusts Heaven to keep her alive; she is wise enough to see that a turn away from virtue is the only real disaster. Just as the natural world awaits spring's renewal, the good person calmly awaits Heaven's vindication.

> Appraisal 9: Waiting, twisted up like a cripple,
>   Heaven strikes his forehead.

> Fathoming 9: That the waiting cripple is struck
>   Means: In the end, he is incurable.

Due to a spinal deformity, the cripple always appears to be looking defiantly toward Heaven. In his arrogance, the moral cripple with his deformed soul also challenges Heaven to punish him. When Heaven moves, so crippling is the blow that the individual never recovers.

Ts'ung
No. 19. Following
March 13–March 17 (a.m.)

Correlates with Heaven's Mystery; Yang; the phase Water; and the I ching Hexagram no. 17, Pursuit; the sun enters the Straddler constellation, 10th degree

HEAD: Yang leaps into pools, into marshes, into fields, into mountains. Things are all poised to follow.

As yang *ch'i* grows steadily stronger, its presence is felt in every corner of All-under-Heaven, from the lowest to the highest. No longer confined below earth, yang *ch'i* expresses its newfound freedom with a joy conveyed by the verb "leap," usually reserved for activities associated with good fortune, with energy and health, with "feeling one's oats," and with eager and lively spirits. Therefore, the myriad things can expect a long growing period of spring and summer, which will prompt their own development.

As yang is to the myriad things, so the virtuous individual is to ordinary people. Lesser mortals "crane their necks" and "stand on tiptoe" to catch a glimpse of the noble man, anxious to express their loyalty and to become like him. In the triadic realms of Heaven-Earth-Man, then, all are ready to obey the Good; hence, the tetragram's title.

> Appraisal 1: The sun, unseen, espouses it.
>   The moon, in darkness, follows it.
>   This is the foundation.

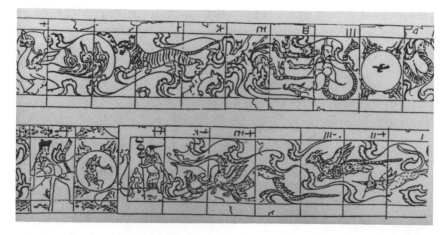

Figure 7. The sun and moon from a Han dynasty depiction. The sun is identified by the black crow; the moon, by its resident frog. The swirling cloud forms are meant to represent the Milky Way ("Heaven's Barge" or the "Silver River" in Chinese), which is mentioned in Tetragram 76.

Fathoming 1: The sun takes a wife, the moon follows.
Meaning: The subordinate's response is the base.

Appropriately enough, Appraisal 1 describes the "marriage" of sun and moon that takes place on the first day of the lunar calendar when sun and moon are conjoined. Immediately after this union, on the succeeding days of the lunar month, the moon (when viewed from stationary Earth) appears to follow the sun faithfully in its westerly course. This provides a model for the wife's faithfulness to her husband, or a subject's to his ruler. To further the simile, the moon, like a self-effacing wife walking slightly behind her husband, seems to lag somewhat behind the sun until the new marriage at the beginning of the next lunar month. The natural accord between yin and yang, leader and follower, represents an eternal constant, which in turn serves as the basis of all social relations. Although its ultimate motive force remains shrouded in mystery ("in darkness"), we know that compliance cannot result from coercion by the leader (yang, male, sun, ruler), but from a recognition of shared goals.

> Appraisal 2: In dawn's first light, things barely emerge.
> Pairing, following, they gather by type.

> Fathoming 2: Barely emerging, following by pairs
> Means: They do not know their destination.

Han literary convention typically employs the new dawn to signify auspicious beginnings. By the same token, the *Changes* phrase, "things gathering by type" (W, 280), usually celebrates the orderly division of cosmos and society into successive related units. However, these lines (correlated with yin) are clearly inauspicious. Perhaps the first light of dawn is too feeble to provide sufficient illumination. Therefore, the myriad things in a benighted state pick partners (and by extension, directions in life) without ever really understanding the choices before them.

> Appraisal 3: Men do not attack him.
> They are drawn to follow.

> Fathoming 3: That men do not attack him
> Means: This, in itself, is proof of Virtue's power.

The good person appears inviolable, since good manners and self-deprecation forestall the attacks of others. Insofar as he himself follows the Right, others are drawn to follow him, thanks to the force of his charismatic example. The comparative ease with which the good person confronts life's difficulties is compelling proof of Heaven's favor and Virtue's efficacy.

> Appraisal 4: The call to follow is improper.
> A woman takes his bloodied basket.
> Lost.

> Fathoming 4: Loss following the call
> Means: How can theirs be a worthy match?

A passage in the *Changes* reads:

> The woman holds out the basket,
> But there are no fruits in it.
> The knight stabs the sheep,
> But there is no blood.
> There is nothing which this favors.
> (W, 212)

In the *Mystery*, matters are, if anything, worse, due to the reversal of traditional male/female roles. The woman, rather than the man, tries to offer the blood sacrifice, although it is her place to offer fruit only. What, we may ask, is lost in consequence? Husband and wife may both have neglected the ritual proper to the service of the gods (the basket, then, "is lost"). Or, possibly the woman keenly feels the loss of her husband, for the blood-soaked basket signifies death, perhaps following a disastrous military expedition. Earlier "cries to follow" were inherently no good (inappropriate or ineffective). Unfortunately, those lacking in virtue often seek to hide their own shame by inducing others to emulate their bad example.

> Appraisal 5: Follow the example of water
> Which goes to fill the hollows.

> Fathoming 5: To follow water filling the holes
> Means: He does not overstep himself.

Readers are enjoined to follow the pattern provided by water, which seeks the low places, moving on only after the hollows have been completely filled. These lines clearly allude to the philosopher Mencius, who says:

> Flowing water does not go further forward until it has filled all the
> hollows. A gentleman in his pursuit of the Way does not proceed unless
> he achieves a beautiful pattern (7A/24).

By following ritual patterns, the good person molds herself until she is in perfect conformity with the Good, just as water meets the outline of the hollow. In that way, she reaches a stage where she can act without overstepping moral boundaries or infringing upon others. Self-cultivation, like water's flow, is gradual and modest, but effective.

> Appraisal 6: Following his eye,
> He loses his belly.

> Fathoming 6: The eye followed and the belly lost
> Mean: He indulges his desires to excess.

As in earlier tetragrams, the eye stands for what is outer; the belly, for what is inner ("inner virtue," according to one commentator). Also, the eye stands for intellectual appreciation or sensual desire, as opposed to the belly, which stands for the instinctual gratification of basic needs for food, sex, and community. Here desire develops at the expense of the body's basic instinct for self-preservation. The desire for novelty, for example, may cause the individual to choose bubblegum ice cream or the latest theory over more nourishing fare for the mind and body. This fundamental inability to set the right priorities in life can only end in disaster.

Appraisal 7: Shaking off the foul in him,
He allows the good to grow:
Realgar eats away the flesh.

Fathoming 7: Shaking corruption, following the pure,
Means: He is saved from bad luck.

Traditionally, Chinese doctors applied disulphide of arsenic (realgar) to
"corrupt flesh" (including carbuncles and sores) on the principle that "poison eats poison." Healing could then take place. By analogy, harsh self-criticism permits self-renewal to occur. With Appraisal 7 near the end of the tetragram, relatively drastic measures are needed if the patient's prognosis is to improve.

Appraisal 8: The tainted is allowed.
Calamity, flying out, cannot be contained.

Fathoming 8: Following corruption
Means: Calamity cannot be argued away.

This individual follows evil companions or an evil course of action willingly; no reform is attempted. Like the evils in Pandora's box, calamity soon flies out beyond his control. All are deaf to his pleas for help.

Appraisal 9: Follow what is most commendable.
Then and only then will he climb the stairs,
Ascending to the proper end.

Fathoming 9: Following the model of perfection
Means: Later, he gets results.

Ideally, education trains youths to emulate what is most admirable (Confucian tradition and the example of the ancient sages). The cultivated individual can then embark upon a distinguished career in public service (signified by the flight of steps) that will benefit the entire community. This image leads naturally to the following tetragram, entitled Advance.

Correlates with Heaven's Mystery;
Yin; *the phase Fire; and the* I
ching Hexagram *no. 35, Progress;*
the sun enters the Straddler
constellation, 15th degree

Chin
No. 20. Advance
March 17 (p.m.)–March 21

HEAD: Yang, attracting things, advances. Things emerge most prolifically. Like morning light opening, they go forward.

We are approaching the vernal equinox, the first time in the annual cycle when the strength of yang *ch'i* is equal to that of yin. (After the vernal equinox, yang will dominate until the autumn equinox.) Under the beneficent influence of yang *ch'i*, the myriad things, including Man, find their growth enhanced. As days lengthen and the light improves, all things develop. In the human realm, true advance means advance in the Way, predicated on tireless effort but leading to profound personal and societal transformation. Conventional desires for advance sparked by overweening ambition and arrogant pride, however, result in reckless acts.

> Appraisal 1: In darkness, he advances. Obstructions
>   Act as the mother of retreat.

> Fathoming 1: The dark advance obstructed
>   Means: Deflection breeds retreat.

The first Appraisal correlates with the Water phase, whose color is black. But there are additional reasons for darkness here. First, any new endeavor in its initial phase is uncharted. Second, the advance takes place in secret since it is improper. The unmitigated darkness prevents the individual from finding his proper path. Somewhere along the Way, he meets with one or more obstructions, then veers off in the wrong direction. The greater the advance, the greater the retreat from Goodness. In this way, the first obstruction becomes the "mother" of defeat.

> Appraisal 2: To advance using the model of centrality:
>   The singular perspicacity of the Great Man.

> Fathoming 2: Advancing by the Mean
>   Means: The model must be internalized.

Several Confucian Classics emphasize the importance of centrality. In private life, centrality means keeping to the ideal Mean of good conduct (an idea similar to the Aristotelian Mean). In the public sphere, centrality implies the unique position held by the ruler as focus for his subjects' talents and aspirations. In that any noble act is prompted by the fully developed conscience, which internalizes the model of the sages, individual "centeredness" cannot be counted as something external.

Appraisal 2 is usually assigned to commoners, yet the *Mystery* here speaks of the Great Man. The theme of this tetragram is advance. Through sustained efforts to embody the Mean, any person can advance to become a sage.

> Appraisal 3: Impetuous and most presumptuous,
> He cannot find the center path.

> Fathoming 3: That he is wildly unstable
> Means: His advance is not centered.

Appraisal 3 marks the transition from Thought to Action. Aligned here with inauspicious Night, it describes reckless advance in disregard of the conventions. Confucius advocated moderation ("the center path") to his headstrong disciples.

> Appraisal 4: The sun in its flight dispels darkness.
> The myriad things are suffused with joy.

> Fathoming 4: That the sun's flight dispels darkness
> Means: The way of the ruler flourishes.

The sun (often called the Red Bird) is compared to a gigantic bird whose flight through the heavens brings light and warmth to regions that would otherwise languish in darkness. The sun, of course, symbolizes the able leader for several reasons. Their positions are correspondingly high. Both shine equally on all regions as they progress through their respective realms. Both bring light and enlightenment to those below. As the good leader's suasive example helps followers who would otherwise remain benighted, he may also be said to "dispel darkness." Responding to such beneficent influences, all the myriad things of the cosmos reach a state of perfect harmony.

> Appraisal 5: He advances by patronage.
> Some support him like a crutch.

> Fathoming 5: Advancement by connection
> Means: He is constrained by his patron's house.

Appraisal 5, in its central position, is ruler (i.e., dominant image) of the tetragram. In a yin (even-numbered) tetragram such as this, a yin line is unlucky. An angry complaint is lodged against two common means of advancement: patronage and factionalism. Those who have won their place unfairly often render poor service to the community, since they feel constrained by loyalty to their own corrupt patrons.

> Appraisal 6: Advancing by the lofty and illustrious,
> In receipt of blessings without bounds.

> Fathoming 6: Advancing by what is high and light
> Means: This Way is far-reaching.

The deserving person advances because she imitates the lofty and illustrious way of the ancient sages embodied in ritual. Her efforts are repaid by high position and extraordinary blessings. (In an alternate reading of the Appraisal line, "she advances and so is lofty and illustrious.") Thus her influence becomes far-reaching in at least two senses. First, her moral influence permeates every aspect of contemporary society. Second, her descendants will receive the benefits of this vast store of accumulated *ch'i* for generations to come.

> Appraisal 7: He cannot sustain his advance.
> Hearing blame, he stops up his ears.

> Fathoming 7: Advance perverted
> Means: Detractions grow ever more obvious.

In the *Mystery* schema, Position 7 is the Beginning of Calamity. This benighted individual, whose advance has come at the expense of the greater good, finally meets severe criticism. Incapable of reform, he can only expect disparaging remarks and disaffection to increase.

> Appraisal 8: Advancing into a deep pool,
> The noble man uses a boat.

> Fathoming 8: To advance in pools using a boat
> · Means: He proceeds by the Way.

The boat stands for all the civilizing inventions of the sage-kings of antiquity, whose utility stems from their imitation of fundamental cosmic patterns. The wise individual who faces potential danger (the deep water) strictly follows the tradition of the sages as outlined in the Classics. Otherwise, progress becomes difficult, due to moral ineptitude.

> Appraisal 9: Heading upstream, barefoot over mountains:
> In three long years he has not returned.

> Fathoming 9: Climbing against current and crag
> Means: In the end, it cannot be prolonged.

In a contrast to the preceding verse, the subject of this final Appraisal sets himself a series of nearly impossible tasks (possibly out of blind perversity or a regrettable love of physical daring). Unfortunately, he does not know enough to employ the tools at hand to his advantage. Although he expends great effort, few, if any, gains result. His failure is all the more regrettable in that it is completely unnecessary. A wiser individual uses available resources, like the Classics, to persevere in the Way.

Correlates with Heaven's Mystery; Yang; *the phase Wood; and the* I ching *Hexagram no. 40, Deliverance; the sun enters the Wall constellation, 3d degree; the Dipper points due east; the musical note is E-flat; the spring equinox begins with Appraisal 3*

Shih
No. 21. Release
March 22–March 26 (a.m.)

HEAD: Yang *ch'i* to effect harmony strikes open the round casing of yin, warming and releasing things, so that all shed their withered husks and are delivered from their shells.

Previous tetragrams, including the Head text of Tetragram 10, consistently associate yin with what encircles, encases, or wraps around things, thereby hampering their growth; hence my translation. However, this Head text could also read, "Yang *ch'i* harmoniously catalyzes. Round and warm, [the sun] releases things so that all shed their withered husks." Either version emphasizes the generative influence of yang *ch'i* at the transitional vernal equinox. Once yin and yang have come into balance, yang *ch'i* is strong enough to break yin's hold on the myriad things. Like thunder, the "release of Heaven-and-Earth," yang *ch'i* catalyzes productive growth so that seed pods now break open; animals and insects, shaking off hibernation, begin to stir. As a host of creatures emerge from their shells, husks, and moltings to the clear light of day, we may expect moral renewal in mankind as well. A boundless potential for good opens up, with a focus on lightening the burdens of others. Inappropriate release entailing careless or remiss behavior, however, leads inevitably to loss.

Appraisal 1: Movement, though nameless,
      Leads to achievement.

Fathoming 1: Moving, without a name
Means: Indescribable are its glories.

Appraisal 1, representing the Beginning of Thought, is here aligned with auspicious yang. By convention, both the Tao and the sage are "nameless" in the sense that their greatness cannot be reduced to one or more discrete attributes. The virtue of the ancient sage-king Yao, for example, was "so boundless that the people could not find a name for it" (A 8/19). And although the patterns they establish help lesser creatures realize their innate potential, both the Tao and the sage prefer to operate behind the scenes, without drawing attention to themselves. In consequence, few among us can fully recognize, let alone name the extent of their innate power. They are at once "ordinary" (because existence without them seems impossible) and "extraordinary." No wonder their achievements cannot be adequately described.

Appraisal 2: Movement yields echo and shadow.

Fathoming 2: Movement yielding only echo and shadow
Means: It is not worth noting.

Echo and shadow usually symbolize the mysterious but powerful attraction between things in categorical sympathy. These same images can also suggest the close conformity of the superior man to cosmic norms, of inferiors to true superiors, and so on. Here, however, the point is decidedly different: While the unseen Tao produces manifest achievements, self-important operators produce no tangible benefit, either because their nature is fundamentally derivative (like echo and shadow), or because they grasp at transitory goals of no greater substance than an echo or a shadow. As the Chinese proverb says, "They would chase the wind and catch the shadow."

Appraisal 3: The wind moves and thunder rouses.
Follow their lofty and exalted natures.

Fathoming 3: Wind moving, thunder rousing
Means: Their movements have purpose.

Appraisal 3 corresponds to the Wood phase, to East, and to spring. Since antiquity, the Chinese have assumed that spring thunderstorms stimulate the proper growth of things. The good leader is like a force of nature in that his catalyzing activity seems irresistible. In contrast to the Taoist sage, who practices "nonaction," the Confucian sage works with the purpose of improving and elevating others.

Appraisal 4: In moving up to the highlands,
He loses friends from the lowlands.

Fathoming 4: Moving to the highlands
Means: He is in danger of losing his base.

Appraisal 4 marks the Beginning of Good Fortune; unfortunately, here it is aligned with inauspicious Night. In climbing from a low post to a high one, the individual neglects his old base, whether it be former allies, the support of followers, the teachings of the Confucian masters, or simply the attachment to right conduct. For this reason, he is likely to be toppled from his position of prominence.

Appraisal 5: Like healing salves, the ruler's virtue
Soothes the Four States.

Fathoming 5: The salves that smooth and release
Mean: The people's joy knows no bounds.

A standard metaphor compares precious unguents to the ruler's gracious virtue. Just as unguents smooth and heal the broken skin, the ruler's right conduct restores life to the body politic and obviates political friction, even beyond the borders of the Central Kingdom. For this reason, the ruler's subjects can look forward to a period of unparalleled peace and joy.

Appraisal 6: Thunder at court
Destroys harmony and propriety.

Fathoming 6: Thunder at court
Means: Both harmony and rectitude are lost.

Thunderclaps express divine anger and, by extension, the wrath of the Son of Heaven. They also suggest new developments, which frighten rather than soothe. Finally, repeated thunderclaps may symbolize self-promoting ministers who make the people quail in fear as they abuse the authority of their offices. Anger, innovations, and arrogance are all out of place at court. For this reason, "harmony and rectitude are lost."

Appraisal 7: Thunder crashes, again and again,
Washing away his shame.

Fathoming 7: Repeated thunderclaps, no disgrace,
Means: Shame is excised from everywhere.

In the *Changes*, repeated thunderclaps convey a salutary shock to the system:

> Thunder repeated: the image of shock. In fear and trembling, the noble
> man sets his life in order and examines himself (W, 648–9).

The right response to bad omens is to resolve upon self-reform. Then, paradoxically, "shock will bring success" (W, 648). These same lines, however, according to certain commentators, describe the righteous indignation felt by the superior individual toward those who dare to blame or insult him. Whatever their charges, he remains unsullied as anger purges the shame.

> Appraisal 8: Driven by profit, he falls
> Flat on his face, then dies.

> Fathoming 8: To be driven by profit
> Means: He walks together with death.

Conventional wisdom equates the good life with the acquisition of wealth. Confucius derided lesser men who go to a great deal of trouble "to discover what will pay." Running after profit all too often ends in the death of the soul.

> Appraisal 9: Today accused, tomorrow blessed.
> In the end, he's freed from his chains.

> Fathoming 9: Today accused, tomorrow blessed
> Means: By that, he's released from calamity.

As one Chinese philosopher noted, "It is never anyone's proper destiny to die in chains." Appraisal 9 is the last Appraisal; hence, the reference to a final release from danger. The vague wording of the end line of the Fathoming tends to focus the reader's attention on the question, "What can one use to release oneself from calamity?" A passage in the *Changes* supplies the answer. Strict adherence to moral standards obviates the need for most constraints, physical and mental, used to train or curb lesser men (W, 22). Proof of the blessings associated with morality is supplied by the story of good King Wen of Chou, who was released from jail even under the evil last king of the Shang dynasty.

Correlates with Heaven's Mystery; Yin; the phase Metal; and the I ching *Hexagram no. 34, Greatly Strong; the sun enters the Wall constellation, 8th degree*

Ke
No. 22. Resistance
March 26 (p.m.)–March 30

HEAD: Yang *ch'i*, internally strong, can offer resistance to the many manifestations of yin. Repelling them, it forces them to withdraw.

As the first tetragram following the vernal equinox, Resistance signals a dramatic shift in the cosmic balance. For the first time in the lunar year, yang *ch'i* is slightly stronger than yin, although yin's influence is still manifest. Yang *ch'i* begins its assault on yin, propelled perhaps by the tetragram's alignment with Metal, the stuff of weapons. Still, at this point in the annual cycle yang *ch'i* is merely internally strong. Only in later tetragrams will yang confront yin externally. This relative weakness of yang *ch'i* is not the primary reason, however, why the Appraisals below do not celebrate warlike postures. As the *Changes* tells us, "The petty person uses his strength, but the noble man does not act in this way." True resistance entails perseverance, not brute force. Developing strength and power in these initial stages depends on distancing oneself from impropriety, while staying close to integrity.

The character used for the title depicts a length of wooden board that demarcates space and separates objects. Footboards and backboards in carriages, window sills, cupboards, animal enclosures, and fences use the same word. The texts that follow emphasize appropriate separation, distancing, and resistance.

> Appraisal 1: Sealing off inner Goodness,
> Propriety fails, Goodness is lost.

> Fathoming 1: Sealing off inner Goodness
> Means: The center cannot assimilate the Good.

The first position, which marks the Beginning of Thought, depicts the inner workings of the heart/mind where seeds of Goodness are implanted, as well as impulses toward evil. If an individual assiduously works to develop the Good within, she will grow in moral strength and eventually innate evil will be overwhelmed. If, however, the individual fails to develop her potential for Good, the conscience as moral center will no longer review her daily conduct, nor will it be able to "assimilate the Good." The individual thereby loses all chance to cultivate her humaneness, the virtue that distinguishes her from the brutes.

> Appraisal 2: Sealing off internal evil
> Makes propriety profound.

> Fathoming 2: Sealing off internal evil
> Means: Hidden propriety is marvelous.

In a contrast to the preceding verses, this poem presents a good person, who steadfastly contains her evil impulses, lest her moral courage be sapped. As the individual becomes more fully human, she finally achieves that mysterious charisma associated with the ancient sage-kings. The most significant acts of resistance, then, often take place in the hidden recesses of the heart and mind.

> Appraisal 3: Shunning belt and hook,
>   He is as loose as his garments.

> Fathoming 3: No belt or hook for his trousers
>   Means: There are no means of restraint.

Personal appearance (including the disposition of one's garments) reflects the inner self. If the individual refuses to accept customary restraints upon his person (i.e., the belt and hook), inevitably the beauty and order embodied in ritual patterns are disturbed. A breakdown of the all-important Five Relations (ruler/subject, father/son, husband/wife, elder sibling/younger sibling, and friend/friend) ensues. With relations shattered, chaos follows.

> Appraisal 4: The net deters.
>   There is a right way to capture birds.

> Fathoming 4: That the net prevents capture
>   Means: Rectify the role of law.

With both Appraisal and Tetragram allied with Metal and punishments, the penal code is the subject of these verses. Using the stock metaphor of the net of the law, the constructive aspects of the legal system are considered. The largest birds of prey (i.e., the worst criminals) are caught by the very same net that allows the smaller birds (i.e., the ordinary people) to go free. In some cases, the very presence of a net may also act as a deterrent to ward off potentially destructive animals, obviating the necessity to take any future action against them. When the law functions in this careful way, criminals are captured and the innocent protected.

> Appraisal 5: If glue and lacquer loosen,
>   The bow does not shoot,
>   For horn and wood have split.

> Fathoming 5: That glue and lacquer loosen
>   Means: Promises do not stick.

One early commentator offers a complicated explication of the images employed here: the loosening of the lacquer symbolizes the indiscretions of the ruler; the wooden bow stands for the subordinate; the horn, for the king's own person. In that case, the text means, "If the ruler is indiscreet, he loses his official" (W, 307).

Although Appraisal 5 signifies the ruler, the poem may simply describe any situation in which the bonds of mutual trust have been broken. Just as the failure of the glue renders the bow unusable, lack of good faith undermines the utility of all social institutions. Clearly, the primary responsibility for establishing group cohesion rests with the elite, whose members must continually and publicly reaffirm their absolute commitment to justice and the common good. It is this attitude that works as "social glue."

> Appraisal 6: Waxing metal, waning stone.
> What's gone is small; what comes is great.

> Fathoming 6: Waxing metal and waning stone
> Mean: Excellence daily grows greater.

Although metal and stone are both aligned with West and autumn in the Han system of correspondences, here they clearly function as opposites. After all, there are certain important differences between the two materials. Metal shines, while unpolished stone is dull; metal alone suggests glory and enlightenment. Metal is also more "productive," valuable, and frequently of greater beauty. Finally, metal seems almost indestructible, while stone can be eroded. In short, "metals means good, and stone, evil" so an increase in good, rather than in evil, is predicted.

> Appraisal 7: In rejecting his most valued men,
> Seal and sash are endangered.

> Fathoming 7: Rejecting his most valued men
> Means: He loses the means to correct the self.

Seal and sash are emblems of political authority that derive from inner integrity and strong commitment to the public good. Since the state is not "one man's possession," its leader must consult with others to learn how best to promote a community of interests. Here, however, the leader endangers the state by ignoring good counsel.

> Appraisal 8: Reluctant to fasten tight that belt,
> The superior man finds timely opportunity.
> The petty man, aggrieved, is blocked.

> Fathoming 8: Reluctance to cinch that belt
> Means: It is fitting that he cannot act.

The same act, a refusal to gird the self, may have different implications when carried out by the immoral individual (as in Appraisal 3) or by the moral superior (as here). The leather belt specifically signifies office-holding, with all its implied constraints. The superior man resists taking office on principle until he is prepared and the time is right. The inferior man, in contrast, may find his career blocked by his own mindless nonconformity.

Appraisal 9: It widens its eyes, raises its horn,
And so its unlowered body is struck.

Fathoming 9: Widened eyes and a raised horn
Mean: It brings harm back on itself.

With Appraisal 9, which corresponds after all to the extreme point of
Resistance, the situation moves far beyond righteous indignation. The eyes
are wide with anger and a desire for vengeance. Eager for conflict, the
animal raises its horn. Here, in the extreme situation, the emotions clearly
rule, rather than the conscience or good sense. With more humane solutions
available, offensive and arrogant stances, stubbornly maintained despite the
possible consequences, can only bring harm to oneself in the end.

Correlates with Heaven's Mystery;
Yang; *the phase Earth; and the* I
ching *Hexagram no. 34, Greatly*
Strong; *the sun enters the Wall*
constellation, 12th degree

Yi
No. 23. Ease
March 31–April 4 (a.m.)

HEAD: Yang *ch'i* injures and cuts off yin so that it succumbs to a debilitat-
ing illness. Things as a rule are balanced and at ease.

Continuing its assault on yin, yang *ch'i* seriously weakens yin; as yin can no
longer hope to save itself, it reluctantly releases its hold on the myriad
things, which now escape its ruinous clutches. Both the initial injury and the
resultant ease are suggested by the character chosen for the title, which has
three main meanings: (1) "to injure or harm," (2) "to level" (both in the
sense of "to put in balance" and "to flatten by force"), and (3) "to ease." The
Appraisals below suggest the complicated ties that relate ease to injury.

Appraisal 1: At first, secretly of two minds,
He grasps what eases his inner self.

Fathoming 1: Initial confusion, then equanimity
Means: This relieves his inner self.

The phrase "to be of two minds" is sometimes a synonym for
"duplicitous." More often, however, it suggests the conflicting impulses to
uphold social duty and to serve self-interest. The notion of divided alle-
giances, can also be applied to a subordinate serving two masters. All these

situations stem from the mind's secret struggle over priorities. If wise and good, the individual orders his goals, ranking inner happiness above conventional goods and communal needs above selfish desires. A calm, yet resolute mind is the key to the internal equilibrium that promotes the healthful circulation of the "ever-flowing *ch'i*."

> Appraisal 2: Secretly injured,
> He blunders into Heaven's net.

> Fathoming 2: Secretly hurt, crashing into the net
> Means: "Though loosely woven, it does not fail."

"Heaven's net" is the conventional phrase for "cosmic retribution," the Chinese counterpart to the recording angel of the Judeo-Christian tradition. The coarse mesh of the net signifies Heaven's desire for leniency. Yet justice demands that the net catch every wicked individual, so that virtue and fate will roughly correspond. As the *Lao tzu* says:

> The net of heaven is cast wide. Though the mesh is not fine, nothing ever slips through (ch. 73).

For the Chinese, talk of Heaven does not necessarily imply a transcendent being as judge. Perhaps the evildoer is naturally caught in entanglements of his own creation, as his lies and cruelty isolate him from the community.

> Appraisal 3: After three days of wailing,
> The frail infant is far from hoarse.

> Fathoming 3: The infant's continuous wails
> Mean: The center heart is in harmony.

Another image from the *Lao tzu* proves the invincible nature of inner oneness by the well-known example:

> The newborn baby howls all the day without its voice cracking once.
> This is because it is harmony at its height (ch. 59).

The *Mystery* agrees with Lao tzu on two points. First, external weakness is not always an accurate indicator of internal weakness. Second, inner peace of mind gives the individual a mysterious power. Still, the *Mystery* does not advocate a complete rejection of civilization, of maturity, or of social duty.

> Appraisal 4: After grinding flat his teeth,
> Some try to feed him dirt.

> Fathoming 4: That his teeth are leveled
> Means: Food no longer appeals.

The teeth are ground down, either by repeated acts of gluttony or by "chomping at the bit" for riches and high rank. Once the teeth are gone, the individual lacks a basic tool for survival. No longer whole himself, the individual is soon devalued by others. Paradoxically, then, self-indulgence leads to a situation where certain basic desires (such as those for food and community) can never be satisfied.

Appraisal 5: With inner ease, nothing but profit.

Fathoming 5: The benefits of inner ease
Mean: Its paths are many.

The person who maintains the peace of mind associated with single-mindedness dedication to the Way finds all roles and opportunities open to him. Just as the one Tao spawns the myriad things, single-mindedness leads to many paths for several reasons. After the arduous task of building a broad moral foundation, acquiring the expertise needed for a specific task is relatively easy. The moral person has already developed the self-discipline needed for lesser tasks. What's more, inner wholeness attunes the individual to the Tao, so that she is particularly sensitive to changing scenes and unfolding situations. As the *Changes* promises:

> By means of what is easy and simple, we grasp the order of All-under-Heaven (W, 286).

Appraisal 6: He is injured in the hut.
His house stands empty as a mound.

Fathoming 6: Injured at the hut
Means: His virtue is lost.

It is said that the virtue of humaneness provides the only secure and happy dwelling for mankind. Those who abandon the struggle to follow the true path of Goodness leave themselves unprotected. Here, either the individual is "injured" or his dwelling is "leveled" (an alternate reading of the Appraisal). With "his virtue lost," he can only wander among the "hills and ruins." As soon as the individual lays waste to his virtue, all true security evaporates.

Appraisal 7: The trunk is pliable and weak,
Yet wood in contact dulls the metal saw.
Such is leveling.

Fathoming 7: That the trunk is weak
Means: "The weak overcome the strong."

To the Chinese, wood is known for its pliability while metal exemplifies durability and strength. Yet wood dulls the metal saw. By analogy, gentle virtue proves more compelling than brute force.

> Appraisal 8: In wearing down its horn
>   There is danger.

> Fathoming 8: Injuring its horn
>   Means: It is wounded by the use of awesome force.

The animal's horn symbolizes brute strength and aggressive behavior. Here the horn has been worn down by repeated use until the animal can no longer defend itself.

> Appraisal 9: The benefits of ease in old age:
>   It is right to be respected when aged and infirm.

> Fathoming 9: The propriety of ease in old age
>   Means: Retired, he hangs his carriage at home.

Since Appraisal 9 represents extreme ease, it properly addresses the subject of old age and retirement. After years of loyal service, the aged official is allowed to retire quietly to his native place, where his official carriage hangs on the wall, no longer in use. The old man wants only to live out his days in peace and honor; he makes no effort to influence others by flaunting his former position. The Chinese Classics label the last of life's blessings "coming to a good end." Here, the individual has clearly accomplished this.

Correlates with Heaven's Mystery; Yin; the phase Water; and the I ching Hexagram no. 16, Amusement; the sun enters the Stomach constellation, 5th degree; the Dipper points ESE; the musical note is E

Le
No. 24. Joy
April 4 (p.m.)–April 8

HEAD: Yang begins to emerge from obscurity. Unrolling what had been folded up, it thereby gains harmony and ease so that all things are filled with joy.

Once again the expansive nature of yang *ch'i* contrasts with yin's propensity to cramp things under its influence. As the gentle spring rains begin, yang *ch'i* not only "begins to emerge from obscurity," but also "begins to put forth warmth" (an alternate interpretation of one part in the Head text). Warmth unfurls the tightly curled leaves of vegetation and prompts hibernating animals to stretch their limbs in preparation for leaving their dens. In fact, the warmth of spring elicits expansive feelings of delight in all living creatures. Since many of these feelings are spontaneously expressed in ecstatic cries, including mating calls, the tetragram is equally associated with music, which functions as outlet for and moderating influence on the emotions. (It is worth recalling that both "joy" and "music" are written with the same graph in Chinese.)

Given the tetragram title, the reader might expect this tetragram to be full of happy overtones, but Yang Hsiung uses the Joy theme to portray the evil consequences of overindulgence in pleasure. In this he follows the imagery of the correspondent hexagram, which cautions against enthusiasms that create remorse. As the *Odes* say, "Let us not be wild in our love of enjoyment." True happiness, as the *Changes* shows, depends upon integrity, perseverance, and adherence to ritual.

Appraisal 1: Solitary pleasure is pleasure confined.
Its reach does not reach far.

Fathoming 1: Solitary pleasure is pleasure held in.
Meaning: It dissipates his inner self.

Although the commentators quarrel over the right pejorative to characterize solitary enjoyment, the general message is clear: to the Chinese, pleasure is essentially a social feeling. The inner soul is ultimately destroyed by solitary pleasures, which neither enhance mutual regard between individuals nor promote communion with the great men of the past (through appreciation of their painting or calligraphy, for example). In short, personal greatness can only be achieved through interaction with others. As one Confucian master wrote:

> It was by sharing their enjoyments with the people that [the ideal] men
> of antiquity were able to enjoy themselves. . . . There is just one thing in
> which the ancients greatly surpassed others, and that is the way they
> extended what they did (Mencius, 1A/2).

The noble person shares pleasure for practical as well as moral reasons. The *ch'i* aroused by pleasurable emotions must find suitable outlets in ritual and music (both essentially public activities) if it is not to harm the body. Also, taking the Tao as model, the noble person makes every effort to encourage others to reach their full potential. As a result of these two factors, communal happiness soon replaces solitary enjoyment. In contrast, the petty person is too selfish to accord others the same opportunity for pleasure that he enjoys.

Appraisal 2: The time for unimaginable joy
Is set in Heaven.

Fathoming 2: Joy that is unimaginable
Means: Use the seasons and the year.

It is in the individual's best interests to adjust his actions to prevailing cosmic trends, thereby multiplying the efficacy of his own labors. Having done that, he can look forward to success. The joy he will receive is "unimaginable" in two senses: first, it exceeds all expectations; and second, its ultimate source cannot be located.

Two commentators would have us relate these lines to the traditional Chinese program of "virtuous government." According to early Chinese thinkers, the ruler should employ the people in corvée labor and military service only during slack agricultural seasons. In this way, state service will never threaten the people's livelihood. While the state grows rich from taxes, the people grow content, without ever giving it much thought. After all, "the best of all rulers is but a shadowy presence to his subjects."

Appraisal 3: All composure is gone.
Weeping, howling, wailing figures
Lean in doorways.

Fathoming 3: Not at ease or refined
Means: Rites and music have been abolished.

The Appraisal uses no fewer than six onomatopoeic characters, whose exact meanings are disputed by the commentators. All six may be read as mournful sounds, but some or all may also convey "sounds of merriment." In a sense, it hardly matters what particular emotion each character signifies. The unmistakable impression is one of a babble of incoherent and distressing noises. Such excessive displays of emotion directly contravene the rites; uncontrolled outbursts can only end in disgrace. Therefore, the Appraisal ends with "leaning in doorways." This can mean misfortune is at the very doorstep. Otherwise, it probably refers either to public expressions of bereavement, or to degraded women selling their bodies.

Appraisal 4: Discarding his ties,
Severing his bonds,
He eases his godlike heart.

Fathoming 4: Breaking free of ties and bonds
Means: The heart truly rejoices.

Contrary to popular belief, steadfast adherence to the Way does not cause the principled person to feel constrained by ritual precepts. Rather, the good person finds regulated conduct eminently satisfying for both aesthetic and practical reasons. Free at last of ungovernable desire for external objects, the individual is finally in control of the "unmoved" heart/mind. He can rest content, having achieved inner equanimity.

> Appraisal 5: Rich harmonies of bell and drum,
>   Then mournful pipes and strings—
>   For them, decline may follow.

> Fathoming 5: Bell and drum sounding in unison
>   Means: After joy comes grief.

The proverb says, "With extreme pleasure, sorrow arises." In typical court performances, bell and drum, with their bracing airs, are followed by the thin whine of pipes and strings, which tend to arouse uneasy longings in the listener. By analogy, the petty person (be he emperor or commoner) who indulges his senses courts disaster. For one thing, an overpreoccupation with pleasure precludes full participation in social and political activity. It may also weaken the body.

> Appraisal 6: Let joy and music swell, filling every gap,
>   To the delight of commonfolk and gods and birds.

> Fathoming 6: Great joy and music filling every space
>   Means: Joy embraces all and everything.

In even-numbered tetragrams, Appraisal 6 corresponds to the ruler; hence, this classic description of the joy that pervades the kingdom ruled by a sage. In contrast to Appraisal 1, which describes the misguided individual (possibly the ruler) who refuses to extend his pleasures to the people, here the benefits of sagely rule accrue not only to human subjects, but to all living creatures. By the end, each thing in the triadic realms of Heaven-Earth-Man is joined in ecstatic union. This is proof that the charismatic individual's influence is felt throughout the cosmos. No absolute barrier acts to separate mankind from the gods.

> Appraisal 7: People sigh, ghosts sigh
>   Over limitations fixed by Heaven.

> Fathoming 7: Ghosts and people sighing
>   Means: They proclaim the end of happiness.

The preceding Appraisal posits the fundamental unity of all things. Now the otherworldly and human realms are joined in sorrow, rather than in joy. The operation of cosmic cycles may undercut the best-laid plans. Evildoers, who have temporarily eluded cosmic retribution, must now accept their punishment. Meanwhile, those who are good face old age and death. The very presence of ghosts indicates some kind of cosmic imbalance.

> Appraisal 8: Heaving sigh after sigh, fearing his own faults,
> He forgets the errors and deceptions of others.

> Fathoming 8: Sigh after sigh, he fears the self.
> Meaning: In the end, he protects himself.

The subject of the previous Appraisal wastes time bemoaning his fate, but here the protagonist works hard to overcome his own faults in order to insure his own protection. So intent is he upon self-improvement that he ignores the faults of others. Meanwhile, such good conduct replenishes the individual's store of the life-giving *ch'i*.

> Appraisal 9: His joy nearly complete,
> Grief comes before day is done.
> He sighs and snivels as he weeps and wails.

> Fathoming 9: Nearly absolute joy
> Means: Truly, this is cause for regret.

Appraisal 9 marks both the culmination and the end of Joy. With it, comes danger, so that ultimately the incautious individual is plunged into great sorrow, with "sighing and sobbing, snivel and snot" (W, 177).

Cheng
No. 25. Contention
April 9–April 13 (a.m.)

Correlates with Heaven's Mystery; Yang; the phase Fire; and the I ching *Hexagram no. 6, Conflict; the sun enters the Stomach constellation, 9th degree*

HEAD: Yang *ch'i* overflows everywhere. It is "neither one-sided, nor partial," so that things vie against one another in competition, with each one following its own proper model.

Yang *ch'i* functions like the true king described in one chapter of a Confucian Classic: it is "neither one-sided nor partial" in its dealings with subordinates, for "to show no favoritism" is divine (LT, ch. 79). Early Chinese thought generally assumes that the Tao and the good ruler are alike in allowing each thing to develop its distinctive nature. That each thing "follows its own model," then, is the natural consequence of good rule, rather than its repudiation. Consequently, "At the birth of the myriad things / Each gets what is suitable for it." In gratitude for this impartial treatment, the myriad things, like the king's subjects, are eager to transform themselves through its good graces.

Since each creature acts according to its better nature, the tetragram can only be considered generally auspicious, despite its title. Still, just as the Joy Appraisals were less happy than might be expected, those in Contention are less evil than might be thought. Under certain conditions, conflict and contention play a positive role, whether in the law courts or on the battle-field. In some cases, punishment, even war, represents the only viable way to suppress evil and advance the cycle. In making this argument, the *Mystery* shifts the emphasis from the *Changes* hexagram, which condemns almost all forms of conflict.

> Appraisal 1: Contend best by not contending.
> Retire to obscurity.

> Fathoming 1: In contending, not contending
> Means: This is the normal course of the Way.

The opening line of both Appraisal and Fathoming literally reads, "Contend not contend." The commentators give four possible interpretations of the line: (1) "Contend before the occasion for contention becomes apparent to obviate the need for obvious contention"; (2) "Contend best by not being quarrelsome"; (3) "To fight on incontestable ground" (i.e., on the basis of the Confucian Classics), so that "nothing can overcome [him]"; and (4) "Able to fight, but choosing not to fight," a reading that emphasizes the latent power of the good person.

The first interpretation clearly draws upon early Taoist and Legalist texts, which enjoin the superior man to solve problems before they become apparent. This fits well with Appraisal 1, since it focuses on the beginning of the cycle. The second reading recalls the nature of Water (the Appraisal's correlation), by showing it to be soft yet forceful in eroding other things. The ritual act, which always exemplifies courtesy and humility, makes the actor equally gentle yet compelling. Since courtesy and ritual constitute "the normal course of the Way," we find that "the gentlest gamester is the soonest victor."

> Appraisal 2: A weakling tries to shout back the River.

> Fathoming 2: A weakling shooing the Yellow River
> Means: How can such a man be relied upon?

The weakling, seriously miscalculating his strength, thinks he can intimidate the Yellow River by his shouts. The futility of the act should be obvious to all, although the weakling is blithely unaware of his own incapacities. What's more, the Yellow River is seen as a storehouse of blessings by agrarian China, since it is the mighty fountainhead of the waters of the North China plain that bring life-giving water to the crops. The weakling's posturing against it, then, could hardly be more inappropriate or even self-defeating. Compare the *Chuang tzu* story (ch. 17), where a stupid owl tries to "shoo away" a spirit-bird:

> In the south there is a bird called the Yüan-ch'u . . . [which] rises up
> from the South Sea and flies to the North Sea, and it will rest on nothing
> but the [marvelous] Wu-t'ung tree, eat nothing but the fruit of the Lien,
> and drink only from springs of sweet water. Once there was an owl who
> had gotten hold of a half-rotten old rat. As the Yüan-ch'u passed by, it
> raised its head, looked up at the Yüan-ch'u, and said, "Shoo!"

Both the poem and the story mock ludicrous acts of physical courage. As Confucius said, "The man who is ready to 'beard a tiger or rush a river' . . . that is the sort of man I would not take" (A 7/10).

Appraisal 3: Archers amiably contend.

Fathoming 3: Amiably contending in archery
    Means: The noble man yields to his neighbor.

Confucius remarked:

> Gentlemen never contend. You will say that in archery they do so. But
> even then they bow and make way for one another in going up to the
> archery-ground, when they are coming down, and at the subsequent
> drinking bout. Thus even when competing, they still remain gentlemen
> (A 3/7).

Ritual archery contests, in fact, provided a public arena for the display of gentlemanly conduct. The superior man competes, but his way of contending takes a completely different form from that of a lesser man. Although his fellow competitors may not recognize it, the true gentleman is only concerned lest he be unable to compete in Goodness (A 15/35). Therefore, the noble man yields graciously to his neighbor, as distinct from the petty person intent on success at any price.

Appraisal 4: Those who battle for petty profit
    Never achieve propriety.

Fathoming 4: Attached to petty profit
    Means: The Right Way is then obscured.

Although desire for wealth and rank is perfectly natural, as even the most strait-laced Confucians admit, it should not override righteousness in cases of conflicting goods. What does it profit a man to win wealth if the Way of true humanity is lost?

Appraisal 5: Taking a stand at the crossroads,
  Yields benefit on every side.

Fathoming 5: Contending at the crossroads
  Means: The place to fight is the center.

The best policy is not predisposed toward any particular line (although it faithfully follows the Good); good policy responds flexibly to each contingency as it arises, thereby achieving the Mean. The crossroads represents the central junction of some nine major highways. Since the king customarily locates his capital at the crossroads, it signifies the leader's central and centralizing role in his organization. It also suggests that consensus should be reached after all arguments regarding specific policy proposals have been submitted to the king and debated at court. As a result of statewide cooperation and consensus, the leader's subordinates gravitate to him. The leader, then, secures his own strategic advantage by being equally open on all sides.

Appraisal 6: Biceps and forearms as thick as shanks,
  Thighs and calves bloated:
  These are surely bodily ailments.

Fathoming 6: Shanklike upper arms and lower limbs
  Mean: The subordinate is too prominent.

The early Han statesman Chia Yi (200–168 B.C.) described the disproportionate strength of the feudal kingdoms vis-à-vis the imperial domain:

> The empire suffers from a kind of bloating illness, in which the shin is
> nearly big as the waist, and the finger nearly as big as the thigh.

In other's words, the trunk (the emperor) is weak when compared with the secondary appendages (the feudal lords). The *Mystery* inveighs against any subordinate who usurps his leader's power. Also, all secondary goals (e.g., those for wealth, position, and fame) should be abandoned in favor of the primary goal of keeping to the Way. Why? In the words of one Han philosopher,

> The small is properly adjunct to the large. . . The important and the large
> should have the means to control the unimportant and the small.

Appraisal 7: Contend with shield and lance and helmet,
  But place them in the king's heralds' service.

> Fathoming 7: Contending with shield and lance
> Means: They protect the ruler's person.

Weapons are properly employed when used for the public good; their use for selfish gain or for revenge is strictly forbidden. The king's advance riders protect the royal person as he makes his progress through the empire, so their martial spirit is rightly celebrated. The *Odes* praise "the lead chariot of the king's host" and "the commander ... who is a pattern to all the states."

> Appraisal 8: The wolf fills its mouth,
> With the arrow at its back.

> Fathoming 8: The wolf cramming its mouth
> Means: He does not turn to see the harm.

Wolves epitomize all that is wicked and rapacious to the sedentary farmers of north and central China. Here greed comes at the expense of wisdom. So intent is the wolf upon devouring its prey that it fails to notice the angry hunter or his bow. (The image probably comes from the Chinese constellations, where the Wooden Bow lies directly behind the Wolf. And certainly, talk of greed is also appropriate to the Stomach constellation aligned with this tetragram.)

The moral is clear: greed is risky, since it works against one's long-term interests. As the Han proverb says, "In carrying out early matters, don't forget the later ones." Or, in the words of Aesop, "False confidence is the forerunner of misfortune."

> Appraisal 9: Two tigers, teeth bared.
> Whichever holds back survives.

> Fathoming 9: Two tigers, teeth bared,
> Means: The victor knows what to restrain.

Appraisal 9 represents extreme Contention. Two tigers face off, poised for the attack. Fully cognizant of the gravity of the situation, the wilier of the two opponents chooses retreat, for a vicious mauling means certain death. In this, the cunning tiger follows military strategy, which advises, "When pitted against an equal, better retire." After all, as the *Lao tzu* asks, "Which is dearer, your name or your life?" (ch. 44).

Wu

No. 26. Endeavor

April 13 (p.m.)–April 17

Correlates with Heaven's Mystery; Yin; the phase Wood; and the I ching *Hexagram no. 18, Undertakings; the sun enters the Stomach constellation, 14th degree*

HEAD: Yang *ch'i* exerts itself in the task of completing things. All things, conforming their hearts, take control of their own affairs.

Two aspects of yang *ch'i*, both alluded to in the Head text, appear to be somewhat antithetical: the single-mindedness of yang *ch'i* and its fostering of individuality in the myriad things. (This description of yang *ch'i* represents an amalgam of Confucian and Taoist teachings.) The good leader, of course, imitates both aspects of yang *ch'i*. His single-minded devotion to the public good is absolute. So, too, is his determination to provide economic security and social mobility sufficient to insure that each subordinate can fulfill his own potential. Only in that way can the realm of Man become as richly varied as the phenomenal world of Heaven-and-Earth. The success of all endeavors ultimately rests on united efforts drawing upon collective strengths; with proper direction, seemingly miraculous feats can be accomplished.

> Appraisal 1: First endeavors find no focus.
> The petty man is useless after all.

> Fathoming 1: Undirected first endeavors
> Mean: Order is not the province of the petty man.

To initiate a project is an act of creation. In large part, the success of the project will depend upon its sponsor's complete dedication to a fixed vision. By definition, however, the petty person lacks single-mindedness. Whatever thing passes before his eyes, he desires; whatever ambition crosses his mind, he pursues. When sustained effort and a sense of direction are missing, no significant achievement is possible. The petty person may pride himself on his flexibility, but in reality his priorities are confused. Assigning proper relative value to personal goals is the first step toward establishing human order for the early Confucians. Small wonder, then, that the petty person only increases disorder.

> Appraisal 2: Seeking for himself the new and fresh,
> Its fragrance pure, refined, and rare—
> Such is the conduct of the noble man.

Fathoming 2: For himself, seeking the new and fresh
Means: Light and glory suffuse the self.

Many ancient Chinese texts enjoin the would-be sage to "daily renew his virtue" by self-assessment and reform. The good person is also one who seeks to renew the hallowed tradition of the sages by applying their general principles to the specifics of his life. Through this process of cultivation, he comes to epitomize all that is new and fresh, rare and refined. Such moral brilliance, it should be noted, stems from hard work, not from luck or innate genius. Over time, the individual's "fragrance" enhances (i.e., "perfumes") the quality of life in his entire community.

Appraisal 3: If neither fettered nor constrained,
Men's minds rot and spoil.

Fathoming 3: Neither fettered nor restrained
Means: Their bodies are not intact.

The Taoist classics (e.g., the *Tao te ching* of Lao tzu) espouse a return to primitivism and a sublime disdain for conventions and cultural baggage. The *Mystery* argues differently. Without the restraints imposed by education and training in ritual, the discriminating mind remains too undisciplined to develop its capacities fully. When the mind malfunctions, its judgment is clouded; before long the body will succumb to a variety of ills: "Their bodies are not intact." Self-abuse, mutilating punishments, or even execution may be in store for the future.

Since Appraisal 3 is aligned with Wood, one commentator sees a description of a tree infested with vermin or insects ("Its core rots and spoils"). If the tree is to survive, the affected branches must be lopped off. By analogy, the would-be sage ruthlessly cuts off that part of himself that is liable to rot.

Appraisal 4: The arrow seems to fly itself
With the help of feathers.
The canopy is borne aloft, the cart conveys it.

Fathoming 4: The arrow and canopied chariot
Mean: Their Way is exemplary.

Using conventional metaphors of his time, Yang Hsiung suggests the benefits of proper alliance and high position. Although the arrow appears to rise "by itself," it cannot fly unless the feathers on its central shaft are strong and properly arranged. Similarly, the canopy (symbol of political authority) will shade the chariot only if it is connected with a sturdy carriage pole. The lesson is clear: no man, however worthy, can expect to rise if he fails to make useful allies or to position himself correctly. For this reason, friends and associates must be chosen with extreme care.

> Appraisal 5: All the spider's arduous labor
> Cannot match the silkworm's cloth.

> Fathoming 5: The spider's endeavor
> Means: There is no benefit to Man.

Both the spider and the silkworm spin marvelous threads of equal strength, durability, and beauty, but only the silkworm's products are of use to mankind. In addition, the spider's web is designed to destroy, while the silkworm's cocoon fosters its own development. Industry, however admirable, is not equivalent to Goodness. As one Chinese classic says, "Avoid doing whatever does not benefit if it harms that which benefits. Only then will [merit] be complete."

> Appraisal 6: When blossom and fruit smell sweetest,
> That is the time to use them best.

> Fathoming 6: Fragrant blossoms put to good use
> Mean: They benefit the present year.

Flowers and fruits when fully ripe are pleasing to smell and to taste. That is the time they should be eaten. By analogy, the person of true cultivation gives off a kind of fragrance because she is both "refined and of substance" (a pun in Chinese for the binome translated "blossom and fruit"). She also should be put to immediate use by her superiors.

> Appraisal 7: Once its fragrance is lost,
> There is no place to go.

> Fathoming 7: Losing his fragrance
> Means: Virtue thereby fades.

Here the fragrance of self-cultivation is destroyed. The individual lacks all sense of moral direction, as in Appraisal 1. But since the time is late, this now matters more. Decay proceeds from the inner core. It is equally distressing to watch this in an exquisite flower or in a human being.

> Appraisal 8: Yellow Center: he escapes calamity
> Because he is properly aligned.

> Fathoming 8: Yellow Center, avoiding calamity,
> Means: He is attuned and thus upright.

Appraisal 8 occupies the central position in the unit of Appraisals 7–9 assigned to Calamity; hence, centrality is played off against calamity. Yellow, of course, is the color assigned to the center; it is said to harmonize and balance its counterparts. For this reason, the yellow center signifies inner virtue directed by the Mean, which works to establish an equilibrium among the emotions. Calamity may be avoided if we stick to the path of moderation and mediation, even at the perilous end of the cycle.

Appraisal 9: The task complete, he defeats himself.
Raindrops form, only to fall.

Fathoming 9: The task complete, self-defeat
Means: This is not Heaven's Decree.

With Appraisal 9, "endeavor" reaches its culmination. The rainclouds symbolize futile tasks, for as soon as individual raindrops accumulate, they disperse in a shower. When the individual finds that his hard work has accomplished nothing, he should not blame his failure on Heaven or on original sin. The fault lies within himself. Perhaps he tends to arrogance or excess; perhaps he ignores prevailing conditions; perhaps success goes to his head.

Shih

No. 27. Duties

April 18–April 22 (a.m.)

Correlates with Heaven's Mystery; Yang; the phase Metal; and the I ching Hexagram no. 18, Undertakings; the sun enters the Mane constellation, 4th degree

HEAD: Yang *ch'i* greatly stimulates and sheds light on the duties. Things expand and expand according to rule, each one exerting its own strength to the fullest.

Yang *ch'i* waxes ever greater, imparting strength and intelligence to all the myriad things, so that each fulfills its intended role. As yang *ch'i* is to phenomenal things, so the ruler is to the masses. The common people learn their social duties through the suasive encouragement of the ruler. Since a single hexagram provides the prototype for both this tetragram and the preceding one, Tetragrams 26 and 27 are generally similar in message. There is, however, a subtle shift in emphasis: in Endeavor, the focus was on regulating action; in Duty, the main theme is the proper division of social responsibilities.

Appraisal 1: Service, without serving narrow ends,
  Leaves nothing left unserved.

Fathoming 1: Serving with impartial service
  Means: He proceeds by the Way.

Most commentators read the first line of this Appraisal and Fathoming (literally, "Serve without serving") as a celebration of *wu wei* ("nonpurposive activity"). In support, they cite the famous *Lao tzu* passage, "The Way does not act, yet nothing is left undone" (ch. 37). Still, Yang Hsiung's other writings strongly object to *wu wei* in government (what we might call laissez-faire), arguing that *wu wei* can only work in an already perfect society. For that reason, I offer a different reading, one that emphasizes the impartial nature of Goodness. As Confucius said, the good man refuses to align himself with a particular faction or cause; instead, he only sides with the Right (A 4/10). The same lines, however, could also mean that the superior man does not take credit for his merits (serving without [claiming to] serve). Or, that the gentleman acts with such mastery of ritual (in the words of the *Changes*, he is "simple" and "easy") that he serves without [seeming to] serve (W, 286).

Appraisal 2: If, when outcomes hinge on choice,
  He refuses counsel or advice,
  He forfeits any token of his wit.

Fathoming 2: Seeking neither counsel nor advice
  Means: His comprehension is lost.

A single decision could swing the course of events either way; hence, the metaphor of the pivot. At such critical junctures, the wise person consults widely among friends and advisors to devise the correct policy. The Confucian Classics credit the sage-kings of the golden past with culling advice from a wide spectrum of subjects, from humble woodcutters and fishermen, as well as worthy ministers. One famous chapter, for example, tells the ruler to confer with no fewer than four separate classes of advisors: the sacred beings (through turtle and milfoil divination), the chief ministers, the minor officials, and the common people. After all, "He who likes to ask becomes enlarged. He who only uses himself grows small." Confucius himself set an example of "inquiring about every matter." Despite these models, the petty person is too arrogant or too impatient to consult others. Not surprisingly, his plans go awry.

Appraisal 3: Opportunities come and go,
  The gap between them finer than a hair.

> Fathoming 3: Time goes and comes,
> Meaning: He hastens, lest he fail.

Appraisal 3 marks the transition from Thought to Action. By definition, all transitions must be "timely" (W, 326) insofar as time is envisioned as a series of distinct moments separated by imperceptible breaks. Past and future, after all, are divided by that single instant we call the present, whose duration is no greater than a hair is wide. The wise and cultivated person lays the groundwork for swift action that "seizes the moment" when he carefully analyzes the main categorical relations in the cosmos. As timely opportunity approaches, "he hastens, lest he fail," knowing that either premature or belated action may be fatal to the success of his plans. This poem gives a new twist to the Han proverb: "Off by a hair's breadth, / Missed by a thousand miles."

> Appraisal 4: Though men do women's work,
> They cannot substitute in suckling.

> Fathoming 4: That a man does women's work
> Means: He negates his duty.

An outrageous example, that of men suckling children, is meant to prove the natural basis for the social law of strict separation in gender roles and, by extension, all aspects of the social hierarchy. In ancient China, hierarchy was based chiefly on age, gender, and educational attainments, although wealth, of course, played its part. Here, with "men doing women's work," humans consciously overturn the fundamental yin/yang values operating in the cosmos. In consequence, the society has no hope of attaining that ideal state where "each attains his or her proper role" by maximizing the individual's innate potential. The *Tso Commentary* laments any case where

> the woman has her husband's house, and the man, his wife's chamber. . . . Any deviation is sure to lead to ruin.

> Appraisal 5: Serving as duty demands,
> The king grants him provisions.

> Fathoming 5: Doing his duty
> Means: He fulfills the burdens of his office.

Appraisal 5 refers to the ruler. It is the ruler's prerogative and duty to dispense rewards, punishments, and ritual foods to his subjects and allies in order to maximize good order in the state. After the ruler tasted the sacrificial meats offered to the gods, it was customary for him to distribute portions to officials of proven merit. Every ritual act represents an exchange. Officials reconfirmed their allegiance to the ruling house in return for receiving the physical and spiritual benefits derived from supping on the sacred offerings. The ruler, for his part, must take great care to ascertain the true mettle of his men, lest the gods be insulted and the state be ruined by unworthy officials.

> Appraisal 6: Though the burden is great, he shoulders it
>   alone,
> Beset by unresolved problems.

> Fathoming 6: Grave responsibilities, acting alone
> Means: How can this be borne?

The good and wise leader never makes a major policy decision without consulting his subordinates. Since changes in policy usually affect so many others, those in power should not try to bear the responsibility alone. The more the participants in the decision-making process, the fewer the stupid decisions that will be made, for the good reason that "many heads are better than one." Even if the best-laid plans still go awry, at least the positive sense of community engendered by the consultative process will offset some of the distintegrating effects of political failure.

> Appraisal 7: The grown man supports the orphan child.
> The young boy lifts a jar.

> Fathoming 7: The grown man rearing the orphan
> Means: The child knows what to do.

The social structure in China is underpinned by reciprocal, yet hierarchical relations. The doctrine of filial piety stipulates that the child's obligations to its parents are nearly absolute, for the child can never adequately repay his parents for the gift of life. Here an older member of the clan decides to rear an orphan. This implies that he will feed, protect, and educate the young boy. In such a case, the orphan's obligations may exceed even the normal demands of filial piety. As if to acknowledge his debt, the young boy raises the jar, accepting his duty to feed his protector and act as willing servant. When each member of the family acknowledges his or her debts to the others, each responds by making his or her separate contribution to the unit. The ideal ruler/subject relation is analogous. The ruler agrees to provide economic security, physical protection, and a suasive example for his subjects; in return, the subordinates offer loyalty and taxes. Reciprocity is the essential root of Chinese hierarchy.

> Appraisal 8: When women do men's work,
> After ten years, they're still unteachable.

Fathoming 8: That a woman does a man's work
Means: Finally the family will not prosper.

The poem reverses the situation presented in Appraisal 4, although the moral is much the same: men and women should not change roles, lest family harmony and prosperity be undermined. If a young woman were to take the position of family head, she would become unteachable in two senses: first, she would find herself ignoring advice given by those considered to be her natural superiors (adult males in the family, including her husband and father-in-law, and women of the previous generation); second, her initiatives would represent a fundamental challenge to the most basic of what were held to be natural laws by the Chinese. Similarly, the appointed official should never presume to usurp his ruler's position.

Appraisal 9: It offends the ear but sets the toe on track.
The matter will go right.

Fathoming 9: Offended ears, compliant toes
Mean: Contrary talk makes for obedient conduct.

The poetry in Chinese is vivid in its sharp juxtaposition of three verbs of position. Here we see an individual who, after overhearing unpleasant truths about himself, finally corrects his behavior and follows in the footsteps of the sage-rulers. Displeasing talk ultimately brings marked advantages, as "loyal words offend the ears but benefit conduct." After all, strong medicine must be bitter if it is to effect the cure.

Correlates with Earth's Mystery; Yin; the phase Water; and the I ching Hexagram no. 49, Molting [and so Renewal]; the sun enters the Mane constellation, 9th degree; the Ch'ing-ming Spring Festival period

Keng
No. 28. Change
April 22 (p.m.)–April 26

HEAD: Yang *ch'i*, already flying up, alters tendencies and shifts forms. Things change with regard to their spirit potencies.

In Yang's schema, Tetragram 28 begins the second of three divisions of the *Mystery*, corresponding to the triadic realm of Earth. Earth is, of course, aligned with center both in the triad Heaven-Earth-Man and in the five directions and Phases. According to the *Changes*, "What establishes the Way of Earth is weakness and strength" (W, 264). Many texts below elaborate this principle.

This tetragram also corresponds to the Ch'ing-ming festival, in which spring outings give equal attention to the dead (through the sweeping of ancestral graves) and to the celebration of renewed life. Therefore, the tetragram shows life resurgent in the midst of death, and moral life retrieved from evil habits. Yang Hsiung's own autocommentaries give "making new" as the main theme of Change. The earth has escaped the ruinous clutches of winter. The days lengthen, vegetation turns verdant green, and migrating birds begin to return as harbingers of spring. Although change of any kind calls for caution, change at this time opens the way for generally positive developments. As the *Changes* argues, "Only through change and transformation can all things come to perfection" (W, 272). The upward thrust of yang *ch'i* leads many things to rise above their old selves (literally and figuratively), yet the metamorphosis is accomplished naturally, without overt chaos, destruction, or coercion. Tradition says that this is the time when scorpions become dragonflies, field mice turn into quail, and crow's feet are changed into butterflies. In the world of Man, the upward flight occurs through self-cultivation. And just as flight depends upon the interaction of structural patterns (in the wing) and unseen currents (in the wind), the human potential for uplifting oneself relies upon the interaction of visible structural patterns in society and the unseen tendencies in the spirit.

> Appraisal 1: Having evolved in darkness,
>   It is not right.
>   Impropriety seems like second nature.

> Fathoming 1: Darkly changed, proprieties blocked
>   Means: In youth, he alters his course.

Deep at the core of his being, the individual has neglected to develop the potential for Goodness that is endowed with human nature. As he accustoms himself to evil, it becomes his second nature. Such a basic distortion of human nature can seem natural enough, especially when changes are carried out gradually over the years. As one Han philosopher observed,

> Whatever is completed during one's youth seems like human nature sent by Heaven. Whatever is customary comes to seem "natural."

Still, the implications of such changes could not be more profound. Through his failure to develop his innate potential for Goodness, the petty person loses the only characteristic that truly distinguishes him from the beasts. It is especially important, then, to take care at the beginning and attend to the base.

> Appraisal 2: The time is Seven, the time is Nine.
> The carriage rolls on its way.

> Fathoming 2: Timely seven times, timely nine times
> Means: Without fail, he faces change.

By convention, both 7 and 9 as odd numbers symbolize yang *ch'i*. In a nine-part cycle, they would correspond to maturity and decline. There may also be number magic at work here. Since $2 + 7 = 9$, Fire (Phase for Appraisals 2 and 7) and Metal (Phase for no. 9) are in direct opposition, and so change occurs. Still, the *Mystery* seldom discusses maturity, let alone irrevocable decline, this early in its sequence of Appraisals. Probably 7 and 9 merely stand for repetitive change. Like the carriage wheel, life moves inexorably on in its journey. The moral person makes sufficient preparation to insure that the trip goes as smoothly as possible. He also adjusts his conduct continually in accordance with ever-changing cosmic, political, and personal cycles. Then, whether faced with prosperity or material failure, he is able to respond appropriately to circumstances, and is better able to uphold the constant norms underlying phenomenal change. Since the sage is not fixated on a single mode of operation, he can experience endless transformations without damaging the self. In other words, the sage can also be "timely seven times, timely nine times."

> Appraisal 3: White things in mud
> Turn black.

> Fathoming 3: Changing white in mud
> Means: Change does not enlighten.

A popular metaphor compares human nature at birth to undyed silk, which is then colored by training and experience. Moral improvement should work to turn evil into good, black into white. Here, by contrast, material of pristine purity is steeped in filth. This suggests the effect on the soul of bad companions or bad customs. That no good can come from this is clearly shown in a pun by which "black" also means "calamity."

> Appraisal 4: With each change, slight gain;
> In use, nothing but profit.

> Fathoming 4: In change, slight gain
> Means: This is what the people look to.

Appraisal 4 marks the Beginning of Good Fortune. Several types of good fortune may be predicted by these lines. In one reading, the incremental political and cultural changes instituted by the sage-ruler eventually lead to marked social improvements, although the reforms largely go unnoticed by the subject population. Certainly Yang Hsiung strongly opposed major policy changes of no real benefit to the common people. Or, perhaps the good ruler's lack of greed lets him rest content with slight personal gain so long as his policies benefit the common people.

In a second reading, the gradual accrual of seemingly inconsequential acts of courtesy and consideration develops the human character and forges strong community to such a degree that "not a use but profits."

> Appraisal 5: Oxen without horns or horses with them
> Exist neither in the past nor present.

> Fathoming 5: Hornless ox, horse with horns
> Means: A change in Heaven's constants.

A mature ox always has horns while a horse is always without them. So undisputably clear is this distinction that early Chinese Logicians used the figures of horse and ox as stock examples to demonstrate absolutely separate logical categories. Here, eternal constants are overturned, which can only have disastrous implications for human society. With the eternal verities ignored or disputed, society enters a state of chaos, in which few can hope to realize their full potential.

> Appraisal 6: In water, they ride on carts
> Out of water, they go by boat.
> True kings rightly reverse them.

> Fathoming 6: Carts and boats, in and out,
> Mean: His way is change.

The *Changes* in its Great Commentary celebrates the sage-king's invention of various tools, including carts and boats, in imitation of sacred images in Heaven-and-Earth. Thanks to such inventions, mankind has moved from primitive existence to advanced forms of social life. It would be foolish, even dangerous, to ignore the inspired nature of the sages' inventions and try to reinvent the wheel. By the same token, thoughtless changes in customary laws and institutions prove worse than useless, even positively destructive.

> Nothing is as good as a boat for crossing water, nothing as good as a cart for crossing land. Though a boat will get you over water, if you try to push it across land, you may push till your dying day and hardly move it any distance at all.

Effort is wasted and culture disrupted. The sage-ruler acts to restore the perfect harmony between the human and nonhuman worlds.

Appraisal 7: Though change they should, they don't,
And thus create the ill.

Fathoming 7: Change unchanged
Means: They cannot improve themselves.

Appraisal 7 corresponds to the Beginning of Calamity; presumably, some measure of adjustment is needed in these later phases of the cosmic cycle if the balance is to be maintained. In the political world, men should consider the warning of the Confucian master, Tung Chung-shu: "To make government policy, and then not carry it out is very serious." As one famous Chinese text argues,

> As times change, it is fitting to change the laws. It is like a good doctor. As an illness goes through ten thousand changes, so his drugs must make ten thousand changes. . . . The one who makes changes in the law must make changes on the basis of contemporary conditions.

Although the translation follows the reading favored by the commentators, given the linguistic compression of the Chinese language, the Appraisal could also mean:

> To change what should not be changed.
> And so to create infirmity.
> To change what should not be changed
> Means: Unable to improve oneself.

In this second reading, the foolish ruler meddles with just policies or the foolish individual works to change those very qualities (like loyalty and good faith) that are worth preserving.

Appraisal 8: When a team of four won't budge,
One can always change the driver.

Fathoming 8: That the team of four won't budge
Means: Changing the driver will help.

The driver is a stock metaphor for the leader, especially the ruler of the state. When the current ruling house cannot ease societal friction and solve stubborn problems, Heaven's Mandate may soon be transferred to a new dynastic line. Note that the people (in the poem, the team of four) are not blamed for their disloyalty. It is the drivers who are blamed for misrule in the state. The ruler must take full responsibility for his bureaucracy and his subjects' welfare.

Appraisal 9: If he does not persist in virtue,
In three years, he'll be replaced.

Fathoming 9: Flagging virtue replaced
Means: An inability to endure.

Chinese tradition recognizes the need for three years to effect a major change. By the end of this trial period, we see the individual entering the climactic final stages of failure occasioned by his inability or disinclination to reform. If he persists in error, he will lose his authority, possibly even his life.

Tuan
No. 29. Decisiveness
April 27–May 1 (a.m)

*Correlates with Earth's Mystery;
Yang; the phase Fire; and the* I
ching *Hexagram no. 43, Breaking
Through [and so, Resolution]; the
sun enters the Net constellation,
3rd degree*

HEAD: Yang *ch'i* is strong within and firm without so that in acting there can be a decisive breakthrough.

Tetragram 9 earlier in the year spoke of yang *ch'i* as "strong within but weak outside." Now that we are in the latter half of the spring season, the balance between yin and yang that obtained at the vernal equinox has given way to the clear supremacy of yang *ch'i*. With yang in full command of its powers, it also works to "strengthen what is within and firm the outside" of the myriad things, spurring on their development. All this is inherently auspicious, especially because of the perfect correspondence between inner and outer. As the *Changes* tells us (W, 515), inner integrity, strength, and steadfastness are preconditions for growth in the direction of brilliance.

The Appraisals play upon the full range of meanings associated with the characters in the title of this tetragram and with the correspondent *Changes* Hexagram no. 43. The title character for this tetragram means "to cut" and, by extension, "to decide" or "to act resolutely." The same graph can describe the "incisive mind." The graph used for the hexagram title has the root meaning of "to open a passage." From this it has the extended meanings of "to cut off or open" and "decisiveness." It also relates to calls to arms, weapons, captives of war, and cries of alarm, all of which are mentioned below.

Appraisal 1: His resolute heart destroys an ax,
Still he keeps his square and line hidden.

Fathoming 1: The decisive heart destroying the ax
Means: The self is ruled from within.

Since this poem marks an auspicious Beginning of Thought, it indicates a heart that discerns right from wrong, although its standards remain hidden. The will is properly set on the Good, as we see in the reference to a carpenter's chalk-line and square, which both symbolize the ability to apply principles of good order to the tasks at hand. Still, the *Mystery* does not entirely clarify the relation of heart to ax. In this translation, the *Mystery* claims that the cutting edge of the well-ordered mind is far more powerful and incisive than the blade of the ax. Certainly, the Chinese are fond of proverbs where an intangible activity easily vanquishes strong objects, for example, "The mouths of the masses [i.e., their wagging tongues] [are corrosive enough to] melt metal." Still, the first line of both Appraisal and Fathoming could also read, "The decisive heart, the destructive ax," implying a parallel between the two. Do heart and ax act in concert or do they work in opposition? If the ax stands for interdiction or punishment, the ax is the external counterpart to the internal conscience. When the internalization of ritual guidelines is incomplete for any reason, a good penal code and the threat of punishment may motivate the heart to distinguish right from wrong.

Appraisal 2: When dark decisions breed adversity,
The fault lies in stopping up the ears.

Fathoming 2: Obscure decisions obstructing
Mean: The center heart is uncertain.

Western philosophy often assumes that the senses undermine the mind's functioning. Prior to the coming of Buddhism, early Chinese philosophy, in contrast, assumes that perceptual knowledge derived from the five senses is absolutely crucial to the correct operation of the heart/mind. Here one of the five sensory receptors, the ear, has been blocked. In early Chinese tradition, the ear is particularly associated with moral development. When insufficient or distorted information is received by the mind, its powers of discrimination are severely hampered. The mind is thrown into confusion so that its decisions are faulty or it lacks decisiveness. It would be highly dangerous to proceed to act.

On another level, the ears represent good advisors. The poem may describe the failure of the leader to follow the excellent advice of his counselors.

Appraisal 3: Clearing his blocked-up ears and nose
Will help to cure the corruption.

Fathoming 3: Clearing his obstructions
　　Means: Whatever plans he has will benefit.

Those "having plans" are worthy candidates who desire to implement their ideas in public service. The head of an organization rids himself of bad advisors, especially those who wish to block the career paths of better candidates. Or, he excises his own worst impulses, so that he is more receptive to good counsel. Once inner and outer corruption have been cleared, all within the community can benefit from better leadership.

Appraisal 4: If he wrongly decides about us,
　　His undeserved wages bring shame.

Fathoming 4: Wrong decisions about us
　　Mean: Drawing his salary is shameful.

Appraisal 4 in Yang Hsiung's schema is reserved for the ranks of officials; here it also corresponds to inauspicious Night. This official is incapable of devising correct policy. Therefore, he should be ashamed to draw his salary; he should submit his resignation. As the *Odes* say, "Oh, that superior man! / He would not eat the bread of idleness."

Appraisal 5: Once the belly is resolved,
　　The legs are free to act.
　　With the noble man decisive,
　　The little guy survives.

Fathoming 5: Set free through gutsy resolve
　　Means: In decisiveness, order is attained.

Appraisal 5 corresponds to the ruler. Since the belly is both the center of the body and its storehouse of energy, the belly or gut is like the ruler. The thighs stand for his chief ministers, although we would talk of right-hand men instead. The limbs depend upon the belly, just as the ministers depend upon the ruler for guidance; the belly functions as the seat of moral courage while the thighs are vehicles for decisive action. Since this Appraisal is auspicious, belly and thigh act in concert to insure the survival and security of the "little guy."

Appraisal 6: Deciding not to decide
　　With your enemies nearby
　　Later attracts the battle ax.

Fathoming 6: Deciding not to decide
　　Means: Crime overtakes his person.

The large battle ax is reserved for the decapitation of criminals or enemies; it is never employed in peaceful activities, such as farming. The individual who fails to distinguish the right course of action in a timely fashion risks his position, and possibly even his life, as his foes quickly seize upon his hesitation.

> Appraisal 7: When *keng* cuts through *chia*,
>> My heart is steady.
>> Later the glory is ours.

> Fathoming 7: *Keng* cutting through *chia*
>> Means: Duty cuts through human feeling.

In the complex system of Yin/yang Five Phases correlations that link the directions, the calendar, and the virtues, *keng* (allied with Metal, the west, social duty, and punishments) conquers *chia* (allied with Wood, the east, humaneness, and suasive example). Since Appraisal 7 represents the mature phase of the cycle (tied to yin *ch'i*, harvests, and punishments), *keng* is properly in ascendancy.

Humaneness describes acts that acknowledge what is due all men by virtue of their humanity. Social duty, by contrast, refers to the fulfillment of "graded" obligations determined by variations in social and kinship ranks, gender, and seniority. The era has passed when compassion and empathy are appropriate; they have been succeeded by somewhat sterner standards of justice. The *Mystery* probably alludes to a passage in the classic *Book of Documents*: "When sternness overcomes his love, then things are surely brought to a successful conclusion."

> Appraisal 8: He attacks valiant dwarfs,
>> But graciously pardons highwaymen.

> Fathoming 8: Decisions favoring highwaymen
>> Mean: He makes decisions recklessly.

The corrupt or incompetent official oppresses the "little guy," who may run afoul of the law through ignorance, while he lets the the worst offenders go free. Although this official is admittedly decisive, his actions subvert the good society.

> Appraisal 9: The finely honed blade of the ax
>> Is the sign of the carpenter.

> Fathoming 9: The ax so shiny bright
>> Means: It is good for attacking chaos.

Appraisal 9 represents the End or Extreme of Calamity. Although society is already to some degree in chaos, control can still be reasserted, given the availability of proper tools. The blade symbolizes both the army and the penal code, since both entail the use of weapons. That it is highly polished (or, possibly curved) is significant, since that allows it to sever cleanly without slipping. Luckily, the ruler is heir to various good tools, including social institutions and Confucian tradition, which will help restore order without unduly disrupting the lives of the innocent. However, it would have been far better to have used such tools to forestall evil tendencies at an earlier stage.

Yi
No. 30. Bold Resolution
May 6–May 10 (a.m.)

Correlates with Earth's Mystery; Yin, the phase Wood; and the I ching *Hexagram no. 43, Breaking Through [and so, Resolution]; the sun enters the Net constellation, 7th degree*

HEAD: Yang *ch'i* just now comes into its own. Resolutely, it dares to act so that things develop their goals.

This tetragram is associated with east, with Wood, and with spring through its assigned constellation, patron Phase, and season of the year. The conjunction of Wood/east/spring proves so compelling that the last barriers to yang *ch'i*'s beneficial action are removed. Yang *ch'i* now flourishes, with no real impediments to its catalyzing activities. Like Tao, it operates in such a way as to allow each of the myriad things to fulfill its potential on its own distinctive pattern.

The tetragram title, Bold Resolution, suggests gutsy courage that takes the initiative. This is a direct contrast to the usual characterization of Wood, which emphasizes slow growth and pliability. Why such a sudden burst of resolution at this juncture in the spring? Perhaps the Changes supplies the answer when it argues, "A breakthrough results from steady increase" (W, 602). Prior to this, there has been a steady increase in the power of yang *ch'i*. Finally, it is time for yang and the myriad things under its protection to break through yin's obstacles in a display of courage. Wood, after all, is coupled with the virtue of steadfast resolution in early Chinese tradition. Any breakthrough, however, depends upon two preconditions covered by the correspondent Hexagram 43: the first is the need for truthful communication between superior and inferior; the second is the obligation of the leader to "dispense endowments to inferiors and refrain from resting [only] on his virtue." Both preconditions associate resolution with filling up [with information, with riches]; hence, the language of certain Appraisals below. The attempts in Tetragram 30 to redefine the notion of courage are also noteworthy. One component of the graph for the tetragram title depicts an enraged wild boar, yet the *Mystery* despises brute, physical courage uninformed by moral courage.

> Appraisal 1: Harboring what is awesome,
> Emptiness fills him nonetheless.

> Fathoming 1: An all-consuming love of power
> Means: The Way and its Power are lost.

The individual's preoccupation with external displays of force or grandeur leads him to neglect the cultivation of his inner life. Self-importance fills the mind (conventionally termed the Void) with what is inherently empty. Since he fails to develop either his innate capacity for Goodness or his concern for the masses, he is a prime example of the wrong kind of resolution. Any disparity between his public and private personae is inherently dangerous, both to him and to society.

> Appraisal 2: Resolute in mind and belly,
> He is the model of stability.

> Fathoming 2: Resolute in mind and belly
> Means: He is strong and firm within.

If mind and body are equally resolved to pursue the Good, its attainment is assured. As Confucius said, "If we really wanted Goodness, we would find that it was by our very side" (A 7/9).

> Appraisal 3: A crown of power fills his head.
> The noble man thinks, "This is not enough."
> The petty man thinks, "More than enough."

> Fathoming 3: Flaunting power, a swollen head
> Means: Only a petty man finds this superior.

The truly moral person is not content with the external trappings of power. With his singular desire for moral community, he recognizes the magnitude of the task before him: he must wisely employ his authority to transform the daily habits of his subordinates. In the words of Confucius, the good ruler "inspires awe, but is not ferocious; and he is proud, without being insolent" (A 20/2). The petty man, in contrast, worships rank and title. In his arrogance, he parades his symbols of authority, mistaking them for moral authority itself. Lacking inner resources, he relies upon harsh punishments since these appear more impressive than rule by benevolence. All the while, unlike his moral betters, he is supremely confident that he is more than capable of governing well. Self-delusion leads to the collapse of power.

> Appraisal 4: The noble man makes a tool of speech.
> His words are gentle yet resolute.

> Fathoming 4: The noble man's tool of speech
> Means: There is method in his words.

Appraisal 4 is aligned with Metal in Chinese tradition. In the cycle of Phases, Metal corresponds to the mouth and tongue in the body; hence, the reference to speech. The proper balance between gentility and resolution is analogous to the balance implied here between Wood (patron phase for the tetragram) and Metal (patron phase for the Appraisal). Since Appraisal 4 also corresponds to officialdom, the poem probably describes the duties of the advisor: specifically, both honest criticism and loyal obedience are to be offered to the leader. The good advisor should be "conciliatory, but not accommodating" (A 13/23).

> Appraisal 5: Not working the field, but eating the yield,
> He boldly seeks a sinecure.

> Fathoming 5: Not tilling, but reaping
> Means: The wage is not matched by worth.

Despite an obvious lack of cultivation (the pun is intentional), the subject of the poem arrogates high rank and salary to himself. In this, he is like the farmer who expects to gather a bountiful harvest without planting his fields. Only hard work can lead to just rewards. Especially in the service of the state, the good man is "Intent upon the task, / Not bent upon the pay" (A 15/38).

> Appraisal 6: Resolved to serve as ridgepole and pillar,
> He helps secure his great master's place.

> Fathoming 6: Resolved to be pillar and pole
> Means: His strength bears the burdens of state.

Using a stock metaphor, the structural supports of a house are equated with the main supports of the ruling house. The ridgepole probably stands for the chief officer; the pillars, for his high officials. Just as the stability of a house depends upon the strength and placement of its constituent materials, the security of the dynastic house relies upon the development of human resources and the placement of good men in appropriate positions of trust.

Appraisal 7: The big ram may be headstrong
But its bleat is less than bold.

Fathoming 7: The stubborn resolve of a ram
Means: Its speech is no model.

Despite its size and strength, the ram is not regarded as an ideal role model. Like the billy goat of Western anecdote, it appears to be unduly stubborn and ill-tempered, even downright contentious. It is undiscriminating in its eating habits. And its shrill screech, which is unlikely to win any admirers, has no staying power or depth. From this we learn that size and strength alone do not constitute true excellence. One's manner is crucial. The model sages, it is said, "got things by being cordial, frank, courteous, temperate, and deferential" (A 1/10).

Appraisal 8: Bold in the face of calamity, so steady!
This is the base of a noble man's fame.

Fathoming 8: Resolute and steady in facing calamity
Means: His virtue cannot be concealed.

The superior man calmly faces adversity, "knowing his fate and delighting in Heaven." Integrity provides a strong sense of security. Since he can maintain his equanimity, chances are good that he will eventually find a way to extricate himself from present calamity. But should misfortune continue, he can at least hope that human memory or the annals of history will take note of his exemplary moral courage.

Appraisal 9: The boar's resolve lies in its tusks,
Which entice the archer's outstretched bow.

Fathoming 9: The boar's brashness in its tusks
Means: That is what the petty officer hunts.

Appraisal 7 presented a case of physical courage that was distinctly unappealing. By Appraisal 9, the situation is far worse: displays of bravado now wreak destruction. The boar's tusks are rustic symbols for bravery; therefore, every local strongman is intent upon securing a set for himself, the better to advertise his own ferocity. Angry farmers may also take up arms to stop the boar from destroying their crops or goring their animals. Ironically, the source of the boar's courage, the strong tusks that make the boar consider itself invincible, prove to be its downfall. By analogy, the petty individual relies on the appurtenances of power to make himself invulnerable to attack. But this attitude only makes him more liable to assault. As he harms others, so he is harmed.

Chuang
No. 31. Packing
May 6–May 10 (a.m.)

Correlates with Earth's Mystery;
Yang; *the phase Metal; and the* I
ching *Hexagram no. 56, Traveling;*
the sun enters the Net constella-
tion, 11th degree

HEAD: Yang *ch'i* is greatly engaged in affairs. Even so, yin, which is very small, makes its base below. It is packed in readiness, about to depart.

The second Appraisal of this tetragram marks the beginning of the Summer Onset solar period. Paradoxically, just as yang *ch'i* seems ready to take off, we learn of yin's first preparations to rise again. After the summer solstice, yang *ch'i*'s power, although seemingly invincible, will start to wane in the face of growing yin *ch'i,* for "whatever has exhausted its greatness must lose its home" (W, 675). Like the sage, yang *ch'i* recognizes the coming trend, so it wisely begins preparations for its departure. The tetragram Packing, therefore, celebrates providence and far-sightedness, rather than travel *per se.* (Only in modern times, of course, are the delights of travel celebrated.) The migratory birds that appear repeatedly in Packing portend ill more often not. In general, the early Chinese regarded the sedentary life as the basis of their society. The *Changes,* for example, associates wandering with carelessness, lack of discernment, and neglect of the all-important social bonds.

> Appraisal 1: Packing in secret,
>   None see him go.

> Fathoming 1: Packing in secret, so that no one sees
>   Means: The mind is already directed outward.

Appraisal 1 describes the Beginning of Thought. It is also an apt portrayal of yang *ch'i* at this time. Thought, in contrast to action, is typically hidden from sight. The noble person begins his preparations to go out into the world. In his heart he is set upon going. Also, he knows where to go, since he anticipates future trends. At this early stage others still ignore him, in part because he is willing to "hide himself" until he is fully ready to act.

> Appraisal 2: Geese, honking, mourn the coming ice.
>   Setting wings to that southward wind,
>   They yearn for their mates in their hearts.

> Fathoming 2: The grief of the wild geese
>   Means: No joy for hearts filled with sorrow.

As water birds, wild geese cannot survive in bitterly cold regions. Therefore, at the first hint of winter, they fly south to warmer climes in search of food. Geese and ducks are said to be monogamous creatures, for when a goose has lost its mate, it is reluctant to abandon it, even though it must do so in order to survive. The goose confronts the most difficult of human dilemmas: to give up one's heart's desire or to give up life itself.

At first reading, the scene appears to symbolize the faithfulness of devoted marriage partners cruelly separated by adversity or death. A classical treatise on mourning rites cites the reluctance of certain birds and beasts to leave their mates in death as proof of the natural and inevitable character of family feelings. But here the goose may have gone too far, for emotional attachment clouds its judgment. The wise person knows when to leave, and harbors no regrets. The *Changes* (W, 131) warns the petty person: "In waiting to escape, there is affliction. Danger." Even a desirable position should be abandoned when trouble is in sight.

> Appraisal 3: Moving on toward his goal,
> Happiness may well ensue.

> Fathoming 3: Moving on toward his goal
> Means: He meets what he rejoices in.

Despite our empathy for the wild goose in the preceding Appraisal, a less emotional person would realize that the goose should never be deterred from its proper course. So long as the will is fixed on proper goals, it will make progress. Happiness, rather than sorrow, will follow.

> Appraisal 4: *K'un* birds fly out at dawn,
> flocking together in the north.
> "Ying-ying," they call back and forth,
> And never stop singing to feed.

> Fathoming 4: The dawn flight of the *k'un*
> Means: How can they live on so little?

The *k'un* is a mythical bird akin to the roc or phoenix of Western tradition. (Like the phoenix, it is associated with the sun, although some tales identify it as the pet of the immortal Queen Mother of the West.) According to Chinese myth, the *k'un* is distinguished by its enormous size and flying speed. Here a flock of *k'un* birds flies north, although the *k'un*'s natural habitat is the south. The *k'un* sing in harmony, but their calls are confused. They ignore their own basic natures and needs; for this reason, they fail to feed themselves. Their initial difficulty, caused by lack of direction, is made still worse once they are content to remain in an untenable position. Their profound willfulness is clear; perhaps they are also too lazy to change direction. It is even sadder that they encourage one another in fruitless pursuits.

Appraisal 5: The wild swan packs for the Tz'u
Where food and drink are plentiful.

Fathoming 5: The swan packing for the River Tz'u
Means: It fully intends to attain its goal.

The wild swan, the third water bird in this series of Appraisals, is provident, unlike the previously mentioned geese and *k'un*. At this propitious time before the end of the cycle, the swan makes plans to go to the Tz'u River (in present-day Shantung Province), a body of fresh water too large to freeze; food and drink will be available throughout the winter. So it will "eat and drink in concord," becoming a symbol of "good fortune" (W, 206).

The same graph used for "wild swan" means "great" as well. Obviously, these lines apply to the morally great, who are far-sighted enough to anticipate future needs.

Appraisal 6: Through six junctions and round nine roads,
No limits on their route, they ply their trade.

Fathoming 6: Through six junctions
Means: Itinerant merchants conduct their business.

Americans often label untrammeled freedom and reckless individuality as romantic and desirable; the Frontier Myth is still powerful. Early Chinese tradition would have been puzzled by this facile equation of physical mobility with happiness and self-fulfillment; even the "free and easy wandering" advocated by Chuang tzu referred to mind travel, not body travel. The Confucians in particular felt that human development itself depended on siting the individual firmly within a nested series of social relations that teach him basic moral lessons. True self-cultivation means learning to realize the full moral potential inherent in each of the many societal roles played by one person during the course of a life. The very rootlessness of the merchant precludes his learning to become truly moral. Should he wish to do good, he will not gain sufficient practice in a sustained relationship. Should he do wrong, his wanderings will make it that much harder to apprehend and punish him, although the corrective would be salutary. In the worst case scenario, the merchant roams highways and byways, his lack of restraint matched only by his unbounded desire for profit.

Appraisal 7: Packing without a partner:
Better to attack the wicked unencumbered.

Fathoming 7: Packing without a partner
Means: Calamity is imminent.

Chinese tradition assumes that morality is charismatic. A lack of like-minded companions usually suggests evildoing. Since an odd-numbered Appraisal in an odd-numbered Tetragram is generally auspicious (because it is assigned to Day), this translation tries to wrest a good meaning from the text; therefore, it adds the word "unencumbered." Appraisal 4 criticized the misguided impulse to flock together. Here the good person seeks to break free of wicked factions, realizing that personal attachments may simply weaken his resolve to restore the Good. If necessary, when calamity is foreseen, the good person will set out on a solitary campaign against the wicked. Once a stable society has been restored, the possibility for true companionship reappears.

Appraisal 8: The young, strewn like grain
    Across rutted paths
    Weep at sacrifices to the Road.
    With these they send them on their way.

Fathoming 8: The young scattered on the road
    Means: They dispatch them to their deaths.

Here the packing clearly entails tearful preparations for war. The youngest and middle children from many families gather at the crossroads, to witness the sacrifice to the Road. Their elder brothers are sent off, possibly never to return. This Appraisal serves to prefigure Tetragram 32, whose main theme is war.

Appraisal 9: He packs at dusk.

Fathoming 9: Packing at dusk
    Means: He can still escape the worst.

Appraisal 9, of course, corresponds to Extreme Calamity. Still, at dusk there is just enough light by which to execute a last-minute change in plans. It is preferable, of course, to set out on a journey at dawn so as to make as much progress as possible. Although there is little to be gained by a late start (in either moral development or a career), at least this individual escapes to relative safety.

Chung

No. 32. Legion

May 10 (p.m.)–May 14

Correlates with Earth's Mystery;
Yin; *the phase Earth; and the* I
ching *Hexagram no. 7, Troops;*
the sun enters the Triaster
constellation

HEAD: Yang *ch'i* expands to the heights, embracing all equally so that the myriad things everywhere grow bright. Beautiful and large they grow, multiplying into legions.

Like its *Changes* counterpart, this tetragram plays off two separate meanings of "legion": "the multitudes" [i.e., the masses] and "the military unit." The Head text focuses on yang *ch'i*'s role in fostering the growth of many things and an increase in their numbers. The Appraisals consider the masses' role in warfare: small farmers are conscripted into infantry divisions, only to die in bloody pitched battles. The *Mystery,* following ancient precedent, can envision the just war, but more often than not it deplores the devastation visited upon the common people. After the unification of the Chinese empire in 221 B.C., the civil virtues slowly came to be favored over the martial; as a later proverb goes, "No good iron should be used to make a weapon; no good man should be used to make a soldier." This proposition was not much advanced in Western Han, however, when successful military campaigns expanded the influence of the Chinese empire deep into Central Asia.

> Appraisal 1: Secretly the war begins.
> Like fire the news spreads.
> Farming stops. Grain goes to war-horses.
> Soon corpses will litter the fields.

> Fathoming 1: The beginning of the dark war
> Means: Once begun, it only gets worse.

Few are able to identify the factors that will lead to war. Initial preparations for war are state secrets. But once war flares up, the effect is all too clear. The alarm is sounded. Farmers abandon their fields. The able-bodied are conscripted into the army. Those left behind may have to flee their homes in the face of advancing enemy troops. Surplus grain is fed to the war-horses, rather than to humans, so food supplies dwindle dangerously. In short, death reigns where life should be; corpses litter the rice fields. No end can justify such utter confusion, for the natural order of things is disrupted. The *Lao tzu* presents the contrasting case "when the Way prevails in the empire": "fleet-footed horses are relegated to plowing the fields" (LT 46).

Appraisal 2: Weapons have no blades.
No armies are deployed.
Even the gentle unicorn submits
To serve the gentle ruler.

Fathoming 2: That no blades clash
Means: Virtue conquers every quarter.

"Arms are instruments of ill omen, not the instruments of the gentleman. . . . One who exults in the killing of men will never have his way in the empire" (LT 31). The conquest of men's hearts by virtue is far superior to the conquest of their bodies by war. This is proven by the marvelous unicorn. Its sharp horn makes it capable of fighting, yet according to myth, it refuses to attack other animals. The unicorn appears only to herald the rise of a true king who prefers rule by charismatic virtue to war, despite his reserve of power and authority. As the *Lao tzu* says, "One who excels in defeating his enemies does not join issue" (LT 68).

Appraisal 3: As conscripts load the carts
A soldier pushes wife and child away.
While rifts inside grow wider.

Fathoming 3: That some in the army load carts
Means: Councils of war draw harm within.

Carts are being loaded, but we do not know their contents. Are they filled with grain in preparation for war? With corpses? With captured prisoners? Since Appraisal 3 marks the transition from Thought to Action, most likely battle plans have been drawn up, but no engagement has yet been fought. Why does the paterfamilias push his wife and child away? Perhaps through him we see the state's own eagerness to go to war. Perhaps we are led to consider the way in which the ruler ("father and mother" to his people) can harm his "children" (subjects) by war. Perhaps his action mirrors the rifts inside the war room between contending strategists. A bellicose ruler and discord among the generals is enough to spell defeat for the entire state. Hierarchical relations are subverted. Chaos threatens. The portents of disaster are clear.

Appraisal 4: The tiger's roar rouses them to battle.
The leopard rears, its selfish fears
Suppressed.

Fathoming 4: The awesome roar of the tiger
Means: Swift and sure as a hawk in flight.

The *Mystery* celebrates the martial virtue of good leaders. The tiger's roar not only strikes terror into the hearts of its enemies; it also serves to alert its allies to join the fray. In response, the leopard leaps up to volunteer, now that it has overcome its own selfish desires. True martial spirit requires self-restraint and self-sacrifice on others' behalf. Those who take up arms in the proper spirit will find that nothing can withstand their sure and swift advance.

> Appraisal 5: Pitched battles to the din of bell and drum:
> Like bears, like demons they clash.

> Fathoming 5: Locked in combat, clash! clash!
> Means: He is king by brute force alone.

The bad ruler relies upon physical strength alone to enforce his will. Forsaking virtue, he and his men are no better than animals.

> Appraisal 6: The army of the great king
> Thunders in their ears.
> Its only use is to subdue men's hearts.

> Fathoming 6: Armies like thunderbolts
> Mean: Almighty is its awesome strike.

Ancient metaphor compares the awesome quality of the king's presence to thunder. The true king employs his crack troops in order to make men submit to the Good, not to wreak destruction. Sure in his purpose, he moves swiftly, stunning his enemies, who can only cower in anticipation of the impending crash. With such force at his command, the ruler seldom needs to resort to arms to enforce his will; his mighty presence alone acts as a deterrent to evil.

> Appraisal 7: A confusion of pennants and flags,
> Shields and lances in disarray.
> Army wives with child bemoan their loss.
> Wailing, they cast scathing glances
> At the king.

> Fathoming 7: A confusion of pennants and flags
> Means: He incites the great resentment of the people.

The army has suffered a devastating defeat. The dead must now be gathered for burial. The blame for all this rightly rests with the ruler, who ordered his people into war. So resentful are the ruler's subjects that rebellion is likely to follow. He who resorts to war may find himself destroyed by it.

Appraisal 8: The king's armies grow weaker.
   Once he sees their ravaged state
   No more tumbrels will be seen.

Fathoming 8: The decimated ranks of his army
   Mean: No longer will blades be bloodied.

"Carriages full of corpses" are a sure sign of lack of merit (W, 423). The wise ruler recognizes when his army is too ill, too poorly provisioned, or too dispirited to continue the fight. Recalling his troops from the field, the good ruler turns his attention to domestic reforms that will insure the safety and security of his people. The truly great ruler goes one step further: never again does he resort to warfare.

Appraisal 9: The battle-ax blade is broken,
   Its handle is cracked.
   It is right to stop, wrong to attack.
   The advance will be bloody.

Fathoming 9: Blade broken and handle cracked
   Mean: There is not enough to go on.

The man who presses forward despite inadequate tools (where tools suggest prior training) will meet with calamity. Reckless courage, after all, is of little use in any great endeavor. Appraisal 9 represents the Extreme of Calamity. Here we witness the folly of continued aggression.

Mi

No. 33. Closeness
May 15–May 19 (a.m.)

Correlates with Earth's Mystery;
Yang; the phase Water; and the I
ching Hexagram no. 8, Holding
Together; the sun enters the
Triaster constellation, 3d degree

HEAD: Yang *ch'i* draws near to Heaven. The myriad things, budding and flowering, are all closely packed together, with no intervening gaps.

The previous tetragram describes yang *ch'i* merely "expanding to the heights." Now culminating yang begins to "draw near to Heaven," which emphasizes its increased power and fundamental kinship with Heaven. As "the two become one," the bond between yang *ch'i* and Heaven becomes a fit symbol for suitably intimate relations of all kinds, especially the primary bonds

Figure 8. "Peeking through the gap." A winged divinity holds a sacred inscription.

within the family and between ruler and official. The myriad things for their part unconsciously imitate these tight psychic bonds by physical proximity. As they grow larger and more numerous, they crowd against one another until no space is left between.

Tetragram 33 variously applies the idea of "no gap" to cosmogonic stages (where it describes the undifferentiated chaos of primordial *ch'i*); to spatial relations; to unbroken feelings of good fellowship; to political alliances and kinship ties; and to a perfect "fit" between perceptual knowledge and external reality, between human potential and its actuality. "No gap" may also refer to the absolute correspondence between ascribed social roles and individual acts, another "fit" usually identified by the catchword "rectification of names" (*cheng ming*). In all these cases, wherever no gap prevails, the individual, society, and cosmos operate in perfect harmony.

The graph used for the tetragram title conveys "closeness," "fineness" [of weave, for example], and "density." In certain cases, the same graph also means "close-mouthed" or "discreet." The Chinese presume a connection between the two sets of meanings. A prudent disinclination to talk promotes perfect closeness in the community.

Appraisal 1: He seeks a glimpse of the Great Unknown,
But there is no gap in the Gate.

Fathoming 1: Peering into it, there is no gap
Means: It is shut up tight on every side.

The "Gate" probably refers to the border between potential and actual existence, between life and death, between tangible experience and the ineffable. Behind our everyday world lies the inchoate source we call the Tao, from which all patterned and particulate matter eventually emerges. And since Appraisal 1 represents the Beginning of Thought, we imagine a similar barrier behind which hide thoughts that are as yet unformulated or unrevealed. The Tao prefers to hide its origins. Similarly, the gentleperson dislikes advertising his thoughts, in part because "things nearly complete, if not handled with absolute discretion, as a rule will be harmed in their completion" (W, 307). No one has the power to peer either into prior existence or into another's innermost mind, despite a desire to do so. Still, the very metaphor of the gate holds out the hope that eventually we can pass beyond the barrier to enter the Great Unknown—perhaps at death or by a flash of sudden illumination. Until then, we know at least that the ineffable Tao informs and animates our present life, while the unseen mind rules our conduct.

Appraisal 2: If he fails to draw us close,
Our hearts stray far from home.

Fathoming 2: Not close, not friendly,
Means: He turns away from his proper place.

The original poem is careful not to specify who is to be blamed for the psychic distance that prevails, but some read these lines as a warning to the ruler who fails to act as "father and mother" to his subjects. The poem also works as a critique of the individual whose restless ambition or search for novelty causes him to neglect close friends or his psychic "home," the conscience.

Appraisal 3: Being close to our parents
Helps us gain true humanity.

Fathoming 3: Being close to kin
Means: We act to promote the good.

According to the ancient Confucians, the development of humane impulses depends upon the quality of the home environment. To them, it is natural for the child to love the parents, and only by appropriately extending this affection to others can the individual learn to be socialized and truly human. Should the family for any reason fail to instill habits of filial piety and devotion in the child, the growing child will find it very difficult to commit to close relations with others. For this reason, the Chinese *Classic of Filial Piety* states, "Not to love one's relatives, and yet to love other men, this is a perversion of virtue." Learning how to love well, like any other learning, requires a fine balance between open-heartedness and discrimination. These qualities make for the moral life.

> Appraisal 4: After three days close to putrid flesh,
> He fails to notice the stench.

> Fathoming 4: Being close to tainted flesh
> Means: Minor evils are pervasive.

Ordinarily, the rank smell of rotting flesh turns the stomach, but human beings seem to have a remarkable capacity, given enough time, to accustom themselves to anything. Therefore, the person who consorts with evil companions soon "fails to notice the stench."

> Appraisal 5: Intimacy unimpaired,
> You are Heaven's chosen consort.

> Fathoming 5: A tight fit and no rift
> Means: Merit lies in being close to Heaven.

The ideal leader perfectly conforms to Heaven's designs, thereby completing its work on earth. Those of merit find their virtue recognized; they are rewarded with high position. As greater numbers are influenced by the models of perfection, harmony comes to prevail in the entire community.

> Appraisal 6: Associating with great evil,
> His miseries may increase.

> Fathoming 6: Being close to great evil
> Means: Joining the errant, he becomes the same.

Past the halfway mark in the cycle, Appraisal 6 tends toward decline unless it is assigned to auspicious yang *ch'i*. The minor evils associated with bad companions in Appraisal 4 have now become great evils since the allies of the wicked quickly are schooled in evil. Soon they are unable to distinguish between aberrant and correct behavior.

> Appraisal 7: In the net's fine mesh is a tear
> As small as the gill of a fish.
> Great is the ruler who prevents its recurrence.

> Fathoming 7: A fine opening, small as a gill,
> Means: We rely on the ruler for repairs.

If the smallest rift occurs between various groups in society, the great ruler repairs it, then takes steps to prevent its recurrence.

> Appraisal 8: Having filed his teeth, he is left with gums.
> In three years, he will no longer rule.

> Fathoming 8: With filed teeth, depending on gums
> Means: The ruler uproots himself.

The teeth rely on their base in the gums, just as hard yang *ch'i* rests on softer yin. But if the teeth are ground down to the level of the gums (because of self-destructive impulses), they become useless. The adult loses all the advantages of maturity, reverting to the helpless state of a mewling infant. How will he ever manage to keep his strength on a diet of gruel? His large frame inevitably weakens, until the gums and even vital organs themselves are debilitated.

By analogy, the individual or state that grinds down staunch supporters loses the last line of defense. By extension, the state that places a child on the throne is also in grave danger.

> Appraisal 9: In the face of repeated disasters,
> He first bows low, then honorably dies.

> Fathoming 9: Faced with calamity upon calamity
> Means: Finally, he cannot be deprived of honor.

Appraisal 9 must describe the ultimate state of Closeness. Despite its talk of death, it is aligned with auspicious yang *ch'i*. In the face of serial calamities, the individual bows to his fate, but remains steadfast in his devotion to the Way. Or, in an alternate interpretation, he is demoted from office, then executed, despite his innocence. Still, his fame will survive him. In a third reading, the individual recognizes his own moral failings (the inner disasters that have led to visible disasters) shortly before death. He humbles himself and reforms his conduct so that he wrests from life an honorable end.

Ch'in
No. 34. Kinship
May 19 (p.m.)–May 23

Correlates with Earth's Mystery;
Yin; *the phase Fire; and the* I
ching *Hexagram no. 8, Holding
Together; the sun enters the
Triaster constellation, 7th degree;
the Dipper points SSE; the musical
note is F*

HEAD: Yang in every direction is humane and loving. It is completely true, generous, and trustworthy so that all things feel a kinship and are at peace.

By the end of this tetragram, summer is in full force. As yang *ch'i* grows stronger and the days noticeably lengthen, the myriad things bask in its warmth. Since there is more than enough yang *ch'i* to foster growth for all, there is no need for contention among living things. Things consequently are drawn to yang and to each other; in their harmonious union, they come to imitate the perfection of yang *ch'i*.

This tetragram, like its predecessor, is paired with Hexagram 8, called Holding Together. The Appraisals suggest that the habit of according one's own kin proper treatment is the first, crucial step toward forming close bonds with all others (whether in friendships, in political alliances, or in wider family circles). On the other hand, as the *Odes* say, "If you keep your own at a distance, / The people all will act thus [to you]!" The second step is to follow Heaven's example in "treating the virtuous as kin."

> Appraisal 1: If kin are not close, their wills
> Grate like teeth in an uneven bite.

> Fathoming 1: That kin are not as close as skin
> Means: The center heart is closed off.

Unlike the Christian tradition, Confucian tradition does not expect the individual to love each and every other person as himself. Instead, Confucianism asserts that each person owes the greatest loyalty and devotion to family members (and by analogy, to the ruler who truly acts as "father and mother" of the people). These feelings of responsibility are then to be extended, but in ever-decreasing measure, to wider circles outside the family into the village and provincial communities. This poem is perfectly ambiguous in that it gives two related messages. First, unless the habit of respect and love is engendered in the family, the capacities of the innermost heart/mind probably will fail to develop sufficiently. And the second, "If those treated as kin are not of his skin [i.e., his family], / Their ideas grate like teeth in a bad bite" (an alternate reading for the Appraisal). Surrogate family relations, then, cannot be an adequate substitute for real kinship ties. Differing temperaments and interests inevitably lead to wrangling, weakening the bonds between unrelated parties.

> Appraisal 2: Trusting ties of flesh and blood,
> To meet their goals they rely on kin.

> Fathoming 2: Trusting flesh and blood
> Means: No one can come between them.

This Appraisal elaborates the moral of Appraisal 1. The wise person realizes that a tight family unit provides the single best base of support from which an individual can develop. Having learned certain fundamental lessons within the family context (including a good sense of priorities), the individual can then go on to make a mark upon society at large.

> Appraisal 3: The mulberry fly abandons its young.
> The wasp that takes them on
> Does not meet with disgrace.

> Fathoming 3: That the fly ignores its relations
> Means: It fails its own body.

The *Mystery* alludes to Ode 196, which says:

> The mulberry insect has young.
> The sphex wasp bears them on its back.
> Teach and train your sons
> So they will try to be good like it.

The mulberry fly fails to protect its own larvae adequately; instead of housing them in a safe place, the mulberry fly shows no particular familial affection toward its young, leaving them to be preyed upon by its enemies. According to legend, the sphex does not devour the mulberry fly larvae. Rather, acting as surrogate parent, it introduces the mulberry larvae into its own nest, where over time they metamorphose into young wasps. The mulberry fly shows unusual lack of foresight, since its careless behavior deprives it of descendants to carry on the family line. The Ode, then, seems to chastise parents whose lack of care may end in their young identifying with the interests of others. The havoc this could wreak in the family should be an important consideration to any right-thinking individual. In other writings, Yang Hsiung employs the same metaphor to prove the relative importance of nurture over nature in the socialization process.

Appraisal 4: Guests feel like kin in sharing the rites
When food and drink are properly measured.

Fathoming 4: That in rites guests feel like kin
Means: Host and guest come together.

The moral superior uses ritual activity to forge good relations with others. Feelings of good fellowship engendered by the feast promote lasting social ties. Food and drink, then, become the tools, not the goals of ceremony, which is carefully designed to induce conduct that exemplifies the Mean. As host and guest come together in mutual esteem, those who participate in the feast are "fed virtue" as well as ordinary food.

Appraisal 5: Slighting those who deserve his care,
His closest friends shall run away.

Fathoming 5: Slighting those who deserve his care
Means: On every side, he alienates good men.

Relatives "should not treat each other coldly," the Classics say. If a man cannot bring himself to bestow affection and gratitude where they are due, why shouldn't his allies and subordinates desert him, reasoning that "he who slights those he ought to treat well will slight all others, whoever they may be." In contrast, the moral superior graciously condescends even to those with the most distant claims to consideration.

Appraisal 6: Caring for those who deserve it,
The noble man grasps the Dipper.

Fathoming 6: Generous to those who deserve it
Means: He attracts good men from every side.

The leader may be said to grasp the Dipper in two senses. First, he ladles out food and wine to honor his guests at ritual feasts. Second, by virtue of his suasive example he is able to grasp the Dipper (the constellation that is symbol of kingly rule), so that "all the lesser lights will revolve" around him happily (A 2/1).

Appraisal 7: However high and lofty his rank,
He is base in conducting affairs.

Fathoming 7: Rank high but conduct base
Means: His character is inadequate.

Appraisal 7 corresponds to the Beginning of Calamity. Well past the midpoint of the cycle, decline begins to set in. The immoral public servant no longer fulfills his duties well. The gross disparity between rank and character makes this leader's position all the more precarious. Should trouble arise, he will not be able to save himself.

> Appraisal 8: Dried meat shared with close kin:
> Flawlessly, the noble man performs his duty
> To act as trunk of the family tree.

> Fathoming 8: Doing his duty by kin
> Means: He claims no credit for himself.

Family obligation is the "trunk of goodness" (A 1/2), and the family head is "trunk" of the family tree. The ideal family head is careful to fulfill his obligations toward inferiors, dependents, and kinsmen. On appropriate occasions, he sends gifts of dried meat to nourish individual family members and strengthen the bonds between them. As Confucius notes, "When gentlemen are punctilious in regard to their own kin, the people are encouraged to be humane" (A 8/2). On the other hand, to neglect such proprieties would be to risk internal dissension within the clan. As the *Odes* warn, "Loss of kindly feeling may arise from faults in [dispensing] dried meat."

> Appraisal 9: Immature yet close: ill-omened.

> Fathoming 9: A childish intimacy untested
> Means: It turns on its very own roots.

If immaturity is allowed to persist so late in the cycle, the relations built upon it will be fundamentally flawed. Such intimacy cannot stand the test of time.

Lien
No. 35. Gathering
May 24–May 28 (a.m.)

Correlates with Earth's Mystery; Yang; the phase Wood; and the I ching Hexagram no. 9, Small Levies [Taming Power of the Small in Wilhelm]; the sun enters the Well constellation, 3d degree

HEAD: Yang *ch'i* swells hugely, filling out to the very outer edges. Minute yin on a small scale gathers its forces on the inside.

At this point in high summer, the position of yang *ch'i* seems unassailable, yet nascent yin has already begun to gather its forces. Thus does the cosmic cycle alternate between full and empty. With yang *ch'i* swelling out to the edges, yin takes advantage of the hollow space left behind at center to build a base of strength. The myriad things mirror this activity, since much "growth on the outside necessarily leads to hollowness within." Given the danger implied by this imbalance between inner and outer, the moral person is especially careful in how she proceeds. As yin begins to gather force, she finds it most effective to take precautions "at the beginning," before trouble of any kind looms large.

The tetragram's title suggests a gradual increase in the accumulation of yin *ch'i* in the cosmic cycle. It also implies that yin will bide its time, "gathering its forces" until it is powerful enough to launch a full-scale attack on yang. The same graph means "savings" or "stores" (as in money or harvests) and "government levies" or "taxes"—yet another kind of transfer from a greater "outside" to a smaller "inside." The movement implied is from field to barn, or from the people to the court's treasury. The outer/ inner dichotomy lies at the heart of the *Mystery's* portrayal of benevolent government. According to hallowed Confucian tradition, taxes should not exceed a tithe on the value of the harvest. Early Chinese rulers were also told not to overtax their subjects by repeated wars and extraordinary levies, or by exacting corvée labor for construction projects. Like yang *ch'i* at this juncture, such a bloated empire will soon find that it is hollow at its core (in that it will lack support from the people). The best method by which the ruler can come to command vast reserves of wealth and power is not through taxes, but through keeping the people's absolute loyalty. In effect, the ruler stores his possessions in the granaries and barns of his subjects.

> Appraisal 1: Small taxes kept the same,
>   Help the common people feel secure,
>   And rectify the state.

> Fathoming 1: Small taxes kept the same
>   Mean: His way is fitting.

According to legend, in the golden age of antiquity the highest tax exacted by a ruler in years of plenty was one-tenth of the yield; the only permissible variation occurred in times of famine, when taxes were reduced or forgiven, depending on local conditions. The best foundation for a secure rule is the government's provision for the economic security of its people.

> Appraisal 2: Greedy hoarding, bit by bit,
>   Steeps us in impropriety.

> Fathoming 2: Black hoarding, bit by bit,
>   Means: This is not the way to glory.

Squirreling away petty profit is one sure way of habituating oneself to evil. Minor covetous acts may seem inconsequential at the outset, but they result in a slow but steady erosion of one's moral faculties.

> Appraisal 3: Seeing it is small, he eschews its use
> So that we may fully develop.

> Fathoming 3: Seeing the small, he does not use it.
> Meaning: He waits for us to grow big.

Ritual precepts forbid the use of young animals for sacrifice. Such prohibitions teach an important lesson (already known to hunters, fishermen, and subsistence farmers): young and fragile things must be patiently fostered until they mature enough to be put to use. Only an idiot pulls his rice-sprouts out of the ground, mistakenly thinking that he will be able to push the harvest date ahead. By analogy, the person who hopes to cultivate his virtue does not prematurely test himself; nor does the wise leader squeeze those followers who cannot yet make significant contributions.

> Appraisal 4: In gathering profit and reducing punishment,
> Small is the advance and great the retreat.

> Fathoming 4: Gathering profits, reducing punishments,
> Means: His government is in retreat.

Chinese tradition presumes that ordinary people will look to their ruler for their values. Here, the government gives them mixed messages. On the one hand, to reduce punishments suggests that generosity is good. On the other, to raise taxes shows that profit is valued over humaneness. Is it any wonder that the common people are left in utter confusion, and that this government lacks a secure foundation?

> Appraisal 5: Livestock propagate contentedly,
> Snowy white cocoons blanket the fields.

> Fathoming 5: Happy livestock and white cocoons
> Mean: The state does not "steal their time."

Domestic animals (especially the ox) and the silkworm are said to be especially pleasing to the gods of Earth, the patron Phase for the central Appraisal 5. Both agriculture (as men's work) and sericulture (as women's work) appear in this scene of idyllic productivity. Food and clothing, the basic necessities of life, are provided, and there is also silk for the aged and for ritual. Such good order results when the people stick to the "basic" occupations, rather than the merchant or artisan trades. But the Fathoming offers the main reason for this material prosperity: the wise ruler, acceding to the natural rhythms of the universe, is careful not to "steal the time." In other words, from spring planting through the autumn harvest, the state should not employ the common people in war or corvée.

> Appraisal 6: Though small and weak at first,
> Something big begins to grow.
> The petty man fails to take heed.

> Fathoming 6: Warnings about the sick and weak
> Mean: He is oblivious to the first small signs of
> change.

The Great Commentary to the *Changes* defines the gentleman in terms of his superb sensitivity to the practical and ethical implications of the unfolding situation, long before it has fully evolved. As the tradition states, it is advantageous to

> Contemplate difficulty when it is still easy.
> Manage a great affair when it is still small.

In contrast, the petty man, in his self-absorption, lacks awareness of the obvious or the inevitable even when it is right under his nose.

> Appraisal 7: The husband pulls in the cart shafts.
> His wife peels wild and bitter herbs.
> What benefits the king's paternal aunts
> Does nothing for the common run of men.
> An affliction.

> Fathoming 7: Pulling in harness and peeling herbs
> Mean: Wealth is collected from them.

In the *Mystery*'s regular alternation of Day and Night, yin and yang, this Appraisal should be lucky. This appears to be an exception. Both husband and wife are employed in lowly jobs entailing a vast expenditure in energy for very little profit. In happier circumstances, draft animals replace human beings in the traces, and the main meal is grain, not bitter herbs. The tiny sums extorted from the working poor could never fund the state adequately, especially when they are siphoned off by the great families of the realm.

The only good interpretation that is possible for these verses goes like this: If the commonfolk find ways to survive harsh and troubled times, their strength will serve as a kind of resource for the state. Persistence and courage mean that the people do survive their afflictions.

Appraisal 8: Heavy taxes bring down the state.

Fathoming 8: Great downfalls from great levies
Mean: Such collections are wrong.

By Appraisal 8 we are already in the Middle of Calamity. Those in power, rapacious in their demands for taxes, have secured their own downfall. Even the most grasping of rulers should realize the advantages of accepting a lower standard of living in return for the security of his throne.

Appraisal 9: Taxing in season
Helps forestall utter ruin.

Fathoming 9: Collecting taxes when timely
Means: How could disaster be imminent?

In good harvest years, the wise ruler orders a significant proportion of tax receipts reserved as a hedge against bad times. In times of natural disaster or famine, these reserves are redistributed among the common people. He only levies public service during the slack agricultural seasons. And he demands no payment before the harvest. Because he has taken account of the cyclical rhythms of Heaven-and-Earth, he will find that the people have more than enough to support him and themselves in comparative luxury.

Ch'iang
No. 36 Strength
May 28 (p.m.)–June 1

Correlates with Earth's Mystery; Yin; the phase Metal; and the I ching *Hexagram no. 1, Masculine; the sun enters the Well constellation, 7th degree*

HEAD: Yang *ch'i* is pure and hard, dry and firm. Each and every one of the myriad things is strengthened.

The first hints of future trouble for the cycle appeared in the Head text of Tetragram 35. Pure yang *ch'i*, like Heaven, is "strong and untiring" (W, 373). Still, things that grow very strong tend to be overbearing; and things that grow too "dry and firm" suggest stiff corpses. Strength, then, can be good or bad, depending on the situation. As if to ease those apprehensions, this Head text treats only the most positive effects of yang's uninterrupted growth on the myriad things.

Appraisal 1: To be hardheaded is not right.
It makes him utterly useless.

Fathoming 1: To be hard at center
Means: One cannot confer with him.

The petty person tends to be stubborn and unyielding, overbearing and inflexible. Basic cooperation is not an option, let alone a fruitful working relation. The Master himself said, "It is useless to take counsel with those who follow a different way [than ritual]" (A 15/40). By contrast, the ideal friend and ally is both flexible and upright; for that reason, people seek his advice. Strength is a necessary, but not a sufficient cause of greatness.

Appraisal 2: The phoenix spreads its wings in flight.
Noble men approach the proper time:
No one can ever hold them back.

Fathoming 2: A phoenix in flight
Means: Opportunity comes to the noble man.

A truly moral person is like a phoenix. With regard to their respective species, both are equally rare. The patterns of both are pleasing. (The phoenix is famous for its exquisite plumage and fastidious habits. In humans, ritual acts provide the pleasing patterns.) Both are endowed with unusual strength. In taking flight, the phoenix spreads its wings (*hsiu*) to catch the wind (*feng*). By a pun, the truly moral person cultivates herself (*hsiu*) to extend her influence to others (*feng*). So long as adequate preparations have been made and the time is right, they will both soar far above their peers.

Appraisal 3: If pillars are uncentered and beams not high,
The great mansion is laid low.

Fathoming 3: Pillars not centered
Mean: They cannot set the foundation straight.

A house will be stable only if its pillars and beams are measured and positioned correctly. By convention, the ruler's chief ministers were called his "pillars" and "beams." If we follow this architectural metaphor, the ruling house can only remain strong if its chief ministers are selected and employed wisely. In the state, as in architecture, the effect of the whole depends upon the balance between numerous structural parts, but a firm foundation is crucial for both.

Appraisal 4: Keen of eye and ear, there and over there,
His attendants, left and right,
Offer him staunch support.

Fathoming 4: Perceptive aides all around
Mean: From every side, the many knights approach.

The ideal man in office is said to be "perceptive in ear and eye." The good ruler must use all available evidence to judge candidates for office. He is bound to select those who, like him, are keen of eye and ear. The talented, therefore, flock to court, where they can put their perceptiveness to good use in service of the king. Their support strengthens the ruling house.

Appraisal 5: Noble men, when strong, use virtue.
Petty men, when strong, use force.

Fathoming 5: That the petty man is strong
Means: His faults increase as he gains rank.

Given the charisma of rank and riches, it may at first seem difficult to judge a person of position or wealth. Yet, the petty person who has finagled his way into office becomes more overbearing as his arrogance and pride increase. In contrast, the moral superior upon attaining high rank becomes even more conscious of his responsibility to lead others along the path of virtue.

Appraisal 6: Using my strength to "overcome myself,"
The sky is the limit to what I can do.

Fathoming 6: Strength in overcoming myself
Means: Great excellence has no limits.

True excellence depends upon the individual overcoming his own selfish, biased, or arrogant tendencies. He may also decide to "overcome his own strength" (an alternate reading of the first Appraisal line), as he recognizes the wisdom of yielding in many situations. Paradoxically, then, strength comes from conquering the self.

Appraisal 7: Metal is strong but flesh is weak.
Blood flows in the fields.

Fathoming 7: Strong metal and weak flesh
Mean: The laws cause great harm.

Not even the strongest man can withstand a blow by weapons. Knowing the harm that weapons can wreak, the good leader runs his state in such a way as to minimize the need for harsh punishments. Here blood flows even in the rice fields, suggesting the tyrannous nature of this regime and its laws.

Appraisal 8: He strengthens where he fails,
Making an effort where he is weak.

Figure 9. Mt. T'ai, the most sacred mountain of China, which is located in Shantung province, near the home of Confucius.

Fathoming 8: Strong after failure
Means: He works hard to make himself strong.

The moral superior learns to recognize and reform his failings. The best way to do this is to immerse himself in the model of the sages.

Appraisal 9: He pulls Great Mountain up from its roots.
He snaps pillars and beams in two.
Such men stumble, then fall.

Fathoming 9: Mountains uprooted and beams snapped
Mean: In the end, he's undone by violence.

Proverbial strongmen are said to be able to pluck Great Mountain (T'ai-shan, in present-day Shantung province) out from its roots, and still go on to chop whole beams in two, like matchsticks. Unfortunately, those who develop their own physical strength to this degree seldom devote equal time to moral self-cultivation. Since their character is relatively unformed, they invite disaster upon themselves.

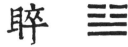

Ts'ui

No. 37. Purity

June 2–June 6 (a.m.)

*Correlates with Earth's Mystery;
Yang; the phase Water; and the* I
ching *Hexagram no. 1, Masculine;
the sun enters the Well constellation, 11th degree*

HEAD: Yang *ch'i* is uniformly pure, clear, and bright, so that things all are
doubly illuminated and protected by its shining light.

As yang *ch'i* approaches its culmination at the summer solstice, yin *ch'i*
appears quiescent (although we know from an earlier Head text that it is
gathering its forces quietly below). As pure yang *ch'i* bathes each of the
myriad things in its cleansing and energizing light, each thing comes to
epitomize that particular form of brilliance consistent with its nature. In
human society, men ideally achieve the brilliance associated with unadulterated virtue.

> Appraisal 1: Pure within,
> He is clear, without stain.

> Fathoming 1: Pure within
> Means: Clear, without a stain.

As if to reiterate the singular perfection of the individual, the Appraisal's
description has been repeated word for word in the Fathoming. Appraisal 1,
tied to the Water phase, suggests that the human heart/mind in its original
state at birth is as pure and limpid as Water. As adults, we can return to that
original purity as soon as we wish for Goodness above all else. Then we
cleanse ourselves of inappropriate desires.

> Appraisal 2: Tainted secretly while feigning purity,
> He is shamed to the center of his self.

> Fathoming 2: A dark mix pretending to be pure
> Means: The center buries itself.

In contrast to Appraisal 1, this poem describes an individual who feigns
integrity but is actually plagued by divided loyalties and contradictory impulses. While others may be taken in by the pretense, his conscience suffers
greatly.

> Appraisal 3: He lifts his eyes up to Heaven.
> He lowers his ears to the depths.
> Such is reverence.

Fathoming 3: Eyes raised and ears lowered
Mean: His powers of perception investigate the limits.

The cosmic patterns of Heaven-and-Earth are perceptible to Man so long as the individual maintains a reverent attitude. These patterns may be adapted to the human order as needed. The *Changes* begins its description of the culture-heroes of antiquity, therefore, with the following passage:

> When in early antiquity Pao Hsi ruled the world, he looked up and contemplated the images in the heavens. He looked down and contemplated the patterns of earth. He contemplated the markings of birds and beasts and the configurations of the soil. Near to hand he applied it [i.e., what he had learned] to his own person; farther way, he applied it to [other] things. And so he invented the Eight Trigrams [of the *Changes* on the cosmic model] to establish contact with the charismatic power of the gods and to categorize the conditions of the myriad things (W, 328–29).

The latter-day seeker after wisdom has two additional ways of perceiving the fundamental cosmic patterns. He can "look up" the Classics composed by the sages; he can "look down" by consulting widely with others, even with the humblest members of society. Once he has carried out his investigations reverently, he can establish fundamental truths for the good of the human race. Then he himself will be worthy of respect.

Appraisal 4: The petty man envies the pure,
And so loses rank and propriety.

Fathoming 4: That small men envy the pure
Means: The Way is not attained.

The petty man, instead of working hard to emulate the pure goodness of the sages, simply envies his moral superiors. In consequence, he fails to reform himself. He may even try to impede the rise of good men. Although sooner or later he forfeits his influence, his misconduct impedes the course of the Way.

Appraisal 5: Pure to the hidden "yellow" core:
Supremely stable, he knows no bounds.

Fathoming 5: Pure in the hidden "yellow" mind
Means: His model is the rectifying Earth.

The phrase "hidden yellow" appears in Tetragram 1, where it signifies the deepest (hidden) recesses of the mind of the centered individual (yellow = the color of the center). The yellow center is associated with Earth, which epitomizes the related virtues of fairness (presumably because all points on its surface lie equidistant from its core), of humility (since the earth is content to lie below our feet), of stability (since the earth never moves beneath our feet), and of openness (since the earth is vast). The man who exemplifies all these virtues is "hidden" in another sense: the full extent of his brilliance will never be known by ordinary mortals.

> Appraisal 6: Great purity gives way to error,
>   And so there is change.

> Fathoming 6: Perfect purity succeeded by error
>   Means: The petty man is overcome.

A state or an individual fails to sustain its earlier virtue. Change and defeat ensue. The only remedy lies in the Confucian prescription to "conquer oneself and return to ritual" (A 12/1).

> Appraisal 7: In his purity, he sees his faults in time.
>   The noble man moves to repair them.

> Fathoming 7: Pure because of timely fault-finding
>   Means: He is good at mending errors.

Although Appraisal 7 corresponds to the Beginning of Calamity, the individual here fortunately manages to correct his faults before it is too late. Perhaps good advisors assist him in reform.

> Appraisal 8: Pure evil, without a trace of good.

> Fathoming 8: Pure evil, without a trace of good
>   Means: Finally, he cannot be helped.

According to Yang Hsiung's theory of human nature, human beings at birth generally fall into three types: the very good, the very bad, and the vast majority who are "mixed" (partly good and partly bad). According to Yang, neither the very good nor the very bad are much affected by education. As Confucius remarked, "The very wisest and the very stupidest [in moral terms] are the only ones who cannot change" (A 17/2). For the truly evil, punitive measures may be necessary.

> Appraisal 9: Pure to the end and forever new,
>   She is propriety exemplified.

> Fathoming 9: Propriety that is pure to the end
>   Means: Truly, this is cause for celebration.

The truly moral person monitors her own conduct each day in order to preserve her hard-won perfection. She is "ever new" because she returns to her roots in filial piety and love of the ancients. Her moral courage untarnished, she deserves the praise of all.

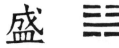

Sheng
No. 38. Fullness
June 6 (p.m.)–June 10

Correlates with Earth's Mystery; Yin; the phase Fire; and the I ching *Hexagram no. 14, Great Possessions; the sun enters the Well constellation, 16th degree*

HEAD: Yang *ch'i,* high and full, fills and stops up every space so that things completely fulfill its intentions.

With summer in full swing, yang ch'i approaches the height of its powers. It fills up every nook and cranny of the cosmos, animating all living things so that each becomes "replete with virtue." Animals grow heavy with maturity; many are ripe with child. Fruits grow heavy on the vine. In the world of Man, the moral person brimming with virtue is ready to "curb evil and foster good" (W, 458). Misfortune comes, however, to those bloated by arrogance or by unhealthy desires for profit or position.

> Appraisal 1: He prospers but not by the line.
> He loses secret virtue.

> Fathoming 1: Prosperous but unprincipled
> Means: At center, he fails to conquer himself.

That already in Appraisal 1 there is talk of prosperity reflects the fullness of yang *ch'i* at this time of the year. Unfortunately, the individual, once so self-effacing, tends to grow careless with prosperity; now self-satisfied, he slips from quiet virtue into immodesty and garrulousness. If he is not careful, such errors will grow. For this reason, as the proverb says, "Prosperity is the beginning of decline."

> Appraisal 2: Acts that do not depend on reward
> Can lead to great riches.

> Fathoming 2: Acts independent of ends
> Mean: This we call "Mysterious Power."

The *Lao tzu* praises the Tao, saying that it

Gives birth, but does not take possession.
Benefits, but does not depend.
Acts as steward, but does not take control.
This is called "Mysterious Power."
(LT 10).

The *Mystery* describes the good person who, in imitation of the Tao, pursues the moral course without thought of reward or recognition. His focus on Goodness should be enough to achieve great virtue (one kind of riches). But in the process, the individual may also attain material success "incidentally" (A 2/18). At the very least, since he has no desire to compete with others, he will make no enemies as he goes through life.

Appraisal 3: Love of profit fills the breast.
    It does not profit the common good.

Fathoming 3: Love of profit swelling the breast
    Means: It builds private gates.

According to most ancient works of Chinese philosophy, the common good should take precedence over private benefits in areas of moral conflict. The Chinese language has no exact equivalent for our generally positive notion of privacy. The term translated as "private" (*szu*) carries the perjorative sense of "selfishness." Those who love profit serve private "gates" (for example, private patrons or heterodox schools of philosophy) rather than the common good, which calls for selfless devotion to duty.

Appraisal 4: In slight prosperity, subservience
    Functions as gateway for great men.

Fathoming 4: Minor prosperity, proper subservience,
    Means: He serves the worthy and humane.

The theme of subservience appears appropriately in Appraisal 4, assigned to members of the bureaucracy. The Chinese graph for "subservience" shows a figure with the head bowed low and the eye turned in. The individual is fit for office only after humility, obedience, and the powers of self-reflection have been developed. In the desire to discharge his obligations to others, the individual comes to disregard his own prosperity. But others, coming to admire this unselfishness, propel him to higher position. Paradoxically, the individual who humbles himself attains still greater success.

Appraisal 5: Failing to bear good fortune lightly,
    He picks up ill and is then ensnared.

Fathoming 5: Bearing good fortune and raising ill
Mean: Such is the way of the petty man.

Good and bad fortune are frequently intertwined. As good fortune becomes a heavy burden, calamity is "picked up" or "raised." There are two ways to account for this. If the leader parades his own wealth and power, the envy and malice of all around him are excited. Or perhaps the individual is not up to the job; in Chinese parlance, his shoulders are not broad enough to bear weighty responsibilities.

Appraisal 6: Granting him glory, Heaven
Opens wide all borders to him.
In modesty, there are rewards.

Fathoming 6: That Heaven grants him glory
Means: Modesty increases what he has.

Appraisal 6 in an even-numbered tetragram corresponds to the Son of Heaven as recipient of Heaven's mandate. So long as the ruler conforms to Heaven's will with due modesty, there are no theoretical limitations on his power and authority.

Appraisal 7: As summer's fiery heat mounts up,
It calls forth winter's icy springs.

Fathoming 7: With mounting fires, that springs grow cold
Means: Calamity is not far away.

Appraisal 7 represents a triple conjunction of Fire; it is the second Fire line in a Fire tetragram. Appraisal 7 is also the Beginning of Calamity. The line, then, follows tradition in predicting that an excess of fiery yang *ch'i* at the summer solstice must give way to the waxing power of destructive yin. (The cold springs of winter bring to mind the Yellow Springs, the underground region inhabited by the shades after death.)

Appraisal 8: He damps down the full blaze
As collapse is about to begin.

Fathoming 8: Drawing off from the brim
Means: He barely escapes from danger.

One early Chinese proverb compares the immoral person to a fool asleep on a lighted pile of wood. A fire in full blaze is dazzling and dangerous; if a person is not careful, the beauty of the fire makes him forget its essentially destructive nature. The wise individual always withdraws to a safe distance in the presence of danger. The conscious decision not to "play with fire" makes good sense at any time. Here, however, the individual saves himself only at the last moment. Still, two benefits have come from damping down the fire: the fire is put out with water from the jar; and since the jar is now less than full, the water no longer spills so easily. By analogy, two benefits come from curbing one's volatile emotions: rage or arrogance no longer consumes the individual; and human desire is safe within acceptable boundaries.

<blockquote>
Appraisal 9: The greatest prosperity does not save.
Calamity is sent down from Heaven.
</blockquote>

<blockquote>
Fathoming 9: That extreme fullness has no power to save
Means: Heaven's Way is disobeyed.
</blockquote>

Lacking the will to be good, the individual is prey to all the traps that success brings to mind and body. Calamity strikes at the height of prosperity, revealing the hollow nature of material success. As always, the root of the problem lies within the self; Heaven cannot be blamed when Man chooses to disobey the cosmic laws.

Chü

No. 39. Residence

June 11–June 15 (a.m.)

Correlates with Earth's Mystery; Yang; the phase Wood; and the I ching *Hexagram no. 37, Family Members; the sun enters the Well constellation, 21st degree*

HEAD: Yang on all sides occupies the outer rim. Awesome and formidable, it serves as the inner and outer walls for things so that all the myriad things receive its protective frame.

Yang *ch'i* moves to take up residence at the outside of things. Like a frame or shelter or city wall, it surrounds and protects things, strengthening their defenses so that all things feel "safe at home" under its influence. As the *Changes* states, "When the house is set in order, the world is set on a firm course" (W, 570). Until yin grows stronger, the potential for Good seems unlimited.

At the same time, the architectural metaphor suggests that yang *ch'i* will soon reach its natural limits. Walls and frames are useful constructions, but their firm structure works against open-ended potential. Also, wide outer frames by definition are inherently weaker than the inner core, where strength can be concentrated. As yang *ch'i* moves to a position at the outer rim, it empties out from the core of Being, leaving behind a vacuum to be filled by yin *ch'i*. (Compare the description of male as "outer" and female as "inner" in W, 570). Danger lies in neglecting what is fundamental (or inner) while attending to the secondary (or outer).

Appraisal 1: Not giving or receiving praise or blame,
He thus preserves his house.

Fathoming 1: No praise or blame
Means: His Way is constant.

Appraisal 1 is associated with the Water phase, with silence, and with the tranquil inner mind. Only those who are self-motivated are single-minded enough to pursue the Good. Unconcerned with others' praise or blame, the good person follows the Right assiduously, acting with equal nobility both in public and in private. At the same time, he may aptly be called a conformist in that he bends his will to the constant norms enshrined in the Confucian tradition. Preoccupied with his own moral quest, he has absolutely no desire to criticize others, so nothing makes him stand out from the crowd. In this way, he preserves his family line.

Appraisal 2: The household has no flasks.
The wife supplants her elders.
She errs, washing them in mud.

Fathoming 2: A house without flasks
Means: It lacks the means to carry on.

Many family rituals preserved in the Confucian canon are designed to balance hierarchy with reciprocity, so that both respect and love, as well as order and intimacy, prevail in the home. This household has no flasks for water and wine, so neither mundane tasks (like drawing water from the well) nor ritual duties can be carried out properly. Worse, in utter disregard of Chinese custom, the young wife refuses to defer to the senior women of her husband's household; instead, she tries to take over the household management in a virtual usurpation of her elders' power. Misrule reigns in the family; even ordinary values are overturned as muddy water is mistaken for clean.

Appraisal 3: With young and old in proper order,
The son can sustain the father.

Fathoming 3: Sons carrying their fathers
Means: Only then can there be renewal.

The fundamental paradox of Chinese hierarchy is that its very survival depends upon adequate provision for mobility and change within that hierarchy. Before his parents' death, the filial son is subject (with very few reservations) to the will of his parents. Upon the death of his father, however, he succeeds to a higher position as paterfamilias. Households and individuals survive only when they take into account both eternal constants and changing realities.

> Appraisal 4: A pig appears in the audience hall,
>   With a puppy following in its tracks.

> Fathoming 4: A pig in the audience hall
>   Means: Their presence is unlucky.

In any private residence, the audience hall as the main public room serves a variety of important functions. The ancestral tablets are arranged on an altar in that room, making one corner of the hall a kind of chapel dedicated to the dead. The audience hall also serves as a living room, where family, friends, and guests gather for meals and other ritual occasions.

The Chinese graph for "house" (*chia*) depicts a pig under a roof; as wealth "on the hoof," the pig should reside somewhere inside the family compound. But the pig is dirty and smelly, despite its long domestication. Such a creature has no place in the most sacred room of the house. Still less should the dog be there. Although European—especially English— tradition has elevated the dog to man's best friend, in China the dog has remained a lowly watchdog, whose rightful post is outside the main gate. Even worse, the dog is in hot pursuit of the pig. Once the dog catches up with it, there is sure to be a tussle. According to Chinese divination texts, a fight between a dog and a pig is a bad omen signifying lack of discipline in the household, especially in sexual matters.

> Appraisal 5: Rudders and oars steady the ride.
>   They are good for riches and stability.

> Fathoming 5: Peace and harmony through rudder and oar
>   Means: The ride is smooth to the borders.

The boat is a miraculous conveyance since it combines the convenience and safety of an earth-bound residence with the capacity for travel on water. This image, then, emphasizes stability in the midst of change. Top and bottom, rudder and oar, work in concert, just as upper and lower ranks in a community must cooperate to create a just and safe state. The safety of the boat depends in equal measure on the initial construction of the boat and the skills of its captain. By analogy, the just society requires both good institutions and a capable ruler. Once it is properly launched and piloted, the heavy frame of the ship glides easily over the waves, just as the ship of state "rides on" the masses. Riches and security come to all who avail themselves of it.

Appraisal 6: He who sets his well and stove apart
In three years, only sees his family's back.

Fathoming 6: To put out well and stove
Means: In three years, no feasts are enjoyed.

To set the well and stove apart signifies the decision to split the extended family household into separate units based on the nuclear family—a decision typically made by the restless younger generation. Each time someone from one of the new, smaller households goes to its own separate well and stove to fetch water and cook, it reinforces the group's refusal to cooperate. Discord in the family predictably ends in three related disasters. First, family elders, who usually counsel against a split, are increasingly ignored by the younger generation (so they only "see the backs" of their insubordinate family members). Second, the initial division of communal family property generates greater mutual antipathy. Third, the property division works against future cooperation between family members, no matter how mutually advantageous such cooperation might be. A single act of rebellion makes the entire community suffer.

Appraisal 7: The old man pulls the cart.
The young girl raises the jar.
Both benefit the ancestral house.

Fathoming 7: An old fellow pulling a cart
Means: Only then do their bodies grow strong.

The old man is apparently still vigorous enough to pull a cart by a large rope looped around his arm. The elder's job, as he sees it, is to "carry the young," both physically and emotionally, until they are old enough to assume some responsibility for themselves. A younger member of the family, ever conscious of her debt to the family head, feels solicitous toward him, despite his evident strength. With no mind to dally, the young girl hastens to raise a wine or water jar to his lips in a gentle gesture of good will. The lesson is clear: the major responsibility for the family is given to the elders, while those who are young or weak repay their elders with respect and love. Since the generations behave well toward each other, the family line is likely to prosper; the advantages of a tight family unit become obvious when each performs his or her role.

Appraisal 8: His stools upended, and his ladles in pairs:
His household is no good.

Fathoming 8: Overturned stools, too many ladles by twice,
Mean: Family usage is not right.

In early China, the Chinese sat on mats placed on the ground, although a stool was provided for the elderly as a mark of respect. (The chair was a Western import that gained popularity later in T'ang times.) An upended stool signifies disrespect for the aged.

At the supper table, a single ladle was commonly reserved for the host's use when serving soups or stews. To double the number of large spoons implies one of three conditions, all undesirable: unwonted luxury in the household, a strong challenge to the prerogatives of the paterfamilias, or the doubling of the women in the household (presumably because of the age-old comparison of the spoon to the womb). Since all respect and probity within the family have been undermined, the family cannot continue strong.

> Appraisal 9: If the stump produces new shoots,
>   Its kind is not cut off.

> Fathoming 9: A stump producing new shoots
>   Means: Only then does its type last long.

After a tree is felled, new shoots sprout from the stump. By analogy, after the demise of the head of the household, the birth of one or more sons promises new life for the genealogical line.

Correlates with Earth's Mystery;
Yin; *the phase Metal; and the*
I ching *Hexagram no. 48, The Well;*
the sun enters the Well constella-
tion, 25th degree

Fa
No. 40. Law or Model
December 15 (p.m.)–June 19

HEAD: Yang suspends its law on high. Things [in response] lift their gaze to their own models so that each and every one takes on pattern.

With the next tetragram, we will have arrived at the summer solstice, the annual culminating point for yang *ch'i*, which accounts for the repeated references to yang's high position. With yang *ch'i* providing the model of perfection, all things measure and adapt themselves according to cosmic law. This tetragram's title refers to models and patterns of any kind (even ritual pattern), as well as to the penal code. In the earlier Appraisals, which we would expect to be more auspicious, the focus is upon various models hallowed in Confucian tradition: the ruler's model by suasive example, the model provided by the Confucian Classics, the sagely model of the culture-heroes of antiquity. But in the first yin line past the midway point, when the power of inauspicious yin is growing, the Appraisals shift to consider the place of penal law. In general, Confucianism admits that even sages may be forced to apply the penal code to particularly recalcitrant cases, although suasive example is preferable in dealing with most humans, both because it is more humane and because it is more effective. In comparing the law to the well of Hexagram 48, this tetragram tries to emphasize one aspect of the law: like the well, the law should not change; only if the law is known to all and fairly applied will it serve the community adequately.

Appraisal 1: The model he builds is an unfit model.

Fathoming 1: That the model built is no model
Means: It is not worth using.

Yang Hsiung's other neoclassical text, *The Model Sayings,* laments the fact that "there are many such cases where a model which is not a fit model, and a pattern is not a fit pattern." Unsuitable models prove worse than useless for the individual or society, for they convey the wrong values or techniques. One example might be that of an evil father, who sets a pattern of inattention or even abuse for his children, which is then replicated in succeeding generations. Since Appraisal 1 corresponds to the Beginning of Thought, these lines also caution that if the mind uses the wrong mental construct to view a certain situation, succeeding decisions about suitable responses are sure to be inappropriate.

Appraisal 2: He copies the model by centering,
And so he overcomes.

Fathoming 2: To pattern oneself on the Mean
Means: It is revered by all the masses.

The cosmic model has been reproduced in the social institutions, ritual precepts, and practical inventions of the sage-kings of antiquity, whose conduct provides the correct model for Man. All these models teach the individual to center himself by keeping to the Mean.

Appraisal 3: Failure to start with level and line
Ruins his settings of compass and square.

Fathoming 3: Level and line not at the start
Means: It is their use that is at fault.

A Han proverb laments the ease with which we compound initial errors by the slogan, "Off by a hair's breadth [at the beginning], missed by a thousand miles [in the end]." Any initial miscalculation, however slight, is compounded with each subsequent measurement. To stray ever so slightly from the Way, then, is to risk grave moral error. The metaphor implies that there is nothing wrong with the base material; the problem arises when the individual decides he need not use available tools. By analogy, there is nothing inherently wrong with human nature; we fail to be good when we fail to use the tools provided by the sages.

> Appraisal 4: Level, line, compass, square—
> None work against our applications.

> Fathoming 4: Level, line, compass, and square
> Mean: They each proceed from the self.

A worthy official (since Appraisal 4 corresponds to the bureaucracy) uses great care to insure that each plan he devises is in exact conformity with the models presented by the sages of antiquity. In this, he is like the good carpenter who continually checks his constructs against level and line, compass and square. When such precautions are carried out over a period of time, the correct models are fully internalized.

> Appraisal 5: The well rope is short, too short.
> The water jar is full.
> Though the well is deep and wide,
> In the end, it cannot slake our thirst.

> Fathoming 5: That the jar is already full
> Means: This is not the way to study.

The proper source of all learning is the Confucian Classics, whose truth is as deep and refreshing as water from the well. To avail himself of the Classics, however, the individual must adopt the proper attitude toward learning. First, the individual must apply himself to the task of how best to plumb the depths; in other words, he had better master the use of the rope. Second, the individual must devote his entire attention to Confucianism. If the individual has drunk too deeply of heterodox texts, there will be no room left for the teachings of the sages. In other words, he will be like a jar that is full to the brim. Confucianism is sufficient for all our human purposes, just as water from the well is sufficient to slake any thirst. Our trouble is, we do not know how to use the resources at our disposal.

> Appraisal 6: In the lead thread, in the guide rope
> Propriety's glories are shown.

> Fathoming 6: Lead thread and guide rope
> Mean: The Grand Rule is made clear to us.

The ruler exemplifies for his people the underlying principles of the integrated cosmic and social fabrics (in Chinese terms, the lead thread and the guide rope). Once the good ruler orders his person and his clan, he proceeds to institute the Grand Rule, an ideal state in which all humans develop in their social roles. The orderly reign redounds to his glory; his name goes down in history as a sage.

> Appraisal 7: If fine nets are cast on deep pools,
> This does not benefit the fish.

> Fathoming 7: Fine nets on deep pools
> Mean: Tyrannical laws spread wider.

In this first yin line past the midpoint of the cycle, the *Mystery* turns to consider the penal code in society. The fine net refers to penal law that is unusually harsh; a wider mesh would allow the "small fish" to escape. Those who give it any thought know that if all the fish are taken, none will be left for later. The moral is, unmitigated severity destroys the very thing it intends to preserve. When minor infractions of the law are punished with undue severity, the people become less rather than more law-abiding.

> Appraisal 8: He corrects those of us with faults
> Until we have no depravity.

> Fathoming 8: Righting those faults
> Means: He urges us toward perfection.

The true moral superior continually corrects his inferiors until they attain perfection. Ideally, as one Confucian Classic says, "Through punishments there may come to be no punishments."

> Appraisal 9: If the well has no rail,
> Water spills straight over.
> With no valley or gorge,
> It will end in a flood.

> Fathoming 9: Wells without railings
> Mean: Laws are unduly excessive.

Water's propensity to flow beyond the confines of the well is compared to the potential of a harsh penal code to engulf all in its ruinous flood. Two remedies exist: the first is to strictly circumscribe the operation of the law (the metaphorical equivalent to putting a railing or collar around the well), so that it does not wreak havoc in the community; the second is to provide as a backup an alternate channel to help prevent excess (an equivalent to the valley or gorge). In human society, the alternate outlet is provided by the ritual system.

應 ䷀

*Correlates with Earth's Mystery;
Yang; the phase Earth; and the I
ching Hexagram no. 30, Adherence; the sun enters the Well
constellation, 29th degree; the
Dipper points due south; the
musical note is F-sharp; the
summer solstice solar period
begins with Appraisal 5*

Ying
No. 41. Response
June 20–June 24 (p.m.)

HEAD: Yang *ch'i* culminates on high. Yin faithfully germinates below. High and low mutually respond.

Tetragram 41 corresponds with the summer solstice, one of two "centers" of the lunar year. As if to emphasize this quality of centeredness, Yang Hsiung has arranged the *Mystery* in such a fashion that Tetragram 41 represents a triple conjunction of centers. With eighty-one tetragrams as his total, Yang Hsiung assigned the first twenty-seven tetragrams to Heaven, the second group of twenty-seven to Earth, and the final third to Man. Tetragram 41 is assigned to the exact center of the "Earth Mystery" (Tetragrams 28–54), which itself holds the center position in the triadic realms of Heaven-Earth-Man. This tetragram is also assigned in the sequence of the Five Phases to the cosmic agent Earth, said to occupy the center of the four points of the compass. So much centeredness cannot help but promote the Good.

The title character Response conveys four related meanings: (1) to re-spond or react, (2) the right or inevitable response in a specific case, (3) conformity to natural patterns in the cosmos and in society, and (4) harmonious union. The Appraisals, playing upon the full range of these associations, generally focus upon the paradigmatic relations between Heaven and Earth, ruler and subject. According to Yang, conformity with the Way is a necessary precondition for successful interaction. Once Man conforms with the Tao,

> Heaven and Earth will unite
> And the sweet dew will fall.
> The people will be equitable,
> Though no one so decrees.
> (LT, ch. 32)

Each of Yang's texts also refers to one or more of the glosses given by Han scholastics for the title of the correspondent Hexagram no. 30: (1) "adherence," (2) "jointure," (3) "brilliant light," (4) "enlightenment,"

(5) "dispersal/separation," or (6) "nets" [for hunting and fishing]. Given the auspicious nature of most of these associations, it should come as no surprise that even the Appraisals assigned to inauspicious Night seem somewhat less dire in their warnings. Still, Yang cautions us about the dangers inherent in florescence. At the very point of yang's culmination, the summer solstice, the contrary power of yin begins to grow. By analogy, we know that the roots of decay are often planted in present prosperity.

Yang's characterization of yin *ch'i* is crucial to our analysis of the larger cyclic patterns at work. Yang chooses to describe yin's activity as *hsin,* a graph that can be understood in at least three ways. *Hsin* may mean "faithfully" (i.e., without fail), as in this translation. The climax of yang *ch'i* above "without fail" spontaneously provokes the birth of yin *ch'i* below. This definition underscores the regularity and inevitability of cosmic response, a theme emphasized by the Head text of Tetragram 1 assigned to the winter solstice. But assuming that Yang's language plays off both Tetragram 1 and the *Changes,* we may also wish to read *hsin* as "expanding." Those texts remind us that the alternating expansion and contraction of yin and yang *ch'i* provide the momentum for all phenomenal change through time and space. Finally, there is a gloss offered by the Sung commentator Ssu-ma Kuang, which, in the absence of any context, may well refer to the fuse of the firecracker. A fuse is an excellent metaphor for the catalyzing properties of nascent yin *ch'i,* for its modest start will in time produce the most startling of changes. Like most Han thinkers, Yang Hsiung subscribed to prevailing beliefs about the sacred origins of language; for him, moral connections are often revealed by such word plays. It is tempting, then, to apply all three descriptions to yin's activity.

> Appraisal 1: Six, as trunk, sets the pattern,
> Making Five, the branches, well-arranged.
>
> Fathoming 1: Six, as trunk, setting patterns
> Means: He adheres to the ruler.

The number symbolism used here is somewhat confusing. According to the Great Commentary to the *Changes,* the number 6 corresponds to yin and Earth, while 5 is assigned to yang and Heaven. If we assume that Yang adopts the *Changes* numerology, then we must read these lines as proof of Yang's eclectic philosophy, for they make yin *ch'i* the ineffable fountainhead of all the various yang manifestations, as in classical Taoist philosophy.

I suggest a simple solution. Each Appraisal in the tetragram is assigned to one of the Five Agents in succession. Six, then, as in other Han writings, represents the higher One—a kind of internal pun for the ruler. Yang Hsiung can be said to typify Han classicism in his preference for divine Oneness over that which is varied or multiplicitous. Here the one ruler's influence spreads throughout the empire, transforming it. Only the ruler, the One Man as he is called, can accomplish this, since he alone provides a unifying vision of the Way to counter multiple claims based on self-interest. So long as the leader addresses the needs of his people, they will offer him their complete allegiance. In this way, the branches depend upon the trunk in the same way that subjects depend upon the ruler.

Appraisal 1 is assigned to the cosmic agent Water. The superiority of the Way over other techniques of rule is like the supremacy of a great ocean over the small streams crossing the land.

> Appraisal 2: The calendar lays it out above,
> Below, the pitchpipes are attuned to it.
> If not, the union of spheres is blocked.

> Fathoming 2: What is set out above is harmonized below.
> Meaning: Otherwise, how could we think them
> correct?

The calendar and pitch standards suggest the full range of inventions, cultural patterns, and institutions bestowed by the sage-rulers upon human society. The calendar regulates agricultural and ritual activity. Music allows men to express their emotions in a socially productive manner that fully satisfies their inborn natures. Since the calendar is tied to movements in the heavens and the pitchpipes are tuned by earthly configurations, the sage-ruler clearly models himself upon the constant patterns of Heaven-and-Earth (W, 294). Each ruler has the solemn responsibility to interpret cosmic norms for the benefit of the common people through wise and natural government policies and institutions. Should he ignore that responsibility, he does not deserve, nor will he win, the support of the common people.

> Appraisal 3: In length and in breadth,
> Heaven's Net is vast.

> Fathoming 3: In length and breadth
> Means: Warp and woof are properly placed.

The phrase "Heavenly Net" refers to the tightly woven social fabric, to the cosmic fabric, and more particularly, to divine justice. Yang Hsiung's writings are preoccupied with the society/fabric analogy. Both society and fabric function by holding together a variety of disparate strands in harmonious pattern. The social fabric ultimately depends, of course, on hierarchy, just as the lead rope of the net pulls the secondary lines.

The cosmic Net also provides each individual with external checks upon his conduct, which come in the form of portents. With the combined help of

the Classics and such omens, the person intent upon self-reform should have
no trouble learning to conform to the divine Way. But all this potential for
social and cosmic harmony is ravaged by the disruptive penal system mentioned in Appraisal 4 below.

> Appraisal 4: Setting nets and snares to catch us,
>   Entangling lines stretch to the wilds.

> Fathoming 4: Laying traps for us
>   Means: He is incapable of ruling humanely.

Appraisal 3, allied with the Wood phase and the virtue of humaneness,
emphasized the supportive structure of the social fabric provided by benevolent Heaven in concert with the sage-kings of old. With Appraisal 4
allied with Metal (signifying war and harsh laws), Yang denounces the
tyrannical ruler's overreliance upon punishments to effect his will. Legend
says that good King T'ang purportedly constructed hunting nets open on
three sides in order to give every wild animal the maximum opportunity to
escape. On the same principle, he made his laws intentionally easy to
follow, so that the common people would not run afoul of them through
ignorance. Confucius insisted that punishments alone cannot effect good
order:

> Govern the people by regulations, keep order among them by chastise-
> ments, and they will flee from you and lose all self-respect. Govern them
> by moral force, keep order among them by ritual and they will keep their
> self-respect and come to you of their own accord. . . . If it is really
> possible to govern countries by ritual and yielding, there is no more to
> be said (A 2/3).

Unfortunately, the ruler portrayed in this Appraisal has decided to forego
rule by humaneness—with disastrous results.

> Appraisal 5: The dragon, in soaring to Heaven,
>   Rightly fears for its scales.

> Fathoming 5: The fear of the soaring dragon
>   Means: At the peak, it fears a fall.

Appraisal 5 in the tetragram represents the apogee of development, especially when it is correlated with auspicious Day. Typically, it is assigned to
the Son of Heaven. As in Tetragram 1, the dragon symbolizes the ruler for
three reasons: first, both dragon and ruler are said to be formed of the
essence of yang *ch'i*; second, the dragon brings fructifying rain to the crops
below, just as the ruler showers blessings on his lowly subjects; third, the
dragon in flight rides invisible currents of wind, just as the ruler "rides" the

intangible support of the common people. At the height of his powers, the good and wise ruler continually checks the popular reaction to his policies, for fear of finding himself without support. In this he follows the *Changes* injunction to be "mindful of danger in the midst of security" (W, 341). The most efficient way for the leader to assess the security of his position is to examine his own conduct in light of the constant patterns of Heaven-and-Earth. Once this self-examination and necessary corrections have been completed, the leader can continue to soar unimpeded. Should he fail to reform himself, however, by his own arrogance he will fall like Icarus.

> Appraisal 6: Blazing heat is sustained in Heaven,
>   While icy yin germinates in Earth.

> Fathoming 6: Sustained in heaven, germinating in earth,
>   Means: Yang begins its retreat.

With Appraisal 6, we pass the day of the summer solstice. These verses reverse the description of the germinating yang *ch'i* found in Tetragram 1, which was assigned to the winter solstice. Although yin *ch'i* appears to be completely vanquished by the strength of yang, it begins gathering its strength deep in the recesses of earth below. As mirror images, Tetragrams 1 and 41 remind us of the absolute complementarity of yin and yang *ch'i*, which in turn provide a pattern for reciprocal relations among men. Still, we cannot call these verses entirely auspicious, since light and enlightenment are henceforth in retreat.

> Appraisal 7: Each day he overcomes his faults.
>   Good omens increase in response.

> Fathoming 7: Daily stronger where once he was weak
>   Means: He hates whatever defeats the good.

Appraisal 7 describes the good person's determination to correct himself; the Fathoming, his abhorrence of unworthy men or evil impulses capable of subverting his concerted efforts. According to tradition, "If the gentleman can daily overcome his failings, then those who respond to him will be numerous." Daily renewal is sure to bring prosperity.

> Appraisal 8: Culminating yang summons yin.
>   In less than a day, it responds.

> Appraisal 8: That extreme yang summons yin
>   Means: In response, it emerges.

Like Appraisal 6, this poem is designed to show that responsiveness does not in every case necessarily tend toward the good. Once again, sober reference is made to the growth of yin *ch'i*, which paradoxically begins just at the point when yang reaches its apogee. Given the inauspicious associations of yin, some might wish that it were slower to respond to yang's cyclic activity. If we apply the metaphor to human existence, we learn that any manifest success contains the seeds of its own destruction, for success tends to breed arrogance and recklessness. This may explain the precipitate rise and fall of dynasties, families, or individuals.

> Appraisal 9: With a culmination of great light,
>   The noble man responds with Grand Decline.

> Fathoming 9: The culmination of great light
>   Means: It would not be right to stay this process.

Appraisal 9 aptly describes an extreme Response. Fortunately, it correlates here with auspicious Day. The earliest commentators tend to see in this poem a reference to the selfless leader ceding his throne to a worthy disciple in order to prolong the era of supreme brilliance (the great light) beyond his own allotted lifespan.

These lines may, in fact, have no political import at all. The *Changes* includes a striking image, in which

> Men either beat the pot and sing or loudly bewail the approach of old
> age in the shimmering light of the setting sun (W, 120).

Human mortality stands in stark contrast to the regular and eternal movements of the universe that surrounds us. As the poet Catullus wrote, "Suns may set and rise again. For us, when the short light has once set, there remains to be slept the sleep of one unbroken night." The petty man feels ill-used by what he sees as the essential unfairness of Time's actions. The superior man, in contrast, is defined by his ability to respond productively to the entire range of changing situations. He is wise enough to accept his old age and impending demise as part of the larger eternal pattern. Rather than railing against the inevitable, he uses the precious time that remains to him to benefit society. In this way, he exemplifies psychic equilibrium and inner peace.

Ying
No. 42. Going to Meet
June 24 (p.m.)–June 28

Correlates with Earth's Mystery;
Yin; *the phase Water; and the* I
ching *Hexagram no. 31, Influence;*
the sun enters the Ghost constella-
tion, 1st degree

HEAD: Yin *ch'i* takes shape below. Things all turn toward it to welcome it.

This tetragram begins the second half of the *Mystery,* which is assigned to the latter half of the calendar year. In this period, yin *ch'i* grows stronger every day. In contrast with Head texts of the preceding forty-one tetragrams, each Head text from now on will open with the phrase "yin *ch'i.*" Still, aside from this, there are few indications in this season of late summer that yang *ch'i* is losing control. For a while longer, yang will seem to continue at the height of its powers. The myriad things, in consequence, must go against the apparent prevailing trend in order to align themselves with this new cosmic trend as they come to maturity; hence, the reference to "turning" back to welcome yin *ch'i.*

This tetragram, like its predecessor, considers the themes of stimulus, response, and mutual influence; it presumes that change in one part of the universe immediately alters all other entities that are categorically related to it, by simple laws of mutual attraction and mutual repulsion. (See "Key Terms" on correlative thinking.) Here the *Mystery* mainly focuses upon aspects of physical and political responsiveness, which correspond to two paradigms of strong sympathetic response: sexual relations between husband and wife, and the mutual dependence of ruler and subject. While the spread of mutual influence is often slow, as the imagery emphasizes, influence is eventually pervasive.

> Appraisal 1: Meeting another, he does not respond.
> Lacking the good, he is perverse.

> Fathoming 1: In meeting another, not responding
> Means: He is not one whom you should join.

For some reason, a preliminary meeting between potential partners fails to induce a climate of mutual sympathy. At least one of the parties must be at fault since a true meeting of the minds depends on virtue. It would be counterproductive, as well as wrong, to form an alliance with an evil person. The gentleperson is careful to make friends only with people of his or her own sort.

Appraisal 2: The scaly dragon, plunging to the depths
Induces its eggs on the heights to quicken.
Though some men talk in darkness,
The Hundred Clans respond to them.

Fathoming 2: Transformations by dragons in hiding
Mean: The center essence is integrity.

According to legend, the female scaly dragon leaves her watery home in
the abyss to deposit her eggs on a mountainside before returning to deep
waters. Miraculously, at the right time the eggs hatch spontaneously, revealing in each a tiny, but fully individuated dragonlet—all without direct inter-
vention by their mother. A second legend says that the egg of the scaly
dragon is produced from the mating of snake and pheasant. The egg is then
drawn irresistibly to watery pools, where the egg metamorphoses into a
dragon. Both traditions reflect the Chinese notion of mutual interaction by
category, by which transformations over time and space take place by laws
of mutual sympathy, rather than Newtonian laws of direct cause-and-effect.

The dragon, of course, stands for the moral superior, especially the ruler;
the egg, for the less developed human being. Although both parties seem to
inhabit entirely different spheres, the moral superior miraculously affects
others, who learn by suasive influence to develop properly into full human
beings.

Appraisal 3: The quintessential stuff of things
Travels subtly back and forth.
Ill omens precede the quickest senses.

Fathoming 3: The essence, all unseen, goes back and forth.
Meaning: Evil omens are proof of blame.

Since each of the myriad things is composed of numinous *ch'i*, in some
sense all parts of the cosmos can resonate with others because of their underlying sympathy. The gods and spirits are only the most exquisitely sensitive
(and therefore, reactive) members of the universe since their constitutive *ch'i*
is particularly subtle and concentrated ("quintessential"). By definition, the
sage has acquired similar divine powers of perception. Omen theory tells us
that the gods, spirits, and sages react immediately to the slightest moral shift
on the part of human beings. Even such swift reactions, however, lag behind
the spontaneous production of portents in the cosmos. The merest inclination
toward evil on the part of those in power, for example, produces serious
dislocations in the starry heavens. In this Appraisal, dedicated to the transition
from Thought to Action, we are reminded that our innermost thoughts soon
prompt visible reactions. We must take special care, then, not to depart from
the Way, lest we disorder the entire cosmic fabric.

Appraisal 4: For trousers, there are always tops,
        And for men with eyes as shiny as pearls,
        Women with lashes curving like hooks.
        This is right and good.

Fathoming 4: Trousers matched to tops
        Mean: Yin stimulates yang.

Sexual attraction is proper and natural, so long as the partners are suitably mated; without it, the human race could not continue. Here, the luminously clear pupils of the man's eyes indicate his upright character, while the gentle curve of the woman's lashes suggests her willingness to respond. Several points in the poem should be noted. Trousers and tops refer to penis and breasts, but the Chinese assumed that it is the woman who often takes the role of sexual initiator. Then comes the play upon pearls and fishhooks: both belong to the watery realm, and sexual intercourse promotes the production of watery fluids. Finally, the fishhook is used to catch fish and oysters, while the seductive curve of the eyelashes "hooks" a man.

Appraisal 5: When yellow rides high,
        It obstructs the good.

Fathoming 5: That yellow's rise bodes ill
        Means: One cannot make friends with it.

Yellow as the color assigned to the center is usually auspicious. Here, the problem is that yellow mounts to the top position. (This may refer to the ascendancy of yin *ch'i* following the summer solstice.) Yellow no longer knows its place, so its characteristic virtues of self-abnegation, loyalty, and good faith fail utterly. Perhaps a trusted subordinate intends to usurp his superior's position, for the word for "rises" also means "to bully." Those with great ambitions make the worst allies.

Appraisal 6: Black Heaven meets Yellow Earth,
        Their ideas interact, one upon the other.

Fathoming 6: Black and yellow meeting
        Means: They respond by type.

Black is the color of Heaven; yellow, that of Earth. The interaction of these two cosmic powers is said to produce the timely wind and rain, which all the myriad things depend upon for life. As the *Changes* says,

> Heaven and Earth come together, and the myriad things are transformed
> and purified. Male and female mix their essence, and the myriad things
> are transformed and born (W, 342–43).

All successful relations between partners are modeled on these momentous cosmic meetings. Since all things respond by type, the good person cannot attract evil friends, any more than the mating call of a warbler could attract a hawk.

> Appraisal 7: From a distance, he glares in anger.
> Coming nearer, he knocks him down.
> To meet with a father should be happy.

> Fathoming 7: Glaring from afar, striking when near,
> Means: He has lost the idea of "father."

By rights, the bond between parent and child should be the most intimate of all human relations. Here instead, father and son are estranged, presumably because of the son's lack of virtue. (A truly virtuous son would continue to esteem even the worst father, as the ancient sage-king Shun is said to have done.) So serious is the estrangement that a blow is struck. This injustice indicates the bitter enmity that prevails between superior and inferior at all levels.

> Appraisal 8: Seeing blood pour through the gates,
> He keeps it away from center court.

> Fathoming 8: Seeing blood enter the gates
> Means: By worthiness he protects himself.

Trouble appears on the scene. The wise person prevents more pervasive disaster (the inner courtyard symbolizes the inmost self and the core of any social unit) by virtuous action and the reliance on good advisors (i.e., by using one's own worth and that of others).

> Appraisal 9: Damp that meets the foot of the bed
> Seeps into the adjoining room.

> Fathoming 9: Damp meeting the foot of the bed
> Means: The collapse occurs within.

Like damp spreading throughout the house, contagion is now pervasive. Since the problem is water (aligned with yin *ch'i*), the problem may well have arisen because of evil women or subordinates. Although the change has been gradual, by the end of the cycle in Appraisal 9, the inner bases of self and society are so completely rotten that evil cannot be easily destroyed. Such ruin is total in that it involves all parts, both high and low; the imminent collapse will soon engulf all members of society.

Yü

No. 43. Encounters

June 29–July 3 (a.m.)

Correlates with Earth's Mystery;
Yang; *the phase Fire; and the*
I ching *Hexagram no. 44,*
Encountering; the sun enters the
Willow constellation, 1st degree

HEAD: As yin *ch'i* starts to come, yang *ch'i* starts to go. Going and coming, they encounter each other on the way.

Shortly after the summer solstice we see yin *ch'i* begin to wax in power (i.e., it "comes"), although much of its activity still goes largely unnoticed. Remember, as early as Tetragram 31, entitled Packing, yang *ch'i* had been making preparations to depart. One commentator attributes yang's earlier dilatory action to its increasing enfeeblement, but now it is forced to leave under pressure from its opponent, yin *ch'i*. On the model of yin and yang, certain kinds of imbalance, if mediated by ritual, can lead to productive situations: for example, the ruler condescends to humble himself before his officials, and the groom abases himself in welcoming his new bride to the household. However, imbalance that ignores ritual is inherently unlucky; hence, the Appraisals depict various encounters with all types of evil men, including bullies, slanderers, and unfilial children.

> Appraisal 1: Meeting the gods in darkness
>   Until even dreams instruct,
>   This is a good sign.

> Fathoming 1: Meeting the gods in secret
>   Means: Thoughts attain the proper pattern.

Appraisal 1 often describes hidden or formless thoughts that have not yet been translated into action. Dreams clearly reveal the hidden preoccupations of the heart and mind. For most of us, our dreams seem wild and disordered since we fail to perceive the fundamental patterns underlying phenomenal existence. But dreams of the truly good reflect an intuitive knowledge of cosmic order, leading one to further careful consideration of the Way. One early text asks,

> Can you concentrate? Can you adhere to the Unity of Nature? . . . Think about it! Think about it! And think of it again! Then the ghosts and gods will teach it. It is not actually that the gods and gods will teach it, but that it reflects the culminating development of the essential *ch'i*.

> Appraisal 2: To come upon a conceited child,
>   Who rejects teachings prescribed for him.

Fathoming 2: Encountering the fractious child
Means: He is an unworthy son.

Immature, truculent, and conceited, the youth knows nothing, yet he resists all attempts at instruction. How can he prove himself worthy to carry on the family name? The moral foundation of the adult is built by proper molding of the child within the family circle.

Appraisal 3: They neither meet illicitly
Nor do they think at all of gain.
Such is good conduct for knights and ladies.

Fathoming 3: Neither going nor seeking
Means: This is the rule for gentlefolk.

Ritual dictates that the gentleman cannot act as his own matchmaker, nor can he promote himself at court. Similarly, a real lady does not seek out her own husband. This reticence stems from three causes: First, it would appear arrogant to put forward for consideration one's own claims to merit. Second, most adult relations are strictly ruled by hierarchies of gender, age, and status; self-promotion undercuts those necessary orders. Third, the truly superior person devotes his or her whole self to Goodness, rather than to external accomplishment.

Appraisal 4: Utterly exhausted, the "opener,"
Having brought the rain, is endangered.

Fathoming 4: That the "opener" encounters rain
Means: It turns out he harms himself.

In ancient China, in times of drought it was customary for important religious leaders (magicians and sometimes even kings) to expose themselves in a courtyard or square. The theory was that the gods, taking pity on their wretched naked state, would shower rain down upon them. It was also the custom for magicians and shamanesses to perform rain dances. Paradoxically, perhaps, the one who forces the skies to open may harm him- or herself in the process: either the frenzied dancing works so well that a cold shower of rain ends in giving the dancer a bad chill, or the "opener" deludes himself into thinking that by his own actions he can command the gods. The opener, then, could symbolize two different flawed personality types. The first secures his own downfall by acting without sufficient forethought. The second mistakenly takes undeserved, even coincidental success as a mark of his own inherent superiority.

Appraisal 5: Out hunting, he comes upon game.
None forbid his taking it.

Fathoming 5: That the hunter chances upon game
Means: It truly is encouraging.

In a yang tetragram, Appraisal 5 depicts the culmination of good fortune. The hunter inadvertently stumbles across his prey. No one would prevent him from taking advantage of his good fortune. By analogy, the truly good person in single-minded pursuit of the Way may somehow stumble upon high office and riches in the process of self-cultivation. Although the good person does not make material success his primary goal, all right-thinking people take pleasure in cases where virtue is rewarded.

Appraisal 6: The lowly spider, in weaving its web,
Comes upon a wasp.
However great the profit,
It cannot follow through.

Fathoming 6: The lowly spider's web
Means: Harm is not far away.

Obviously, the spider weaves its web to catch small insects. However, a wasp in the web spells trouble, partly because of its disproportionate size, and partly because of its stinger. Since the spider cannot disarm its victim without risking injury to itself, the spider's very success leads to its possible destruction. The lesson is clear: do not be indiscriminate in the pursuit of profit; otherwise, your most successful schemes may backfire. Even the greatest prize may conceal a deadly barb.

Appraisal 7: He brandishes his horn, eager to defend
Ruler and father from further insult,
Though such a fate is undeserved.

Fathoming 7: Raising his horn
Means: Straight on the Way he proceeds.

The image of "brandishing the horn" comes from the correspondent hexagram in the *Changes:*

> Coming to meet with his horns. Humiliation. No blame . . . At the top, utter humiliation (W, 613).

Appraisal 7 marks the Beginning of Calamity, but in this tetragram it is aligned with auspicious Day; once again, we can expect no blame. Righteous anger is displayed in the defense of worthy superiors. Although the loyal subordinate faces possible death, he never swerves from duty. In the approach of calamity, we detect the growing influence of yin *ch'i*, associated with decline and sorrow.

Appraisal 8: Two wild oxen clash in battle.
The one that loses its horn
Will not conquer death.

Fathoming 8: Two locked in mortal combat
Means: Lost weapons spell certain death.

The strength of the wild ox or rhinoceros (early texts do not clearly distinguish between the two) resides in its horn; that's what gives it sufficient confidence to engage its foes in battle. Here two opponents, evenly matched at the outset, meet in bloody battle until the loss of one animal's horn renders it completely defenseless in the fray. Certain death follows for the loser. From this we learn that it is dangerous to miscalculate our strength or the strength of an opponent.

Appraisal 9: The enemy's blow, though deflected,
Hits lower by chance, wounding the foot.

Fathoming 9: Fending off its horn
Means: How can one escape unscathed?

Near the end of the cycle, a person is lucky if she manages to escape total destruction.

Correlates with Earth's Mystery; Yin; the phase Wood; and the I ching hexagram no. 50, Tripod; the sun enters the Willow constellation, 6th degree; the Dipper points SSW; the musical note is G

Tsao
No. 44. Stove
July 3 (p.m.)–July 7

HEAD: Although yin, being moist, would sprinkle them, yang, still hot, would blend them.

Appraisal 7 of this tetragram sees the end of the Summer Solstice solar period. The influence of yin *ch'i* waxes steadily while that of yang continually wanes. Still, at this point, the heat of yang is so intense that it apparently continues to affect the growth of the myriad things, despite yin's counterimpulses. The stove is the place where flavors are blended. In Chinese terms, flavors are characterized as "cold" or "hot," by analogy with yin/yang. The stove serves, then, as an apt symbol for the characteristic mixing of yin and yang that now occurs. The stove also signifies the har-

Figure 10. A tripod. One early text talks of "a divine tripod, which cooks without fire and produces the Five Tastes spontaneously." Another talks of magical tripods "that boil, though they have not been fired, that put themselves in storage, though they have no been lifted, that transport themselves, though they have not been moved."

mony and material wealth associated with the extended family unit. Finally, in certain early texts, the master of the stove, the knowledgeable chef, becomes a metaphor for the perfect ruler. This metaphor presumes the *Changes'* remark that cooking has two main purposes: to prepare sacrifices to the gods and to feast worthy officials at court. Accordingly, this tetragram examines the true king's care of worthy officials, although it omits all explicit reference to state religion.

In the Chinese mind, the tripod and the stove on which it sits are inextricably connected. (Compare the title of the correspondent *Changes* hexagram.) Out of the tripod come marvelous, even demonic things, as out of a great primordial soup. Along with its ancient religious significance, the tripod also represents the conferral of legitimate political authority, as with the famous Nine Cauldrons of the legendary sage-ruler Yü (see page 201). Cast bronze, of course, was a luxury item whose use was reserved for the political elite. But bronze cauldrons in their technical perfection also symbolized the full range of social and legal institutions provided by the sages to enable many different types of people to coexist successfully. Ultimately, bronze ritual vessels suggest close cooperation between the ruler and the gods, ancestors, and common people, while the three legs of the tripod specifically recall the interdependence of the triadic realms of Heaven-Earth-Man and the king's three chief ministers. Finally, the circular forms of the tripod's looped handles promise eternity through cyclical renewal; for this reason, the tripod "means taking up the new" (W, 641). Each of these associations comes into play in the Appraisals below.

> Appraisal 1: When there is no food in the stove,
> He begs from neighbors.

> Fathoming 1: The empty stove
> Means: He bears an empty reputation.

The interpretation of this poem depends upon a pun: the Chinese character for "food" also means "substance" or "authentic nature." Since the sole function of a stove is to cook food, a stove that lacks food is like a person who lacks fundamental integrity and merit. After all, the sole function of Man is to realize his inherent potential for Goodness, turning his "uncooked" or "raw" capacities into a finished person of self-cultivation. Therefore, a person who appears to be human but lacks true humanity is no less dysfunctional than a stove without food. Although the individual may win material wealth or high position, he holds an empty, borrowed reputation. No help from friends or allies can do him any permanent good. Bad luck surely follows, as in the related omen of the "basket with no fruit in it" (W, 212). Only the person who hungers to be filled may improve over time.

> Appraisal 2: The golden tripod is immense,
> Its center bowl matches its size.
> Still, they do not eat nor do they drink.
> Truly, there is no harm.

> Fathoming 2: An immense golden tripod
> Means: At center, incorruptible and good.

In antiquity, the polished bronze tripod was reserved for luxury items, such as meat stews or warmed wine, to be consumed either by the gods or by high-ranking members of the court. The tripod may be compared to the charismatic virtue of a good person in that it represents an inexhaustible store of riches, always ready for use, which sustains others. So mysterious and great, in fact, are the tripod's powers (and those of Goodness, by analogy) that ordinary individuals need not actively resort to it to receive its benefits. Advantages multiply throughout society precisely because the good person conforms to the wisdom of the ages no less perfectly than the bowl of the tripod conforms to its outer shape.

Still, the exact connotation of the line, "They do not drink, nor do they eat," may be debated. At least we know it cannot imply praise of asceticism *per se,* since that is an idea foreign to pre-Buddhist China. Since Appraisal 2 corresponds to those of low rank not yet in service, perhaps they "do not dare to eat" (of official salary) because the time is still too early.

> Appraisal 3: There is no firewood in the stove.
> The golden vessel is set aside.

> Fathoming 3: That the stove lacks wood
> Means: What one has cannot be used.

Here the *Mystery* plays upon another pun, with a synonym for firewood meaning "talent" or "capacity." Even the best of rulers must depend upon worthy officials to disseminate his policies among the common people. In this, the ruler is like the stove, which requires firewood to function, no matter how fine it is.

> Appraisal 4: Eating food from the tripod steamer,
> He gains the strength to toil.

> Fathoming 4: Eating the steamer's food
> Means: It is offered to us in time.

In contrast to Appraisal 3, here the wise individual has properly prepared and used his cooking utensils. Seeds have been planted, food harvested, and brushwood gathered to make a fire. When the proper time comes to employ his strength, the individual will not only experience no difficulty in securing his just deserts; he will also find that he has grown from his efforts, just as rice doubles or triples in bulk when cooked. The moral person can expect good results when following the Way of the sages.

> Appraisal 5: The large tripod can be used as goblet
> But this is neither pious nor dignified.

> Fathoming 5: The large tripod serving as goblet
> Means: The feast then lacks all meaning.

Appraisal 5 describes the Son of Heaven. In antiquity, Heaven conferred upon the emperor Yü a set of nine Great Tripods as symbols of legitimate authority. When the Son of Heaven in turn wished to confer special favors upon his vassal lords, he also had ritual vessels cast in commemoration of his subordinates' meritorious service. The bronze tripod, then, as a mark of supreme favor and legitimate appointment is reserved for the most sacred of ceremonies; it should not be used for more mundane purposes by those who are "neither pious nor dignified." In this case, perhaps those in power are besotted with drink. Certainly, they fail to understand the importance of making distinctions. If they mistake a tripod for a goblet, they are likely to mistake great for small in moral and political matters as well.

> Appraisal 6: The Five Tastes are blended properly,
> The flavours are balanced and fine.
> A feast fit for the great man.

> Fathoming 6: A feast where flavours are harmonized
> Means: This is the duty of ministers.

The pot stands for society or the state. The Five Tastes are its various components. "Great man" is a term used either for the ruler or for the noble men in his service. By a pun ("minister" = "butcher"), the chief minister acts as chef-manager for the feast.

Numerous classical texts urge the leader to seek out worthy helpers, who can aid him in the difficult enterprise of ruling. The day-to-day job of coordinating the diverse talents of these great men is delegated to the second-in-command.

> Appraisal 7: The fattened ox is perfectly plump
> But if cooked in an unwashed pot,
> Retching and gagging result.

> Fathoming 7: A fattened ox, then retching
> Means: Impure are their goals.

Animal fat imparts tenderness and flavor to the dish. Here the animal has been prepared for the feast, but the cook ignores simple precautions in its preparation. As a result, sickness, rather than satiety and good health, follows. Since no flaw exists in the basic material, one's actions must be at fault. If one's intentions are bad, even a ritual gift will provoke revulsion. Extreme caution must be exercised when offerings are prepared, lest bodily harm result.

The metaphor applies to the political sphere as well. Rulers can secure the help of worthy candidates for office only if they first make sufficient preparations in self-cultivation. High salary alone cannot induce good men to put up with a ruler whose conduct disgusts them.

> Appraisal 8: If he eats what he has stored,
> Despite an outcry, no harm is done.

> Fathoming 8: Eating what he has stored
> Means: He is lavished with his ruler's favor.

Stored grain implies the prosperity and security brought about by providential behavior. The good farmer need not want for anything so long as he consumes only what he has earned. Similarly, the good official enjoys his ruler's favor because of his hard work. Although others, acting out of envy, may object to his high rank and salary, it is no more than the helpful aide deserves.

> Appraisal 9: Once the fire in the stove is put out,
> Nothing but disaster comes to the house.

> Fathoming 9: That the stove's fire is extinguished
> Means: It takes away from the state.

Traditionally, when a family line was destroyed, its stove was dismantled. And when a dynastic line was destroyed, its conqueror laid waste to the altar sites where burnt offerings had once been made to the patron gods of the former ruling house. Destruction of the stove represents final death for the family and state; no hope for revival remains. It is now far too late to apply the earlier, relatively simple solution of "using firewood" (i.e., worthy talent) to fire up the stove.

Ta
No. 45. Greatness
July 8–July 12 (a.m.)

Correlates with Earth's Mystery;
Yang; *the phase Metal; and the I*
ching *Hexagram no. 55, Abun-*
dance; the sun enters the Willow
constellation, 10th degree

HEAD: While yin empties out what is inside, yang increases what is outside. Things are like basins and canopies.

Despite its apparent strength outside, yang *ch'i* is steadily drained by yin's inexorable increase. The particular form of the interaction between yin and yang *ch'i* mimics, as it happens, the archaic character meaning "to join", which shows a covered vessel. The universe itself is envisioned as a canopy or inverted basin, with the broad sweep of the late summer sky sheltering the blasted earth below. The myriad things in imitation grow hollow inside and overextended outside.

Such images may be important for several reasons. First, Hexagram 55 in the *Changes,* the counterpart to this tetragram in the *Mystery,* repeatedly mentions things (such as curtains and underbrush) that screen off the light, obscuring heavenly patterns. The canopy in particular, of course, is an apt symbol for late summer, since heat and glare prompt its frequent use. Second, insofar as the myriad things' functioning depends on maintaining Tao as center, they are like a canopy that revolves around a central fixed point.

Third, the astronomical theory originally favored by Yang Hsiung imagined the heavens as a giant canopy arched over the Earth, with the cosmic axis as handle; once again, this cover extending over emptiness is positioned by its center. Centrality and emptiness, then, are two of the main themes of the Appraisals below.

> Appraisal 1: The pool so deep and broad
> Cradles all sides in darkness.

> Fathoming 1: The deep, broad pool
> Means: It envelops an infinity of things.

Appraisal 1 corresponds to Water; hence, the metaphor of the pool. It also signifies beginnings: on the personal level, the Beginning of Thought, and on the cosmic level, the primordial *ch'i* of the mysterious Tao from which all forms evolve. Since the pool (the mind, the Tao) is infinitely vast and deep, its life-giving substance can nourish all living things; it can never run dry. Yet it draws no attention to itself.

> Appraisal 2: In enlarging its ambitions
> The self grinds itself down.

> Fathoming 2: His growing ambitions
> Mean: He is harmed by his thoughts.

Appraisal 2 describes the ordinary fellow, who in his egotism considers his own mind to be a wondrous pool infinitely "deep and broad." Unfortunately, his actual abilities and rank are inadequate for his grand schemes; he is incapable of handling even the situation at hand. For this reason, the petty person wears himself down in vain attempts to grasp power or solve problems on his own. He would do better to devote his time to study and then apply the ancient models of good behavior to himself. As Confucius remarked, "To think without studying [the Way of the former kings] is dangerous" (A 2/15).

Convention compares the process of self-cultivation to the grinding, polishing, and carving of fine jade, which only enhance the value of the precious material. The petty person who intends to refashion his life never learns to use the right tools if he ignores the sagely models. Like the careless jadecutter, he gouges himself. Inexperience and ineptitude can only harm the self.

> Appraisal 3: Treating the small as great
> Helps in becoming great.

> Fathoming 3: Making great use of the small
> Means: Taking the small as the base.

The first lines of Appraisal and Fathoming read literally, "Great not great." Obviously, these lines are open to interpretation. Appraisal 3 marks the transition from Thought to Action, so probably the *Mystery* intends to teach a familiar lesson: by definition the truly wise pay close attention to the first small signs of change, since no one has sufficient strength to single-handedly defeat a well-developed trend. The sage looks at small details overlooked by lesser individuals, making them the secure foundation of his visionary rule.

The commentators unanimously prefer a different reading, however:

> The great do not view themselves as great.
> It helps to use [this way] to become great.
> The great do not view themselves as great,
> Meaning: They use "keeping small" as the foundation.

Either reading is possible. (Compare with Appraisal 6 below.)

> Appraisal 4: He enlarges his gates outside the city,
>   Though he fails to get the knife he needs.
>   Such fame is empty.

> Fathoming 4: Enlarging his gates in suburbs
>   Means: As real worth goes, the name comes.

Appraisal 4 corresponds to official rank. In imperial China, strict sumptuary rules limited the use of high gates to the inner circle of the emperor. Enlargement of the gates, a public display of enhanced status, should come only after outstanding merit has been proven. The petty man, however, typically is bent on advertising himself, although this means that he fails to focus on fundamental self-cultivation. His preoccupations are far from central, as is indicated by the gates' location out in the country.

The greatness of any house lies in its ability to concentrate its resources. The sharp knife signifies the sharp mind able to frame good decisions that benefit the community. A knife could also signify money since certain ancient coins were made in that image. Apparently, this house lacks both leadership and material resources. How long can it sustain itself before its reputation is shown to be hollow?

> Appraisal 5: By using the Mean, he draws the outlands
>   Into his realm and so is victorious.

> Fathoming 5: Bringing them in by centering
>   Means: He oversees the Nine Barbarians.

Appraisal 5, aligned with Earth, the center, and humaneness, depicts the good leader as the binding agent for society, for the good leader upholds the

Mean in order to center himself and others. As even the barbarians feel the attraction of his charismatic power, the true sage eventually gains power and authority over all four corners of the earth, acting as center pivot or *axis mundi* for the rest of humanity. In return for their allegiance, his loyal followers are shielded from harm by the royal person, which enfolds them in a warm embrace like that of a "father and mother."

> Appraisal 6: The great fail because of the small.
> The many, because of the few.

> Fathoming 6: The great failing the small
> Means: Disaster comes from the smallest part.

When an unwise individual in high position ignores what appear to be only insignificant problems, he allows unhealthy trends to develop. The true sage, by contrast, is always on the lookout for the first signs of trouble. By taking immediate steps to remedy the situation, he can both adapt to and manipulate the evolving situation for the benefit of the Good. This is no less true in the private world of the heart/mind than in the public world of bureaucrats.

> Appraisal 7: Great indulgence leads him astray.
> When he limits his cups of wine,
> Others may increase his portion.

> Fathoming 7: Indulging to excess, then depriving himself
> Means: He is able to fault himself.

This individual is drunk on wine or self-importance. Self-indulgence currently clouds his judgment, but once he curbs these tendencies to excess, he is bound to find others happy to reward him.

> Appraisal 8: The immense wall with narrow base
> For three years goes without repairs:
> Collapse.

> Fathoming 8: A narrow base for the great wall
> Means: Collapse is not long in coming.

This individual of high rank and wide fame lacks sufficient moral cultivation to acquit himself honorably. Lacking a broad moral base, he inevitably comes to ruin. Just as earthen walls must be repaired regularly, continual self-strengthening (accomplished by daily reform) is needed if one is to continue to survive in such a precarious situation. "Collapse" may point specifically to the ruler's demise.

> Appraisal 9: A Great End gained by self-denigration.
> Evil is forced out beyond the heavens.

Fathoming 9: Great Ends gained by abnegation
Mean: Modesty is the stuff of greatness.

The Great End may refer either to a good end (i.e., an honorable death) or to the attainment of life's central ambition. Any person can achieve both of these desirable ends only if he or she is willing to yield when appropriate, rather than push forward regardless of consequences. Paradoxically, the greatest goods come to those who minimize their own importance.

Correlates with Earth's Mystery; Yin; the phase Water; and the I ching *Hexagram no. 55, Abundance; the sun enters the Willow constellation, 15th degree*

K'uo
No. 46. Enlargement
July 12 (p.m.)–July 16

HEAD: Yin *ch'i,* concealed, gathers them in. Yang, still enlarging, opens them up.

Despite its growing strength, yin *ch'i* is still too weak to prevent a final burst of activity and development by the myriad things. Yang *ch'i* in late summer still operates with relative freedom, so that the myriad things enlarge until harvest or hibernation time. Yin *ch'i,* then, is pictured as a kind of "unmoved mover," which acts to counter all tendencies toward proliferation and expansion.

The character used for the tetragram title originally referred to the outer city walls built for defense; hence, the Appraisals' repeated references to architectural forms. It was typical in ancient China to construct the outer city walls first, allowing room for later population growth. For this reason, the tetragram talks of large, even bloated forms encasing empty spaces. Not surprisingly, classical texts use the same graph to describe that individual who combines self-aggrandizement with ignorance. The proverb tells us that, "The largest vessel fills most slowly." Rapid expansion often undermines internal solidity. Such lessons apply to the self-cultivation of the individual, of course, as well as to issues of statecraft.

Appraisal 1: He enlarges and extends it,
But the base was not built straight.

Fathoming 1: Enlarging and extending it
Means: From the first, the base leans.

The classical *Doctrine of the Mean* stipulates a fixed order for reform: the individual must first rectify herself, then the household, then the state, and finally All-under-Heaven. Here the individual enlarges her power base before achieving full mastery of the Way. Since her base is not "straight" (i.e., in accord with Tao), whatever security she builds is likely to collapse under pressure, just as a physical structure constructed on a faulty foundation is sure to collapse.

> Appraisal 2: Gold posts and jade props
> Stand large in inner city walls.

> Fathoming 2: Gold posts and jade frames
> Mean: Many are the supports and uprights.

Posts and props are structural units required in the construction of the strong tamped-earth walls used in all major public works projects in early China, including palace complexes. The excellent material employed in their construction insures durability, strength, and impregnability. The presence of rare gold and jade also points to the singular importance of the site and structure. We should also note that the reference is to *inner* defensive walls. Primary attention is focused on internal, rather than external matters. From this we see that the wise person intent on constructing a strictly upright moral life is absolutely dependent upon "golden" advice from the sages, whose collective wisdom will help her secure and enhance her position.

> Appraisal 3: Though enlarging, she bears no son.
> He beds a barren wife.

> Fathoming 3: Great but not with child
> Means: How can he get descendants?

In Appraisal 3, the transition from Thought to Action, the individual seeks to enlarge his power base, but lacks the means to bring his plans to completion. The metaphor used is easily understood: the husband, intent upon producing an heir, mistakenly weds a "stone wife," a term that can refer to a barren woman or possibly (more literally) to a stone sculpture carved to commemorate chaste wives. Two lessons are taught here: first, initial miscalculations about one's capacity may preclude final fruition, no matter how many attempts are made; second, apparent capacity should not be confused with real capacity.

> Appraisal 4: Enlarging his gates and doors,
> He protects himself from robbers and rogues.

> Fathoming 4: Enlarging the gates and doors
> Means: He extends what he plans and builds.

Since the height of gates and doors is strictly regulated by sumptuary laws, raising the height implies a significant improvement in both the resources and the status of the household. At the same time, an enlarged entry implies increased contact with the outside world. Such contact can continue in safety so long as the basic structural elements of the house are strong. By analogy, so long as the good person is strongly committed to the Way, she need not fear that the achievement of various goals will bring greater danger in the future.

> Appraisal 5: Heaven's gate is opened wide,
> Extending the steps of its hall.
> This may give rise to error.

> Fathoming 5: That Heaven's gate is opened wide
> Means: Virtue cannot fill the sacred hall.

Heaven wishes to favor those below, so its gate is opened wide to promote free communication with those on earth. That the steps extend straight to the formal audience hall signifies the relative ease with which humans can accomplish their fundamental task of bridging the realms of Heaven-and-Earth through "godlike" sagehood. Unfortunately, many lesser human beings lack the requisite virtue to act as partner to Heaven; ignoring Heaven's manifest desire to help, they make no effort to grow in wisdom or truth. Instead, they view every natural advantage and possible opportunity as a way to increase their hold over others. Sooner or later, it will become obvious that they cannot measure up in terms of virtue. However powerful they are, such people may have "ascended to the hall," but they have "not entered the inner sanctum" (A 6/15).

> Appraisal 6: With plenty the norm, how lofty his reign!
> The Hundred Lords give staunch support.
> It is that which his virtue begets.

> Fathoming 6: All abundant and all lofty
> Means: This is what we mean by the Great Peace.

Through the exercise of his charismatic virtue, the good ruler consolidates the peace. First, he insures material prosperity (plenty) for his chief advisors (the Hundred Lords). Second, he educates them by providing a lofty moral example for all to see. Since his store of virtue is sufficient to the task, his reforms win the support of those below. Over time, there occurs in all his subjects a fundamental moral transformation that brings peace and harmony to the entire state.

> Appraisal 7: Outside he is high and mighty.
> At center, though, he fails.
> Noble men are sent to the wilds,
> While small men enter his chambers.

Fathoming 7: The outside high and mighty
Means: At center he has no men worthy of the name.

The phrase "no men" traditionally refers to a dearth of good and loyal supporters, rather than to a complete absence of subjects. As one Chinese philosopher wrote,

> As a rule, a state without law-abiding families and reliable
> officials . . . will perish.

An evil king may appear all-powerful to others, but his rule will ultimately fail if he exiles worthy men from court and surrounds himself with petty sycophants.

Appraisal 8: Enlarging their outsides, hollowing their insides
Is best for drums and signal-bells.

Fathoming 8: Enlarging the outside, emptying the inside
Means: Only then can they be heard.

Like a master of Zen philosophy, Yang Hsiung seeks to upset our conventional expectations. Most of the Appraisals in this tetragram have warned against enlarging the exterior while ignoring the crucial interior. But then, just as we are tempted to make a hard and fast rule, the *Mystery* reminds us to measure all conduct against the specific case at hand. In some instances, an object's effectiveness depends entirely on the felicitous conjunction of large outsides and empty insides. And so we are led to a more subtle understanding of the two terms "greatness" and "emptiness." Greatness implies power, but power can make its base in virtue or in misguided notions of self-aggrandizement. Emptiness can convey either an admirable receptivity to the Tao or an empty-headed unconcern for the one, true Way.

Appraisal 9: Building the largest of very high walls:
In three years, no servants.

Fathoming 9: Maximizing the size of the wall
Means: In the end, none are willing to serve.

Appraisal 9 corresponds to the Height of Calamity, so the *Mystery* depicts the extreme situation in which the leader loses all popular support because he does not know "when to stop" (LT 44). The high walls may signify the enormous construction projects typically associated in Chinese history with megalomaniacal tyrants. Or, the walls may signal the leader's unwillingness to preserve lines of communication with those below. Finally, the high protective walls may hint at the relative poverty of the leader's inner soul, as opposed to his external power. The *Changes* clearly states, "To be in high position, yet lack the people's support, . . . that person will have cause for regret at every turn" (W, 383). . .

Wen
No. 47. Pattern
July 17–July 21 (a.m.)

Correlates with Earth's Mystery;
Yang; the phase Fire; and the I
ching Hexagram no. 59, Dispersal;
the sun enters the Star constella-
tion, 4th degree

HEAD: As yin gathers their plainness to itself, yang disperses their patterns.
"The plain and the patterned are interspersed" so that the myriad things
grow bright and beautiful.

The Head text explores one of the most fundamental patterns in the
Chinese universe: yin is associated with the unadorned, hidden, inner
core, while yang is tied to the multiplicity of forms that evolve from it.
Pattern (especially, the relation between the societal patterns we call
"culture," the behavioral patterns we call "conduct," and the cosmic patterns we call "portents") is perhaps the single most important preoccupation of Han thinkers. Even thought itself is basically conceived of as the
process whereby underlying, significant patterns are extracted from the
many disparate bits of information fed to the heart/mind by the sensory
organs. This process produces an evaluating mind able to judge proper
moral direction. Once each phenomenon is assigned its correct categorical (or correlative) value, events and things are seen to operate by invariable cosmic patterns. Many early Chinese thinkers were intent upon
discovering the cosmic laws in order to find ways of manipulating the
course of future events, but the *Mystery* focuses upon a series of state-
ments drawn from the Confucian Classics that relate pattern to culture
and sagehood.

Four passages are most important to understanding this tetragram. The
first characterizes ritual in terms of pattern:

> Tzu-hsia asked the meaning of the poem,
>
> Oh the sweet smile dimpling.
> The lovely eyes so black and white!
> Plain silk that you would take
> For colored stuff.
>
> The Master said, "The painting comes after the plain groundwork." Tzu-hsia
> said, "Then ritual comes afterwards?" The Master replied, "Ah, . . . At last I
> have someone with whom I can discuss the *Odes*" (A/38).

A second quotation describes the noble man as one who (not unlike the
cosmos) represents a balance between the plain and the patterned:

> When natural substance prevails over ornamentation, you get the
> boorishness of the rustic. When ornamentation prevails over substance,
> you get the pedantry of the scribe. Only when ornamentation and
> substance are duly blended do you get the true gentleman (A 6/18).

A third passage compares the gentleman to two animals known for their
beauty and strength:

> [He who effects] great change is like a tiger, his patterns
> distinctive. . . . The superior man changes like a leopard, his markings
> fine. The small man [merely] changes his spots (W, 192).

The fourth depicts the sage as one who has fully internalized the cosmic
patterns and so is able to induce societal order among his fellow men:

> [Only the sage] could copy it [the patterned nature of Heaven] . . . .
> Sublime are his achievements, dazzling the manifestations of his
> [internal] pattern (A 8/19).

This series of four quotations reveals a kind of progression, which mirrors the development of the individual soul. Achievement necessarily begins
with attention to the "plain groundwork," that is, building a solid basis in
integrity. Next comes the pattern, for "a gentleman in his pursuit of the Way
does not get there unless he manages to exemplify a beautiful pattern." If
the human being goes on to fully develop his innate potential, we have the
brilliance of the sage, who draws his inspiration for cultural patterns from
the regular movements of Nature. The course of humanity is thus to "first
cultivate the self and later make it pervade [the outer world]."

These quotations, however, do not provide an answer to the fundamental
question, "How can a person distinguish the right patterns of the moral superior
from the deceptively pleasing patterns of the petty individual?" Part of the
Mystery's answer can be gleaned from the arrangement of the Appraisals. In
general, the vigor of the early lines is associated with plainness. As the tetragram
moves toward the end of the cycle, ornate pattern takes over, becoming ever
more complicated until it threatens to obscure the basic substance entirely. This
has implications for the development of the heart/mind, of course, but also for
government policy. The Appraisals suggest that the court forego excessive expenditure on finery and palace carvings, both to conserve wealth for more
important uses and to set a proper example for its subjects.

> Appraisal 1: For collar and lapel, why use undyed silk?
>   For its jadelike purity.

> Fathoming 1: For collar and lapel, why the undyed silk?
>   Meaning: Its pattern lies within.

Appraisal 1 typically describes the shadowy, undeveloped inner core of the human being. Here it contrasts the undyed silk used for interfacing with the figured silk preferred for the outer clothing. Plain raw silk is like the unadorned substance in human nature at birth. The subtle patterns of the silk that lie within the lining material give shape to the whole, although the surface patterns of dyed silk are much more obvious. By analogy, the good person builds upon the innate potential for Goodness when striving to internalize the pattern of the sages; later, plain thoughts can be translated into the brilliant insignia of culture. As the story cited above shows, just as the painting comes after the groundwork, ritual comes after the proper internal attitude is established.

Appraisal 2: The pattern is richly figured,
But the base material is bad.

Fathoming 2: Embellishments without substance
Mean: Both cannot be equally fine.

Confucius once said of a lazy student, "Rotten wood cannot be carved nor a wall of dry dung trowelled" (A 5/9). Outward embellishment cannot hide a lack of inner quality. Real cultivation (defined as attaining the pattern of true humanity) is possible only when it develops from a firm core of integrity. This is a different point from that made by Lao tzu and Chuang tzu, who suspect embellishment in all its forms, preferring the unadorned, which they associate with spontaneous Nature, to the "artificial" products of society.

Appraisal 3: The greater the pattern, the simpler it seems.
The great seems truly inadequate.

Fathoming 3: In patterns, plainer is greater.
Meaning: It has more than enough substance.

This lucky set of verses presents a paradoxical truth: the greater the man, the simpler he appears to be. By extension, the greater the institution or tool, the more naturally it appears to function. For this reason, "vast virtue seems inadequate" (LT, ch. 41). The average person fails to appreciate the miraculous nature of either the sage or sagely institutions. This is both because the inherent modesty of the sage prevents him from parading his achievements, and because the petty mind mistakenly assumes that great tasks and talents require extraordinary complexity. Confucius himself confessed to a similar misapprehension when assessing the character of his best disciple, Yen Hui:

> The Master said, "I can talk to Yen Hui a whole day without his ever differing from me. One would think he was stupid. But if I inquire into his private conduct when he is not with me, I find that it fully demonstrates what I have taught him. No, Hui is by no means stupid." (A/29).

Appraisal 4: Ornate patterns are overembellished.
>   If tiger and leopard were patterned thus,
>   It would not please Heaven; it would be bad.

Fathoming 4: That ornament obstructs
>   Means: How is it worthy of praise?

A passage in the *Changes* compares the distinctive markings of the tiger and leopard to the superior patterns of cultivation displayed by the truly noble person. If their bold markings were indistinguishable from those of lesser beasts, the tiger and leopard would no longer be fit analogues to the superior person. Overly ornate patterns, in fact, recall the petty man, who is hardly worthy of praise.

Appraisal 5: Bright and bold:
>   Brilliant the patterns upheld
>   When chariots and robes are fully used.

Fathoming 5: What is bold is on high.
>   Meaning: Heaven's patterns are most bright.

In the very first chapter of the *Documents,* an ancient sage-king bestows upon various officials "chariots and robes according to their services." Sumptuary regulations combined with liberal rewards were considered important tools of good government in China. Through them, the government hoped to teach its subjects the relative worth of various contributions to society; by making virtue and duty the "root of profitable action," the court strove to encourage good behavior and discourage the bad. In theory, once each shining model of good behavior receives munificent awards of chariots and robes, even the lowest type of person may wish to emulate the good example. Therefore, the ruler of true cultivation employs sumptuary regulations (one pattern) bestowed in court ceremonies (another pattern) to enforce cultural values (still another pattern) derived from Heaven (the ultimate source of divine pattern).

Appraisal 6: The pattern of wild geese in flight
>   Is no model for man.
>   They fly as they wish toward the river.

Fathoming 6: No rule to the patterns of geese
>   Means: They go wherever they please.

In China, as in the West, migratory birds are thought of as portents, due to their uncanny ability to predict the onset of cold weather. However, the wild goose often breaks rank as it flies south, stopping off at river banks. Thus, no "great pattern" marks its behavior. In this it is like the individual of some talent whose desires lead him to disregard proper social constraints.

> Appraisal 7: While pheasants win no favor,
> Chickens are lavished with grain.

> Fathoming 7: That pheasants win no support
> Means: It is hard to feed those in hiding.

Because of its patterned plumage and rich taste, the pheasant should be valued far above the lowly chicken. Nevertheless, the pheasant's refusal to be domesticated makes it an unreliable source of food or feathers. Given this, it is hardly surprising that the inherently less valuable but domesticated bird is offered the grain.

Since official salary was paid in grain, the verse is a thinly veiled comment on political life. The two birds, of course, symbolize the worthy and the mediocre candidates for office. If noble men avoid government service, only mediocre talents will be left for the ruler to appoint. For this reason, the good man should not regard himself as too pure to accept patronage from others, nor should he forsake the court in periods of decline.

> Appraisal 8: Intricate carving and grain-patterned cloth
> Squander the farmers' time.
> With patterns, then chaos.

> Fathoming 8: Patterns of intricate carving
> Mean: They only waste their days.

The *Mystery* encapsulates the famous argument made by an earlier Confucian master, Chia Yi (200–168 B.C.), in a memorial to the throne: the production of each and every single luxury item represents a severe loss to the state, since it diverts manpower from the production of such basic goods as grain and plaincloth.

> Appraisal 9: Extremely complex patterns:
> Changed to the bolder ax-and-stripe.

> Fathoming 9: That the ultrapatterned is exchanged
> Means: They match it to the substance.

Appraisal 9 as the last poem of the tetragram reflects extreme patternization. The auspicious character of the line correlated with yang *ch'i* requires a retreat from extreme embellishment and a return to greater simplicity of pattern. Accordingly, the sacrificial robes are patterned with bold figures rendered in dramatic colors. This change in clothing signifies a fundamental change of heart. The private person returns to ritual as the basis of self-cultivation. Meanwhile, high officials restore the essentials of government, including an emphasis on ritual and agriculture.

Correlates with Earth's Mystery;
Yin; *the phase Wood; and the* I
ching *Hexagram no. 10, Step; the*
sun enters the Spread constellation,
2d degree; the Dipper points SSW;
the musical note is G

Li
No. 48. Ritual
July 21 (p.m.)–July 25

HEAD: Yin is in the low regions while yang is on high. If high and low right [their] bodies, things join in having ritual.

The Great Heat solar period, when yang *ch'i* blazes most fiercely, opens with Appraisal 3 of this tetragram. Despite this, the decline of yang *ch'i* has already begun. Yin is poised below in the lower regions, ready to advance, while yang, still on high, prepares to leave. Thus, the two complementary configurations of energy now appear in a dancelike counterpoint of rhythm and pattern. In the world of Man, this pattern of interdependence and complementarity finds its analogy in the delicately balanced rituals that rule relations between host and guest. On that model, all significant exchanges (e.g., the exchange of gifts or of verbal communications) take on correct ritual postures appropriate to their times.

"Ritual" (*li*) is the word the Chinese gave to any symbolic act that marks a significant interaction between two or more parties (e.g., between the gods and man). According to Confucius, the physical enactment of ritual becomes fully compelling only if it reflects a profound integrity of the spirit; it is this perfect harmony of form and heart that infuses each gesture with dignity and direction. Ceremony that is perfunctory or gestures that are mechanical, even if they mimic ritual well, are unworthy of the name. Insofar as ritual implies spiritual wholeness, the graph for "ritual" relates to the cognate graph "body," which describes corporeal completeness.

In the centuries after Confucius, the word for "ritual" takes on ever wider associations. In many ways, it comes to embrace not only all "rules for living," but also all cosmic interactions. In short, it comes to be synonymous with Tao. For this reason, the Head text can speak of the myriad things participating in ritual activity in company with human beings. Correct ritual performance is said to make for good community and fair government. And it also intimates the ineffable that would remain otherwise unknown, while providing numerous opportunities for aesthetic and moral appreciation. However, the forms of ritual—at least initially—place fundamental constraints on the heart/mind and the body. Long hours of disciplined study and intensive training are required if one is to truly master them and make them instinctive. The *Changes* hexagram aligned with this tetragram speaks of conditions "subject to restraint" (W, 435). The *Mystery* will develop that theme below.

> Appraisal 1: Stepping on tiptoe,
> He leaves his forebears behind.

> Fathoming 1: Raising his heels
> Means: He makes his own family retreat.

Because of a phonetic identity between the two graphs, many early dictionaries define "ritual" (*li*) in terms of behavioral "steps" (also *li*). To readers in the West, stepping on tiptoe often indicates extreme deference, on the presumption that a mincing step minimizes the obtrusive character of a person's advance. (Of course, stepping on tiptoe can also indicate a certain degree of furtiveness.) In China, however, stepping on tiptoes is equated with "high-stepping"; it is the outer expression of inner arrogance since, in the words of one commentator, the desire to raise the heel reveals a person's ambitions to "force to a high point what is [naturally] positioned below." For this reason, such a step becomes "a symbol of the usurpation of a superior's [place]." Here, arrogance and ambition threaten the entire family hierarchy, for the youngster forgets even the most basic filial duties owed the living and the dead.

In ancient China, those who looked toward the future with eager anticipation were also said to "stand on tiptoe." So much attention directed to the future can lead one to forget the past. That this individual forgets even the ancestors, from whom life itself derives, is clear proof of utter self-absorption. At Appraisal 1, which indicates either the beginning of a cycle or very low social position, the individual already congratulates himself on being a self-made man. Such a fundamental mistake can only bring trouble in future.

> Appraisal 2: With a gaze most deferential,
> With reverential steps,
> Only then is he shot through with integrity.

> Fathoming 2: Most deferential, most grave
> Means: Respect issues from the heart.

The *Analects* of Confucius repeatedly identify respect as the first, crucial step on the road to moral perfection. Inevitably, a reverential attitude toward moral superiors results in outward displays of virtue. Here inner and outer correspond perfectly; eye and step, intention and act, move easily in ritual forms.

> Appraisal 3: The portrait is perfect in form,
> But in truth, it lacks perfection.

> Fathoming 3: The portrait, perfect in form,
> Means: It is not true to its source.

As in English, in Chinese the words for "faithful" and "true" denote both the accuracy with which an artist's image reproduces reality and the integrity of one's inner psychic state. A painting, however good, can never really come to life; it is two-dimensional, even curiously flat, rather than multifaceted. In that, it is fundamentally different from the real object on which it is modeled. Only very stupid people would confuse the painted representation with the real thing. No less benighted are those who presume that the outer forms of ritual constitute the "real thing" in its totality. Those who intend to convey true humanity through the forms infuse each ritual act with a sacred character; it is this inner commitment to Goodness, not the mechanical imitation of certain prescribed gestures, that endows the ritual with power. Simply going through the motions teaches nothing, nor does it forge true community. How, then, can it be equated with true ritual? As the Confucian Classics say, "In small particulars, he practices deportment as if that were all important. Is that not far from saying that he knows ritual?"

This verse does not criticize imitation *per se*. Faithful imitation of the ancients' intentions lies at the heart of good ritual.

> Appraisal 4: The stately demeanor of peacock and goose
> Helps when mounting the steps.

> Fathoming 4: The decorum of peacock and wild goose
> Means: They can be used as models.

Both the peacock and the wild goose are rare birds. In both species, the plumage of the males is brilliantly colored in intricate patterns. Therefore, in ancient times, their beautiful feathers were used in the insignia of rank on ceremonial caps. The wild goose was admired for its uncanny ability to fly at the correct time in orderly fashion; the peacock, for the stately sweep of its majestic walk. For all these reasons, the two species were associated with impressive ceremony. From this poem we learn that the wise leader on the rise, if sufficiently schooled in correct ritual pattern, can lead his followers to a profound moral transformation.

Appraisal 5: Harboring his rebellious intent,
He smashes his ladles in error,
Then ruins the gift of Nine Arrows.

Fathoming 5: Rebelliously breaking ladles
Means: He reduces his own dignity.

Appraisal 5 corresponds to the ruler. In the ritual enfeoffment of his vassal lords, the Son of Heaven confers upon his chief supporters nine symbolic gifts of investiture (the so-called Nine Conferrals), including a bundle of arrows, sacrificial wine, and ceremonial clothing, all of which symbolize the ruler's absolute trust in his subordinates. For example, trustworthy officials are said to be "straight as arrows"; hence, the gift of arrows. Such important gifts are presumably reserved for those who, mindful of ancient precedents and family honor, can be depended upon to sacrifice their very lives to protect the ancestral house.

Here, the disrespect shown the Son of Heaven by one or more enfeoffed lords is evident. The subordinate who lacks virtue rises up in revolt. The outward sign of his inner rebellion is his willful destruction of the ritual gifts received at his appointment. Rebellious subordinates soon lose their "dignity," a term that in archaic usage refers to high rank and a generous stipend.

Appraisal 6: Having ranked them in order like fishscales,
Only then does he grant them largesse.
By this, like a lord, he rises to Heaven.

Fathoming 6: Serried ranks like fishscales
Mean: Noble and base take their places.

Ideally, the imperial bureaucracy is a tight, orderly formation that functions as one, although ritual stipulates that separate duties and prerogatives be assigned to each official grade. Therefore, many early Chinese writers compare the bureaucracy to the overlapping scales on a fish's back. Careful gradations in rank supported by ritual prerogatives clarify proper standards of conduct for All-under-Heaven. Ritual pattern, by its very integrity and cohesiveness, makes usurpation unthinkable and unworkable. The most important task of the sage-ruler, then, is to employ ritual to make appropriate distinctions among his many subordinates, so that each person receives a rank commensurate with his ability and merit.

Appraisal 7: Overstepping ritual:
"One who knows no fear enters fearsome situations."

Fathoming 7: Fearlessly overstepping ritual
Means: This is what all other men reject.

Ritual is the root of all productive social activity, for ritual is the most effective means to secure the goodwill of family and friends. To abandon ritual is to turn to "rule by punishments," a policy that ultimately undermines state order, according to the Confucians. On the other hand, to go beyond ritual (in other words, to be overelaborate in one's practices) is to muddy the clear message ritual normally conveys. Excessive ritual also represents an unjust burden in terms of time and money. For this reason, in the case of ritual, "to go too far is as bad as not to go far enough" (A 11/16). Whoever ignores due consideration for others, as expressed in ritual, can expect to be abandoned by those for whom he has demonstrated contempt. As the *Documents* says, "One who knows no fear enters fearsome situations."

Appraisal 8: His cap is full of holes,
His shoes are in good repair.

Fathoming 8: The cap is full of holes
Means: Clearly, the cap must go on top.

Those who occupy the top positions have failed, while those below still perform their jobs admirably. Despite the better condition of the shoes (i.e., those below), shoes cannot be worn atop the head. The metaphor suggests that social status and political position are to some extent predetermined for some fixed period of time by the Mandate of Heaven. Just because an subordinate demonstrates marked ability, it does not follow that he can immediately challenge his superiors. Instead, he should patiently await Heaven's commands.

Appraisal 9: He wears a hat, but has no head.
Of what use is high rank to him?

Fathoming 9: Having no head, he wears it still.
Meaning: Where is he going to go?

Appraisal 9 always describes extremes, and so we hear of the head. If the ruler has no head for ruling, what does it matter that he wears the crown as symbol of his authority? And if the ruler loses his head through his own ineptitude, still less will the crown or rank matter.

T'ao

No. 49. Flight

July 26–July 30 (a.m.)

*Correlates with Earth's Mystery;
Yang; the phase Metal; and the I
ching Hexagram no. 33, Retreat;
the sun enters the Spread constellation, 6th degree*

HEAD: Yin *ch'i* manifests its strength. Yang *ch'i* plunges into retreat. The myriad things are about to be destroyed.

It may seem premature to predict the death of the myriad things immediately following the Great Heat solar period of late summer, but this tetragram is allied with Metal, the "killing" or "punishing" Phase; hence, the imagery of battle. The tetragram's title, Flight, predicts a quick retreat by yang *ch'i* as soon as yin *ch'i* reveals its strength. In response, the myriad things will be destroyed. After all, as the *Changes* reminds us, "Things cannot abide forever in their place" (W, 550).

Since the Head text characterizes initial retreat as the first important step toward ultimate destruction, it is notable that the *Mystery* talks of flight as both auspicious and inauspicious in the Appraisals. Enforced flight is inherently dangerous because it leaves one's flanks exposed, but voluntary retreat from a position (as, for example, in certain acts of courtesy) can actually prove of benefit to the superior individual.

> Appraisal 1: Retreating waters as they level
> Obliterate the tracks they made.

> Fathoming 1: Leveled by retreating waters
> Means: The tracks are not recut.

Appraisal 1, at the beginning of the cycle, is allied with the Water phase. It is the property of water to level through erosion and flooding. The poem must be auspicious, since it is allied with Day and yang *ch'i*. In this translation, escape becomes possible once the fugitives have fled through water, which erases all evidence of their flight. By analogy, self-cultivation acts like water to cleanse the self of all traces of one's former bestial impulses. The same poem also works as a description of the mysterious Tao, which erases the present moment as the future unfolds.

> Appraisal 2: Preoccupied with worries,
> He fails to notice the ditch,
> Though shod in golden slippers.

Fathoming 2: The very troubled mind
Means: Righteousness does not advance.

Not unlike Freud, the ancient Chinese insisted that unconscious or inadvertent slips reveal our innermost state of mind. In the vast majority of cases, they reasoned, luckless individuals can learn to exercise greater caution to improve their fate. The most famous anecdote illustrating this is that of music master Tzu-ch'un, who stubbed his toe one day. Tzu-ch'un responded to the minor accident by retreating to his bedroom for an entire month to consider the possible disgrace that might result from similar acts of carelessness.

Unfortunately, the hapless subject of this poem pitches headlong into a drainage ditch, sullying his finery. His lapse in judgment seems more serious when we remember that golden shoes indicate high rank and status.

Appraisal 3: Clenching his thighs, whipping his horse,
With bandits watching his door,
It's best for him to flee.

Fathoming 3: Kneeing and whipping the horse's rump
Means: He sees what's coming.

Appraisal 3 marks the transition from Thought to Action. The horse's owner, seeing the robbers case his house, recognizes the danger he is in. Salutary fear galvanizes him into action. Fortunately, he has a means of escape. He flees on horseback, digging his knee into the horse's haunches and wielding his whip to make the horse run faster. Thanks to his quick response, he manages to slip away, although his escape is narrow.

Appraisal 4: The trees though tall are but tips at top.
The birds in flight pass over them.
Some stop and then alight.

Fathoming 4: Birds in the tall trees
Mean: Wanting to stop, they drop down.

One popular anecdote of Han times tells of a flock of birds in flight that decide to rest in what appears to be an inviting grove of tall trees. But when the birds alight on the trees, the fragile treetops cannot support their weight, and the boughs swing down under them. Some birds plunge to their deaths. Others die when the tips snap back, stunning the birds, which are then easily picked off by crafty hunters. It is also possible that the lush forest conceals hunters' traps. This cautionary tale teaches two main lessons: first, we must all learn to distinguish external appearance from internal substance; second, we must never let down our guard in the face of alluring prospects and desires, especially in midflight.

Appraisal 5: Falcons are seen massing in woods
　　Otters plunge into deepest pools.
　　An attack is imminent.

Fathoming 5: The sight of falcons and otters
　　Means: To flee bad luck, hide in the deep.

When great danger looms, the wise individual knows enough to retreat. Falcons and otters often signify cruelty since both prey on smaller creatures. In this case, however, even strong falcons and otters scurry away rather than face impending doom.

Appraisal 6: With so many fields unplowed,
　　He wastes the work we put into footpaths.

Fathoming 6: Many fields, as yet unplowed,
　　Mean: He wastes strength and loses merit.

The early mention of "many fields" leads the reader to expect great wealth or vast territories, such as might belong to members of the ruling elite. Initial preparations for a good harvest have been made. A group of conscientious farmers have constructed raised footpaths between fields. These footpaths, which look like low dikes flattened at the top, serve two main functions. Water collects between them, facilitating the irrigation process. They also allow the farmer to tend his crops without trampling tender shoots underfoot. Despite these preparations, the farmer in this poem fails to hitch his oxen to plow the fields. From seed sown in unplowed fields, he can hardly expect great profits, even with his vast holdings. The fields, in effect, become a dead loss; the vast labor already expended fails to further production.

　　With regard to self-cultivation, a man cannot expect to develop his talents unless he is willing to harrow his soul. This poem may also apply to the ruler who, in ignoring hardworking advisors (symbolized by the farmer's oxen), ultimately fails to use his kingdom's resources to the full.

Appraisal 7: By keeping an eye on the fowler's net,
　　Later the bird can fly.

Fathoming 7: Keeping the rope in sight
　　Means: It is not quite high enough.

The wise individual keeps danger in sight, so that he can effect an escape if necessary. Like the bird, this individual nearly fails to fly high enough to escape harm's way. Luckily, the rope is not thrown high enough to snare the bird.

Appraisal 8: The neck is pierced by an arrow
And the wings are bound by its string.

Fathoming 8: The neck hit, the wings bound,
Means: Do not struggle in vain.

The hunter attaches a string to his arrow because it helps him locate his prey after the hit. The string also serves to bind the catch. The bird, if shot, may still have sufficient strength to flap its wings, but once its wings are bound, it can never hope to fly off to safety. As the poem indicates, all further struggle is futile.

Appraisal 9: It's best to flee, even on calloused feet,
When bands of thieves surround the city walls.

Fathoming 9: That thieves and knaves besiege the walls
Means: Where on earth can a person flee?

Appraisal 9, although aligned with auspicious Day, also represents the culmination of Flight. The individual realizes he is under seige since evil men now surround his stronghold. Despite his evident panic, he manages, after much travail, to escape with his life, although there is no promise of a more secure future.

T'ang
No. 50. Vastness/Wasting
July 30 (p.m.)–August 3

Correlates with Earth's Mystery; Yin; the phase Earth; and the I ching Hexagram no. 33, Retreat; the sun enters the Spread constellation, 11th degree

HEAD: Yin *ch'i* increasingly comes; yang *ch'i* increasingly goes. Things are on the verge of dissipation.

At this point in the yearly cycle, autumn will soon be upon us. Things move inexorably past ripeness to spoilage. The range of meaning for this tetragram's title bridges the transition from admirable maturity to first decay, for its associations are both good and bad. On the one hand, the title can mean "vast" or "great," especially with reference to capacity (in both senses). But closely related to vastness is the idea of "what is wasted." (Compare English, where "vast" and "wasted" are both from a single Latin root, *vastus.*) By a series of small extensions, the same graph comes to mean "to flee," "to drift," "to toss about aimlessly," "to feel unsettled," "to experience loss or

failure," "to act in vain," "to suffer decay," and "to be emptied or exhausted."
It signifies the wanton and dissipated, the exaggerated and the unrestrained;
therefore, it is used in connection with abrupt, boastful, rude, or preposter-
ous acts that defy ritual.

> Appraisal 1: When inner restraints are absent,
> Do not act. Danger.

> Fathoming 1: Unrestrained within
> Means: He holds to no principle.

Appraisal 1 corresponds to the beginning of the cycle and to first thoughts;
hence, the focus on the inner workings of the mind. The mind of the unprincipled individual will not direct the body properly. Surely this is dangerous.

> Appraisal 2: When adrift and in the dark,
> It helps to set out for the East.

> Fathoming 2: Help for drifting in the dark
> Means: The bright path is beneficial.

Dark and light are contrasted here. After the sun rises each morning
from the vast, dark pool located beneath the horizon, the myriad things,
formerly condemned to darkness, are flooded with brilliant light. If we wish
our minds to be similarly enlightened, we must move in the direction of an
equally bright path, the Way, as embodied in the Confucian Classics.

> Appraisal 3: To be oversimple is improper.
> Lost is that rhythmic sound of jade.

> Fathoming 3: That there is no measured sound of jade
> Means: He is not your haven.

One who values rustic simplicity over the refinements of the civilized
life cannot provide a sure model for others.

> Appraisal 4: Broadminded, with no predilections,
> The Way and the Right are his lords.

> Fathoming 4: To be greatly without bias
> Means: He sides only with righteousness.

A famous passage in the Confucian *Analects* (A 4/10) says that the truly
superior person is simply "on the side of what is right," and so is without
particular predispositions. Similarly, the "Great Plan" chapter of the *Documents* identifies this fairmindedness with the King's Way.

Appraisal 5: He sets the deer to running
While clasping a mouse to his breast.
What he gained has no value.

Fathoming 5: A deer on the run and a mouse at the breast
Mean: This is not enough for merit.

Because of a pun, the deer (*lu*) represents any piece of great good fortune (*lu*). Attaining the throne, then, in early slang became "catching the deer." A wise man always foregoes petty profit for the sake of a larger gain. Here, however, we see a foolish person, who wastes time and effort in vain pursuits, ignoring great opportunities. If we consider study, for example, the only learning worth pursuing is the Way of the ancient sage-kings. If we consider official appointments instead, only virtuous candidates are worth pursuing. Were it not so tragic, this inability to distinguish good from bad would be ludicrous.

Appraisal 6: The great do not hoard their sufficiencies.
Like Heaven, they disperse their wealth.

Fathoming 6: That the great do not hoard
Means: No trace of selfishness marks their faces.

In general, Confucian philosophers were suspicious of those who act alone rather than in concert with family or friends. To monopolize resources, to be independent-minded, or to claim to be a self-made man, all these acts represented challenges to societal cohesion. This is one reason why, as the *Analects* holds, "Virtue never dwells alone" (A 4/25). All human beings, even the leader, must acknowledge their dependence upon others.

Appraisal 7: Shooting one arrow at three birds in flight:
Though he sets forth by dawn's first light,
At day's end, he has not returned:
Lost.

Fathoming 7: One shot for three birds
Means: He strikes out aimlessly.

These verses demonstrate the utter uselessness of unfocused or misguided activity. Although an entire day has been spent in frenzied pursuit of a goal, no obvious gain results, despite many opportunities. Alternately, the same lines can describe a hunter who loses himself in the pleasures of the chase. Far better "to concentrate the mind and unify the will" in a single-minded search for the Way, since this holds out the promise of success.

Figure 11. Shooting arrows at birds.

Figure 12. Shooting arrows at birds and harvesting the fields.

Appraisal 8: The great accept official posts.
    Ghosts at the shrine cease wailing.
    Some gain their blessings.

Fathoming 8: That the great accept posts
    Means: They restore what had been lost.

The main theme of the verses is clear, although the specific identity of the great is open to question. Once good leaders take up (or, are restored to) office, the local patron gods cease their weeping and wailing, in expectation of renewed good rule and the reinstitution of regular sacrifices. The common people also expect to benefit from the new administration, and so "some gain their blessings." Both the gods above and the people below rejoice in the facility with which the truly great restore what had been lost.

> Appraisal 9: Bright pearls used for birdshot.
> Even if flesh by chance is struck,
> It will not repay the outlay.

> Fathoming 9: Lustrous pearls used for shot
> Means: The expense is not recouped.

Pebbles would work as well as pearls in shooting game birds. What's more, pebbles, when compared with pearls, are of relatively little value. Therefore, the hunter can afford to lose any number of pebbles; he cannot afford to lose a single pearl. Once again, the reader is urged to carefully consider which acts are truly worthwhile. As the *Mystery* implies, when precious human life is to be employed in the pursuit of a goal, the Way is the only goal that can repay the requisite effort. Unfortunately, the petty person typically pursues the vastly inferior goals of fame, fortune, and sex.

Correlates with Earth's Mystery; Yang; *the phase Water; and the* I ching *Hexagram no. 32, Duration; the sun enters the Spread constellation, 15th degree; the Dipper points WSW; the musical note is G-sharp*

Ch'ang
No. 51. Constancy
August 4–August 8 (a.m.)

HEAD: By yin one knows the subject; by yang one knows the lord. The Way of ruler and subject remains unchanged for ten thousand ages.

The Autumn Onset solar period, usually regarded as the juncture between summer and autumn, takes place with Appraisal 6 of this tetragram. Here, then, we have another critical meeting point between yin and yang. Since this is the last opportunity yang will have to lord it over yin, it is appropriate that Yang Hsiung should discuss the relations of the ruler (whose correlate is yang) and the subordinate (identified with yin). That autumn follows summer is an invariable rule of nature. Following this immutable pattern, all subjects, including court officials, must follow the ruler.

Hierarchy functions as the necessary basis for enduring and productive relations; as the *Changes* argues, the four seasons keep to their constant course only when the "strong is above and the weak below" (W, 546). Not surprisingly, the need to recognize one's proper place in the hierarchy is a theme of this tetragram. So long as a just hierarchy is preserved, the worst calamities associated with yin *ch'i* may be avoided. This may explain why the penal code associated with the autumn season is represented in a positive, rather than a negative light.

> Appraisal 1: Holding up the ink-line of the gods,
>   He follows the sacred model.
>   Using the One to pair ten thousand,
>   To the end, his light does not fade.

> Fathoming 1: Upholding divine measure
>   Means: He embodies the form of the One.

Because its primal Oneness produces the myriad things, the Tao in its totality lies essentially beyond mere human comprehension. Certain broad patterns of cosmic activity, however, are discernible to Man. For example, the superior man takes primal oneness as his model when dealing with others. Single-minded in his pursuit of moral understanding and unshakeable in his integrity, he "holds fast to the One" Way. Applying the single tool of categorical logic to the entire universe, he comes to grasp all the myriad things within his mind, so all-encompassing is his understanding. Conformity with such sacred norms gains him charismatic power that will work to effect a perfect union of all the myriad things in the cosmos around him; in the words of the *Changes*, "The movements of All-under-Heaven when aligned correctly become uniform" (W, 326). Above and below, inner unity brings the union of all.

> Appraisal 2: With little constancy within,
>   Female chastity is in danger.

> Fathoming 2: Inner constants undeveloped
>   Mean: The women are not upright.

"Inner" often refers to women or the women's quarters, since only men participated in "outer" (i.e., public and social) lives in early China. The husband/wife relation was viewed as one of great, constant patterns in human relationships. Like the ruler/subject relation, it presumed a hierarchical structure tempered by mutuality. It was believed that the entire hierarchy would collapse, however, if women were unchaste before or after marriage. Clear lines of patrilineal descent had to be assured for both religious and economic reasons. Unfortunately, bastard males passed off as legitimate heirs would participate as adults in sacrifices to ancestors in the patrilineal line. Since tradition insisted that the ancestors would accept no sacrifices from those of different surnames, the prosperity of the clan might be jeopardized for generations by a single illicit liaison. Furthermore, female infidelity demonstrated a fundamentally rebellious attitude toward husbands, to whom women owed loyalty. Such a cavalier attitude could ultimately infect the rest of society. Since women who were less than "upright" undermined the entire "eternally correct" social structure, female sexual and political intrigue was a source of considerable concern to strict Confucian scholars.

> Appraisal 3: The sun makes its virtue constant
> By not eclipsing for three years.

> Fathoming 3: The sun, making its virtue constant,
> Means: The Way of the Ruler shines forth.

Appraisal 1 compared the truly good person to a sun that never sets. Appraisal 3 presents a variation on this astronomical motif. In Han omen literature, eclipses of the sun and moon were thought to presage disorder in the apartments of the king and queen respectively. Often the solar eclipse portended usurpation of the royal power (yang) by ministers or consorts (both of whom were yin). In folk tradition, "three" stands for "many." If no eclipse occurs for many years, the sun's uninterrupted light shines brilliantly on all below. The charismatic ruler, by analogy, enlightens others, with no fear that he will be eclipsed since he has made his virtue constant.

> Appraisal 4: The moon is inconstant.
> She sometimes strays from her course.

> Fathoming 4: The inconstant moon
> Means: The minister errs in his course.

The moon symbolizes the minister for several reasons. First, the moon's light entirely depends upon the sun for its brightness, just as the minister's authority derives entirely from his ruler. Second, the moon shines less brightly than the sun, just as the minister is less glorious than his ruler. Third, the moon, even to the naked eye, appears to wobble occasionally in its course. The Chinese took this irregular motion of the moon to mean that an evil minister with designs upon the throne wavers in his loyalty. One early astrological text predicts that

> when the state is controlled by ministers . . . the movement [of the moon] inclines sometimes toward the south and sometimes toward the north. Irregular motion of the moon, whether fast or slow, indicates excessive power held by relatives of the empress.

Appraisal 5: Whether up, down, or sideways in his course,
  He takes Heaven and Earth as his constants.

Fathoming 5: His vertical, his horizontal
  Means: The order of ruler and official is constant.

The early commentator Fan Wang says, "Heaven is vertical; Earth, horizontal. This is the constant way." Man moving in horizontal and vertical directions suggests the fundamental interconnectedness of the three realms of Heaven-Earth-Man. Elaborate patterns in the night sky and geological configurations are studied by the sage intent upon devising models for human culture; the sage hopes to recreate in human society that marvelous interdependence that proves so productive in the phenomenal world. Patterns in Heaven-and-Earth, then, suggest the norm for ruler and official.

Appraisal 6: Having reached Seven, he tends toward Nine.
  Weakness stirs in what was once firm.
  He cannot overcome the rule for him.

Fathoming 6: Getting Seven and becoming Nine
  Means: Abundance is left as he rides to decay.

Why this talk of seven and nine in Appraisal 6, which marks the transition from beneficial Action to Calamity? Beneficial yang *ch'i* is said to culminate by the seventh position, and to decline by the ninth. Yin, of course, is "weak" while yang is traditionally characterized as "firm." Given the ongoing cycles of the constant, yet everchanging Tao, whoever grasps at good luck ("abundance") finds bad luck later in the cycle. Only the wise individual who knows when to stop is likely to maintain his present position. He contentedly cultivates his virtue while regarding material success with an unmoved mind.

Appraisal 7: Back and forth, forever it flows.
  Those most constant, coming together,
  Can carry on in propriety.

> Fathoming 7: Ever flowing, back and forth,
> Means: He takes the Right to confront the wrong.

In this auspicious Appraisal aligned with Day, the flowing water calls to mind the desirable qualities of floodlike *ch'i* associated with integrity, a power at once gentle and inexorable in its effect. At the same time, the flow suggests the passage of time. When good men come together, early errors give way to rectitude.

> Appraisal 8: Constant illness not seen as illness:
> Blame complete, yet uncondemned.

> Fathoming 8: Chronic illness not seen as such
> Means: He is unable to cure himself.

The individual's persistent evildoing is likened to a chronic illness. The individual who has grown accustomed to moral or physical disease forgets what health was like. No cure is possible if the individual fails to see himself as sick. As the *Lao tzu* advises,

> One must be sick of illness
> If one is to recover from illness.
> (LT, ch. 71)

> Appraisal 9: Seeing his illness as illness,
> Magician-healers will not fail.

> Fathoming 9: Seeing the illness for what it is
> Means: He can serve as his own doctor.

In contrast to Appraisal 8, this individual does not gloss over the serious nature of his chronic lapses. Once he has diagnosed himself correctly, he can certainly effect a cure. Good advisors and the Confucian Classics, after all, exist to help in the process of healing the soul.

Tu

No. 52. Measure
August 8 (p.m.)–August 12

Correlates with Earth's Mystery; Yin; *the phase Fire; and the* I ching *Hexagram no. 60, Regulation; the sun enters the Wing constellation, 2d degree*

HEAD: Yin *ch'i* daily leaps up. Yang *ch'i* daily yields ground. Leaping and more leaping, receding and more receding, each attains its proper measure.

At this point of the year, yin *ch'i* leaps into prominence above ground, while yang hastens its retreat below earth. In effect, yin's rapid advance has stopped the progress of yang *ch'i*. Since waxing and waning occur in proper measure, the continuation of the eternal cycle is assured.

This tetragram and its allied *Changes* hexagram (Regulation) emphasize certain values: "stopping in an appropriate place," "recognizing one's place," "remaining central," and "accepting the superior's position above" (W, 696–97). In Chinese political theory (Confucian or Legalist), "measure" refers to the institutions by which the ruler maintains good order and unifies his empire. By tradition, fixing standardized weights and measures throughout the land was viewed as the first step in the establishment of universal morality. As seen below, the successful construction of a city (especially the capital) was also taken as proof of the king's ability to correctly appraise situations in accordance with natural and human requirements. The capital recreates on a human scale the significant features of the cosmos—the better to convey to the populace the king's charismatic sway over the triadic realms of Heaven-Earth-Man. Therefore, the well-designed capital illustrates the true king's capacity to take the proper measure not only of mankind, but also of the universe.

> Appraisal 1: He consistently fails
> To measure by the Mean.

> Fathoming 1: That measures at center only fail
> Means: There can be no success.

The measures at center point to the individual conscience, which uses the Mean as its standard. As soon as the conscience fails to distinguish right from wrong, the individual cannot possibly attain full Goodness. For this reason, the Classics advise us to conduct our internal measurements with extreme care:

> Be like the forester, who when he has adjusted the spring, goes to
> examine the end of the arrow to see whether it is placed according to
> rule, and only then lets it go.

> Appraisal 2: Like waters that do not recede,
> The center measure is hidden.

> Fathoming 2: Waters not receding
> Mean: Only then can there be rectitude.

Here the individual conscience is likened to a stream whose strong yet reliable flow brings health and refreshment to all who take advantage of it. That the wellspring is hidden only testifies to the depth and purity of its source. In moral development, the person intent upon improving herself through assiduous study of the Classics will discover that her unseen conscience never fails her, and that blessings wash down on her in one continuous flow.

*Figure 13. Tamping earth (*hang-t'u*) in order to provide a secure foundation for major public buildings.*

Appraisal 3: Each small measure,
      Slightly more off than the last:
      Steps toward great disaster.

Fathoming 3: Small errors in measurement
      Mean: Great calculations are overturned.

An initial miscalculation eventually leads to disastrous departures from the Way. As an oft-quoted Han proverb has it,

Off by a hair's breadth [in the beginning],
Missed by a thousand miles [in the end].

Therefore, even a small oversight leads to major damage. Since Appraisal 3 marks the transition from Thought to Action, this is a timely warning.

Appraisal 4: Post and upright help in building walls.

Fathoming 4: The benefits of post and upright
      Mean: These benefit the building.

In ancient Chinese architecture, sturdy posts and uprights are used first to compress and mold, and then to support the tamped earth used in major construction works, including palace complexes. Walls serve several crucial functions. They protect the inhabitants from the elements and from intruders. The space they enclose provides a focus for the community, thereby strengthening the bonds between men. In teaching men how to make crucial divisions of space, they also signal the civilized need for less tangible demarcations like hierarchy. Secure walls, therefore, make the entire state secure.

If the wall stands for the state, the sturdy posts and uprights represent the ministerial advisors to the king. They help the ruler both to bear the crushing weight of his responsibilities and to construct wise policies. Just as the wise builder checks that he has enough material for construction, the good leader makes sure that he has an adequate provision of good advisors. If the wall is a symbol for civilization as a whole, the posts and uprights stand for ritual.

> Appraisal 5: If the posts do not act as posts,
> It spells disaster for buildings.

> Fathoming 5: That posts are not posts
> Means: There can be no security.

Appraisal 5 corresponds to the Son of Heaven. Once again, the ruler's posts are his close advisors, drawn from his chief ministers and close relations. If their talents are inadequate to the task, the entire ruling house will collapse (literally and figuratively), in part because the example of the ruling elite is imitated by all the king's subjects. As errors multiply throughout the kingdom, its peace and security are destroyed. For this reason, the wise ruler is careful to select the best possible material for government service.

> Appraisal 6: Examine great measures again and again.
> In heaven, the images are revealed.
> Elicit the models from them.

> Fathoming 6: Great measurements taken with great care
> Mean: The images drawn down are reliable guides.

The sages are said to apply cosmic standards to human predicaments. In the heavens, the greatest of all measures is the Big Dipper, symbol of the ruling house and focus of the entire night sky of constellations and planets. Heaven displays this image to suggest the natural character of hierarchical patterns. With these to guide him in the dark, Man can learn to build correct social relations. As the *Changes* describes the sages,

> Looking upward, they contemplated the images in the Heavens. Looking downward, they examined the Earth's patterns. . . . From the heavens there hang images that reveal [the correct models for mankind]. The sages imitate them (W, 320, 294).

Without such guides, the fragile seeds of Goodness innate in each person can never develop along the lines of Heaven's manifest intentions for the world.

> Appraisal 7: To draw guidelines without measuring
> Brings down the instant ridicule of ghosts.

Fathoming 7: Unmeasured guidelines
Mean: Those with keen sight only laugh.

Those who fail either to take the proper measure of a situation or to apply the guideline of the sages to a problem deserve our blame. Ghosts represent the shadowy spirit world. With their special insight into human affairs, they are able to discern such failures more quickly than ordinary individuals. As support is withdrawn from the individual who refuses to reform, disaster surely follows.

Appraisal 8: Red from the stone cannot be pried apart.
Equally ingrained is the knight's integrity.

Fathoming 8: The indelible nature of the stone's red
Means: Covenants are possible with him.

The early Chinese Logicians were intrigued by the relation of the separate attributes of a thing (e.g., the color of a stone) to the thing itself. Playing off the language of the Logicians, the *Mystery* uses this familiar vocabulary to imply the priority of certain Confucian values. Stone is known for its firmness and durability, two desirable qualities in candidates for office. The color red often signifies good faith and loyalty. If redness is an integral part of the stone, then, good character equally defines the essential nature of the gentleperson. Since the most famous red stone in China, of course, was cinnabar, a chemical base for the production of the elixir of immortality, perhaps the *Mystery* also means to remind us that good character can win us lasting fame, which is itself a type of immortality.

Appraisal 9: When error comes from repeated faults,
Ten years is too short to restore true measure.

Fathoming 9: Those cumulative mistakes
Mean: Constructive action is precluded.

Appraisal 9 signifies action that comes too late in the cycle. As faults are compounded over time, the person is led ever further from the True Path. The *Changes* says of such a situation,

> He misses the return. Misfortune. There will be disaster. . . . For ten years, it will not be possible to go forward again. Such is the opposition to the way of the noble man.

Yung

No. 53. Eternity

August 13–August 17 (a.m.)

Correlates with Earth's Mystery;
Yang; *the phase Wood; and the* I
ching Hexagram no. 32, Duration;
the sun enters the Wing constella-
tion, 6th degree

HEAD: Yin seizes by force of arms. Yang endows by civil means. The Way can be made to last forever.

In Han thinking, yin *ch'i* is allied with punishments and with war, while yang is associated with the gentler rule of suasive example that gradually habituates creatures to the norms of civilization. Since autumn has begun, the Head refers to the killing power of yin *ch'i* exemplified by the harvest. (Until now, the warmth of yang has promoted only growth and renewal.) As the Head text makes plain, cosmic balance requires both yang and yin *ch'i*, spring/summer and autumn/winter, suasive example and punishments, give and take.

An equally significant aspect of Tetragram 53 is the identification of "eternal rules" that "make [things] endure" with traditional hierarchy in the family and state. The Appraisals therefore discuss patrilineal succession and the so-called Three Guide Lines of ruler-subject, father-child, and husband-wife. These hierarchies are said to be eternal in at least two senses: first, they are modeled upon preordained cosmic patterns that operate throughout all time; second, adherence to these norms creates an orderly society that can attain lasting peace.

> Appraisal 1: Not to demote the heir or fault his claim,
> Choosing the eldest son is the constant rule.

> Fathoming 1: Neither deposing nor faulting
> Means: To preserve forever the ancestral line.

In commoner families in ancient China, the principle was equal inheritance among the sons. At the imperial court, however, one important controversy focused on the best way to decide the apppointment of the heir apparent. Many Confucian scholars argued that the eldest son, regardless of his mother's status in the hierarchy of the back palace, should inherit the title and responsibilities of his father; his mother's eventual elevation to the rank of empress would naturally be arranged "on account of the son." However, other scholars, equally eminent, defined the eldest son quite differently. For them, only the eldest son of the principal wife could become the legitimate heir, regardless of his age relative to other royal sons. Only a very few scholars argued that the most meritorious of the royal sons should be appointed heir, in imitation of practices attributed to the Golden Age of the past.

Yang Hsiung's talk of the eldest son clearly opposes the principle of imperial succession based on merit. The absence of strict guidelines for the succession led to competition between brothers during the ruler's lifetime; often it led to chaos after his death, when rival factions put forward different candidates for the throne. Rules for succession should always adhere to age as the chief criterion, lest the entire royal court be plagued by internal disputes.

> Appraisal 2: Longing to demote the heir and invalidate his
> claim,
> Forever lost are the blessings of propriety.

> Fathoming 2: Longing within to demote or find fault
> Means: How can the line be made to last?

Here, Yang Hsiung criticizes the benighted family head who disinherits the eldest son, thereby overturning the natural preordained order of succession. With such a negative example, how can the royal house be expected to maintain its power for long?

> Appraisal 3: Eternal is his Way.
> Achieved, the blameless state.

> Fathoming 3: Eternal is his Way.
> Meaning: Truly, this can be preserved.

The *Analects* (15/29) insists, "It is not the Way that makes human beings great, but human beings who make the Way great." Here the individual has dedicated himself to absolute conformity with the Way. Because he is good, he avoids unlucky blame (the enmity of his fellow men). Through his steady accumulation of virtue he himself partakes of the eternal nature of the Tao. Worldly success, however, is by no means promised.

> Appraisal 4: The succession order is set aside.
> To favor secondary wives
> Means eternal loss for rightful masters.

> Fathoming 4: That the order of sons is disordered
> Means: This is no way to make it eternal.

The disruption of the natural order of succession undermines the fundamental principles embodied in sacred ritual. Although a favorite may persuade the ruler to name her son as heir, such an unlawful appointment spells lasting trouble for the entire family.

All extant commentaries read the lines somewhat differently:

> The order of sons is disordered.
> When the guest goes first, the host is lost forever.
> The order of sons is disordered.
> Meaning: This is not the method [to insure] eternity.

By this reading, disorder inside the family finds its parallel in discourteous relations between guest and host. After all, the conventions are equally ignored when the guest takes the lead in a ceremony and when a younger son claims the title of heir.

> Appraisal 5: The Three Guide Lines attain Center Perfection.
> Heaven makes eternal its good fortune.

> Fathoming 5: Eternal through the Three Guide Lines
> Means: Their Way lasts forever.

At least since the time of Tung Chung-shu (176?–104? B.C.), the term "Three Guide Lines" has been used in China to signify the all-important social relations between ruler/subject, father/child, and husband/wife, which in theory balance rights and responsibilities to the mutual benefit of all parties. The fundamental importance of these three social relations is suggested in two ways: first, their collective name identifies them as what gives shape to the social fabric; second, the relations are treated here in Appraisal 5, the central position of the tetragram. Through repeated ritual acts the good ruler promotes the values embodied in the Guide Lines. By the time all have learned to emulate his example, the ruler himself has reached that state of godlike perfection called *chung-chi* ("Center Perfection"), so that he henceforth functions as *axis mundi* for the entire universe. Harmony and good fortune will prevail, once mutual obligations are supported by ritual behavior.

> Appraisal 6: The great presume good fortune eternal.
> Returning to an empty court, he enters
> The great darkness he brought on himself.

> Fathoming 6: In greatness, thinking good fortune eternal
> Means: Good fortune turns to ruin.

Like its prototype, the *Book of Changes*, the *Mystery* cautions all fortunate people to proceed with great care, lest they bring about their own downfall by arrogant behavior. There is only one sure way for the great to extend their good fortune and protect themselves against ruin: to pile up more virtue through ritual observances (the only secure kind of good fortune). Those less fortunate will then respond with love and respect, rather than with hate and fear. The subject of these verses forgets this simple lesson. Thus he is totally unprepared for the calamity that he has brought upon himself. That his courtyard (his mind? his physical home?) is empty suggests that he deserves to have no loyal adherents. His life is also empty in that it lacks lasting achievements. Had he only upheld the eternal standards embodied in the Three Guide Lines, ignominious defeat could have been avoided.

> Appraisal 7: By the old tree new sprouts grow,
>   Which eternally twine its hollows.

> Fathoming 7: That an old tree grows the "time"
>   Means: Eternal is its body.

Appraisal 7, well past the halfway mark, depicts an old tree well past its prime. Fortunately, the Appraisal corresponds to auspicious Day, so we can expect some kind of restoration. Either new sprouts spring from old wood, as many commentators assume, or the green tendrils of the "time plant" wind round the old wood, binding its hollows together and extending its lifespan. The support of the young gives the old a new lease on life.

> Appraisal 8: Permanent lapses lead to ill fortune,
>   Bringing ruin down on one's heirs.

> Fathoming 8: Persisting in error
>   Means: His decree is cut by half.

Repeatedly the petty man leaves the path of Goodness. His persistent errors can only lead to ruin, since no lasting good fortune can come from abandoning the Way of the ancients. Repeated evil acts, however, not only affect the present life of the wicked individual, but they also damage the lives of his descendants. Besides transmitting a bad example to junior members of the family, parental misbehavior depletes the portion of vital life-force available to descendants in their patrimony. Thus the sins of the father are likely to be visited upon the sons, according to Chinese notions of collective responsibility.

> Appraisal 9: Always, at the end, conform to the beginning.

> Fathoming 9: Ends that always conform to beginnings
>   Mean: Prolonging joy and true ease.

Appraisal 9 marks the end of the cycle, yet, in a seeming paradox, the *Mystery* writes of the joys associated with new beginnings. The truly moral person feels a kind of inner strength and vitality akin to that of youth, even when facing his own end. This strength, of course, comes from continual efforts at self-improvement. He takes care to act to follow the ancient injunction:

Translation of the Mystery

> You should make your virtue ever new. At the last, as at first, have this
> as your one object: daily self-renewal.

As he orients himself by the Way, itself the origin of all things, he returns to
the beginning, even at the end.

昆　☷☰

K'un
No. 54. Unity
August 17 (p.m.)–August 21

Correlates with Earth's Mystery;
Yin; *the phase Metal; and the* I
ching *Hexagram no. 13, Fellowship
with Men; the sun enters the Wing
constellation, 11th degree*

HEAD: Yin is about to divide them, but yang still unifies them. The Way of
Unity exalts sympathetic union.

In general, it is the physical *ch'i* that allows the separate properties of a
thing to cohere; it is also *ch'i* that contains the properties that differentiate
one thing from another. The *Mystery* credits yang *ch'i* with the nurturing
impulse to keep things intact; this in turn counters the disintegrating impulses identified with yin *ch'i*. At this point in the annual cycle, just prior to
the autumn equinox, yin and yang are almost in balance. A kind of stasis has
been achieved, which makes for cohesion, at least temporarily. Since unity
by definition is entirely good, according to the *Mystery*, the Appraisals must
depart from their usual format designed to illustrate both good and bad
connotations of the term employed in the tetragram's title.

Yang *ch'i* epitomizes undifferentiated love in the cosmos. Like a good
ruler, yang fosters a strong sense of community in fragmented things as it
responds to their needs, forging an effective whole. Specifically, in the realm
of Man, the Appraisals suggest that three main factors contribute to unity:
(1) the elite's empathy for those in trouble, (2) a necessary consensus on
morality, and (3) an equitable government policy in the public interest.
Once achieved, unity becomes the single most important factor in stabiliz-
ing political rule. With a true meeting of all minds, unity and good fellowship can reign supreme.

> Appraisal 1: United with the black,
> He does not know the white.

> Fathoming 1: At one with the black
> Means: He is not fit to be called "human."

For the good Confucian, it is the potential to be Good that distinguishes
the human being from the beast. This potential develops when the powers of

242

discrimination basic to the heart/mind are habitually employed. Most commentators, therefore, apply these lines to benighted individuals who fail to distinguish good (the white, the pure, and knowledge) from bad (the black, the impure, and stupidity), even when confronted with glaring examples. In embracing the wicked, such individuals lose any vestige of true humanity.

The contrast between black and white, however, need not only refer to morality. The lines function equally well as a critique of predetermined or biased views. Only an open-minded person "who sees a question from all sides" (A 2/14) is fit to be called truly "human."

> Appraisal 2: White and black intermingle.
> Three birds, one beak, same tail.

> Fathoming 2: For three birds, one beak
> Means: There is no harm in their hearts.

Confucius said:

> The noble man, though in harmony [with others], does not [always] agree [with them] (A 13/23).

That white and black comingle indicates the rich variety that can coexist in a society. But if harmony is not to be threatened by variety, those in the group must believe that they share a common foundation and goals (here, a common beak and tail). As one commentator puts it, "[Their] forms may differ but [their] heart's desires are the same." This sharing strengthens the communal bonds between men, so that they flock together as naturally as birds.

The same lines, as Ssu-ma Kuang points out, could also describe the ability of the superior human being to live among lesser mortals without fear of corruption by association. Moral superiors may sometimes find it expedient to join with lesser men in defense of life and property. (In terms of the metaphor, they may use the same beak.)

> Appraisal 3: United with the white,
> Lost from not being black.
> No point of connection.
> For one tail, three beaks.

> Fathoming 3: Joining the white, not the black
> Means: Neither feels kin to the other.

As the commentators offer no convincing explanation for these lines, my translation is necessarily tentative. For one single end (the tail), there are numerous approaches (the beak). Apparently, no single meeting point can be found between various groups in opposition. Such uncompromising attitudes naturally preclude the formation of real community.

In an alternate reading, the individual who initially joins with the white comes to congratulate herself simply on not being "black," and so makes no real effort to improve herself.

> Appraisal 4: Birds trust their nests to the thickets.
> Men trust their fates to just regimes.

> Fathoming 4: Birds entrusting their nests
> Mean: Where there is justice, there are no poor.

Good government acting in the public interest unifies the community. The just state acts to protect its fragile subjects from economic ills, just as the sturdy thicket serves to protect its fragile bird nests from the elements. In return for this support, the common people give their allegiance to the ruler.

> Appraisal 5: The hub is no hub
> With spokes unevenly spaced.
> Many hairline cracks ruin the jade.

> Fathoming 5: Hubs with spokes unevenly spaced
> Mean: How could they ever be even enough?

As luxury items, both carriages and jade objects are reserved for members of the ruling elite. Appraisal 5 usually refers to the Son of Heaven as center of the state. The carriage wheel is a particularly apt symbol for state unity, since it functions well if its many different parts (the spokes) are bound to a common center. The ruler is like the wheel hub in that all his subjects must revolve around him; it is he, in turn, who gives shape to their efforts. The ruler's person can serve to focus his subjects' many talents, however, only to the degree that the ruler is evenhanded in his treatment. Should the ruler distribute his favors unfairly, the state will soon break down as a result of many small rifts between ruler and individual subject, each seemingly unimportant in itself. The analogy is to the numerous hairline cracks that mar an otherwise valuable piece of jade.

> Appraisal 6: Uniform measures for well and market;
> Writing made standard, and also the carts.

> Fathoming 6: Uniform measures at well and market
> Mean: All share a single order.

Wells and markets, writing and carts, are four institutions created by the sages according to divine cosmic patterns. The well and market exemplify the interdependence of various groups in a good society, since these are places where villagers tend to congregate. In an ordered society, farmers (the well) and merchants (the market) meet to exchange basic commodities.

The sage-kings are said to have perfected material culture by a second series of inventions, including the writing system and the cart. Wise rulers in later times mandated a single writing system and a standardized system of weights and measures (which regulated even the length of cart axles so that roads and wheel ruts would be of uniform width). Culture is likely to advance only if the writing system is unified; economic and cultural exchanges are likely to flourish only if transportation improves; and cardinal virtues like honesty will prevail only if a single pricing structure is introduced. Although such reforms represent major changes in government policy, the common people do not regard these changes as unwelcome interference in their lives; instead, they accept them as natural. Thus is the ideal community fostered.

> Appraisal 7: Pushed to the side, covers don't cover,
> Nor can they shield him from evening rain.

> Fath 7: That canopies askew do not cover
> Means: The disposition is not equal.

Virtue acts like a canopy to shield one from calamity. One-sided prejudice, however, leaves the individual open to disaster. For this reason, the wise ruler protects himself and his people by equitable treatment.

Several commentators disagree with this reading. For them, both the canopy and the rain signify the ruler. Like the ruler, the canopy shelters those below; like the ruler's favors, the rain showers down. Here, however, the canopy provides inadequate shelter. Similarly, the evening rains are in some way too inadequate to save the crops from destruction. (An alternate interpretation of line 2 would be, "The evening rains do not save.") All these failings suggest the ruler's stinginess in dispensing gifts and appointments. Neither reading bodes well for the health of the body politic.

> Appraisal 8: He joins in danger and disaster,
> Then defeats them, making it safe.

> Fathoming 8: Safety from danger and disaster
> Means: Throughout he extends humankindness.

Paradoxically, whoever is willing to risk his life to help others will find that this insures his own safety. Because of his real concern for his fellow man, he snatches moral victory from danger and defeat. At the same time, the good man can be trusted to return good for evil, so his enemies are dissuaded from causing further harm.

> Appraisal 9: Uniting with death,
> He leaves to bandits all that is left.

Fathoming 9: Joining with death
Means: Giving up on his heaven-sent person.

Although the *Mystery* does not tell us his motives, it makes it perfectly clear that this individual has thrown away his life. Perhaps suicide is the only course open to him, either because he has acted despicably or because he has valued his own life so little that he put himself in peril. Had he only acted more prudently, he might never have needed to waste the precious gift of life, endowed by Heaven and bestowed by his parents.

Correlates with Human's Mystery; Yang; the phase Metal; and the I ching Hexagram no. 41, Decrease; the sun enters the Wing constellation, 15th degree; the Dipper points WSW; the musical note is A-flat

Chien
No. 55. Diminishment
August 22–August 26 (a.m.)

HEAD: Yin *ch'i* waxes; yang *ch'i* wanes. Yin prospers; yang declines. The myriad things by this process are stunted in their growth.

This tetragram opens the third and final phase in the Triadic *Mystery* of Heaven-Earth-Man. Not surprisingly, in view of Man's many imperfections, this final phase of the *Mystery* generally marks the least auspicious of the three phases. Many of the verses belonging to Tetragrams 54–81 assigned to Man specifically address individual human responsibility in the face of contrary trends and an unhappy fate.

It is autumn. The decline of the myriad things is increasingly evident. In the midst of growing troubles, the wise person does well to remember that there is "a time for decrease . . . and a time for increase. In decreasing and in increasing, . . . one must go with the time" (W, 590). Self-restraint, perseverance in the Good, and "a decrease in faults" are advised by the *Changes*. Only by such methods can one hope to escape the downward course associated with the end (whether the end be the end of the annual cycle, the end of a lifespan, or the end of a project).

Appraisal 1: Good at diminishing, and so undiminished.
A mystery deep and dark.

Fathoming 1: That good diminishing does not diminish
Means: Constantly to empty oneself.

Appraisal 1 corresponds to first thoughts, the Water phase, and to the lowest social rank. Individuals should imitate water, whose nature it is to seek the low places. By shunning the limelight and cleansing the self of egotistical impulses, the individual can avoid the calamities that result from arrogance and notoriety. Paradoxically, such decrease brings only increase in the end. As the *Lao tzu* writes:

> He does not show himself
> And so is conspicuous.
> He does not consider himself right
> And so is illustrious.
> He does not brag
> And so has merit.
> He does not boast
> And so endures.
> (LT 22).

Appraisal 2: A heart diminished will strike itself
So as to punish his own person.

Fathoming 2: That a heart reduced inflicts the self
Means: He confines it at center.

Evil acts that ignore the conscience diminish the heart. As the moral will is weakened over time, the body's physical store of *ch'i* is gradually depleted. Once inner weakness affects the entire body, the damage becomes obvious to all. Then "what truly is inside takes form on the outside." Although the petty man tries to attribute his failing powers to an innate incapacity for Good, the truth is that he himself has stunted his own development by hampering his conscience.

Appraisal 3: Decreasing his decorum
Helps to bring light to the steps.

Fathoming 3: Decreasing ceremony
Means: He wishes to restrain himself.

In most cases, decorum and ceremony have positive connotations in ancient China, but here the *Mystery* calls for a decrease in pomp and ceremony. The steps symbolize advancement in the official bureaucracy. Therefore, the verses may decry those in high position who use elaborate ceremony simply to distance themselves from those below. For members of the ruling elite, a desire for less formality (the initial act of self-restraint) may set the pattern for even greater acts of renunciation, as "higher-ups" accept the frank remonstrances of those below. Then if they respond by reforming themselves, advancement in the Way (and often, incidentally, in their careers) follows quickly.

> Appraisal 4: Good order diminished
> Reduces his position.

> Fathoming 4: Decreasing order
> Means: This is no way to regulate the masses.

State control is justified insofar as it relieves the masses from crippling insecurities (such as those prompted by crime or natural disasters). If the government cannot insure good order, however, it no longer deserves the support of the masses. Here the petty man in high office can neither control disorder nor hold onto his own position. How, then, can he hope to transform the masses through the suasive force of his moral example?

> Appraisal 5: Decrease: the proven good of Yellow Earth.
> When the low receives from the high: true peace.

> Fathoming 5: Decrease as Yellow's virtue
> Means: The subordinate's Way is now proper.

Appraisal 5, of course, corresponds to the ruler or leader. Yellow (or gold) is the color identified with desirable Centrality and with Earth. The good leader acts as the center for her community, provided that she distributes her favors fairly among her subjects, while downplaying her own elevated position. In this, she mimics Earth's own propensity to level itself. In return for such humility, she wins the maximum cooperation from those below. This makes for peace and social order.

> Appraisal 6: Obscuring what was clear,
> He amasses but never reduces,
> Ungiving as a stone.

> Fathoming 6: Obscuring, ungiving
> Means: His favors do not bring balance.

The wise ruler distributes just rewards to those below, with several aims in mind: (1) he wishes to focus attention on examples of model conduct; (2) he wishes to "share his pleasures" with the common people; and (3) he wishes to teach them the virtues of cooperation. This individual, intent only upon adding to his coffers, fails to reduce taxes or bestow bounties on the subject population. Since the stingy ruler fails to teach his people the benefits of generosity, they not unreasonably feel that they owe him no more loyalty than they do a stone.

Appraisal 7: Decreasing his infirmities,
And so diminishing his cares,
The danger thus is stayed.

Fathoming 7: Decreasing his infirmities
Means: He brings no danger on himself.

In the *Changes*, the phrase "decreasing his infirmities" signifies the noble man's reformation of his faults (W, 593). Through continual reform, the individual is brought to the state where his health (moral, mental, and perhaps physical) improves. Now in his prime, the individual is strong enough to withstand difficulty; thus, he avoids danger.

Appraisal 8: Its flowing out in floods
Brings loss to life's root.

Fathoming 8: Flowing, ever flowing
Means: The living root is destroyed.

In living plants, vigorous growth depends upon strong, healthy roots. If the sap gushes out from the plant, the death of the plant inevitably follows. By analogy, in the individual conscience, the roots of moral action must be nourished by repeated noble acts. If violence is done to the conscience, it is soon destroyed.

Appraisal 9: Decrease at the end
Helps in ascending West Mountain
And overseeing Great River.

Fathoming 9: Ascent by decrease at the end
Means: Truly this can be done.

Climbing mountains to oversee great rivers is "using the tall to oversee what is low." West Mountain is said to be the site of the Chou royal family's ancestral tombs; as such, it represents their great patrimony of charismatic virtue. In popular tradition, West Mountain is also said to be the sacred abode of the immortals under the Queen Mother. Finally, West Mountain is the home to which the sun daily returns after it sinks below the horizon. The mountain, therefore, links immortality with constant virtue, especially at a time of decline. The Great River is apparently no less sacred. The *Changes* literature calls it a place "beneficial to cross" (W, 411). Perhaps it is the river that separates life from death; perhaps it refers to the waters that lie below the surface of the earth.

In several works, Yang Hsiung explicitly denies the possibility of immortality. The good person, in acknowledging the larger cycles operating in the universe, comes to calmly accept his own impending death, trusting that his virtue may secure him a kind of immortality.

Chin
No. 56. Closed Mouth
August 26 (p.m.)–August 30

Correlates with Human's Mystery;
Yin; *the phase Fire; and the* I
ching *Hexagram no. 12, Obstruc-*
tion; the sun enters the Axletree
constellation, 3d degree

HEAD: Yin does not transform it; yang does not bestow it. The myriad things are each closed shut.

The metaphor of the closed mouth alludes to all kinds of closedness, such as the unwillingness to engage in orderly social intercourse or the inability to speak or eat. More positively, it may refer to reservoirs of any kind (e.g., those of *ch'i*, blood, or water). Since the *Mystery* equates human achievement with making contact, closed entities are generally regarded as unlucky. Tradition supports Yang, describing the superior man as "silent, but not close-mouthed." With unity the ideal, communication is its necessary vehicle. Admittedly, when things are no longer united, the superior man has no recourse but to "fall back upon his inner worth in order to escape difficulties" (W, 448), hoping that stagnation will finally revert to good fortune.

At this point in the annual cycle, the myriad things seem dead, although we know that even the minimal presence of generative yang *ch'i* (which itself appears to be closed shut) guarantees their continued existence. Since the normal process of growth depends upon the comingling of yin and yang, this tetragram emphasizes the dangers of separateness.

> Appraisal 1: Close-mouthed and ungiving,
>   The husband takes the wife's place.

> Fathoming 1: Close-mouthed, ungiving
>   Means: This is what men find abhorrent.

There is both a sexual and a social metaphor here. According to traditional Chinese notions of sexuality, the male deposits his fluid in the vagina like a gift. The female in response sustains male virility by releasing generative fluids in the vagina that bathe the penis. Together, the comingling fluids produce the embryo. Here, the husband does not initiate the process, with the result that no fluids are exchanged; possibly he is impotent. His failure to take part in the exchange overturns all sexual conventions about the proper roles of yin and yang. This reversal of conjugal roles recalls the overturned norms of the winter season, when yin seems to dominate while yang shrinks back.

These same lines also describe the man who prefers seclusion within the home (traditionally, the woman's place) to fulfilling his public responsibilities as paterfamilias. As the *Changes* writes, "Not to venture outside the gate and courtyard is unlucky" (W, 696). Failure to uphold one's prescribed societal role is abhorrent to others, an offense against the human order.

> Appraisal 2: The blood, if closed off,
>   Nourishes dry bones.

> Fathoming 2: The closed system of blood
>   Means: The emaciated body grows fat on its own.

These lines clearly refer to ancient Chinese medical concepts that recognize the life-giving properties of blood. If the individual can master various techniques to promote internal blood circulation, he can restore vigor to the system, rather than succumb to the progressive desiccation of the bones, body, and spirit associated with old age. In effect, the individual learns to "nourish himself and keep himself intact." By analogy, these lines also describe the superior man who learns to revitalize his spirit through mastery and promotion of the Confucian Way. As the "Great Learning" says, "Riches enrich the house; virtue enriches one's person."

> Appraisal 3: His demeanor is standoffish,
>   He stammers at the mouth.
>   Closed off, he has no words.

> Fathoming 3: Disengaged from others
>   Means: The way of Man is slighted.

In ancient China, Man was thought to be unique in his ability to create a meaningful community through the vehicle of speech. The individual described here refuses to use that gift, thus diminishing the true way of humanity. Yang Hsiung clearly criticizes those recluses who claim to serve higher goals than mere social cohesion. Insofar as their conduct undercuts the very basis of society, it makes hermits less than human.

> Appraisal 4: Shutting up his stores of grain,
>   He defies custom by failing to save
>   Even the old and members of his clan.

> Fathoming 4: Closing off his grain
>   Means: They cannot look to each other with hope.

According to Yang's schema, this set of verses should be auspicious. Therefore, some interpretations of the Appraisal depict a providential head of the household who prudently decides to reserve stores of grain for those deserving of special consideration: the aged and fellow clan members. For "not to relieve would not be customary, as it would affect the aged, even of the clan" (an alternate reading of the second and third lines of the Appraisal).

The most natural way to read these lines, however, is as inauspicious; hence my translation.

> Appraisal 5: Keeping neither to center nor the Mean,
> He harvests rotten vermin.

> Fathoming 5: Neither centered nor moderate
> Means: His close-mouthedness is wrong.

The evil man commits one of two errors, both of which are indicated by Yang's ambiguous phrasing. Either he has hoarded his grain so long that all he finds in his storehouse are the bloated corpses of dead rats who once feasted on his stores. Or, in his inveterate stinginess, the miser himself becomes a rat. He has forgotten that the sole purpose of accumulation is to allow for the eventual dispersal of grain and goods to achieve good ends. That is why, "though the superior man accumulates, he is also able to disperse."

> Appraisal 6: The spring at its source, full to overflowing,
> Is held in reserve on the hill in the park.

> Fathoming 6: The closing off of the source of the spring
> Means: It cannot be criticized.

Appraisal 6 corresponds to the Water phase; hence, the watery metaphor. Powerful abundant force is indicated by the swelling waters; the source of the spring recalls the conscience as site of the "ever-flowing *ch'i*" that endows the entire body with physical and moral strength. The hill described in the poem is specifically a high mound depressed at top so that it forms a natural reservoir; by analogy, the conscience keeps men's thoughts at a high level. Deep waters collect, held in temporary reserve for the time when they will be needed, just as the good person awaits the time when she will be called to useful service. This is a case where holding back is praiseworthy.

> Appraisal 7: Closed off in the four limbs,
> The Yellow Flesh decays.

> Fathoming 7: Blocked in the limbs
> Means: Bones and flesh are harmed.

Appraisal 7 represents decay. The color yellow always refers to what is central, possibly the marrow or the innermost muscles. If the circulating *ch'i* and blood are held up in the appendages, the internal parts of the body cannot be nourished adequately.

If we apply this metaphor to the body politic, it describes the unhealthy situation in which all resources of the state are siphoned off by a few at court, preventing an equitable distribution of wealth. Political harmony is consequently ruined. Of course, the same metaphor can be applied to human relations as well as the state.

> Appraisal 8: Blocked, he meets with calamity.
> By offering an ox he expiates his blame.

> Fathoming 8: Blocked and facing calamity
> Means: The great expense is justified.

When a wise man meets calamity, he takes steps to remedy the situation. First, he acknowledges his faults, then he tries to make reparations for his crimes. He reverently undertakes sacrifices to the gods, sparing no expense, to expiate his sins. Since closed-mouthedness is associated with the miser, Yang also advises the reader to counter calamity with a generous spirit.

> Appraisal 9: Closed skies do not rain.
> Dried meat is dried out more.

> Fathoming 9: Blocked, no rain,
> Means: What can one hope for?

Rain signifies a balance between yin and yang. Here a serious imbalance has occurred, with the drought lasting for weeks on end. Since moistening of all types symbolizes the grace of the ruler, the ruler has also become estranged from his people, so that they no longer look to him with hope and love. From now on, their conduct will be marked by increasing desperation.

Correlates with Human's Mystery; Yang; the phase Wood; and the I ching Hexagram no. 12, Obstruction; the sun enters the Axletree constellation, 6th degree

Shou
No. 57. Guardedness
August 31–September 4 (a.m.)

HEAD: Yin guards the door; yang guards the gate. No things make contact.

Yin guards what is relatively inside; yang takes care of what is comparatively outside. Thus, yin may be said to keep watch over Earth, while yang watches Heaven. With both yin and yang at their separate stations, there can be no mutual contact, for each defends its own territory. That means that the marvelous capacity for interaction is also lost to the myriad things. In consequence, things can no longer germinate or grow.

Appraisal 1: Shut the double windows
To guard first possessions.

Fathoming 1: Shutting the double windows
Means: He is good at keeping what he has.

Since Appraisal 1 refers to the Beginning of Thought, the "double windows" most likely refer to the eyes and ears as primary vehicles for sensory contact with the outside world. In general, Han philosophy does not celebrate denial of the senses for its own sake. At the same time, many texts recognize that sensation-seeking deters one from reverent attention to social duty. Driven by desire, a person "is agitated, with his thoughts helter-skelter" (W, 124). One classical text says:

> The people are born good. It is because of [desires for] external things that they change.

If this is so, then to preserve Man's original potential for Goodness, the individual must learn to lessen desire. The good man keeps unnecessary distractions at bay, the better to dedicate himself to pursuit of the Way.

Appraisal 2: To blindly preserve the self
Is not as good as "maintaining the One."

Fathoming 2: Blindly bent on self-preservation
Means: At center, he lacks a way to sustain himself.

In Confucian terms, to abandon moral considerations in order to save one's own person demonstrates a kind of blindness. Paradoxically, in the desire to save himself, the individual loses all sense of self. His principles will be thrown to the winds as soon as real or imagined danger appears. The individual would do better in both moral and practical terms to keep to a steady course of action, in which he "firmly grasps the One" by single-minded devotion to the Way.

Appraisal 3: Neither losing nor gaining,
He comes and goes in silence.

Fathoming 3: Neither losing nor gaining
Means: He maintains his original state.

The *Changes* associates "neither losing nor gaining" with good order (W, 185). The noble man disregards material gain or loss, praise or blame, since he cares only for the Way. This insures that he maintains his original potential for Goodness endowed by Heaven.

Appraisal 4: Images of snarling dogs on guard.

Fathoming 4: Guarded by a make-believe dog
Means: Integrity has nothing to rely upon.

Han dynasty buildings were frequently decorated with painted or sculpted images of guard dogs designed to scare away thieves. (Door knockers, for example, were made in this shape.) Such models prove ineffective since even the stupidest robber can easily tell the difference between an image of a dog and the real thing. The poem mocks those who believe that others cannot see behind their public masks to their true intentions and character.

Appraisal 5: Guarding center by harmony,
In covenants with marquises,
He is tried and true.

Fathoming 5: Holding the center by harmony
Means: The feudal lords turn to him.

Appraisal 5 represents the Son of Heaven and center. According to Han readings of the "Great Plan" chapter of the *Documents*, the emperor holds fast to the Way of Centrality and Harmony through ritual action. As his word can be trusted, the feudal lords acknowledge his sovereignty through various covenants.

Appraisal 6: The carriage rests upon the block.
Jade tablets and disks gather dust.

Fathoming 6: The carriage on the block
Means: He fails to contact his neighbors.

The carriage symbolizes contact through trade, war, and diplomacy. The jade tablet and round *pi* disk are associated with both state sacrifice and high office. Although the two most important affairs of the ancient Chinese state are said to be sacrifice and war, here the state neglects its functions. No meetings are held; no tokens of good faith are exchanged. Ritual obligations (both public and private) are ignored. Since the ruler no longer extends his civilizing influence to others, neighboring fiefs no longer benefit from his proximity. While Lao tzu celebrates states that express no interest in their neighbors (in ch. 80, for example), the *Mystery* equates lack of contact with calamity.

Appraisal 7: The many yang greatly defend
The male offspring's propriety.

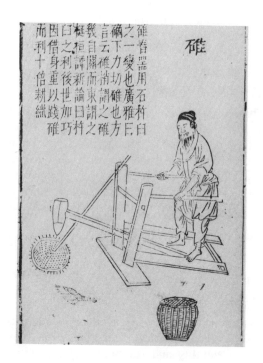

Figure 14. The tilt-hammer (sometimes called the treadle) used in pounding rice.

Fathoming 7: The defense by various yang
    Means: He guards propriety and good faith.

The commentators offer little help here. It seems that the active nature of male yang (as opposed to the quiescent nature of yin) leads it to defend (while yin tends to thwart). The Head text talks of yang guarding the gate. Images of guarded passageways appear also in Appraisals 1 and 4. As the male heir moves out into his proper sphere in the public world, his acts of virtue will summon the vitality, strength, and creativity of yang *ch'i* in its many aspects to protect him.

Appraisal 8: The mortar lacks a pestle.
    His treadle is raised.
    The sky clouds over but no rain falls:
    Glaring sun and blazing heat.

Fathoming 8: To be without a pestle
    Means: What he preserves is poverty.

The basic tools to secure a livelihood are lacking: even the mortar lacks a pestle. What's more, the tools at hand are used improperly: the treadle is raised rather than rammed down. At the very least, the individual is confused. What is worse, he may be lazy. Such a person can expect no help from Heaven. But without Heaven's help, a drought will blast the crops, so that only poverty is preserved.

> Appraisal 9: Joining the white-haired in their principles,
> He rejects the young with their coal-black hair.
> He is not in danger.

> Fathoming 9: Joining the aged in having principles
> Means: The old excel the new.

In China, men of experience tend to be valued over strapping youths. One chapter of the *Documents* has a wise ruler saying,

> Henceforth I shall take advice from the aged and then be free from error. Those white-haired officers whose physical strength is failing, I would rather have. Those dashing brave officers, though faultless in shooting and charioteering, I would rather not have.

Correlates with Human's Mystery; Yin; the phase Metal; and the I ching Hexagram no. 57, The Penetrating; the sun enters the Axletree constellation, 11th degree; the Dipper points due west; the musical note is A

Hsi
No. 58. Gathering In
September 4 (p.m.)–September 8

HEAD: Yin as it comes moves against change; yang as it goes adapts to transformation. Things retreating, descend below to gather together.

At this time of the year, yin waxes while yang wanes. Since yin *ch'i* rises from below (contrary to the action of yin's ally, Water, which flows downward), it may be said to go against natural change. It can also be said to move against change insofar as it harms other things. Yang *ch'i* now descends from on high, in an action opposed to the characteristic activity of its allied phase, Fire, whose nature is to rise up. Still, yang may be said to adapt to transformation, either because it continues to foster growth or, as seems more likely, because it accedes to yin's temporary rule.

One of Yang Hsiung's autocommentaries takes "entering" as a gloss for the tetragram's title. Some read the title as "joining." As the harvest is gathered in, things shut down, after which they hibernate or withdraw into their shells. After being gathered in, then, things all join together in entering a state of rest.

> Appraisal 1: Wildly they clash in the dark,
> Closing on their goals.
> Though they wish to wander freely,
> Heaven does not foster them.

> Fathoming 1: Thrashing in the dark
> Means: Heaven is not yet with them.

Appraisal 1 usually describes first thought. Here various conflicting desires and ambitions contend for dominance in the hidden recesses of the mind. In the ensuing confusion, personal goals are somehow constrained, because the person is hampered from seeing self-cultivation as the only goal worthy of his efforts. Just when the season calls for "gathering in" (i.e., conserving rather than expending valuable resources), the mind wastes itself on undirected activity. Heaven frowns upon the individual's lack of direction and restraint. Such profound ignorance of Heaven's patterns does not augur well. Only minds with a unified vision in accord with cosmic laws can hope to succeed.

> Appraisal 2: Gath'ring in at the dark center,
> He aims for what is tried and true.

> Fathoming 2: Into the dark center
> Means: He corrects the self.

The individual maximizes his own charismatic force by focusing on his "dark center," the hidden conscience, wellspring of all good action that reflects the dark center of phenomenal existence, the Tao. Once his thoughts focus on the Way, succeeding actions will not go astray, just as a careful aim in archery insures an accurate shot. This directed devotion to the Right contrasts with the aimless activity described in Appraisal 1.

> Appraisal 3: All intent on eating, gobble gobble.

> Fathoming 3: Intent on gobbling
> Means: Profit for him is like a ritual dance.

Appraisal 3 describes the person who is "advancing." The individual's desires and ambitions are insatiable, as indicated by his hasty gobbling of the food put before him. As one commentator remarks, "[This is] an image of one who will go absolutely anywhere [in avid pursuit of profit]." In contrast, the true gentleperson who eagerly follows the rituals "never goes on eating until she is sated"; from ritual she learns useful self-restraint.

> Appraisal 4: Closing its wings
> Helps it to rise.

> Fathoming 4: Closing in on what raises him
> Means: This is the aid of true friends.

In Chinese, as in English, "raising" or "rising up" is associated with elevation in official rank no less than with physical movements. The graph for "wings" is cognate with that for "protection" or "support"; for this reason, it often appears in the titles for the king's officers. Chinese tradition suspects the self-made man, arguing that a man of true virtue attracts worthy friends to support and protect him. The wings folded in, therefore, suggest the good man's rise to power through the concerted efforts of true friends.

> Appraisal 5: He draws in his belly
> To avoid the grain.

> Fathoming 5: Collapsing the belly
> Means: This is no way to build a reputation.

The belly is commonly identified in Chinese philosophy as the seat of the physical appetites for food and sex. These lines probably mock the benighted individual who denies himself various human pleasures in the vain hope of attaining immortality through a strict regimen. No enduring reputation can be gained by either asceticism or eremitism since both defy the ritual norms.

> Appraisal 6: A golden heart and vast wings
> Draw in to Heaven.

> Fathoming 6: The golden heart and vast wings
> Mean: They help in getting her support.

The golden heart, of course, refers to the heart/mind of one who exemplifies good faith, the virtue associated with Yellow and Center. The vast wings suggest unusual strength that may be employed to shield others from harm. If the heart refers to the king, the wings are his worthy officials. It is equally possible, however that perfect virtue and great strength are here conjoined in a single individual, whose efforts will be blessed.

> Appraisal 7: Drawn in the arrow's string—
> Ah, how pitiable!

Fathoming 7: Grief from the string drawn in
Means: He is caught in the net of harm.

The hunter ties a string to his arrow for three good reasons: first, the fallen prey is then more easily located by the hunter; second, the arrow is then preserved for future use; and third, the string comes in handy when the hunter goes to pin back the pitiful wings that still struggle to fly. The bird shot down in midflight is effortlessly pulled toward the archer, who easily binds its wings, making escape impossible. By analogy, the person in midcareer is easily felled by a calculating enemy, who renders his prey utterly helpless.

Appraisal 8: He shakes off the net,
Breaking its meshes:
A close call.

Fathoming 8: Shaking nets and cutting cords
Means: In danger, he manages to go on.

Although the hunter's prey is already ensnared, it manages to struggle free. Such a narrow escape must strike the victim's heart with fear. If the individual is thereby inspired to reform his behavior, initial calamity can end in good fortune.

Appraisal 9: He brandishes his horn,
Using it only to attack his kin.

Fathoming 9: Brandishing its horn
Means: He exterminates his own kind.

Provocative acts often bring down destruction not only upon oneself, but upon one's relatives. This was especially true in ancient China, where the law mandated collective responsibility for all serious crimes. The violent criminal might find his entire clan exterminated and his ancestors forever deprived of sacrifices. In this way, evil persons draw disaster into their own homes.

Chü
No. 59. Massing
September 9–September 13 (a.m.)

Correlates with Human's Mystery;
Yang; the phase Earth; and the I
Ching *Hexagram no. 45, Gathering*
Together; the sun enters the
Axletree constellation, 15th degree

HEAD: Yin *ch'i* gathers and masses together. Yang does not prohibit and prevent [anything], so that things mutually peak [in their] accumulation.

The myriad things at this time of year mass together. Either they are stored together after the harvest or they flock together in preparation for winter. In this, they follow the action of yin *ch'i*, which is now dominant.

In the world of Man, Yang Hsiung relates massing to religious activities, a topic seldom discussed in earlier passages of the *Mystery*. Elsewhere, Yang Hsiung explicitly states his doubts about the existence of a supernatural world. Here, he follows tradition in referring to ghosts and spirits who require sacrifice. In this he apparently follows the correlate *Changes* hexagram entitled Gathering Together, which is filled with talk of ghosts and spirits. That hexagram shows the ruler praying at the ancestral temple; by satisfying the ancestral spirits gathered there. the ruler is "armed against the unseen" (W, 614–16). If selfish aims divide the worshipers, however, mass religious activities lead to inauspicious frenzy and confusion, rather than an affirmation of proper ritual. Unity of mind and purpose, then, becomes no less important in religious sacrifice than in the conduct of war, a related activity.

> Appraisal 1: Ghosts and spirits use the invisible
> So numinous are they.

> Fathoming 1: Ghosts and spirits, formless and numinous,
> Mean: Their forms are unseen.

Appraisal 1 is aligned with Water, whose source and power are invisible. Also hidden at this time of year are the myriad things, as they burrow down, retreat, or die. With all "things reverting to their base," the discussion naturally shifts to ghosts and gods, whose operations are by definition unseen, although the results of their operations are manifest to all. Apparently, the perfect efficacy of ghosts and spirits depends upon this unseen quality, for paradoxically whatever has form has severe limitations. For this reason, the superior man chooses to operate as much as possible behind the scenes to effect his will.

> Appraisal 2: At the banquet they gather,
> Titter, titter.

Figure 15. A Han dynasty banquet. Note that the guests are seated on the floor. Chairs, which were imported from the West, became popular only in the T'ang dynasty (618–906).

Fathoming 2: Laughter at banquet gatherings
    Means: In their pleasure, they go to excess.

The ordinary fellow wants to meet with boon companions in his pursuit of pleasure. Ignoring the constraints of ritual, he easily lapses into drunken laughter and stupid excess. It could also be that his mediocrity and crudity prompt the ridicule of others.

Appraisal 3: He reveres his own elders
    As gateway to the many ghosts.

Fathoming 3: Revering his own elders
    Means: The ghosts await respect.

For the ancient Chinese, piety toward living and dead forebears was the foundation of all morality. Family feeling should inform each ritual act so that the individual is naturally schooled in a properly reverential attitude, an attitude that could then be extended to other authority figures outside the family. Many also regarded ancestor worship as a prerequisite for good fortune, since the ancestors could intercede on a person's behalf in the spirit world, thereby securing the favor of the gods in Heaven. Here the *Mystery* shows the aged to be only one step away from the ancestors; a single barrier (the gate of death) separates the living from the dead. Members of the household should treat their elders with respect, then, for both practical and moral reasons.

> Appraisal 4: Leading sheep to show to the thicket god,
> Extending the left thigh, tablet in hand.
> Both are uncouth.

> Fathoming 4: Leading a sheep to the thicket
> Means: This is hardly worth glorifying.

The Fathoming offers severe criticism, but the commentators cannot agree on the specific nature of the ritual lapses cited here. Apparently, the right thigh, rather than the left, should be extended when bowing to the emperor during a formal audience. But it is less clear what is wrong with "leading the sheep." One commentator, Ssu-ma Kuang, believes that it is inappropriate to offer the sacrifice of a sheep to the god of the soil, represented by the thicket of trees. Perhaps an ox should have been slaughtered, rather than a lowly sheep. A modern commentator, Cheng Keng-wang, finds an additional flaw in the proceedings: no blood sacrifice is offered; the gods are only "shown" a sheep. In any case, when mistakes mar the rituals, rituals are of no use to man or the gods; no good can come from them.

> Appraisal 5: With *yu* herbs in the tripod's blood,
> And good ties for nine degrees of kin,
> Only then does real trust exist.

> Fathoming 5: The *yu* in the tripod
> Means: There is trust in the king's decree.

Appraisal 5 corresponds to the Son of Heaven, who mixes an herbal infusion in the tripod with the bloody meats as an offering to the ancestors. This ceremony concludes the pact between members of the king's clan, who partake of his charismatic authority as they share the sacrificial meats. Through a single ritual act, then, the entire political structure is cemented and the king's power extended.

> Appraisal 6: Fearing his ghosts, honoring their rites,
> Wanton acts cause benightedness.
> By excess, he will be ruined.

> Fathoming 6: Reckless acts in fearing ghosts
> Means: He goes beyond what is right for him.

Many Han thinkers explicitly denounce the popular fear of ghosts, arguing that excessive sacrifices and weird cults both deplete household funds and disorder human relations. They base their arguments on passages in the Classics, such as the *Tso Commentary*:

> When a country is about to rise, it listens to its worthy men. When the
> country is about to fall, it listens to the spirits.

Similarly, the *Record of Ritual* warns that "excessive sacrifices bring no
good fortune." Those who merely fear the unknown show little inclination
to embrace the sacred cosmic norms. They splurge on sacrifices, presumptu-
ously apply for help from gods above their own station, and neglect their
regular duties. All such activities would anger, rather than satisfy the inhabitants of the otherworld. Real love and honor inject an element of solemn
restraint into the ritual process. In actuality, these cowards cheat the dead
out of the true devotion that is their due.

Appraisal 7: Duly reverent, they gather at the hillside grave.

Fathoming 7: Reverently gathering at the hillside grave
    Means: Ritual is not forsaken.

The grave sited on a hill is regarded as especially favorable by geomantic
specialists, who regard the grave as a symbol both of individual death and
family continuity. Here sacrifices to the dead ancestors proceed with the
utmost reverence. As one treats the dead, so is one likely to treat the living
members of one's family and, by extension, other figures of authority. We
may therefore expect good fortune to result.

Appraisal 8: Owls and pigeons in the forest
    Scare off many other birds.

Fathoming 8: Owls and pigeons in the forest
    Mean: This is frightening to many.

The Chinese consider the owl and the pigeon robber birds since they
feed upon smaller birds, fledglings, and eggs purloined from nests. Defenseless birds of other species are afraid to enter the forest, lest they be killed.
By analogy, in the world of Man the vicious or violent individual (especially the slanderer) may cause widespread panic.

Appraisal 9: Snivel dripping collects at the nose.
    The family gathers together.

Fathoming 9: Snivel dripping and collecting at noses
    Means: A timely fate is cut off.

According to Yang's own schema, these lines should be auspicious; they
should also convey an extreme example of massing. Still, it is more natural
to read these lines as a description of mourners gathered for a funeral. Death
itself is an extreme example of massing; in death, the body collapses, pull-

ing in on itself. These lines are auspicious only insofar as death rituals bring the kinship community together.

Chi

No. 60. Accumulation

September 13 (p.m.)–September 17

Correlates with Human's Mystery; Yin; the phase Water; and the I ching Hexagram no. 26, Great Provisioning; the sun enters the Horn constellation, 3d degree

HEAD: Yin is about to largely close things. Yang is still slightly opening things. Mountains, valleys, wetlands, and marshes, to them the myriad things return.

Creatures return to their nests or lairs in preparation for the approach of winter. In the world of Man, it is now time for humans to consider their center, their conscience. As the days darken and inauspicious yin *ch'i* accumulates, the psychic journey "home" (i.e., to one's conscience) becomes at least as important as any physical retreat. Periodic returns to the inner self are necessary for the proper functioning of each and every living thing. At the same time, continuous accumulation that knows no retrenchment tends to be fraught with danger. (The single exception is provided by virtue, the steady acquisition of which promotes physical safety and psychic security.) A good example is provided by the heedless accumulation of various luxury items like jade and silk. Not only are such luxuries easily lost to thieves or robbers; their very possession may threaten the soul. More is not necessarily better.

> Appraisal 1: Accumulating evil in the dark
>   Creates the basis for what will be clear.

> Fathoming 1: Darkly hoarding evil
>   Means: Putting oneself in the wrong from the first.

Although the petty person repeatedly does wrong in secret, the ill effects of his crimes will soon become obvious to all.

> Appraisal 2: Accumulating the useless
>   And so coming to great use:
>   Such is the stout heart.

> Fathoming 2: Amassing the useless
>   Means: It cannot be circumscribed.

Early Taoist texts extol the "usefulness of being useless." According to their arguments, only the truly useless person can avoid relentless exploitation by others. The *Mystery*, however, subtly shifts connotations of the phrase so that the poem means something like,

> Accumulating [virtue, though] it is unused.
> And so to come to be of great use:
> Such is the stout heart of the noble man.
> Accumulating the [temporarily] unused
> Means: It cannot be circumscribed [so great is it].

Unlike the petty person, the morally superior individual accumulates wisdom and experience long before her appointment (i.e., when such knowledge is apparently useless), to better serve her community in the future.

> Appraisal 3: Collecting stones she does not eat
> Wastes her efforts and strength.

> Fathoming 3: Piling stones that none will eat
> Means: Nothing can be harvested.

The wise individual makes sure that her energies are expended to secure certain benefits. It only makes sense, then, for her to invest her time and effort in ways that are most likely to bring a sure return. Only the accumulation of merit carries with it an inevitable reward. Acquisition for its own sake profits the individual nothing.

> Appraisal 4: Piling up good, the noble man
> Gains a carriage with "ears."

> Fathoming 4: Nobility amassing good
> Means: And so he comes to prosper.

The superior person grows gradually in wisdom and truth until his reputation for virtue insures an appointment to public office under a good leader. The carriage indicates his high rank and imperial favor; its panels remind us that virtue acts like a screen insofar as it protects the individual from corruption.

Figure 16. A Han dynasty official's carriage. While the illustrated carriage is enclosed on three sides, a carriage "with ears" has two large side panels, but none in back. These "ears" shield the occupants of the carriage from curious eyes. Insofar as they create a visual separation, they assert the occupants' privileged status. In an ideal Confucian world, such privilege is reserved for those of special merit and virtue.

> Appraisal 5: When stores are not full,
> Theft brings no gain.

> Fathoming 5: Full stores and robbers in full supply
> Mean: As it turns out, it harms the self.

Appraisal 5 corresponds to the Son of Heaven, so the failure of central government is likely to be the subject here. Because of puns, however, there are no fewer than three related ways to understand these lines. The first reading criticizes the bad ruler who exploits his subjects through taxation and corvée labor, never understanding that his interests are identical with those of the common people: "[The common people's] stores are not full / [Yet the ruler] steals what is in short supply." A second reading advises the ruler to share his wealth with the common people so as to forestall all attempts at usurpation, for "when stores are not full / Stealing is no gain." A third reading emphasizes that the ruling elite's obsession with material goods not only depletes the treasury, but also attracts thieves to court: "When [the ruler's] stores are not full, robbers are few / . . . When stores are full, robbers are many." The sage-master Confucius once told a local magnate that the best way to rid himself of burglars was to excise his own thieving tendencies: "If only you yourself were free from desire, they would not steal even if you paid them to" (A 12/18). The bad ruler soon learns, "Too much stored / will end in immense loss" (LT 44). Only a leader's lack of cupidity sets the proper suasive example for his subjects.

> Appraisal 6: Great and full he grandly disperses,
>   So in getting men, he has no peer.

> Fathoming 6: Great, full, grand, and giving:
>   Means: He is the one to whom all men come.

Han scholars defined the king as "he to whom men gravitate." Having accumulated sufficient charismatic power, the true leader disperses goods and favors to worthy subjects, both to improve the caliber of his supporters and to incite lesser men to virtue:

> The humane [ruler] employs his wealth to distinguish himself. The
> inhumane [ruler] employs his person to accumulate wealth. . . . Virtue is
> the root; wealth is secondary. If [the ruler] makes the root a secondary
> goal, he will only compete with the people and promote thievery.

> Appraisal 7: How grand the display
>   With jade and silk arrayed!
>   Desires cut loose only summon thieves.

> Fathoming 7: "How grand his display!"
>   Means: Thieves it attracts.

Numerous Warring States and Han thinkers inveighed against lavish display of any kind (even in the case of funeral rites), reasoning that any conspicuous display of wealth provokes greed and violence. Therefore, the *Changes* says, "If a man carries a burden on his back while riding in a carriage, he encourages thieves to draw near. . . . Carelessness about stored [items] tempts thieves [to steal]" (W, 307–8).

Appraisal 8: Though he piles up good,
    The hour is calamitous,
    Only because of his forebears' crimes.

Fathoming 8: Accumulated good and calamitous times
    Means: It is not his fault.

The Chinese were hard pressed to provide a reasonable explanation for cases where the good individual meets with a bad fate. The *Mystery* falls back upon one standard solution to the problem of evil: the family is collectively responsible for individual fate. After all, as the *Changes* says,

> The house that accumulates good is sure to have a surplus of blessings; the house that accumulates evil is sure to have a surplus of ills. When a subordinate assassinates his ruler or a son his father, it is not a matter of a single day's or night's events. The root causes build up gradually (W, 393).

Appraisal 9: Petty men's accumulated wrongs
    Are brought home to their progeny.

Fathoming 9: Piling up evil in the petty
    Means: They are perverted by calamity.

Appraisal 9 represents Extreme Calamity. Surely evil is extreme when it blights not only the individual's own life, but also the lives of his descendants as well.

Correlates with Human's Mystery; Yang; the phase Fire; and the I ching Hexagram no. 45, Ornamental; the sun enters the Horn constellation, 7th degree; the Dipper points due west; the musical note is A; the autumn equinox solar period begins with Appraisal 6

Shih
No. 61. Embellishment
September 18–September 22 (a.m.)

HEAD: Yin is white while yang is black. Separately they perform their respective tasks. Whether going out or entering in, they are most embellished.

This tetragram marks the autumn equinox, when yin and yang, equally strong, are in exact opposition to one another. The *Mystery* conveys this stark

contrast through the colors black and white. Given the Han system of correspondences, where winter (as a time of extreme yin) is symbolized by black
while autumn (a time when yang is relatively greater) is white, the commentators clearly feel the need for some explication of Yang's color symbolism.
The late Eastern Han exegete Sung Chung (d. A.D. 219) reasons that yin now
begins to come out into the clear light of day, while yang retreats below into
shadowy realms; therefore, yin is white and yang is black. His near contemporary Lu Chi (d. ca. A.D. 250) adds, "Yin *ch'i* rules the west; hence, the
talk of white [the color associated with the west in Five Phases thought].
Yang retreats to the north; hence, it is said to be black." A final exegesis is
given by a late commentator, who suggests that in this time of yin's dominance, yang *ch'i* attempts to take on the protective coloration of yin.

It is also possible that the black and white color scheme is used to recall
the elaborate patterning of certain court robes used in antique ceremonies.
Ornamentation in general fulfilled an important function in ancient Chinese
society. Strictly regulated by sumptuary laws, ornamentation was thought to
promote good order since it drew attention to the secure social status of
those singled out as moral exemplars.

Appraisal 1: Speaking by not speaking,
He does not use speech.

Fathoming 1: Speaking by not speaking
Means: Being silent, he is to be trusted.

In one sense, we regard speech as a characteristic ornament of human
existence. On the other hand, early Chinese philosophers emphasized the
impossibility of capturing in speech the ineffable nature of Tao or Heaven.
The true sage, then, models himself upon Heaven, which "does not speak"
but reveals itself in its deeds. Confucian texts in particular tend to be wary
of speech for an additional reason: grand words ring especially false when
they do not translate into brave deeds. The wise person does not boast of his
talents, bray about his accomplishments, or promise more than he can carry out.

Appraisal 2: The ornament lacks substance.
With pattern put first, faulty robes follow.

Fathoming 2: Without substance, emphasizing pattern
Means: He loses all propriety.

Numerous debates appear in early Chinese philosophy about the proper
balance between ornamentation and substance. [See No. 47, page 211.] Classical Taoist thinkers often argued that the plain and the rustic most nearly
approach the "natural" Way, but thinkers associated with the Confucian
school tended to equate the Way with certain schematized patterns, especially ritual activity. True Confucians, however, also insisted that ornamen-

tation should not prevail over substance, since that would be to prefer the secondary over the fundamental; as Confucius taught, "the pattern comes *after* the plain groundwork" (A 3/8). To illustrate this principle, the *Mystery* employs clothing as a metaphor.

> Appraisal 3: Sticking out yellow tongues
> And grasping golden brushes
> Help to show the men of wisdom.

> Fathoming 3: The benefits of tongue and brush
> Mean: They help us see the men who know.

It is easy to estimate the true moral worth of a person by what he says in person or on paper. For,

> Speech is the music of the heart. Writing is the painting of the heart.
> Once the musical notes and paintings take form, the [difference between]
> the noble and the petty person is apparent.

Here speech and writing "express the beauty within" (W, 395), as a golden yellow signifies what is good, central, and in accord with the Mean.

> Appraisal 4: Sharp tongues toady for profit.
> This is a sure sign of merchants.

> Fathoming 4: The sure signs of toadies
> Means: This is profit for business.

Love of profit often interferes with pursuit of the Right. Merchants succeed best when they use smooth but "twisty" speech that flatters the customer. The would-be sage, however, finds the merchant's glib disregard for truth abhorrent.

> Appraisal 5: Humble words are like water,
> And true to Heaven's Female.

> Fathoming 5: A flow of humble words
> Means: He is able to empty himself.

The leader is advised to act like a female. In other words, he should condescend to his subordinates and humbly ask their advice. A modest stance may indeed secure greatness.

> Appraisal 6: Pointless speech, when suppressed,
> Still goes flying off.
> The great man shakes the wind.

> Fathoming 6: Speech that runs on
> Means: Suppressed, it rises up again.

A Chinese proverb says, "No team of four horses can overtake a tongue." Ironically, the empty speech of the petty man often "flies" better than the weightier speeches given by a truly noble person. But in these lines we see the virtuous person about to blast the idle prattler from the scene.

> Appraisal 7: Talk of current affairs is taboo.
>   Fine subtlety in phrasing, though,
>   Shows suspect points to those on high.

> Fathoming 7: Times when one should not speak
>   Mean: How else can it be clarified?

There may be times when the loyal subordinate is forced to speak on forbidden topics. Since this is likely to irritate her superior, the wise subordinate takes special care in her phrasing so that she conveys all her points successfully without drawing the superior's ire down upon herself. (Interestingly enough, the text leaves open whether subtle phrasing refers specifically to allusive indirection or just finely crafted rhetoric.)

> Appraisal 8: The cicada cries *yung yung,*
>   As blood spurts from its mouth.

> Fathoming 8: The shrill cry of the cicada
>   Means: The mouth wounds itself.

However loyal the remonstrant, he would be unwise to harp upon the faults of his audience; adopting a shrill, accusatory tone will only provoke anger, just as the incessant din of the cicadas irritates the listener. If the audience moves to punish the remonstrant, he will soon learn that the mouth can harm itself.

> Appraisal 9: The white tongue that labored
>   Is drawn back to its roots
>   When noble men are not trusted.

> Fathoming 9: A plain tongue that presses on
>   Means: Integrity can be prolonged.

Two commentators assume that the white (i.e., "clear" and "honest") tongue belongs to the truly good person, who in better times would hasten to offer loyal advice. In a benighted age, however, such a person checks his speech since remonstrance, however loyal, would prove useless. As the *Changes* says, "When what is said is not believed, those who value talk are confounded" (W, 625).

Yi
No. 62. Doubt
September 22 (p.m.)–September 26

Correlates with Human's Mystery;
Yin; the phase Wood; and the I
ching Hexagram no. 57, Laying the
Offering; the sun enters the Horn
constellation, 12th degree

HEAD: Yin and yang grind against one other. Things all wither, then disperse. Some seem to be right, some seem to be wrong.

By midautumn, open hostility between yin and yang *ch'i* brings on the withering and decay of the myriad things. All of creation at the autumn equinox is evenly divided between yin and yang, night and day, right and wrong; this confusing situation may well account for increasing doubt. Yin's cyclical rise to prominence seems to undercut the true and natural state of things, in which yang should take the lead; this may also lead to doubt. And finally, there is another doubt associated with yin: although it now holds sway, yin *ch'i* is suspicious about yang's future course. Will it continue to cower in submission or does it only await a future opportunity to undermine yin's dominion?

> Appraisal 1: In doubt and confusion, he
> Loses what is tried and straight.

> Fathoming 1: To lose the Right in perplexity
> Means: How could it be settled in his mind?

If it is to function properly, the mind must be calm. The individual beset with doubts about the proper course of action can never hope to act effectively. All doubts can be resolved, however, by applying the Way of the sage-kings to present-day problems.

> Appraisal 2: In doubt, return to the self.
> In truth, it is no distance.

> Fathoming 2: In times of doubt, reversing the self
> Means: Return to what is clear and still.

This set of verses advises those in doubt to "return the self" in three related stages: (1) to recover one's inherent goodness by a process of (2) self-examination that ends in a decision (3) to reverse one's previous course of action. By this act of will, the individual consciously rejoins the larger cosmic Tao, which is "clear and still" (LT 45). The mind, reflecting the Tao, will then become perfectly lucid and unmoved (meaning both unflappable and unbiased). For this reason, one early philosopher, Mencius, defines "supreme courage" in terms of this ability to "return to the self."

> Appraisal 3: Doubts overcome clarity.
> He suffers mounting distress
> In his heart it advances.

> Fathoming 3: Doubts stronger than clarity
> Mean: The center heart grows dim.

An earlier clarity of the heart/mind succumbs to doubt. As a result, the conscience weakens.

> Appraisal 4: In cases of doubt, examine the old
> To meet the tried and true.

> Fathoming 4: In cases of doubt, to examine the old
> Means: First ask.

Chinese tradition emphasizes the unassuming nature of the true gentleperson. Confucius himself, although an expert on ritual matters, was always careful to "ask for information" from local elders and other potential instructors. Because this way avoids unnecessary mistakes, "he who likes to ask is blessed as a rule."

> Appraisal 5: Mistaken hopes that orpiment
> Holds gold at the center.

> Fathoming 5: Doubts about the center
> Mean: Crooks steal from the upright.

Orpiment (arsenic trisulfide, also called pigment of gold) is a yellow crystal of pearly lustre frequently found in gold and silver mines. Although somewhat like gold in appearance, its properties are quite different. Gold is harder than orpiment. Gold also has no cleavage, unlike orpiment, which has perfect cleavage in one direction. Gold is insoluble in acids (except for aqua regia) while orpiment is soluble in sulphuric acid or potassium nitrate. Thanks to their alchemical experiments, all of this was known to the early Chinese. Any learned person, then, who looked beyond the surface could be expected to see the difference between real gold and its imitator. Those of little discernment, however, mistake the base for the precious. Since Appraisal 5 describes the leader, his failure to distinguish good from evil men is particularly decried. (More specifically, this poem may criticize members of the elite, including many emperors, who favored alchemists and immortality-seekers over sober scholars.)

Appraisal 6: Honest oaths are fit to be heard.
For doubts they have the ring of truth.

Fathoming 6: Proper oaths worth hearing
Mean: They are decrees of enlightened kings.

As written or verbal compacts, oaths provide a standard by which all doubts may be resolved to the satisfaction of the parties concerned. Wise rulers learn early to be careful in how they frame their words.

A well-known story recorded in the *Garden of Sayings* speaks to this: King Ch'eng of Chou (tradit. r. 1115–1079) as a child was out playing with a friend. In jest, he cut a leaf from a pawlownia tree, then announced, "I use this to enfeoff you." Later, when the story was reported to the regent, the regent insisted that the king's word must be kept; therefore, the king's playmate was duly awarded a fief.

Appraisal 7: "Are there ghostly souls
That sigh and sough?"
The arrow aimed at crows in trees
Strikes at the fox in its lair.
To overturn the eye and ear brings danger.

Fathoming 7: Doubts about ghostly souls
Mean: Truly, they cannot be believed.

Imagine a late autumn evening. (After all, the tetragram is allied with autumn; this appraisal, with night.) Will-o'-the-wisps dance by; the wind rustles the trees and whistles through caves, making weird keening sounds. Perhaps the anxious hunter mistakes the sound of woodland creatures for a ghost. Frightened by the prospect of a haunting, he takes up his weapons to kill the phantoms, since they portend evil. He may be so rattled that he confuses the fox and crow, although the size, coloration, and habitat of the two animals are completely different. In any case, he shoots by sound, rather than by sight. With both the eye and ear fooled, the mind can no longer be sure of what is real and what is not. Such confusion is dangerous.

Appraisal 8: Confounded by doubts, yet
So able are the clients that he meets
That three years hence, he's still not tired.

Fathoming 8: Confounding doubts by receiving guests
Means: This is very much worth our respect.

The wise leader makes every effort to resolve his doubts by seeking experts who can enlighten him. Having found good counselors, he is delighted to talk with them and take their advice. The host who recognizes the value of wise guests or clients merits our respect.

> Appraisal 9: In the final appraisal, doubt without trust.
> Drawing the bow, the deer—presumed there—is not.

> Fathoming 9: Final doubts but no faith
> Means: In the end, he lacks what it takes for fame.

By a pun, to "aim at the deer" means to "aim for good luck" or even for supreme power. Efforts are wasted when the goal is misplaced. An atmosphere of suspicion and doubt can never lead to a secure reputation.

Shih

No. 63. Watch

September 27–October 1 (a.m.)

Correlates with Human's Mystery; Yang; the phase Metal; and the I ching Hexagram no. 20, Contemplation; the sun enters the Gullet constellation, 4th degree

HEAD: Yin forms the corporeal soul while yang forms its dying counterpart. All the external forms and appearances of things can be observed.

After the autumn equinox, yin *ch'i* shows its true corporeal form; it takes the lead, while yang, now relatively less powerful, only retreats. Yin's robust appearance contrasts with yang's present frailty. The devastating effect of this cosmic shift is apparent in all things as they become hollow shells of their former selves and die.

> Appraisal 1: Keeping his light within,
> He does not use its brilliance.

> Fathoming 1: Keeping his light within
> Means: His eyes peer into the depths.

The noble man by definition is engaged in a continual process of self-examination. He does not focus his inner light on others' foibles; he prefers to correct his own. As a result of this process, he achieves a state of full enlightenment. Once enlightened, he does not advertise his achievement; he is content to hide his inner light, especially in a troubled age or when a display of talents would be premature. But thanks to his powers of self-perception, he need not seek for the sometimes feeble outside light provided by public opinion.

Appraisal 2: The noble man looks to the inside.
The petty man looks to the outside.

Fathoming 2: The petty man watching externals
Means: He is incapable of seeing the heart.

Two important differences between noble and petty people are suggested here. First, when mistakes are made, the moral person looks to his own heart to find fault, while the petty man blames others for his failure. Second, in judging others, the moral person looks beyond surface appearances to the inner heart, while the petty man, like Shakespeare's Polonius, focuses on outward appearance.

Appraisal 3: Making his virtue seen,
He is fit to support
The realm of the king.

Fathoming 3: Supports whose virtues are revealed
Mean: Only then can perfection exist.

Appraisal 3 represents completed thought about to be translated into action; it also symbolizes advancement. Inner virtue, having been perfected, is now properly revealed to one's superiors, so that it can be used for the community's benefit.

Appraisal 4: He powders his forehead and cheeks.
It rains on his dyed beard:
A sight utterly lacking in charm.

Fathoming 4: Powdered heads with rained-on beards
Mean: One cannot bear to look.

A heavily powdered man encounters a rainstorm. The pale powder washes down his face, dyeing his beard white, the color of old age, death, and mourning. (Perhaps the dye from his beard also runs onto his cheeks.) Before long, he is too hideous to gaze upon. By analogy, the petty man attends only to the externals (the "powdering" and the "dyeing"). As soon as he meets with even a minor mishap, he is shown in his true colors. No wonder others turn away from him in disgust.

Appraisal 5: *Luan* and *feng* in great numbers,
Their virtue is dazzling.

Fathoming 5: Many magical birds in pairs
Mean: Virtue's light is dazzling bright.

The *luan* and *feng* (male and female of the same species of marvelous birds), like the phoenix in Western culture, are said to possess extraordinary powers. Highly discriminating in their habits, these birds alight "only where the light of virtue shines." Their beauty dazzles the beholder, demonstrating the compelling aspect of charismatic virtue. Such auspicious omens occur in great numbers only at the court of an enlightened leader to whom good advisors flock.

> Appraisal 6: A plain cart with a canopy
> Of kingfisher feathers—
> Just to see it harms propriety.

> Fathoming 6: A feathered cover for a cart that's plain
> Means: There is only love of externals.

According to Chinese sumptuary regulations, the commoner rode in an undecorated carriage, while great officials, who presumably exemplified the highest virtue, rode along in a carriage decorated with a canopy constructed from the brilliant blue-green feathers of the kingfisher bird. The owner of this plain cart is common, even base, but he pretends to virtue and high rank.

> Appraisal 7: Looking to his flaws,
> He finds no taint.

> Fathoming 7: Seeing to his flaws
> Means: He can correct himself.

The good person assiduously attends to his own cultivation.

> Appraisal 8: Kingfishers in flight
> Have their wings ensnared.
> The furs of fox and sable
> Rob their very selves of life.

> Fathoming 8: Kingfisher, fox, and sable
> Mean: What is loved makes for blame.

Were the kingfisher's feathers less brilliantly colored, no nets would be set to trap it. Were the fur of the fox and sable less warm and lustrous, no traps would be laid to catch them. It is, paradoxically, our delight in them that endangers them.

> Appraisal 9: The rays of the setting sun
> Flood the eastern sky with light.
> By this we watch its beginning.

Fathoming 9: That the sinking sun sets the east alight
Means: At the end, look back to beginnings.

Appraisal 9 marks the end of the cycle. As dusk falls, the eastern sky is flooded with light cast back by the setting sun. This warm light at sunset prefigures the brilliant rays cast by the rising sun on a new day. A good end points to the new beginning.

Ch'en

No. 64. Sinking

October 1 (p.m.)–October 5

Correlates with Human's Mystery; Yin; the phase Water; and the I ching Hexagram no. 20, Contemplation; the sun enters the Gullet constellation, 7th degree

HEAD: Yin is held to the bosom of yang, and yang is held to the bosom of yin. Their wills are set upon the Mysterious Palace.

The verb "to hold to the bosom" conveys a sense of the inextricable bonds between yin and yang *ch'i*, whose patterns of development are mutually dependent. Yet at this point in late autumn, yin and yang "have gone their separate ways for a long time." At the autumn equinox their powers were evenly balanced; now each feels the loss of the other. Both anticipate their eventual reunion at the Mysterious Palace, a location far in the north where yang is born and yin achieves its maximum effect.

The title of Tetragram 64 apparently refers to "sinking one's sights" to look below. Like the preceding tetragram, Tetragram 64 in its Appraisals makes reference to various birds, but this time they are ominous birds of prey, whose actions symbolize the increasing depradations of inauspicious yin *ch'i* upon helpless yang.

Appraisal 1: Inclining an ear to the women's rooms,
He does not hear the good.

Fathoming 1: Immersing himself in the back rooms
Means: He loses what embodies virtue.

Some early Chinese thinkers assumed that women were inferior in virtue. Others explained women's supposed propensity for gossip, intrigue, and trivial pursuits as the inevitable result of their confinement within the women's quarters. However, Chinese moralists perceived a clear need for chaste women to provide an heir to carry on the religious and economic activities of the family. To this end, the rites stipulated the strict segregation of the sexes, except in the conjugal bedchamber. Given women's general exclusion from public affairs, the man who preferred to "incline an ear" to the women's ward (by eavesdropping, engaging women in idle chatter, or participating in "feminine" pursuits) could never hope to learn enough about public affairs. Still worse, overindulgence in these yin activities might lead to poor health, even death. For this reason, the *Record of Ritual* insists that "what is said within the women's quarters shall not become known outside; what is said among men outside shall not be divulged to the women."

> Appraisal 2: Sinking his gaze
>   To see himself better
>   Is wiser than the skew
>   Of one blind in one eye.

> Fathoming 2: A deeply penetrating look
>   Means: He gets to be upright and fine.

The good person examines his conscience daily. In contrast, the petty person only perceives the faults of others and fails to see his own. In this he is like the half-blind man who looks askance at others.

> Appraisal 3: He sinks into beauty,
>   Losing the tried and straight.

> Fathoming 3: Immersed in beauty
>   Means: This makes us deaf and blind.

To sink into beauty is to be hopelessly enthralled by beautiful women and sensuous music. As the *Lao tzu* writes,

> The Five Colors make people blind in the eye.
> The Five Notes make people deaf in the ear.
> (LT 12)

With the mind besotted with sensory delights, no time or energy remains for the "tried and straight" Way transmitted from the ancients. Adherence to the Tao eventually yields more reliable pleasures for the individual. To be oblivious to the greater moral good makes us in effect deaf and blind to its many advantages.

> Appraisal 4: The *wan-ch'u* lowers its gaze,
>   Eating the bitter bamboo, as is right.

> Fathoming 4: A fledgling phoenix drops down to look.
>   Meaning: This is the way it selects its food.

The singular purity of the mythical *wan-ch'u* is proven in Chinese tradition by its unerring taste for the finest. It is said that

> In the south there is a bird called the Wan-ch'u, which alights only on
> the rarest of trees, eats nothing but the fruit of the Lien, and drinks only
> from springs of sweet water.

The moral person is equally choosy when it comes to selecting who and what will sustain him.

> Appraisal 5: Eagle and hawk soar high
>   But sink their bellies low.
>   They prefer newhatched things
>   And disdain good rice gruel.

> Fathoming 5: That eagle and hawk soar high
>   Means: They fasten on rotten stuff.

The eagle and hawk are among the most majestic of birds. Due to the power and size of their wings, they easily soar high above ordinary birds. In this, they are like the person ambitious for high position. Unfortunately, high position is no guarantee of right conduct. In certain cases, a propensity for "high-flying" may be coupled with a vicious or perverse nature. The eagle and hawk prefer carrion to the rice gruel fed to domesticated fowl. They are like evil leaders who use their positions to advance the equally corrupt.

> Appraisal 6: He views each kernel as a pile.
>   Clear on profit and right for king.

> Fathoming 6: Seeing the kernel as a pile
>   Means: His Way is clear.

The virtuous person considers each kernel of grain (and by analogy, every minor event or insignificant person) as a thing of enormous importance. The good ruler, therefore, weighs each and every exaction from his people with the utmost seriousness. Otherwise, ill-considered demands certainly will lead to great troubles.

> Appraisal 7: Like a net, like a snare,
>   Red flesh spells danger for kites and owls.

> Fathoming 7: Nets and snares, bloody flesh,
>   Mean: They eat what is unclean.

Nets and snares are baited with red meat to catch evil birds of prey. Greed overcomes good sense when the lure of bloody flesh overcomes the birds' survival instincts. The moral is, the compulsion to satisfy one's worst desires is in itself a deadly trap.

Appraisal 8: He hopes to get his medicine
To help in corrective campaigns.

Fathoming 8: Looking for his medicine
Means: This is good for campaign marches.

The punitive campaign and the march symbolize the individual's crusade for moral righteousness. The individual decides to cure his own illnesses first, the better to improve his defenses against the many evils outside.

Appraisal 9: Bloodstained, the hard steel
Sinks into the forehead.
First a master, but later ruined.

Fathoming 9: Bloody steel sunk in the head
Means: In the end, defeated by greed.

Blood has the dual associations of desire and death. The ruthless individual eventually is undone by his own greed for power.

Nei
No. 65. Inner
October 6–October 10 (a.m.)

Correlates with Human's Mystery; Yang; the phase Fire; and the I ching *Hexagram no. 54, The Marrying Maiden; the sun enters the Base constellation, 4th degree*

HEAD: Yin, leaving its inside, goes to stay on the outside. Yang, leaving its outside, goes to stay on the inside. The myriad things come to completion.

With Appraisal 3, the Cold Dew solar period begins. As yin *ch'i* completely fills Heaven and Earth, and yang returns below, transition becomes an appropriate theme for the tetragram. In particular, this tetragram focuses on one transition point, marriage, which parallels yin's current position as it experiences the onset of full maturity. Marriage, as the *Changes* tells us, is simultaneously "end and beginning," "transitory yet eternal" (W, 664). Rituals often acknowledge the confusion of such transitional times by reversing some aspects of customary order. In both the betrothal and nuptial ceremonies of ancient China, for example, when the bride is introduced to the groom's house, she finds her future husband giving precedence to her. In all human relations (whose basic model is husband and wife), there is a need for such periodic reversals if one wishes to establish great harmony and productivity.

The reversals begin in the Head text, which shows yin *ch'i* (usually associated with what is hidden or inside) moving into an outside (i.e., visible) position, while exhausted yang *ch'i* retreats to some place out of sight. The myriad things now approach completion, in which full maturity leads to death or hibernation. With yin now clearly dominant, the tetragram considers the rightful place of women, aligned with yin and the inner (or private) worlds, contrasting it with men's outer (or public) selves.

> Appraisal 1: Careful about consorts:
>   To be chaste at first
>   Makes for later peace.

> Fathoming 1: Careful about his consorts
>   Means: He begins with women of proven worth.

Along with filial piety, female chastity was one of the main supports of the patriarchal system in China, since a single act of infidelity could confuse the direct line of patrilineal descent ever after. All order requires self-restraint exercised in the interests of the larger community; therefore, good order in the household is an important first step toward order in the community and even the cosmos. For these reasons, a woman chaste in both mind and spirit is needed for the "inner apartments" if harmony is to prevail after marriage. If care is taken at the start of any marriage, the end is likely to be good.

> Appraisal 2: Depraved is his wife.
>   He puts her away from that Yellow Couch.

> Fathoming 2: Depravity in the inner chambers
>   Means: He is far from at peace in his mind.

The Yellow Couch usually refers to the imperial couch, although it may simply be a flowery term for the conjugal bed in the inner apartments. Yellow, of course, signifies the central virtues of moderation and humility, while the couch symbolizes ease and harmony, as well as conjugal love. The wife here ignores proper conjugal relations, which are to be ruled by moderation, and wallows in depravity. Lest her behavior infect the entire household, the husband shuns her, thereby insuring peace in the household. The husband is acutely aware of the distance between his actual situation and the ideal family life.

> Appraisal 3: Despite your courtesy, she grieves
>   As she approaches our western steps.

Fathoming 3: Your decorum and her sorrow
Mean: This is how it feels to replace a mother.

In the ancient Chinese marriage ceremony, the future mother-in-law descends the western steps to indicate that she will soon give way to the younger generation. The bride then mounts the steps of the ancestral hall to show that she and her progeny will ultimately replace the older generation. Thoughtful newlyweds cannot but feel some sorrow at the implications of their marriage ceremony. The joyful prospect of new children to continue the ancestral line is offset by an acute awareness of the increasing age and approaching death of the present family heads. Marriage typifies times of transition, which are usually marked by mingled joy and sorrow.

Appraisal 4: Loving the petty, loving the perils,
Losing even his cloak of hemp.
Danger.

Fathoming 4: Liking the petty and perilous
Means: This is not worth glorifying.

Warm clothes are one of the basic necessities of life. As winter approaches, the wise person is provident enough to prepare sufficient food and clothing to sustain his or her family. In contrast, the petty person, having flirted with danger, loses every single possession, down to the coarsest of cloaks. (Is there a hint of a sexual adventure here?) Such improvidence will surely ruin the entire family.

Appraisal 5: The dragon lowers itself to the mud.
Noble men profit when taking on wives
If they meet them by custom as equals.

Fathoming 5: A dragon descends to the mud.
Meaning: Yang goes below yin.

The dragon, of course, may refer to the dragon ruler, the Son of Heaven who flies high above the common run of men. But the dragon is also a symbol of the virile male at the height of his powers. As winter (aligned with yin and the female) draws near, the soaring dragon is said to burrow into the mud. Clearly, a concerted effort to level differences often produces harmonious union and mutual benefit. This is true not only for male-female relations but for those between leader and subordinate.

Appraisal 6: At dusk in midflight,
He draws in his wings.
Though he wants the palace full,
He will not see his woman.

Fathoming 6: In yellow dusk, drawing in his wings
Means: He is unable to restrain himself.

The winged creature (possibly a dragon?) suggests any "high-flyer" of power and ambition. In the half-light of dusk, his thoughts turn toward home. Sexual desire fills his breast; he wishes his home were full of luscious beauties. But this very preoccupation with sex, ironically enough, prevents him from finding a suitable mate with whom he could find true satisfaction.

Appraisal 7: A crumbling wall grows foxtail shoots.
When grizzled heads bring home young wives,
Their wives are soon with child.

Fathoming 7: That the crumbling wall grows foxtail shoots
Means: This is a sign of felicitous things.

The *Changes* envisions great prosperity as "an old fellow taking a young woman to wife" (W, 527). Appraisal 7 typically marks the onset of old age, but here a fruitful marriage brightens prospects for the future.

Appraisal 8: Inside, not to subdue one's wife
Lays waste to home and state:
Wading through depths unfathomably deep.

Fathoming 8: Women inside who are uncontrolled
Mean: These are calamities for the state.

The wife, who is "inner," should submit to her husband, who is "outer," in all public matters. If the wife insists on taking her pleasures where she chooses, in utter defiance of her husband and her sacred duty, her promiscuity spells ruin for the family line, whether she is a commoner or a member of the royal line. To allow her to produce illegitimate children (an alternate reading for "calamities" in the last line) is a self-destructive impulse, like wading into a deep body of water.

Appraisal 9: Rain falls onto the land.
It cannot stop, it cannot exceed.

Fathoming 9: Rain falling on the land
Means: Favor comes in goodly measure.

The fertility of the loess soil in the Central Plain region of China depends upon abundant rainfall. In consequence, the pouring rain comes to symbolize all types of favors bestowed, including the king's benefactions to his subjects and the husband's gift of semen to his conjugal partner. Here rain (grace and favor, even semen) showers down from above upon a yin figure (Earth = yin; women relative to men; and subordinates relative to their leader.) Grace in proper measure imparts new life.

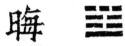 ☶

Ch'ü

No. 66. Departure
October 10 (p.m.)–October 14

*Correlates with Human's Mystery;
Yin; the phase Wood; and the* I
ching Hexagram no. 25, Unex-
pected [Wilhelm: Innocence]; the
sun enters the Base constellation,
9th degree

HEAD: Yang takes leave from its yin. Yin takes leave from its yang. All things are disappointed and perturbed [with no sense of belonging to either].

In the previous tetragram, yin and yang abandon their usual bases. Now, in this tetragram, they even abandon their partnership. No chance remains for harmonious union. The myriad things feel only despair, for they are left without a sense of belonging or direction. The tetragram is correlated with a *Changes* hexagram, whose title was interpreted by Han Confucians to mean "no hope" or "no expectations," and whose theme was the loss that accrues from "reckless behavior." This tetragram's assignment to Wood underscores the contrast between the present, desiccated condition of all things and their former luxuriance. Given the unfavorable trends of the time, the wise person thinks she has done well enough if she is able to extricate herself from complete disaster.

> Appraisal 1: He leaves this Numen Pool
> To dwell in that withered garden.

> Fathoming 1: Quitting this Numen Pool
> Means: He does not proceed with modesty.

Appraisal 1 corresponds to Water; hence, the reference to restorative waters. The exact meaning of the term "Numen Pool" is not certain. Most likely the pool refers to the innermost heart/mind, the reservoir of effective thought and the conscience. The withered garden, apparently on high ground, presents a striking contrast. The garden lacks moisture (a symbol for fecundity and grace), so it can provide nothing. By analogy, the petty man, ever intent on climbing high in the social and political worlds, fails to cultivate those virtues, in particular humility, which would yield good fruit.

> Appraisal 2: He leaves that withered garden
> To dwell below in the Numen Pool.

Fathoming 2: Dwelling in the Numen Pool below
Means: Such is the light of humility's Way.

Appraisal 2 clearly reverses the preceding verses. Humility and a well-kept conscience provide the best preparation for future glories.

Appraisal 3: Raising high his step
In going to the hall,
He is somewhat exposed.

Fathoming 3: High steps and exposure
Mean: He proceeds wantonly.

For the ancient Chinese, as for Freud, physical gestures indicate inner states of mind. "High-stepping," for example, betokens overweening political ambition. The final Appraisal line then gives a compound term, which can be construed either as "There is dew" or as "There is [something] revealed." If dew soaks the hem, we know that the individual has taken insufficient care of his person. However, dew may also soak the road, signifying that the path to power is a slippery one. In any case, the wicked individual now finds his evil intentions exposed to others.

Appraisal 4: Quitting as son,
He becomes a father.
Quitting as subject,
He becomes a ruler.

Fathoming 4: Leaving as son to become the father
Means: It is not what he had hoped for.

In this tentative translation, the lines illustrate the unsought but inevitable changes in status that occur with increased maturity. Such changes parallel yang's temporary abdication to yin at this season of the year. However, the Sung commentator Ssu-ma Kuang reads the Appraisal as, "Leaving the son to go to the father / Leaving the subject to go to the ruler." To him, this suggests a proper understanding of and acquiescence in hierarchical order. Such model behavior is rewarded, he argues, "beyond his wildest dreams" (an alternate reading for the final Fathoming line).

Appraisal 5: Hiking up his skirt
He goes to the court,
Where wild grasses grow.

Fathoming 5: Hoisting the robes where grasses grow
Means: They, for their part, should also be feared.

Appraisal 5 plays upon Appraisal 3. Once again, the subject of the verses raises something (here, the hem of his robe). As he crosses the courtyard, he discovers wild grasses and brambles that threaten to snag his robes or his flesh. The courtyard (and the court) should be more orderly; the individual (a high official, judging from his long robes) should have taken greater care. Perhaps he has been exiled to the wastelands because of depraved behavior? By any reading, this image spells disaster.

> Appraisal 6: He freely leaves his achievements behind.
> Heaven will grant him its name.

> Fathoming 6: Willing to leave his success behind
> Means: He declines to occupy a position.

The Taoist sage Lao tzu equates Heaven's Way with "retreating when the task is accomplished" (LT 9). Chinese tradition in general praises wise persons who readily give up their positions once their objectives have been achieved. The best example was provided by the illustrious Duke of Chou (11th c. B.C.), who stepped down as regent once his young charge, King Ch'eng, was mature enough to take up his responsibilities. The texts celebrate those "without prideful presumption" or "contentious desire" for reputation. History (or "Heaven") will reward them.

> Appraisal 7: Having left his virtue and propriety,
> Even three deaths do not clear his name.

> Fathoming 7: Departing from virtue and propriety
> Means: In the end, he dies an ugly death.

The number three signifies "many" deaths. Here death comes first to virtue, and then to one's person and reputation. The evil that men do lives on in popular memory and historical record.

> Appraisal 8: The moon is a crescent on high
> And Fire is about to descend.
> He cannot use them to move
> For in movement there lies fault.

> Fathoming 8: Crescent moon and hanging Fire
> Mean: He fears to suffer blame.

The crescent moon appears in the final third of the lunar month. The Fire Star (Antares, the central star of the Chinese Heart constellation) is suspended just above the horizon in the tenth month, near the end of the year. Both indicators, then, point to the end of the phase and the inevitable dying of the light. The proper time for initiatives has already passed. The wise individual avoids all precipitate action, lest she fall into error; the noble man waits for Heaven to improve the situation, knowing that he himself is powerless.

> Appraisal 9: He seeks me with no success
> Since my turn to the northwest.

> Fathoming 9: Seeking, but not getting me
> Means: How can it last long?

Weak yang *ch'i* makes a turn northwest, the direction of yin's maximum activity. This suggests the many changes brought about by the cycle, some of which may usher in welcome events. Yin's domination, for example, seems absolute now, but it will not last. Soon nascent yang will reappear, giving hope to all.

Hui
No. 67. Darkening
October 15–October 19 (a.m.)

Correlates with Human's Mystery; Yang; the phase Metal; and the I ching Hexagram no. 36, The Light Injured; the sun enters the Base constellation, 13th degree

HEAD: Yin ascends to yang's usual position; yang descends to yin's. Things all are losing light.

The *Changes* hexagram correlated with this tetragram sets the tone for the Head and Appraisals:

> "Darkening" means "damage," "injury.". . . Expansion will certainly
> encounter resistance and injury (W, 564, 566).

The Image text attached to the same hexagram tells us that the primary technique the noble person uses to deal with such situations is to "veil his light" (i.e., hide his superiority) in order to live out his days unharmed among the benighted (W, 565).

In the natural world, there remains only the gloomy crepuscular light of winter. The myriad things, which depended on yang *ch'i* for their light and vitality, are in decline now that yang retreats far below earth.

> Appraisal 1: Together in the dark,
> Seclusion is proper.

> Fathoming 1: In common dark, the only one to see
> Means: At center, he is singularly brilliant.

In a benighted age, when all seem equally in the dark regarding moral values, enlightenment is still possible for the individual intent upon Goodness. However, the humane person who is out of step with his neighbors may choose to temporarily hide his light, in order to preserve himself in a time of chaos. Only an inner light shines forth in all its brilliance. After all, in Appraisal 1, it is still too early for action that may reform the world.

> Appraisal 2: Blindly forging ahead, he meets with
> obstructions.

> Fathoming 2: Blindly marching into obstacles
> Means: Clearly, he does not see the Way.

The rash individual forges ahead, oblivious to all the difficulties that lie ahead. But in reality, he is no better able to see the one true Way than a "blind man tapping his cane to find the road." Only study of the ancients can provide sufficient guidance for life, yet this individual claims to know it all.

> Appraisal 3: Yin proceeds while yang follows:
> Good for making what is not bad luck.

> Fathoming 3: Yin proceeding with yang following
> Means: The matter must go outside.

Appraisal 3 marks the transition from Thought to Action. Normally, yang initiates activities to which yin responds. However, by this time of the year, their characteristic activities have been reversed. In certain circumstances, the priority of yin is now accounted good. For example, a good woman may lead her husband to virtue. In another case, the conscience (which is yin because it is inner) motivates the individual's action (yang, because it is outer). In all such cases, an internal change will have its external effect.

> Appraisal 4: Confusing his categories,
> He loses the golden casket.

> Fathoming 4: Dim about categories
> Means: Laws and institutions decline.

In early Chinese thought, categorical thinking provides the key to all logic. If a suitable analogy to the sage-rulers' precepts can be found, then complicated moral issues can be untangled with ease. The wise individual, therefore, closely guards the "golden casket," the precious strongbox where important records and state documents are kept for reference. But woe to the individual who "confuses the categories," who reasons, in other words, by improper analogy or faulty precedent. Such muddleheaded thought undermines legal, institutional, and ethical systems, whose very existence requires the consistent use of a body of precedents.

> Appraisal 5: With the sun at noon
> And the moon quite full,
> Noble men dim themselves
> So as not to enter extremes.

> Fathoming 5: The noon sun and the full moon
> Mean: Bright fears of extermination.

Appraisal 5, midpoint of the tetragram cycle, corresponds to the sun at high noon and the moon in midmonth. (Such brilliant light may recall the Son of Heaven, usually assigned to this Position.) The noble man at the height of his powers should consider "hiding his light" in order to preserve himself as the cycle begins its downturn. By reclusion, either physical or psychic, the moral superior can evade the decline that typically follows great florescence. One who is truly "brilliant" would never endanger the self by pressing for further growth or advantage.

> Appraisal 6: The Dark Bird is filled with worry:
> The light slips down into hiding.

> Fathoming 6: The Dark Bird filled with grief
> Means: He is about to descend to the dark.

The Dark Bird usually refers to either the swallow or the crane, migratory birds thought to "worry" at winter's approach. Here, however, given the puns on light and enlightenment, darkness and moral benightedness, the Dark Bird may refer to the black crow, symbol of the sun.

> Appraisal 7: In darkest night, a light is raised.
> Some follow it and go forth.

> Fathoming 7: Raising a light at darkest night
> Means: Virtue will soon go forth.

The worthy individual "raises a light" for her fellow men, either by the force of her example or by recommending worthy candidates for office. Some follow her lead and embark on the path of Virtue, so that enlightenment eventually spreads throughout the land.

> Appraisal 8: Seeing what is not his truth
> Harms his own right eye.
> It destroys the state and ruins the house.

Fathoming 8: That seeing wrong harms the eye
Means: By this, the state is lost.

This individual fails to discern the difference between true and false. Acting on false assumptions ("seeing what is unreal"), her judgment is hampered. Perhaps she also ignores the advice of friends and elders, so that she calls ruin down on all around her.

Appraisal 9: In a dark age, seeing dimness for itself
Helps propriety in an unenlightened age.

Fathoming 9: The benefits of dimming in darkness
Mean: It is no use to be brilliant alone.

The early sage Chi tzu is said to have "veiled his light" (by feigning madness) in order to escape execution by the final evil ruler of the Shang dynasty. The latter-day gentleperson, when faced with insoluble difficulties, recognizes his own inability to induce an immediate improvement; one enlightened person cannot light the whole world. Rather than draw undue attention to himself, which might prove dangerous, he bides his time, cultivating his virtue until such time as he can act more effectively. Seeing dimness for what it is, then, may lead to greater enlightenment.

Correlates with Human's Mystery; Yin; the phase Earth; and the I ching *Hexagram no. 36, The Light Injured; the sun enters the Chamber constellation, 3d degree; the Dipper points WNW; the musical note is A-sharp*

Meng
No. 68. Dimming
October 19 (p.m.)–October 23

HEAD: Yin marches to the south; yang marches to the north. Things lose light and proper orientation. Not a one but grows increasingly dim.

This tetragram is the twin of the previous one, since it is paired with the same *Changes* hexagram; therefore, the images of darkening and damage continue. Yin and yang *ch'i* have reversed their usual orientation, with yin in the south and yang in the north. Confusion reigns as the Winter Dew solar period yields to Frost fall. All sentient beings grow dim and feeble as the light fails. Human hearts as a result become ignorant of or insensible to the value of tradition. All things enter that dreamlike state where reality and illusion are confused.

Appraisal 1: The belly dim, he glimpses Heaven,
But fails to see its borders.

Fathoming 1: Dim-bellied and sky-glimpsing
Means: He lacks all ability to see.

The belly refers to the seat of the emotions (elsewhere located in the heart/mind). With its own powers of perception beclouded, the self cannot hope to imagine the full range of marvelous reality. Even a brief glimpse of the divine cannot end in full illumination. Ignorance and insensitivity continue to reign.

Appraisal 2: Lucid at heart, he glimpses Heaven,
Seeing clear its very roots.

Fathoming 2: Bright-bellied and sky-glimpsing
Means: At center, exceptional brilliance.

This Appraisal reverses the message of the previous Appraisal, predicting the most profound insight.

Appraisal 3: Blind masters: some teach archery
But fail to hit their target.

Fathoming 3: Instruction by the blind
Means: They lack the means to discriminate.

Appraisal 3 marks the transition from Thought to Action. Lacking sufficient clarity himself, how can the teacher enlighten his pupils? As the philosopher Mencius wrote,

> Men of worth use their light to enlighten. Nowadays some would use their benighted state to enlighten.

Appraisal 4: With Right as his mirror, he does not stray.
To others, he is one to rely on.

Fathoming 4: The Right reflecting true
Means: Integrity can be trusted.

Whoever takes the sages for a model provides contemporaries with a perfect "mirror" of good conduct.

Appraisal 5: Turning his back on what is bright,
Going against the light,
He hits enveloping darkness.

Fathoming 5: Against the bright, against the light
Means: This is what others turn against.

Appraisal 5, corresponding to the Son of Heaven, is ruler of the tetragram. The arrogant leader refuses to take good advice from his supporters, for he believes himself sufficiently enlightened. It will not be long before others rebel against him.

Appraisal 6: From the dark going to the light,
    Reluctant to dazzle and charm.

Fathoming 6: The dim light of day
    Means: The center is not blinded by light.

Meeting with a benighted age, the noble person hides her light, since the world is not used to such brilliance.

Appraisal 7: Dimming the good,
    They bring to light what they abhor.

Fathoming 7: Evil in obscuring the good
    Means: Their unenlightened state is all too clear.

Appraisal 7 reflects the failure of will to do good. The individual's evil propensities grow increasingly obvious over time.

Appraisal 8: Dusk is a time that benefits the moon.
    A small good omen, but too soon for stars.

Fathoming 8: That dusk favors the moon
    Means: Still there is something to be hoped for.

As we near the end of the cycle, the dim light of dusk sets the stage for the moon. Sometime soon, the stars will come out. There is reason for hope, but we must be patient for now. Although the dark age would profit most from the great light provided by the sage, a lesser light can still do some good.

Appraisal 9: Drawn-out sighs at the time
    Do not secure the good.
    The male breaks a hairpin.
    The wife changes her luck.

Fathoming 9: Not capturing their good
    Means: The husband dies, his wife sighs.

Death is the extreme case of dimness and insensibility. When a husband dies, his hairpins are broken to signify that he will no longer be using them. His widow changes her hair ornaments to don mourning, showing that her luck has changed for the worse. (By a pun, "luck" and "hair ornaments" are read interchangeably in the fourth line of the Appraisal.)

Ch'iung
No. 69. Exhaustion
October 24–October 28 (a.m.)

Correlates with Human's Mystery;
Yang; *the phase Water; and the* I
ching *Hexagram no. 47, Hemmed
in; the sun enters the Heart
constellation, 2d degree*

HEAD: Yin *ch'i* fills the eaves as yang loses its place. The myriad things are exhausted and agitated.

The tetragram title can describe a variety of situations where the individual faces a symbolic or actual dead-end, including the absolute exhaustion of physical powers and utter impoverishment. Not surprisingly, the tetragram, like its correlate *Changes* hexagram, is generally inauspicious in tone, with gloomy predictions of "perplexity," "distrust," "losing one's way," physical dangers, and psychic discomforts. However, the same character may be given the more positive meaning of "reaching the culmination." To reach moral perfection is the aim of the would-be sage; nobility of character, in turn, insures that ultimate victory can be snatched from temporary defeat. As the *Changes* tells us, only the noble person "is capable of being in straits without losing the power to succeed" (W, 624) because in times of crisis she is prompted to undertake a thoroughgoing reform. Consequently, the virtuous individual not only survives present difficulties, but even prospers as soon as the times turn more favorable.

The Head text contains an internal pun: the myriad things are not only agitated and exhausted because they have lost their master, yang *ch'i*, they have also "run out of places" where they can hide. The Appraisal texts focus on examples of those who have no haven to which they can escape. Occasionally, even meritorious individuals find themselves caught up in wider cycles of inauspicious fate.

>   Appraisal 1: He sees his limits as limits,
>   So people embrace him as center.

>   Fathoming 1: Recognizing his own limits
>   Means: Emotions dwell at the center.

The first lines of the Appraisal and Fathoming talk literally of "seeing his extremity as extremity." One interpretation for the lines (reflected in this translation) presumes that the truly superior human being exerts all his charismatic powers to attract, then utilize talented supporters, who regard him as "center."

Two other interpretations for the same lines are equally possible, however, given such a wide range of meaning for the word "extremity." In one alternative, the noble man "sees the limits of his desperate straits." The moral superior faces present calamity with perfect equanimity, in part because no misfortune exists that can deter a truly determined would-be sage from achieving moral perfection. As the *Analects* says, "The superior man can withstand extreme hardships. It is only the small man who, when submitted to them, is swept off his feet" (A 15/2). Once the individual approaches the perfection of the sage, he then employs suasive example to rouse others to redirect their attention to the core values that constitute the Good in Confucian tradition.

In yet another reading, the person of virtue "pushes to extremes his own limits" so that he daily improves in virtue. Eventually, having realized the full human potential for sagehood, he becomes a much beloved model for the common people.

> Appraisal 2: Failing to see his limits as limits,
> The people come to reject him as center.

> Fathoming 2: Unaware of his limits
> Means: Deceit can be made to flourish.

This verse is the mirror opposite of the preceding one. As with Appraisal 1, there are three possible readings: (1) the evil individual fails to seek guidance since he does not recognize his own limits; (2) the weak person's good intentions are jettisoned in the face of calamity; and (3) the petty person fails to push his potential for humanity to its natural limits. The result of any one of these three failures is the same: the people will "reject him as center."

> Appraisal 3: However desperate, his thoughts apprehend.

> Fathoming 3: Apprehension in desperate straits
> Means: A tutor resides in the heart.

"Apprehending" for proponents of the Confucian school refers to "apprehending the [Confucian] Way," while true "desperation" is measured in terms of distance from the Way. When a superior person faces a crisis, the inner resources of the heart/mind will see him through. Such resources have been developed by a prior intensive study of various classical precedents, rather than by exhaustive analytical thinking.

> Appraisal 4: The soil is not sweet.
> Trees wither and lose their leaves.

Fathoming 4: A disharmonious earth
Means: Affliction extends to the common people.

When the earth, symbol of all that nourishes, fails to support luxuriant growth, the common people find themselves without sufficient food to eat. Soon famine and its attendant diseases appear. Wise leaders work hard to remedy this situation, for "if the common people have not enough for their needs, the ruler cannot expect to have enough for his needs" (A 12/9).

Appraisal 5: The stew has no ricecakes.
Her belly rumbles *k'an-k'an*,
Empty as a drum,
Yet she does not lose her model.

Fathoming 5: Cooked dishes without rice
Mean: Even so, she does not lose the Right.

Appraisal 5 as the ruler of the tetragram depicts the perfect model of upright behavior in poverty. This individual is so poor that she cannot afford to supplement her meager stew of greens with nourishing grains. Nevertheless, she manages to perfectly embody the ancient models of proper behavior. In this she is like Yen Hui, the favorite disciple of Confucius, of whom the Master remarked:

> Incomparable indeed was Hui. A handful of rice to eat, a gourdful of
> water to drink, living in a mean street—others would have found it
> unendurably depressing, but to Hui's cheerfulness it made no difference
> at all! . . . Hui was capable of occupying his whole mind for three
> months on end with no thought but that of Goodness (A 6/9, 6/5).

Appraisal 6: The mountains have no game.
The rivers boast no fish.
Troubles attack the person.

Fathoming 6: Mountains without beasts
Mean: Trouble to the common people.

In early Chinese tradition, the products of the mountains and rivers are reserved for the common people, who use them to supplement their meager diets and incomes. Evil rulers often claimed these areas as their own property, causing a severe reduction in the people's standard of living. Under such conditions, "While some men can get enough to eat / Few men can eat their fill."

It is also possible that the common people have wrecklessly misused available natural resources; on their own initiative, they have burnt the hillsides to flush out all the game and drained the lakes to catch all the fish.

Despite the magnitude of the initial catch, such wasteful exploitation of limited resources destroys all future food sources.

> Appraisal 7: Though he straightens his step,
> He lands in prison.
> In three years, he sees a pardon.

> Fathoming 7: Righting his foot
> Means: The danger gets him peace.

Appraisal 7 ordinarily represents the loss of one's ambition, but here it corresponds to lucky Day. The subject of the poem modifies his conduct in accordance with the Right. Though he is thrown into prison, his case will be reviewed and he will be pardoned sooner or later. The superior man calmly awaits better times, knowing that ultimately he will be vindicated.

> Appraisal 8: He trudges through frost and snow,
> With his neck bound to his knees.

> Fathoming 8: Bound neck to knee
> Means: After all, life is not worth living.

Frost and snow symbolize danger of every sort since they are difficult to negotiate in the best of times. Now this person, bound neck to knee, faces additional impediments. Even if he survives this ordeal, the pain will be so great that life will hardly be worth living.

> Appraisal 9: Jade circlets are smashed and tablets broken.
> In mortar and stove, frogs breed.
> Calamities from Heaven are loaded on.

> Fathoming 9: Circlets and tablets, broken and smashed,
> Mean: Chance does not favor him.

The circlet and tablet of jade are signs of enfeoffment bestowed upon rulers. Wanton destruction of these insignia suggests a violent breach in the contractual relations binding superior and inferior. As political upheaval plunges all into chaos, entire communities are laid waste, despite the best efforts of some. With the population decimated, the unused mortars and stoves are inhabited by frogs.

Ke

No. 70. Severance

October 28 (p.m.)–November 1

Correlates with Human's Mystery;
Yin; *the phase Fire; and the* I
ching *Hexagram no. 23, Splitting
Apart; the sun enters the Tail
constellation, 2d degree*

HEAD: Yin *ch'i* cuts away at things. Yang's form is hung and killed. In seven days, it will nearly be severed.

This tetragram, like the corresponding hexagram in the *Changes*, equates utter ruin with severed relations: "Splitting apart means ruin" (W, 501). In the phenomenal world, yin and yang *ch'i* are openly antagonistic. With some forty-nine (7 x 7) days left until the winter solstice, when yang *ch'i* will seem to expire under the power of yin, the utter extinction of yang seems a real possibility. After all, the destruction of Hun-t'un, symbol of the primeval chaos, is said to have required only seven days. But however bloodthirsty yin's action may appear, it ultimately (and paradoxically) provokes a stronger yang *ch'i*. Those of true understanding recognize "the alternation of increase and decrease" as "the course of Heaven" (W, 501). They therefore look to patch up serious breaches and estrangements. One good way is for superiors "to give generously to those below," as the *Changes* (W, 501) suggests.

> Appraisal 1: Cutting off his ears and eyes
>   Affects his mind and belly.
>   Danger.

> Fathoming 1: Cutting off ears and eyes
>   Means: The center has no outlet.

The ears and eyes supply the inner organs with perceptual evidence, thereby insuring the proper functioning and protection of the center. The individual who is deaf and blind (either literally or metaphorically) finds it difficult to sustain the self, let alone prosper. Danger lies ahead.

This lesson may be applied to affairs at court. Since the ruler seldom leaves the confines of his palace, he depends upon others to gather information for him. Loyal advisors are likened to the ruler's ears and eyes. Should the ruler punish those who tell him the true state of affairs, he will have destroyed the one tool with which he can correct current policy. In consequence, his throne is endangered.

> Appraisal 2: Cutting off his warts and wens
>   Helps to make him incorrupt.

Fathoming 2: Cutting off warts and tumors
Means: What is loathesome does not grow big.

Warts and tumors symbolize corrupt deeds prompted by greed. When illness pollutes the body, the only hope of a cure may lie in lancing the infected areas. Although hardly pleasant, the benefit of such decisive action is evident: the flesh is no longer plagued by festering corruption. By analogy, the wise individual heals himself by swiftly excising all impurities. The ruler, for his part, expels evil officials from court.

Appraisal 3: Cutting the nose to feed the mouth,
He loses what lets him breathe.

Fathoming 3: Cutting the nose and losing the Master
Means: The loss brings no glory.

In great stupidity, this individual feeds one organ (in Chinese, one Master) to another, forgetting that both are needed if the body is to prosper. Considering the lack of meat on the nose, the act is particularly absurd. Important lessons may be drawn from this. Perhaps the "nose" (i.e., a loyal advisor who smells out trouble) is sacrificed to the unprincipled leader. Or perhaps those above are hurt in order to feed those below.

Appraisal 4: The butcher hacks meat in even pieces.

Fathoming 4: The butcher's even hacking
Means: Perfection can exist.

The good butcher easily hacks the meat evenly off the bones. In this he is like the chief minister, whose job it is to fairly apportion government positions among suitable candidates, or the parent who must apportion the family's goods among several children. Confucius remarked of such weighty tasks, "I do not fear that there are few [resources], but I do fear unjust distribution" (A 16/9).

Appraisal 5: Cutting off his thighs and arms,
He loses the use of his horses in shafts.

Fathoming 5: Cutting off his thighs and arms
Means: Gone are the great officials.

Thigh and forearm symbolize the ruler's chief ministers; "horses in shafts" probably stand for the common people. The poem tells us that the Son of Heaven cannot hope to extend his influence throughout the realm if he severs good relations with his chief ministers. No longer will the leader "ride high" above his subordinates.

Appraisal 6: Though he cuts it, there is no wound.
It satisfies all on all four sides.

Fathoming 6: Cutting without harm
Means: The Way can be divided.

With most entities, a cut or division necessarily entails a wound. The case of the Way, however, is startlingly different. One can apportion courtesy and care to all, without fear of the supply ever running out. Paradoxically, the more generous the gift, the more the giver receives.

Appraisal 7: Violet rainbows, carnelian clouds
Like friends cluster around the sun.
His affliction is not excised.

Fathoming 7: Violet rainbows and carnelian clouds
Mean: He does not know to cut them.

Spectacular rainbows and brightly colored clouds, for all their apparent beauty, lead the eye away from the sun. If brilliant but cunning advisors surround the leader, they may try to compete with him for attention or prevent his light from reaching the common people. Relations with such advisors should be severed immediately.

Appraisal 8: Cutting out the borers,
He gets at our heart's disease.

Fathoming 8: Cutting out the parasites
Means: This is good for the state.

The parasite or borer stands for individuals whose beliefs and actions undermine the healthy state. When the state is rid of such parasites, it will flourish once again.

Appraisal 9: Cutting the flesh to get at the bones,
The crown is drowned in blood.

Fathoming 9: To cut the flesh and drown in blood
Means: He is unable to keep himself whole.

The final Appraisal depicts the harm that comes from too much deep cutting. As muscle and blood vessels are severed, loss of blood and its attendant risk of infection make death almost certain. Applied to the state, the metaphor suggests that the ruler's cruel exploitation of his subjects will end in his own death.

止　　▦

Chih

No. 71. Stoppage

November 2–November 6 (a.m.)

Correlates with Human's Mystery; Yang; the phase Wood; and the I ching *Hexagram no. 52, Resisting; the sun enters the Tail constellation, 6th degree*

HEAD: Yin, enlarged, stops things above, and yang for its part stops things below. Above and below, together they stop everything.

The Winter Onset solar period begins with the last Appraisal of this tetragram. A seventeenth-century commentator describes cosmic trends in this way:

> At this time, the Frostfall solar period is already past. Hibernating insects all hunker down. The magpies have entered the oceans to become oysters. Whatever fat there is in things has turned to yin; with the shrinking and splitting already complete, there is no way [for yin *ch'i*] to requisition more. Therefore, yin quits its tyrannical and bullying rule above, and temporarily stops to calculate [the situation]. Yang likewise stops below in fear of yin's awesome majesty, afraid of its [yin's] destructive action. Therefore, it [yang] hides its shadow in the *Mystery* Palace [far below the earth's surface,] not daring to come out again, hoping in this way to avoid further paring of its resources.

In essence, yin and yang are cut off from each other, although good fortune depends upon their successful interaction. The myriad things as a result are "each stopped in their tracks, so that they do not proceed"; obstructed by yin's growth above, they would retreat to yang below. The *Changes* characterizes human relations in much the same language:

> Those above and below are in opposition and have nothing in common. . . . The superior man does not permit his thoughts to go beyond his situation (W, 652–4).

With both cosmos and society on the verge of an absolute split, the wise person focuses his or her entire attention upon present dangers and "knows when to stop" taking the initiative. Not surprisingly, both this tetragram and its correspondent hexagram tend to focus on the negative aspects of stoppage.

Appraisal 1: Stopping at the stopping place,
There is inner light and no blame.

Fathoming 1: Stopping at the right place
Means: Wisdom enough for enlightenment.

Appraisal 1 corresponds to Water in the cycle of the Five Phases. The cultivated mind, undistracted by inappropriate or excessive desires, reflects Virtue with the same degree of accuracy as a still pool of water. As the *Great Learning* teaches us,

> Know when to stop and then you can be quiescent. Be quiescent and
> then you can be at peace. Be at peace and then you can think. Think and
> then you can achieve everything.

Appraisal 2: Braking the cart, he waits
    For the horse to come to a halt.

Fathoming 2: The carriage braked, he waits.
    Meaning: He cannot use it to go forward.

Appraisal 2 corresponds to the middle stage of the thought process and to the status of the ordinary person. When external constraints are applied, all movement slowly grinds to a halt. Someone with half-baked plans or insufficient wisdom finds himself unable to proceed. For the moment, it is best to focus on self-cultivation and self-restraint. Later opportunities may arise.

Appraisal 3: Closing his gates and doors,
    By this he stops *ku* madness.

Fathoming 3: Closing his gates and doors
    Means: He prevents what is not right.

Ku indicates a variety of virulent poisons associated with sexual indulgence and black magic. The pictograph shows three insects, worms, or reptiles in a bowl, a possible reference to the standard recipe for concocting the poison: Leave several poisonous insects or reptiles in a covered jar until one has devoured all the others, then extract the concentrated poison of the survivor. It is wise to close the mind to all dangerous thoughts, delusions, and heterodox arguments, which poison the perceptions. Lewd and superstitious men should also be shunned.

Appraisal 4: They stop at saplings
    To seek their luxuriant fruits.

Fathoming 4: Stopping by young trees
    Means: Theirs is a fruitless search.

Appraisal 4 marks the initial transition from Thought to Action. However, some prematurely search for perfection and completion. Should further cultivation of the tree (i.e., the heart/mind) be discontinued, the tree may never bear fruit upon maturity; by analogy, the petty man rushes toward an ambitious goal, such as high office, before he is ready.

Figure 17. Ku *poison being expelled by an exorcist from a victim.*

Appraisal 5: Pillars keep the house in place.
Canopies shield the carriage.
Hubs balance the space between.

Fathoming 5: Pillars, canopies, and hub
Mean: Honor the center above all else.

Human civilization depends upon a number of inventions that exemplify the twin principles of "not moving" (i.e., stability) and centrality. The pillars, positioned at regular intervals, bear the weight of the home. The canopy, if properly centered, shelters the entire carriage from the elements. Finally, the hub keeps the spokes and axles in place while the wheels move. By analogy, the good ruler knows enough to promote stability with centrality. He steadies the state like a pillar; he shelters the common people like a canopy; he functions as the hub of his kingdom. He alone has the ability to coordinate his subjects' activities so that their efforts converge productively.

> Appraisal 6: Square wheels and angular axles
> Make for bumpy rides in the cart.

> Fathoming 6: Square wheels and bumpy roads
> Mean: At every turn, he jolts himself.

The early Chinese believed that the sages of old invented certain fundamental tools like carts and roads to facilitate the development of human civilization. That such tools are wrongly fashioned now means that their most basic functions, let alone their divine origins in cosmic patterns, are no longer understood. Just like the ill-made cart lurching along, society muddles along uncomfortably and without stability. Smooth progress in the Way becomes impossible.

> Appraisal 7: When the cart has its wheels tied on,
> And the horse wears out its hooves,
> To stop is good.

> Fathoming 7: The cart tied and the horse tired
> Means: To proceed can be difficult.

Normally, Appraisal 7, although aligned with Defeat, is lucky in an odd-numbered tetragram because it is aligned with auspicious Day. Here, however, the cart is worse than useless. Either it is in such poor repair that its wheels have to be tied on or else its wheels are "tied up" (i.e., clogged) by debris and mud from the road or tangled ropes. Compounding the difficulty, the cart is drawn by an old nag whose hooves have worn thin. The wise person, recognizing the nature of the problem, stops to make major repairs.

> Appraisal 8: Good bows return; so do the bad.
> Good mounts are headstrong; so are the bad.
> Snap the bowstring, smash the cart,
> For this will never stop.

> Fathoming 8: Bows that return and headstrong horses
> Mean: In the end, they are unusable.

The bow and horse symbolize human developed capacities, since a long course of training precedes skilled use of these tools. Even after training, the tools may prove unusable under certain circumstances. For example, the best wooden bow, because of its sensitivity to moisture and heat, may lose its proper tension. Similarly, a spirited horse may at times seem too unruly.

Clearly, poorly made bows and unbroken horses are even less usable. To employ bad tools even temporarily may end in disaster. By analogy, a person's temper must be fully tested if another is to make proper use of her.

Appraisal 9: Broken on a tree stump,
　　　　　　And snagged on knife-sharp stones,
　　　　　　It stops.

Fathoming 9: Broken on trees, snagged on stones
　　　　　　Means: This is where the noble man stops.

As successive calamities befall the journey, the noble man, recognizing the hopelessness of his situation, "knows enough to stop."

Chien
No. 72. Hardness
November 6 (p.m.)–November 10

Correlates with Human's Mystery; Yin; the phase Metal; and the I ching *Hexagram no. 52, Keeping Still; the sun enters the Tail constellation, 10th degree*

HEAD: Yin's form is covered with callouses while yang loses its main function. Things compete in hardening themselves.

The assignment of this tetragram to the patron phase Metal probably accounts for the tetragram's title. With yin building a tough outer casing, yang grows correspondingly weaker until it loses the "main thread" of its existence, its propensity for nurturing. In imitation of yin *ch'i*, the myriad things begin to compete with each other for scarce resources under winter's harsh conditions. In the human realm, as in the natural world of Heaven-and-Earth, both advantages and disadvantages may accrue from this tendency to hardness. A staunch defense of the Good, of course, is commendable, but stubbornness in pursuit of lesser goals is likely to lead to failure.

Appraisal 1: The massive stones so hard inside
　　　　　　Do not change for the good.

Fathoming 1: That massive stones are hard inside
　　　　　　Means: They cannot be transformed.

Appraisal 1 corresponds to the Beginning of Thought. An obdurate massive stone symbolizes a stubborn inability to rethink decisions before embarking upon a disastrous course of action. As Confucius remarked, "It is only the very . . . stupidest who do not change" (A 17/3).

Appraisal 2: Firm and white, the jade form
　　Changes inside for the better.

Fathoming 2: Firm and white, the jade form
　　Means: Changes are rightly made.

In this Appraisal assigned to the Middle of Thought Yang Hsiung clearly refers to a *Changes* passage depicting the heart/mind of the noble person as "firm, fixed, and pure white like beautiful jade" (W, 69). However fine the basic stuff of humanity, it can always be improved, like jade, through polishing. Firmness, then, must be offset by mutability if self-cultivation is to occur.

Appraisal 3: Firmness is not pervasive.
　　Something leaks at its center.

Fathoming 3: Firmness not pervasive
　　Means: It cannot maintain uniformity.

Typically, the petty person has both good and evil impulses. While she may initiate a good act, she lacks the inner strength to carry it through to completion. As thought yields to action, the reader is reminded of the hazards of inconsistency and weakness.

Appraisal 4: Small bees, busy busy,
　　Swarm at their hive
　　To make it firm not big.

Fathoming 4: Small bees, busy busy,
　　Mean: The bees secure their base.

As in Western culture, in China bees symbolize productive community. The base of the hive stands for virtue; its chamber, for the state. Just as worker bees follow the direction of the queen, hard-working members of the community manage to build a firm basis for productive life after their leaders help them realize an important lesson: true security does not depend upon the size of the community but upon its dedication to a common purpose in the Good.

Appraisal 5: The hive is big, the swarm is small,
　　And so it hangs empty.

Fathoming 5: A big hive and a small swarm
　　Mean: The state is empty and hollow.

Appraisal 5 is the ruler of the tetragram; hence, its reference to politics. The bad leader, preoccupied with aggrandizing his position and enlarging his territory, neglects to build up his "base" in virtue. As a result, there are few reliable allies in his inner circle. Soon the empire collapses.

Appraisal 6: The swarm is fine, so fine,
  Suspended over the Nine Provinces.

Fathoming 6: The tiny swarm suspended
  Means: The people are thus at peace.

The wise beekeeper, knowing that bees are docile just after the swarm alights, picks that time to handle them. By analogy, the charismatic individual chooses the right time to effect change so as to retain his followers' allegiance. In this way, his influence is greatly extended.

Appraisal 7: A hardhead smacks into a hill.

Fathoming 7: A hard head pitted against the hill
  Means: He knows not where he's going.

The bullheaded individual who fails to ascertain the proper moral course runs headlong into disaster. Ironically, his very strength of purpose proves to be his ultimate undoing. Blind to the fact that he could easily circumvent many obstacles simply by changing direction, he stubbornly persists in error until it destroys him.

Appraisal 8: Confident and firm in calamity,
  He uses only the *hsieh-chih*'s signs.

Fathoming 8: Secure and strong in calamity
  Means: He uses the straight path.

In Chinese myth, the *hsieh-chih* resembles an ox with one horn. Legend credits it with an uncanny ability to distinguish right from wrong. Therefore, in ancient legal trials it was purportedly employed to determine guilty parties. After the good person uses his conscience and the Classics to determine the Right, he never wavers in his pursuit of it, even in the midst of calamity. Such steadfast service to the Good contrasts favorably with the bullheadedness depicted in Appraisal 7.

Appraisal 9: The bees burning their hive
  Bring ruin to their forebears.

Fathoming 9: Bees burning their hive
  Means: What they relied on is ruined.

Here, at the end of the cycle, supremely arrogant individuals destroy their own community. While the *Changes* likens this to "birds burning their own nest" (W, 219), the *Mystery* compares it to bees burning their own hive. All that has been built over generations is now lost in the general conflagration.

Ch'eng
No. 73. Completion
November 11–November 15 (a.m.)

Correlates with Human's Mystery;
Yang; *the phase Water; and the* I
ching *Hexagram no. 63, After
Completion; the sun enters the Tail
constellation, 15th degree*

HEAD: Yin *ch'i* is pure right now. Yang is stored in the numinous earth.
Things, being rescued, complete their forms.

At this point in the calendar, the warming trends associated with yang *ch'i*
seem to have completely disappeared in the face of fearsome wintry blasts
propelled by waxing yin *ch'i*. Yang now takes refuge far below the surface
of the earth; therefore, its power cannot be completely extinguished by its
opponent. From this underground region it provides enough of the life-
giving impulse to rescue the myriad things from extinction. The tetragram
title, Completion, then, refers to several related phenomena: the utter deso-
lation brought about in the world of Heaven-and-Earth by the complete
separation of yin from yang, the imminent closure of the cycle of eighty-one
tetragrams, and the closing days of human struggle.

> Appraisal 1: Completion seems obstructed.
> Its use, though unending, is hidden.

> Fathoming 1: Completion seemingly obstructed
> Means: This is why it remains undefeated.

The cosmic Tao never draws attention to its cyclic operations, yet nothing remains undone. By analogy, the superior person never parades her
talents and virtues. None credit her with effecting major changes. To some,
her achievements even seem modest. As the *Lao tzu* writes, "Great completion seems deficient" (ch. 45). In this way, the noble person avoids any
situation where she might inspire envy or fear. Thanks to her inherent modesty, she is never harmed.

> Appraisal 2: Tenuous achievements and constant change:
> Before it is done, he grows lax.

> Fathoming 2: Minor achievements, continual change,
> Mean: He cannot keep up with himself.

Repeated change tends to bewilder lesser mortals. For this reason, the
Classics consistently describe the ancient sage-kings' preference for subtle

adjustments, incremental change, and natural inducements to reform. The *Changes* writes, for example, that the sages

> brought continuity to their changes, so that the people did not grow weary. . . . [Only] when one change had run its course did they effect another (W, 331).

Here an individual who claims to be bent on self-improvement finds himself growing weary before his goals and habits have been revised. Far better is the steady, if gradual progress of one whose commitment to Goodness is unflagging.

> Appraisal 3: He completes the leap by drawing back.
> Completing the flight, he is not caught.

> Fathoming 3: Completing the leap by drawing back
> Means: Strength in completing virtue.

In Yang's schema, Appraisal 3 correlates with advancement. The wise person realizes the advantages of restraint before setting out to pursue his goals. He curbs arrogant impulses; he denies excessive desires. Paradoxically, such a person makes tremendous progress precisely because of this "drawing back"; having never pursued wealth or fame, it follows him relentlessly. As the old proverb has it, "Contract the foot before you leap. Fold in the wings before you fly."

> Appraisal 4: On the verge of completion,
> He boasts and so is defeated.

> Fathoming 4: Bragging when nearly done
> Means: Achieving the Way is impaired.

The stupid individual brags about his accomplishments prematurely. By his own words, he is undone.

> Appraisal 5: If his center is complete,
> He alone oversees all.
> Such is greatness.

> Fathoming 5: Singular oversight by a center complete
> Means: He can take the center position.

Position 5 is the ruler of the tetragram. Yang Hsiung borrows the notion of strategic advantage to express a profoundly Confucian message about leadership. The ideal leader completes himself at center as daily self-examination of the conscience leads to moral perfection. The force of his charismatic virtue then makes him center of the entire community.

> Appraisal 6: In completion, so conceited and mean is he
> That completion only garners calamity.

> Fathoming 6: Arrogance in completing
> Means: He fails to employ modesty.

Appraisal 6, past the halfway point of the tetragram, is also paired with inauspicious Night. Overweening arrogance coupled with high position spell ruin for the individual.

> Appraisal 7: Perfection marred, he repairs.

> Fathoming 7: Repairing defects
> Means: Surely it is hard to carry on.

Position 7 corresponding to loss here is aligned with auspicious Day. When major achievements have been sullied by flaws and faults, the superior individual works hard to correct them, lest they continue.

> Appraisal 8: The time is perfect but he is not.
> Heaven rains down no good omens.

> Fathoming 8: Imperfection at the perfect time
> Means: He fails to hit it on his own.

Here, near the end of the cycle, someone fails to avail himself of the opportunity for improvements in society and self. Heaven then rains calamity down upon the unrighteous.

> Appraisal 9: With completion, exhaustion
> Enters defeat, destruction complete.
> The noble man does not complete.

> Fathoming 9: In completing, exhausted and destroyed
> Means: The noble man by this achieves his ends.

Due to the cyclical nature of things, completion ultimately entails defeat. Knowing this, the wise person thinks of his virtue always as incomplete and chooses goals that are not final. Through daily self-renewal and persistent rededication to higher goals, he achieves the good life and a good death.

Chih

No. 74. Closure

November 15 (p.m.)–November 19

Correlates with Human's Mystery; Yin; the phase Fire; and the I ching *Hexagram no. 21, Biting Through; the sun enters the Winnower constellation, 1st degree*

HEAD: As contact between yin and yang falters, each closes in on itself so that it becomes a single entity. Their ill fortune causes the myriad things to weep.

The tetragram title shows "a door tightly shut," a perfect symbol of contact that has been completely "blocked off." As yin flourishes, yang declines. With this reversal of their conventional values, yin and yang falter in their new roles, finally retreating into separate spheres. This radical separation means ruin for the myriad things, whose continued existence depends upon their union, as Tetragram 16, entitled Contact, shows us.

Appraisal 1: Round peg and square socket:
　　Inside is a bad fit.

Fathoming 1: Circle and square, peg and socket
　　Mean: Inside, they miss each other.

These lines give a classic example of a lack of correspondence: the round peg in a square hole. Since Appraisal 1 is assigned to the Beginning of Thought, it is appropriate to contemplate the thought processes, viewed as successive attempts to fit external events into their proper categorical slots. Obviously, the heart/mind fails to function here. This failure in turn precludes the possibility of true human community based on shared moral perceptions.

Appraisal 2: Close with no intervening gap.

Fathoming 2: To be close with no gap
　　Means: The two are as one.

Sageliness depends upon perfectly matching external events with internal moral categories. Right thinking, then, is a kind of psychic union on which true union among men is based. The power of such unions is suggested by the *Changes*, which says,

When two persons are of one heart
They are sharp enough to cut metal.
(W, 306)

Appraisal 3: The dragon steals into another's lair.
  Its light is then lost to the house.

Fathoming 3: The dragon slipping into the wrong cave
  Means: It fails in its constant rules.

Yang *ch'i* (aligned with the dragon, the east, and spring) retreats below ground, although the dragon generally prefers its natural habitat in high mountain peaks wreathed in rain clouds. Even the marvelous dragon can only flourish in the proper environment. Should it steal into the wrong type of cave, it not only endangers itself but also deprives its dependents of its beneficent power. By analogy, the promising individual who accepts an unsuitable position risks disgrace to herself and harm to the community. Since Appraisal 3 corresponds to "Advance," Yang Hsiung's warning is timely.

Appraisal 4: To immerse the nose in fragrant fats
  Is good for beauty and propriety.

Fathoming 4: The propriety of immersing the nose
  Means: He sinks in what is fragrant.

Because fatty meats, fragrant from cooking, nourish our bodies, the correspondent hexagram gives as a good omen "sinking our teeth in tender meat 'til the nose disappears" (W, 492). The good person also exudes a fragrance (a noble "reputation") that sustains while dulling the craving for less savory things. As thought turns to action with Appraisal 4, we should consider how best to immerse ourselves in the model of the sages.

Appraisal 5: Gnawing bones, he breaks his teeth—
  Enough to fill a crock.

Fathoming 5: Gnawing bones and breaking teeth
  Mean: He greatly covets profit.

With Appraisal 5 the ruler of the tetragram, the petty person in high position is willing to inflict any sort of violence upon others in his ruthless pursuit of profit. In this, he is like the rapacious diner who chews even the bones, lest the smallest morsel escape him. Before long, the evil consequences of unrestrained greed become evident. Harm inflicted upon others through greed soon comes back to haunt us; it is like "biting through dried meat to get poison" (W, 88). Broken teeth "fill the crock"; this may prefigure his funerary urn.

Appraisal 6: Lapping up sweat
  To gain its glossy smoothness.

Fathoming 6: Lapping up sweat, slurp slurp,
Means: The Way is worth being relished.

By the sweat of one's brow one secures great good fortune. Oddly enough, profuse sweating after hard work does not unduly tire the person, but instead lubricates the joints, massaging them with precious oils. In this way, sustained effort devoted to the Good ultimately provides refreshment and relief.

Appraisal 7: Despite the breach, forcing a fit:
What's joined at first later splits.

Fathoming 7: Forcing their faults together
Means: Their union falls apart.

When the panels of a traditional Chinese gate are unevenly hung, the gate will not shut tight unless the panels are forced into place every time. Sooner or later, that forcing will ruin the panels. By analogy, defects in a union, initially glossed over, will resurface, causing an irreparable break.

Appraisal 8: He repairs the breaks,
And covers the flaws.
Such a person is dazzling and strong.

Fathoming 8: Repairing breaks and covering flaws
Means: He is still capable of improvement.

So long as the individual dedicates himself to the task of self-cultivation, even at Appraisal 8 it is not too late to reform. The verses also work as a description of the faithful friend who encourages improvement.

Appraisal 9: As yin and yang start to transform,
They change to red and white.

Fathoming 9: Yin turning red as yang turns white
Means: Reaching their limits, they then reverse.

Although the exact significance of this color change is lost to us, the verses probably use an apparent contradiction in the traditional correlations of color magic to suggest an unhealthy disjunction in conventional values. In China, the color white is always used for mourning while the red of the newborn babe is a sign of health and virility. In the same system that correlates winter and *yin* with snowy white, summer is associated with red, with heat, and with yang *ch'i*. Accordingly, as summer yields to winter, red pales to white; as winter reigns supreme, what is fundamentally white glows with ruddy health. With normal values reversed, a new cycle is about to begin. Still such dramatic disjunctions and metamorphoses are inherently dangerous. The wise person takes warning.

Correlates with Human's Mystery;
Yang; *the phase Wood; and the* I
ching *Hexagram no. 28, Great
Error; the sun enters the Winnower
constellation, 6th degree; the
Dipper points NNW; the musical
note is B*

Shih
No. 75. Failure
November 20–November 24 (a.m.)

HEAD: Yin on a grand scale acts like a bandit. Yang cannot gain anything. Things sink into the unfathomable.

With this tetragram we move past the Onset of Winter solar period into full winter, when yang can no longer hope to resist the repeated onslaughts of yin *ch'i*. In this unequal struggle between yin and yang, the myriad things will suffer greatly until greater balance in the cycle is restored. In human life, the suffering occasioned by the internal struggle between good and evil can be mitigated by a return to balance and the reform of one's conduct.

> Appraisal 1: Stabbing at the Void,
> Plunging in the blade.

> Fathoming 1: Stabbing the Void, sinking the blade
> Means: Deeply he ponders his own first signs.

In this Appraisal aligned with the Beginning of Thought, the void refers to the mind. The good person examines her innermost thoughts in order to destroy even the first signs of evil.

> Appraisal 2: Paltry virtue breeds small failures.

> Fathoming 2: Failures from paltry virtue
> Mean: He knows too little to fear first signs.

Appraisal 2, aligned with low position, coincides here with inauspicious Night. The petty person thinks his own paltry virtue sufficient for success. Persisting in his errors, he never acquires sufficient power to realize his goals. Minor errors multiply into major disasters.

> Appraisal 3: Persistent and compliant,
> Anxious and attentive,
> In his heart, he advances.

> Fathoming 3: Persistent and compliant
> Means: He is able to reform himself.

Appraisal 3, correlated with advancement, describes the best attitude for those who intend to progress: each individual must persist in complying with the dictates of the conscience.

> Appraisal 4: Trusting his faults, he does not eat,
> So, like the sun, he sinks from sight.

> Fathoming 4: Trusting faults and unemployed
> Means: He forfeits salary due upright men.

Position 4 corresponds to high officials or the aristocracy. Due to misplaced trust in himself or others, someone of high rank fails, losing rank and salary ("He does not eat.").

> Appraisal 5: The yellow-haired and gap-toothed
> Take to protecting the center.
> By them, the noble man is cleansed of faults.

> Fathoming 5: The aged taking center
> Means: Faults are thereby cleansed.

The leader as center of the community is assisted in his reforms by aged advisors who exemplify wisdom and experience (the "yellow-haired and gap-toothed").

> Appraisal 6: Filling his granary but neglecting his fields,
> He eats their fruits without tending their roots.

> Fathoming 6: A full granary but neglected fields
> Means: He is unable to cultivate the base.

Appraisal 6, past the midpoint of the tetragram, is also paired with inauspicious Night. The petty person, who only considers present benefits, makes no provision for the future. In his short-sightedness, he ignores the root of all happiness, virtue in community.

> Appraisal 7: Sick men as a rule take medicine
> While the shamans pour libations.

> Fathoming 7: Medicine for the sick, libations for shamans,
> Mean: Calamity can be turned around.

Although Appraisal 7 describes loss, here it corresponds to auspicious Day. Plagued by physical or moral impairment, this individual applies every known cure in an attempt to improve. Such persistence is rewarded by a return to good health.

Appraisal 8: The hen cries at dawn.
  The female sports a horn
  And fish inhabit trees.

Fathoming 8: The hen calling at dawn
  Means: What is right for them is reversed.

The constant laws of the phenomenal world have been overturned. Erratic behavior in the animal world reflects disorder in the realm of Man. The crowing of a hen, for example, portends subversion of the family.

Appraisal 9: With days and months passing,
  He changes at death's door.

Fathoming 9: Changing at death's door
  Means: He is still not too far away.

Although the individual does not reform until he is at death's door, he still is accounted a virtuous person.

Correlates with Human's Mystery; Yin; the phase Metal; and the I ching Hexagram no. 28, Great Error; the sun enters the Winnower constellation, 11th degree

Chü
No. 76. Aggravation
November 24 (p.m.)–November 28

HEAD: Yin, coming to an end, weeps copiously that in yang it lacks a great partner. Such is the aggravation of parting.

Even as yin's sway comes to a virtual end, yang is still bereft of power. With no clear force in charge, the cosmic order verges on chaos; hence, the tetragram title, which conveys a sense of "aggravation," "scarcity," "extremity," and "intensity."

Appraisal 1: Bones bind his flesh.
  Darkness within.

Fathoming 1: Bones binding his flesh
  Mean: The thief within is at work.

Typically, bones support the flesh that binds the bones together. Here, the dramatic reversal of their usual roles suggests the degree to which internal problems affect external situations.

Appraisal 2: An eclipse with flowing blood
Is both bad omen and good.

Fathoming 2: An eclipse with blood flowing
Means: The noble man inside sees harm.

The word "eclipse" comes from the Greek for "abandonment," which captures the sense of foreboding felt by many at the sun's vanishing. Like other ancient peoples, the early Chinese feared that the sun or moon would ultimately be devoured by total darkness during an eclipse. In some lunar eclipses, the moon turns blood-red. Here blood appears to pour forth, compounding the inauspicious character of the event. Such a dire omen can only portend the most dramatic of evils. Still, the noble person, recognizing the fearful implications of the eclipse, promptly resolves upon reform. In that way, a bad omen can indeed inspire a change for the better. Good and wise leaders even long for such signs. According to popular tradition, when disasters and prodigies ceased to appear in the Ch'u state, wise King Chuang (r. 836–826 B.C.) was far from delighted. "Am I not doomed?" he asked his courtiers. Thinking that an angry Heaven had abandoned all attempts to warn him against error, King Chuang responded with an ambitious program of reform.

Appraisal 3: Wine makes for loss of virtue.
Ghosts spy upon his house.

Fathoming 3: Wine causing virtue's loss
Means: He cannot take charge of himself.

The Chinese Classics condemn intoxication, attributing to it a loss of virtue in the people and their leaders; although wine was invented to bring men together in ritual acts, drunken misconduct easily breaks communities apart. That ghosts are present suggests both the befuddled minds of drunken fools and the imminent character of the calamity.

Appraisal 4: Eating in times of scarcity:
Parents are urged to take second helpings.
Such is compliant behavior.

Fathoming 4: Compliant though food is scarce
Means: He takes a salary so that he may comply.

Appraisal 4 usually refers to the bureaucracy. The superior man, mindful of his obligation to support his parents in their old age, accepts a less-than-ideal position so that his parents may eat their fill even in times of relative scarcity.

> Appraisal 5: Out into the wilds,
>> He surveys the ruins.
>> A tiger there is herding pigs.
>> He hoists his pantlegs to his jacket.

> Fathoming 5: In the wilds, seeing ruin
>> Means: No place is left to set his foot.

Unfortunately, Position 5 as ruler of the tetragram here is aligned with inauspicious Night. The moral superior witnesses total disorder. A rapacious elite (the tiger) takes charge of defenseless commoners (the pigs). Knowing that there is no place for an honest leader, the good man hikes up his clothes in order to quickly flee the scene.

> Appraisal 6: The Four States prosper.
>> He is their home.

> Fathoming 6: That the States fill his realm
>> Means: They seek a safe home.

In all four directions, the states look to the charismatic leader to protect them. They seek a just state; once they have found one, they feel themselves secure.

> Appraisal 7: How vigorous! how prosperous!
>> Yet he carries the face of calamity.

> Fathoming 7: Vigorous and flourishing
>> Means: He wears clear marks of calamity.

The inner decay (moral or physical) of one in high position or in the prime of life is first betrayed by a facial expression. Although superficially healthy, the petty person is liable to calamity as the cycle approaches its extreme position. As the *Lao tzu* writes, even "the hard and strong" can become "comrades of death" (ch. 76).

> Appraisal 8: A flask secured by a well-rope
>> Is a good omen and fine.

> Fathoming 8: Securing the flask
>> Means: His duties are pressing.

The water flask is secured by a strong rope, so the benefits of fresh, clean water (a symbol for the purifying heart/mind) are readily available without fear of loss. The flask stands for the noble person, who is useful to the extent that he is restrained by the model of the ancients.

Appraisal 9: Like the sea, flocks flying
Cover over Heaven's Barge.

Fathoming 9: Flocks flooding the sky
Mean: The end is unspeakably bad.

At the climax of the cycle, flocks of birds seem to flood the sky, obscuring the usual brilliance of Heaven's Barge (the Chinese name for the Milky Way). As one commentator writes, "This is an image of rain." That inferiors (the rain) hide the light of the greater (the Milky Way) portends ultimate calamity, with subordinates usurping the place of their superiors.

Surely the poem also alludes to the famous legend about the annual renunion on the seventh day of the seventh lunar month of the Oxherd and Weaver, two star-crossed divinities who leave their homes in the Vega and Altair constellations to meet on a bridge of magpies in the clear light of the autumn sky. Since the Milky Way is intimately connected with the rivers, seas, and lakes of earth below, this image may portend great floods as well.

馴　☷

Hsün
No. 77. Compliance
November 29–December 3 (a.m.)

*Correlates with Human's Mystery;
Yang; the phase Earth; and the I
ching Hexagram no. 2, The
Receptive; the sun enters the
Dipper constellation, 3d degree*

HEAD: Yin *ch'i* greatly conforms. Undifferentiated like the primeval chaos and infinite in scope, there are none who see its root.

Yin *ch'i*, nearing the end of its dominant phase, returns to primeval chaos. Since it lacks all boundaries and distinguishing features (in contrast to yang *ch'i*, which is characterized by edges and sharp definition), yin *ch'i*'s hidden source cannot be located with any certainty. Nevertheless, yin has the power to envelop all things in its womb. Concerned less with heroic acts than with the repetitive aspects of the cycle, especially birth and death, yin *ch'i* is largely invisible even as it labors, however essential it is to life itself. At this time, humans are urged to imitate yin *ch'i* by adopting such virtues as devotion, the capacity to nurture, modesty and forebearance, compliance, and receptivity, which are said to "bring sublime success, furthering through perseverance" (W, 386). According to the *Changes*,

Taking the lead brings confusion, because one loses his Way. Following with devotion—thus does one attain a permanent place (W, 388).

Quiet compliance with the rules of society and the laws of nature tends to produce good fortune, so the wise person chooses not to advertise her own merit. In imitation of pure yin and Earth, she works instead to bring others' achievement to completion. In keeping with such prescriptions, this tetragram advocates the slow accumulation of good acts that exemplify devotion to the Way.

> Appraisal 1: Yellow, the spirit of Earth,
>   Is profound. A good omen.
>   Such is compliance.

> Fathoming 1: Yellow, numinous, profound, and true
>   Means: Through compliance it corrects.

Black and yellow in combination often refer to the complementary powers of Heaven and Earth or of yang and yin respectively, as in Tetragram 1. Here, however, the poem talks only of yellow and what is profound (or dark). Yellow probably signifies the propensity of the heart/mind, the human center, to follow the Mean and respond with fairness and receptivity, while "profound" may symbolize the good person's innate modesty. The attainment of such virtues invests the individual with quasi-divine powers.

> Appraisal 2: Bearing the child is the work of women.
>   If she is not still, it will not live.

> Fathoming 2: A miscarriage
>   Means: She could not keep pure and still.

In traditional China, the woman's primary responsibility was to bear male children to continue her husband's ancestral line, so it was her solemn duty to keep herself from physical harm while pregnant. Ideally, she also exposed herself to positive influences, such as soothing music and proper reading matter, so that the embryo might be educated in the womb. Unfortunately, the mother in Appraisal 2 exposes herself to mental or physical disturbances. The results are predictably awful. This metaphor, of course, applies to any project that is "stillborn" due to its promoters' reckless behavior.

> Appraisal 3: True women give constant care
>   And so protect their roots.

> Fathoming 3: True women give constant care.
>   Meaning: They do not forget the base.

Appraisal 3 is aligned with Wood, whose characteristic virtue is all-encompassing benevolence. A mother's ability to nurture her dependents selflessly is a strong force worth imitating. By practicing this virtue, males can easily secure the psychological base of individual, family, or state.

Appraisal 4: Though boasting of his deeds,
He is less heroic than Earth.

Fathoming 4: Boasting of his deeds
Means: He brags of good acts.

Earth fosters all the myriad things without requiring gratitude in return. Similarly, the true gentleman cares for lesser mortals without insisting that they acknowledge his superiority. In contrast, the petty man seeks to draw attention to his merits. Therein lies his downfall.

Appraisal 5: The spirit sack holds all in its embrace,
Its virtue is as precious as gold.

Fathoming 5: The great embrace of the cosmic sack
Means: It does not dare aggrandize itself.

Appraisal 5 as ruler of the tetragram outlines the ideal behavior for the effective leader. By receptivity toward others' suggestions, rather than by coercion, the good leader induces his followers to contribute their talents to his government. Ultimately, he knows that to govern effectively he must have at his command all the ideas of many supporters, so that his own thinking comes to resemble a sack filled with marvelous possibilities. Only then will he have become a sage.

Appraisal 6: The sack fails to hold,
Leaking the precious tools.

Fathoming 6: A sack losing its hold
Means: The subjects' mouths spill forth.

The basic virtue attributed to yin, Earth, and woman is silent devotion. But here Appraisal 6, past the midpoint of the tetragram, is paired with inauspicious Night, making an evil omen. Petty men in subordinate positions cannot be trusted to remain loyal to their master. (This, of course, may well be due to the inadequacies of their leader.) Rumor and advice are offered to rival powers; for "words are the steps that lead to disorder" (W, 307).

Appraisal 7: To be square and firm in opposing compliance
Helps the subordinate prove his mettle.

Fathoming 7: Square and firm in opposing compliance
Means: He preserves correct principles.

When a superior commits herself to some wrong course, his loyal follower bravely points out the error of his ways. The good subordinate is willing to risk his superior's anger, lest important principles be abandoned. Since the wise leader values this outspokenness, she encourages her advisor's independence.

> Appraisal 8: Compliant, he defies the Right.
> He fails to protect its Decree.

> Fathoming 8: Complying with what is wrong
> Means: He lacks the means to unite with the One.

Compliance with the rules of conduct laid down by the sage-kings of antiquity in conformity with Heaven can unify the hearts of men. To acquiesce in what is evil ultimately weakens community and undercuts the Way.

> Appraisal 9: Complying with duty, he forgets life,
> Relying instead on Heaven's good omen.

> Fathoming 9: Complying with duty and forgetting life
> Means: Receipt of the Decree is certain.

The verse plays upon various associations for the word "Decree," including "life" (given by one's parents), "fate" (sent by Heaven), and political "appointment" (mandated by the ruler). Taken together, these three decrees largely determine individual destiny. In recognition of the heavy debt owed to those who have given him physical and social life, the moral superior willingly performs all the duties associated with these decrees, even at the cost of his own life. In return, he may expect a reward, perhaps immortal fame or illustrious descendants.

Chiang
No. 78. On the Verge
December 3 (p.m.)–December 7

Correlates with Human's Mystery; Yin; the phase Water; and the I ching Hexagram no. 64, Not Yet Complete; the sun enters the Dipper constellation, 9th degree

HEAD: Yin *ch'i* completes things to the upper regions. Yang, extending, is about to return to begin them at the lower regions.

Momentous changes are about to occur in the phenomenal world. Yin *ch'i*, which has nearly effected the completion of the myriad things, will soon depart. Yang is about to return to its initial position at the beginning of the cycle. Renewal ultimately stems from such reversals, but given the potential danger inherent in times of transition, the noble man takes particular care to persevere in the course of moderation.

> Appraisal 1: Almost off on a deviant course:
> Initial danger.

> Fathoming 1: About to embark on evil
> Means: Peril predominates.

In this Appraisal corresponding to the Beginning of Thought, the individual is about to set off on a mistaken course that ultimately will endanger him.

> Appraisal 2: Almost without a blemish:
> Initial purity.

> Fathoming 2: Almost without blemish
> Means: Ease is what succeeds.

Here the individual in low position has nearly purified himself of faults. This facilitates later success.

> Appraisal 3: With furnace and wheel not right,
> It would be good to stop.

> Fathoming 3: That furnace and potter's wheel are wrong
> Means: To transform the inside would be harmful.

In early China the furnace and the potter's wheel signify the cosmological processes whereby undifferentiated stuff is fashioned into the fully articulated phenomena of Heaven-Earth-Man. Applied to creative thinking, they suggest the thought processes by which raw sensory information is fitted into proper legal, social, and ethical categories. Here, however, fundamental flaws in the basic tools lead to the misuse of creativity. Like a good workman, the man of virtue must be careful to keep his tools (including his advisors and reasoning methods) in proper working order if he hopes to build upon the model of the sages.

> Appraisal 4: About to fly, he gets his wings,
> Which help in rising to Heaven.

> Fathoming 4: Prepared to fly on new-got wings
> Means: Their support is strong.

Like a fledgling that has only just discovered the use of its newly grown feathers, the good person on the road to advancement finds just how useful good advisors can be. Without such support, all attempts to "fly high" may prove futile.

> Appraisal 5: The great sparrow, about to fly,
>   Plucks out its shaft feathers.
>   Despite a wealth of down, it cannot proceed.

> Fathoming 5: Great sparrows plucking shafts
>   Mean: There is not enough to rely upon.

Appraisal 5 as the ruler of the tetragram describes the leader through a popular pun: "great sparrow" also means "great emoluments" (and by implication, high rank). If one of high rank offends his strongest allies (the "shaft feathers"), he may find it impossible to continue despite the broad support of many (the "down").

> Appraisal 6: The sun slips down in all its glory.
>   The noble man will soon decline and fall.

> Fathoming 6: That the blazing sun slips down
>   Means: Self-generated light is great.

Position 6 is past the halfway point of the tetragram. The sun, still blazing with afternoon heat, begins its decline. The sun stands for the superior individual, especially the ruler, whose charismatic light is shed on lesser mortals. But in what limited sense can the noble man be said to be on the verge of decline? Three answers are possible. In the first reading, the superior man, recognizing death's inevitability, works hard to enlighten others before his own light is extinguished; in the second, he nobly declines a post in acknowledgment of his failing powers; and in the third, he condescends (i.e., "goes down") to meet with inferiors, like the setting sun.

> Appraisal 7: Hurrying the boat or rocking the cart,
>   Harmful effects are not far away.

> Fathoming 7: Hurried boat and rocked cart
>   Mean: He is not far from harm.

Boats and carts are two of the many tools invented by the sages to enhance human existence. As with all human inventions, their proper use implies a certain trade-off. Cart and boat are unwieldy, yet they carry great loads over long distances. Improper use destroys the advantages of such tools.

> Appraisal 8: A small child in a deep abyss:
>   The adult men take out their boats.

Fathoming 8: Adults out in boats
Mean: They would save a drowning age.

A young child who has ventured too far out into deep water will surely drown unless rescued. Luckily, wise adults know how to employ the tools at hand to save him. By analogy, the worthy leader intent upon saving the common people in a benighted age must use the proper tools (for example, study of the Confucian Classics, ritual conformity, and good government).

Appraisal 9: Red silkworms cling to dry mulberries.
Their cocoons will not turn golden yellow.

Fathoming 9: Not yellow on account of the dry
Means: The silkworms' work is ruined.

Silkworms turn red when they are old or diseased. The silkworms' problem is compounded because they have attached themselves to dry and leafless branches. (Since this is Appraisal 9, perhaps it is too late in the season for mulberry leaves?) Such a scant diet cannot produce healthy cocoons of average weight and value, let alone the highly prized, silky golden threads used in ritual. Similarly, the potential for human productivity is ruined when bad timing or misdirected activity is combined with the wrong environment.

難 ≡≡

Nan
No. 79. Difficulties
December 8–December 12 (a.m.)

Correlates with Human's Mystery;
Yang; the phase Fire; and the I
ching Hexagram no. 39, Difficulty
Walking; the sun enters the Dipper
constellation, 13th degree

HEAD: Yin *ch'i* makes difficulties on all sides. Water freezes, the earth cracks. Yang drowns in the abyss.

At the end of the calendar year, marked by the Great Snow solar period, the myriad things keenly feel the cruelty of wintry yin *ch'i* as it culminates. Yang *ch'i,* buried deep below the earth's surface in the watery netherworld, is so quiet that it seems dead, even though it will not be long before yang *ch'i* begins to reassert itself. After all, return or reversal is the movement of the Tao.

Appraisal 1: Troubled am I in deep, dark places.

Fathoming 1: That I am troubled in deep, dark places
Means: Its form is not yet seen.

At the Beginning of Thought, the inner self, mired in doubt and confusion, struggles to reach the true light of understanding before its benighted ideas "take form" in action. In this it imitates yang *ch'i* in winter, struggling to escape its confinement below earth.

> Appraisal 2: As solid ice thaws to slush,
> The crazed horse misses the whip.

> Fathoming 2: A crazed horse missing the switch
> Means: A reckless disregard for life.

Avoiding his master's whip, the crazed horse decides to escape across the frozen river. However, the ice has just begun to melt; as soon as the attempt is made, the horse will plunge headlong into the water to its death. Alternately, the man himself walks across a melting river of ice because he is unable to discipline his horse. Miscalculation combined with heedlessness brings disaster, not freedom.

> Appraisal 3: A center firm and fixed
> Troubles the "inconstant."

> Fathoming 3: A center firmly fixed
> Means: Finally, none are overturned.

Once again, the center refers to the individual's heart/mind, the seat of both the emotions and the intellect. So long as the *hsin* is firmly fixed upon the Good, the person has no difficulty repudiating evil impulses for the "inconstant" (i.e., what is contrary to Heaven's norms).

> Appraisal 4: When the egg breaks against a stone,
> The undeveloped dies.

> Fathoming 4: Rotting embryos from broken eggs
> Mean: The difficulties of the petty man.

The egg represents perfect potential. In the case of humans, this applies to the development of the innate capacity for Goodness. Two readings then follow. In the first, the petty man in the face of difficulties breaks as easily as an eggshell against a stone. In a second reading, the petty man is like a stone and the good person is like an egg. Out of power, the virtuous individual cannot survive the vicious slander leveled by opponents.

> Appraisal 5: No gap between troubles:
> No matter how great, he will not succumb.

> Fathoming 5: Troubles find no gap
> Mean: At center all is tightly blocked.

In both Appraisal and Fathoming, the first line is ambiguous. Either difficulties come in rapid succession with no gap (i.e., interval) separating them, or personal trials leave the individual largely unaffected, since no gap exists in an integrated self to allow evil an *entrée*. As the ruler of the tetragram, Appraisal 5 reminds us that troubles cannot really defeat whoever rules by the conscience, no matter how many calamities come to plague this Job-like figure.

Appraisal 6: The great carriage lumbers on.
Above, it is blocked by mountains.
Below, it runs into rivers.

Fathoming 6: The great carriage lumbering on
Means: Above and below, brakes are applied.

Appraisal 6, which is just past the midpoint of the tetragram, is paired here with inauspicious Night so that it portends ill. The individual who shoulders heavy burdens, like a great cart, meets with repeated delays and numerous obstacles. Just as the size of the conveyance may prove an added encumbrance, high rank or status may make it more difficult for the individual to maneuver.

Appraisal 7: Extracting stones is difficult.
His strength fades, still he persists.

Fathoming 7: Wresting stones free
Means: He takes advantage of the time.

Appraisal 7 corresponding to loss is here aligned with auspicious Day. Clearing a field of stones is tough work even when the stones are smooth. But the individual who intends to persevere in his task will find it much easier if he waits until rain or a thaw has softened the ground. Such are the benefits of acting at the right time. (Compare this message with Appraisal 4 of Tetragram 3.)

Appraisal 8: Crashing against stones, snapping trees in two,
He merely breaks his horn.

Fathoming 8: Stone-crashing and tree-snapping
Mean: This is no way to rule.

To overcome obstacles, this individual uses brute strength rather than calculating intelligence coupled with charismatic virtue. Naturally, he is bound to fail.

Appraisal 9: Leading the *hsieh-chih* to use its horns
Offenders are finally set straight.

Fathoming 9: Making the *hsieh-chih* butt
Means: By this in the end he straightens them.

When the true identity of an offender is unknown, Heaven may help right-thinking men to ascertain the criminal. While the marvelous *hsieh-chih* only appeared in the courts of the sage-kings of antiquity (see Tetragram 72), in the modern age there exist equally infallible guides to conduct, including the Classics of Confucianism and the rituals sanctified by tradition.

Correlates with Human's Mystery; Yin; the phase Wood; and the I ching Hexagram no. 39, Difficulty Walking; the sun enters the Dipper constellation, 18th degree

Ch'in

No. 80. Laboring
December 12 (p.m.)–December 16

HEAD: Yin freezes firm as it is terrified of being wounded on the outside. Tenuous yang lodges in darkness, exerting its strength on the inside.

Yin has already rendered itself immobile, now that the myriad things are frozen. Being immobile, it is particularly vulnerable to attack. Meanwhile, we detect the first hints of yang's latent strength gathering its force in the secret recesses of the Earth. We are nearly now at the winter solstice, the point at which yang will start to wax and yin to wane.

Appraisal 1: Diligence of mind
Obstructs propriety.

Fathoming 1: Diligent but wrong
Means: The center is not upright.

At the Beginning of Thought, the heart/mind is set upon wrongdoing. Under such circumstances, the mind's very diligence is all the more frightening.

Appraisal 2: Laboring from a sense of duty,
And tireless in his diligence,
The noble man has his center.

Fathoming 2: Laboring out of obligation
Means: Diligence rests in emotion.

By definition, the individual "has a [moral] center" once he acknowledges his obligations to a nested hierarchy of social relations, extending from parents to mentors to patrons to the state. Through ritual conduct, which expresses his love and respect for those who have helped him, the individual becomes fully human.

> Appraisal 3: Babes with "bridles" and "horns"
> Insistently weep *ku-ku*
> If unsupported by swaddling.

> Fathoming 3: Babies with "bridles" and "horns"
> Mean: They will not get to live.

"Bridles" and "horns" are the names of the characteristic hairstyles once given female and male babies in imperial China; baby girls sported two small braids (or bridles) while the boys' hair was dressed in a single pony-tail worn at the top, called the "horn." Newborns bawl incessantly until they are wrapped securely in swaddling clothes. Just as a child cannot survive to adulthood without the loving care of parents, our fragile conscience can only develop under the watchful eye of moral superiors.

> Appraisal 4: Diligent in exerting his strength,
> Doubling his efforts, he forgets to eat.
> The great man has this ability.

> Fathoming 4: In diligent labor, forgetting to eat
> Means: Such is the virtue of great men.

In tetragrams assigned to the end of the lunar year, the individual is often instructed to persevere in good conduct, even in the face of calamity. Here the good person redoubles his efforts so that nothing can stop his reforms. One early text describes the sage Confucius in comparable language:

> This is the character of the man: so intent upon enlightening the eager
> that he forgets his hunger, and so happy in doing so, that he forgets the
> bitterness of his lot, and fails to realize that old age is at hand (A 7/19).

> Appraisal 5: Going forth, he stumbles and stumbles.
> Ill fortune is near and good far away.

> Fathoming 5: That he stumbles in going forth
> Means: He keeps his distance from good fortune.

As ruler of the tetragram, these lines describe the individual who is prevented from achieving his goal by repeated missteps. Had he made suffi-cient preparations to advance, he could have proceeded with confidence.

> Appraisal 6: With labor comes success
> Nearly up to Heaven.

Fathoming 6: Success through labor
Means: This is the help that Heaven grants.

Heaven helps the superior individual who has cultivated her original endowment to such an extent that her virtue nearly equals that of Heaven.

Appraisal 7: Working hard to drag it along,
If not by the nose, then by the tail,
He wearies.

Fathoming 7: The weary work of leading
Means: His way is contrary.

The stupid oxherd leads his draft animal either by a rope strung from the animal's nostrils or by its tail. Due to its discomfort, the ox, increasingly angry, resists all efforts to be led. The oxherd fails to reach his goal, then, not because his strength is insufficient, but because he lacks the requisite skill and empathy. The way he has chosen is contrary to both reason and convention.

Appraisal 8: He labors at a breakneck pace,
With a heart at ease.
Crashing through thickets, he does not retreat.

Fathoming 8: Working diligently
Means: He sacrifices himself for the state.

The individual foregoes some comfort, perhaps even sacrifices his life, in service to the state. This description recalls that of the sage-ruler Yü, who is said to have spent eight years selflessly working for the common people of the Central Kingdoms at the time of the primordial great flood. According to Yang Hsiung, the true gentleman is one who "loves what is good for others, but forgets what is in his own interest."

Appraisal 9: So diligent, so diligent!
Holding the cart, he enters deep pools.
Bearing the boat, he climbs up mountains.

Fathoming 9: How diligent, how diligent!
Means: Such hard work brings no gain.

Without some basic understanding of the tools of civilization, the individual cannot hope to gain success through diligence. Misguided labors only end in utter weariness as Appraisal 9 depicts the height of folly.

養

Yang
No. 81. Fostering
December 17–December 21 (a.m.)

*Correlates with Human's Mystery;
Yang; the phase Metal; and the* I
ching *Hexagram no. 27, Providing
Nourishment; the sun enters the
Dipper constellation, 22d degree*

HEAD: Yin, like a bow stretched taut, bulges out to the farthest reaches.
Yang bathes the myriad things [in its energizing solution], turning them red
in the nether regions.

Together, Heaven and Earth provide physical nourishment for all the myriad
things, endowing them with life. As the winter solstice approaches, yang
ch'i from its unseen base below begins to imbue the roots of all the myriad
things with renewed vitality, signified by the color red. On this model, the
truly good person provides spiritual refreshment for lesser mortals. When in
high position, he takes particular pleasure in sustaining worthies while providing for the physical needs of all. Sustenance and support sought in the
wrong places, however, only increase the likelihood of danger.

> Appraisal 1: Store the heart in a deep pool
> To improve its marvelous roots.

> Fathoming 1: Storing the heart in a deep pool
> Means: Divinity is not outside.

The first Appraisal is aligned with the Water phase, which may have
prompted the reference to a pool of infinite depth. The pool signifies the
unmoved mind of infinite capacity, which accurately reflects reality when
functioning properly. Also, appropriate action in later Appraisals must draw
upon depths of knowledge and moral courage. The noble person nurtures
such divine aspects within (the "roots" of Goodness), rather than looking
outside for good luck.

> Appraisal 2: Silently he fosters perversion,
> Harboring impropriety at the start.

> Fathoming 2: In silence promoting evil
> Means: The center heart is defeated.

In an obvious contrast to Appraisal 1, Appraisal 2 depicts the wicked
propensities of those who fail to nourish the roots of Goodness inherent in
human nature. Even before taking action (when still silent), the inborn conscience is silenced.

Appraisal 3: Fertilizer to enrich the hill
　Nourishes its roots and stems.

Fathoming 3: Fertilizing the hill
　Means: At center, the glory is great.

The center, of course, refers to the human heart/mind, the seat of both
the emotions and the intellect. Just as the growth of vegetation depends
upon repeated applications of fertilizer, full human development relies upon
continued exposure to the nurturing qualities of ritual. Otherwise, the fragile
human propensity for Goodness is soon stunted.

Appraisal 4: Swallows feeding everywhere
　For they intend to steal.
　This is good for seizing business.

Fathoming 4: Swallows feeding here and there
　Mean: The will is fixed on gain.

The swallows swoop down to feed. Despite their insatiable appetites,
they appear to have no fixed goal. In this, they are like greedy individuals
who fail to pursue a single good with sufficient dedication, adopting the
philosophy that "more is better." Or they are like crass merchants who care
less for community than for their own profits.

Appraisal 5: With a heart of gold in the belly,
　Even old white bones grow flesh.
　Virtue fostered is not overturned.

Fathoming 5: A golden heart in the belly
　Means: The highest virtue is heavenly.

The heart is golden yellow because it keeps to the Mean; yellow, after
all, is the color of the center. The virtue correlated with the center is
good faith, without which true community falters. Here, the virtue that
fosters sustains the individual until she experiences renewed life (in the
metaphor, dry bones growing flesh) and a fundamental kinship with the
cosmic norms.

Appraisal 6: In quick succession, in a single day,
　　Three blood sacrifices, auguries from sacred oxen.
　Fattened animals bring no benefit.

Fathoming 6: Repeated sacrifices
　Mean: Fat is of no benefit to the self.

According to Yang's system of correlations, Appraisal 6 corresponds to the ancestral temple; hence, the references to sacrifices and Heaven-sent omens. Blood sacrifices associated with heterodox cults are offered repeatedly, which suggests the uneasy state of mind experienced by superstitious petitioners to the gods. The claims of cult leaders are at best presumptuous and at worst a lie. Frequent contact with the gods is itself a mistake: scarce human resources are wasted and the experience of the sacred is cheapened. For these reasons, the offering designed to please the gods, the fattened ox, does not augur well. It would be better to follow the ritual precepts strictly.

> Appraisal 7: A small boy leads an elephant
> A woman ropes a fierce beast.
> Noble men care for the afflicted.

> Fathoming 7: Leading an elephant, caring for the sick
> Means: They have no intrinsic connection.

The small boy symbolizes what is weakest; the woman, what is most gentle. Because of these attributes, these two people are clearly unfit for their dangerous jobs. In this they are like the petty man who does not measure his strength or who is unfit for his responsibilities. In such cases, it is always left to the superior to solve the ensuing problems.

In one interpretation the small boy is compared to nascent yang *ch'i*, which subtly leads the myriad things to fulfillment. In that case, the woman must signify "old yin," which still relies on force. The noble person chooses neither extreme, but flexibly and appropriately responds to each situation.

> Appraisal 8: The fishbone is not dislodged.
> Its poisonous illness spreads.
> Ghosts rise up on the tomb.

> Fathoming 8: An outbreak of illness from fishbones
> Means: He returns to the grave mound.

If the fishbone is not quickly dislodged from the throat, life-giving breath cannot reach the vital organs. Illness and death follow, with death envisioned as a return (*kuei*) to a ghostly (*kuei*) state. Ironically, the subject of this verse only intended to nourish himself.

> Appraisal 9: Like the fixed stars, like the Year,
> Return and continue at the start.

> Fathoming 9: The stars and the Year Star
> Mean: At the end, they foster beginnings.

In the final text of the final tetragram at the end of the lunar year, we have come full circle. Yang Hsiung reminds us of the constant cycles that rule our lives, especially the impressive revolving patterns of the night sky. Just like the heavenly bodies, which keep to their orbits, renewal ultimately depends upon our willingness to adhere to cosmic norms.

* * * *

To provide for a leap year, Yang supplied two additional intercalary lines, which together account for three-fourths of an additional day.

ODD (Or, "DEFICIT")
> Freezing ice ascends Red Heaven,
> Swelt'ring heat enters the Mystery Springs.

Fathoming 1: The freeze mounting Red Heaven
Means: Yin makes a beginning.

Red Heaven refers to the point where yang is maximized, presumably in the highest heavens; Mystery Spring, to yin maximized in the deepest recesses of the earth. Freezing cold and blazing heat represent yin and yang respectively in their essential forms. Yin and yang alternate as they describe their cyclical path through the course of the year.

EVEN (Or, "SURPLUS")
> That one is empty and one overfull
> Is a state produced by unevenness.

> Uneven, uneven for empty and full
> Means: There is succession without an end.

As the days pass one by one, time marches inexorably on in an infinite succession of separate days. The annual discrepancy between the solar and the lunar calendars appears to account for the regular alternation between surplus and deficiency in a world ruled fundamentally by constant norms. If all distinctions were leveled, change would become impossible.

Autocommentaries of the *Mystery*

POLAR OPPOSITIONS OF THE MYSTERY
Hsüan ch'ung

[This section is comparable to the "Sequence of the Hexagrams" (Hsü Kua) section of the Changes *Ten Wings.]*

> If it is Center (no. 1), then yang begins.
> If it is Response (no. 41), then yin is born.

> With Full Circle (no. 2), a return to virtue.
> With Going to Meet (no. 42), a counterturn toward punishment.

> With Mired (no. 3), great woe.
> With Encounters (no. 43), small desire.

> With Barrier (no. 4), isolation, but
> With Stove (no. 44), neighbors.

> Keeping Small (no. 5) means the minute [first signs].
> Greatness (no. 45) means battening.

> With Contrariety (no. 6), internal contradiction.
> Enlargement (no. 46) means external opposition.

> With Ascent (no. 7), coming up against plainness.
> With Pattern (no. 47), increasing artifice.

> Opposition (no. 8) means recklessness.
> Ritual (no. 48) means "squareness" [the correspondence between word and deed].

> If it is Branching Out (no. 9), it comes, but
> If it is Flight (no. 49), it flees.

With Defectiveness (no. 10), selfishness and crookedness.
With Vastness (no. 50), fairmindedness and desirelessness.

Divergence (no. 11) means mistakes, but
Constancy (no. 51) is good.

With Youthfulness (no. 12), to have little, but
With Measure (no. 52), to have no lack.

With Increase (no. 13), the beginning of florescence, but
With Eternal (no. 53), what lasts to the very end.

With Penetration (no. 14), "grasping the One," but
With Unity (no. 54), the Grand Accord.

With Reach (no. 15), daily increasing its kind.
With Diminishment (no. 55), daily depleting its type.

Contact (no. 16) means mutual compliance.
Closed Mouth (no. 56) means no contact.

With Holding Back (no. 17), to have fears.
Guardedness (no. 57) means to be impregnable.

As to Waiting (no. 18), it exits.
As to Closing in (no. 58), it enters.

Following (no. 19) means dispersing, but
Massing (no. 59) means assembling.

With Advance (no. 20), many plans.
With Accumulation (no. 60), much wealth.

Release (no. 21) means a push forward.
Embellishment (no. 61) means a decline.

What Resistance (no. 22) approves is right while
What Doubt (no. 62) abhors is wrong.

With Ease (no. 23), a leveling, but
With Watch (no. 63), a collapse.

With Joy (no. 24), raising high, but
With Sinking (no. 64), hiding below.

Contention (no. 25) means the *shih* are impartial.
Inner (no. 65) means the women are partial.

If it is Endeavor (no. 26), then joy, but
If it is Departure (no. 66), then sorrow.

Polar Oppositions of the Mystery

With Duties (no. 27), esteem for activity.
With Darkening (no. 67), esteem for rest.

With Change (no. 28), with alterations and sharing smiles.
With Dimming (no. 68), over a long time, increasing troubles.

With Decisiveness (no. 29), numerous affairs, but
With Exhaustion (no. 69), not a single happiness.

With Bold Resolution (no. 30), daring, but
With Severance (no. 70), weakening.

With Packing (no. 31), a move home, but
With Stoppage (no. 71), a failure to proceed.

With Legion (no. 32), gentle softness, but
With Hardness (no. 72), cold firmness.

With Closeness (no. 33), no possible gap, but
With Completion (no. 73), no possible change.

With Kinship (no. 34), drawing close to goodness, but
With Closure (no. 74), closing out feelings of obligation.

As to Gathering (no. 35), it is success.
With Failure (no. 75), loss of fortune.

With Strength (no. 36), untiring good.
With Aggravation (no. 76), unending evil.

Purity (no. 37) means the Way of the ruler.
Compliance (no. 77) means the subjects' preservation.

Fullness (no. 38) means the prime of life, but
On the Verge (no. 78) means old age.

With Residence (no. 39), attaining to rank, but
With Difficulties (no. 79), meeting with demotion.

Law (no. 40) means to facilitate union with All-under-Heaven.
Laboring (no. 80) means to lack achievement despite strenuous efforts.

Fostering (no. 81) receives all the rest.

> The noble man fosters good luck.
> That means the petty man fosters ill.

INTERPLAY OF OPPOSITES IN THE MYSTERY
Hsüan ts'o

*[This section is comparable to the "Interplay of Opposites" (*Tsa kua *section of the* Changes Ten Wings.*]*

> With Center (no. 1), it begins.
> With Full Circle (no. 2), it wheels back.
>
> With Defectiveness (no. 10), the crooked.
> With Bold Resolution (no. 30), the straight.
>
> The ways of Purity (no. 37) and Pattern (no. 47):
> Some are simple and some are complex.
>
> As to Strength (no. 36), it is the solidly built.
> As to Waiting (no. 18), it is the weak.
>
> As to Accumulation (no. 60), it is the many, but
> As to Keeping Small (no. 5), it is the few.
>
> As to Watch (no. 63), it is the apparent.
> As to Darkening (no. 67), it is the indistinct.
>
> With Youthfulness (no. 12), having no knowledge, but
> With Fullness (no. 38), having a surplus.
>
> With Departure (no. 66), leaving the old, but
> With On the Verge (no. 78), coming to a new start.
>
> As to Greatness (no. 45), it is the outside, but
> As to Closing In (no. 58), it is the inside.
>
> As to Branching Out (no. 9), it is the advance.
> As to Holding Back, it is the retreat.
>
> With Joy (no. 24), calm and composure.
> With Laboring (no. 80), hustle and bustle.
>
> With Reach (no. 15), thoughts that comprehend.
> With Exhaustion (no. 69), thoughts that confound.
>
> With Opposition (no. 8), at court, but
> With Inner (no. 65), on the [sleeping] mat.
>
> With Divergence (no. 11), self-loathing.
> With Embellishment (no. 61), self-love.
>
> With Resistance (no. 22), intolerance, but
> With Unity (no. 54), magnanimity.

With Increase (no. 13), daily additions, but
With Diminishment (no. 55), daily reductions.

With Compliance (no. 77), orders upheld, but
With Contrariety (no. 6), mutual opposition.

As to Release (no. 21), it is softness, but
As to Hardness (no. 72), it is leathery toughness.

With Ease (no. 23), the level and smooth, but
With Difficulties (no. 79), the going up and down.

With Decisiveness (no. 29), many decisions, but
With Doubt (no. 62), some hesitation.

With Flight (no. 49), there is what one avoids.
With Contention (no. 25), there is what one hastens toward.

With Advance (no. 20), the desire to proceed.
With Stoppage (no. 71), the desire for constraints.

With Enlargement (no. 46), no bounds.
With Endeavor (no. 26), no duplicity.

As to Response (no. 41), it is the present, but
As to Measure (no. 52), it is the past.

With Going to Meet (no. 42), one knows what preceded.
With Eternity (no. 53), one sees the later issue.

As to Following (no. 19), it is dragged along.
As to Guardedness (no. 57), it is secured.

With Mired (no. 3), plucked out from calamity.
With Aggravation (no. 76), lacking any pardons.

With Vastness (no. 50), the infinitely great, but
With Barrier (no. 4), the buried and blocked.

With Change (no. 28), creating the new.
With Constancy (no. 51), cleaving to the old.

With Failure (no. 75), great loss.
With Gathering (no. 35), small gain.

With Stove (no. 44), love of profit.
With Law (no. 40), abhorrence of the cruel.

As to Ritual (no. 48), it is the capital, but
As to Residence (no. 39), it is the home.

With Massing (no. 59), affairs emptying.
With Legion (no. 32), affairs filling.

As to Closure (no. 74), both are shut off, but
As to Closeness (no. 33), all use the One.

With Ascent (no. 7), high ambitions.
With Sinking (no. 64), low ambitions.

With Contact (no. 16), many friends.
With Closed Mouth (no. 56), few allies.

With Penetration (no. 14), a sharp advance.
With Dimming (no. 68), an impeded walk.

With Kinship (no. 34), attachment between [even] distant relatives.
With Severance (no. 70), offense to one's own flesh and blood.

With Encounters (no. 43), coming upon difficulties.
With Packing (no. 31), awaiting the proper time.

With Duties (no. 27), to exhaust oneself.
With Fostering (no. 81), to increase oneself.

As to Resistance (no. 22), it is contradiction, but
As to Unity (no. 54), it is conforming.

With Increase (no. 13), having gains, but
With Diminishment (no. 55), having losses.

What we term Completion (no. 73) is enduring achievements that cannot
be changed.

EVOLUTION OF THE MYSTERY
Hsüan li

[This essay compares with the "Appended Texts" commentary to the Changes
*(often called the Great Commentary). The main idea of the first section is that the
Mystery is both the entire sum of stuff from which all else derives and the fash-
ioner of that stuff into the individual types of existence. Note that the term "Mystery" refers simultaneously to two related phenomena: the book of that name
composed by Yang Hsiung and the cosmic Tao in its mysterious operations.]*

The Mystery of which we speak in hidden places unfolds the myriad
species, without revealing a form of its own. It fashions the stuff of Emptiness
and Formlessness, giving birth to the regulations. Tied to the gods in Heaven
and the spirits on Earth, it fixes the models. It pervades and assimilates past
and present, originating the categories. It unfolds and intersperses yin and

yang, generating the *ch'i*. Now severed, now conjoined, [through the interaction of yin and yang *ch'i* the various aspects of] Heaven-and-Earth are indeed fully provided! As the heavens and the sun turn in their circuits [moving in opposite directions], hard and soft [day/night, yang/yin] indeed make contact. Each returns [within the course of a single year] to its place, so that it is indeed a fixed rule that once ended, the cycle begins again. Now giving life and now giving death, human nature and the Decree are indeed illuminated [through the operations of the Mystery].

[The main idea of the following section is that the Mystery makes Heaven and Earth appropriate patterns for Man. The section ends with references to binary opposition.]

Looking up to contemplate the [starry] images, looking down to view [earthly] conditions, the sage examines human nature and comes to know the Decree. He seeks the origin of beginnings and sees the final outcome. The Three Reigns [Heaven-Earth-Man] share the same standard; thick and thin [yin/yang] intersect each other. Round [Heaven] as a rule wobbles unsteadily. Square [Earth] as a rule conserves. Exhalation [yang *ch'i*] as a rule makes the bodies flow out. Inhalation [yin *ch'i*] as a rule congeals forms. For this reason, what encloses Heaven we call spaces and what opens spaces out we call times.

The sun and moon come and go so that now it is winter and now it is summer. As a rule, the pitchpipes complete things, while the calendar arranges the seasons. The pitchpipes and calendar meet in their paths. The sage uses them in planning. Day he regards as good. Night he regards as bad. Now it is day, now it is night, as yin and yang separately seek out [their respective realms]. The way of night is extreme yin. The way of day is extreme yang. For female and male, there are numerous orientations, so good luck and bad evolve. Then the ways of ruler and subject, of father and son, and of husband and wife are indeed distinguished.

For this reason, the sun moves eastward while the heavens move westward. The heavens and the sun cross paths. Yin and yang alternate in their circuits. Death and life are intertwined. Only then do the myriad things become inseparably bound. Therefore, the Mystery is what seeks to take the correspondent parts of All-under-Heaven and string them together. It stitches them together according to their category. It prognosticates about them according to their norms. It clarifies the very dimmest parts of All-under-Heaven. It illuminates the most obscure parts of All-under-Heaven. What else but the Mystery can do all this!

[The following section speaks of the unfathomable profundity of both the Tao and Yang Hsiung's neoclassical imitation of it.]

Now, as we know, the Mystery hides its position and conceals its boundaries. It stores its great expanse deep and obscures its base. It thrusts aside its own merit and makes a secret of its motive force. Therefore, the Mystery, itself surpassing, really shows Man how far away he is. Itself vast, it really enlarges the chances for Man to be great. Itself unfathomably deep, it really incites Man to be profound. Itself infinite, it really cuts Man off from insignificance. The one that silently gathers all together, that is the Mystery. The one who with grand gestures would disperse it, that is Man.

> Knock on its gate.
> Open its door.
> Rap its knocker.

Only later will the response come. How much less likely is a response for those who do otherwise?

Good is "what people like and have too little of." Evil is "what people dislike and have a surplus of." If the noble man daily strengthens what is deficient in him [i.e., the good], and eliminates what he possesses in surplus [i.e., the evil], then indeed the Way of the Mystery is nearly approximated! Looking up, he sees it located in the higher regions. Looking down, he spies it located in the lower regions. Standing on tiptoes [in eager anticipation], he watches for it to be located in front. Abandoning it, he forgets that it is located in back. Even if he would go against it, he cannot, for it is the Mystery that silently by rule makes each attain its proper place.

[The following section speaks of Man's functional relation to the Mystery. All human virtues are defined with reference to it.]

Therefore, the Mystery of which we speak is the ultimate in utility. To see and to know it is wisdom. To regard it with love is humaneness. To be resolute in deciding to practice it is courage. To rule without distinction, broadly applying it, is fairmindedness. The ability to use it to correlate things is comprehension. To be absolutely free of bonds and impediments is sageliness. To be timely or not is the Decree. What is empty of form and the path of the myriad things, that we call the Way. Continuous development without abrupt change, so that the internal order of All-under-Heaven is attained, that we call Charismatic Power. What orders living things and unites the many so that there is all-embracing love, that we call humaneness. What arranges matches and measures what fits, that we call the Right. Grasping the Way and its Power, humaneness and the Right, and then applying them, that we call the Task. What illuminates Heaven's achievements and enlightens the myriad things, that we call yang [*ch'i*]. What is dark, without form, and of unfathomable depth, that we call yin.

Yang knows yang, but does not know yin. Yin knows yin, but does not know yang. To know yin, to know yang, to know stopping, to know proceeding, to know darkness, to know light—what else but the Mystery [can know all this]?

As what suspends them, it is the balance. As what levels them, it is the steelyard beam. The polluted it purifies. The precipitous it levels. Any departure from [true] conditions it invariably exposes as false. Any departure from falsity it invariably reveals as true. Whenever true and false push against one another, the ways of the noble and mean man become relatively clear. The Mystery of which we speak uses scales to measure.

> The elevated it lowers.
> The low it raises.
> The abundant it takes from.
> The depleted it gives to.
> The bright it tones down.
> The doubtful it clarifies.

To use it as compass is thought. To establish it is duty. To explain it is [true] disputation. To complete it is good faith.

Now Heaven openly shows men the gods. And Earth grandly shows men the spirits. Heaven and Earth have their appointed places. The gods and the spirits make the *ch'i* communicate. There is one, there is two, there is three [in the triadic realms of Heaven-Earth-Man]. Each position is of a different class, but each makes the circuit of the Nine Districts [i.e., the nine Appraisals], so that end and beginning are connected in a seamless cycle, so that above and below make a perfect circle. Examine the patterns of Dragon and Tiger [constellations of the eastern and western sky]. Contemplate the configurations of Bird and Turtle [constellations of the southern and northern skies]. Plot their revolutions with regard to the Seven Regulators [the sun, moon, and five planets], and tie them to the Culmen of the Grand Inception [i.e., the Polestar] there. By this comprehend the system of the Jasper Template and straighten the base line of the Jade Level. As for the grinding of circle and square [Heaven and Earth] against one another, the mutual opposition between hard and soft [yin and yang]: by rule, abundance enters decline and what ends is born again. There is filling up; there is emptying out. It flows or stops; there is no constancy.

[The following section describes the way in which each major pattern of human society derives from natural phenomena in the realm of Heaven-and-Earth.]

Now Heaven and Earth are placed; therefore, the noble and base are ranked. The four seasons proceed in order; therefore, the son inherits from the father. The pitchpipes and calendar are set forth; therefore, relations between ruler and subject are orderly. Constancy and change are interspersed; therefore, the Hundred Affairs are hewn. Simplicity and embellishment take shape; therefore, what exists and what does not is made clear. Good luck and ill appear; therefore, good and evil are revealed. Emptiness and fullness propel one another; therefore, the myriad things are inextricably connected.

If yang fails to culminate, then yin fails to germinate. If yin fails to culminate, then yang fails to sprout. Extreme cold gives birth to heat. Extreme heat gives birth to cold. The way of expansion induces contraction. The way of contraction induces expansion. In its active mode, the Mystery daily creates what it lacks and favors what it renews. In its quiescent mode, the Mystery daily depletes what the world has and diminishes what the world has completed. Therefore, we infer it by the waterclock; we further test it by the gnomon. Back and forth is its sequence; twisting and turning is its path. By them we see the invisible form. By them we draw out the elusive thread. Through it we become part of the continuum of the myriad categories of things.

When above, it is suspended from the heavens. When below, it is submerged in the abyss. So fine is it that it enters a single blade of grass. So vast is it that it encompasses whole regions. Its Way is to wander in obscurity and to ladle out the full. It preserves what should be preserved and destroys what should be destroyed. It keeps hidden what should be hidden and manifests what should be manifested. It causes the beginning to begin. It causes the end to end.

Whoever approaches the Mystery will find the Mystery for its part approaching him. Whoever distances himself from the Mystery will find the Mystery for its part keeping its distance from him. It is like the vast blue of the heavens. It is in the east, in the south, in the west, in the north. Look up and there is no place where it is not. But the moment someone bends down, then it is no longer seen. How could Heaven possibly leave Man? It is Man who leaves on his own accord.

Whatever comes after the winter solstice and midnight is an image of "approaching the Mystery." It advances, but it has not yet culminated. It goes forward, but it has not yet arrived. It is empty and not yet full. Therefore, we call it "approaching the Mystery." Whatever comes after the summer solstice and midday is an image of "distancing the Mystery." Once the advance culminates, it retreats. Once the forward movement ends, it goes back. Once it is already full, it is depleted. Therefore, we call it "distancing the Mystery."

As soon as the sun turns south [from the summer solstice to year's end], the myriad things die. As soon as the sun turns north [from the winter solstice on], the myriad things are born. As soon as the Dipper points north, the myriad things empty out. As soon as the Dipper points south, the myriad things fill up. The sun it its southward path proceeds toward the right [that is, from the west], then returns in a leftward path. The Dipper in its southward path proceeds toward the left, then returns in a rightward path. Sometimes going left, sometimes going right; sometimes dying, sometimes living. The gods and the numinous unite their plans. Only then are Heaven and Earth aligned, so that Heaven is divine and Earth numinous.

ILLUMINATION OF THE MYSTERY
Hsüan ying

[This essay also corresponds to the "Appended Texts" commentary to the Changes. *The opening paragraph describes the origin of the cosmos, tying the* Mystery *text to the mysterious Tao. Succeeding paragraphs outline the most important constant features of the Mystery, as it operates both in this text and in the universe outside the text. Finally, reference is made to certain organizing principles of human society.]*

When Heaven and Earth were severed, space and time broadened out and leveled. The Heavenly Origin [midnight on the first day of the winter solstice that coincides with the first month in the sixty-year cycle] was spanned and paced; the cycle of sun and moon was computed. Completing the [annual] revolution is the calendrical cycle; grouping the social orders are the various ranks. Sometimes there is conjunction, and sometimes separation, sometimes a surplus, and sometimes a deficiency [when solar and lunar years are aligned]. Therefore, I say: "Great indeed are Heaven and Earth, which engulf all development! As in a net, all is cloaked in the Mystery. The end and the beginning, the dark and the light, the Tables [each set of three Appraisals] and Appraisals [correspond to] Heavenly gods and Earthly spirits. As great yang rides on yin, the myriad things are held together. Making a circuit of the Nine Empty Positions [the Nine Appraisals], calamity and good fortune are entangled in the net."

Altogether there are twelve beginnings [one for each month of the calendar year]. With regard to the many orders [of existence], one draws out the end threads. And so there exist 1, 2, and 3, which act to catch [the many orders] as in nets and snares. The arts of the Mystery illuminate it.

The Five Phases of the Vast Base are set out repeatedly in the Nine Positions. Above and below they cleave to one another [in successive cycles, with the various] categories residing in their midst. The arts of the Mystery illuminate it.

Heaven is round and Earth is square. The Culmen [the Polestar] is planted in the exact center [of the cosmos]; the movements [of the stars around it] are fixed by the calendar. Time rides on the twelve [zodiacal sections of the sky, each 30 degrees long]. Thus are established the Seven Regulators [of sun, moon, and five visible planets]. The arts of the Mystery illuminate it.

The Dipper, moving according to the order of the heavens, advances [toward the west]. The sun, going against [the westward spin of] the heavens, retreats. Some move with it and some go against it. Thus are established the Five Indicators [the Year star, moon, sun, stars, and calendrical calculations]. The arts of the Mystery illuminate it.

One places the dial to have it give off a shadow. One drains the clepsydra to figure the quarter-hour marks. [From] dusk and dawn, one empirically establishes the center [position of the circumpolar stars at noon]. Those who create [human institutions] are forwarned by [the information such instruments provide]. The arts of the Mystery illuminate it.

The bamboo of [Music master] Ling-lun [i.e., the pitchpipe] is used to make a tube. Ash housed within [bamboo tubes] is used to make a "watch" device. By it are measured the Hundred Norms. Once the Hundred Norms are in place, the legions of people are no longer in error. The arts of the Mystery illuminate it.

East to west is the woof. South to north is the warp. When warp and woof are interwoven, the deviant and the upright thereby are distinguished, while good luck and ill thereby take form. The arts of the Mystery illuminate it.

Drilling a well supplies water; drilling for fire ignites wood. [Add to Water, Fire, and Wood] molten Metal and molded Earth to correctly apportion the Five Excellent Resources [i.e., the Five Phases]. The stuff of the Five Excellent Resources is used to endow the Hundred Corporeal Bodies. The arts of the Mystery illuminate it.

Odd numbers are used to enumerate yang [*ch'i*]. Even numbers are used to enumerate yin. Odd and even extended and expanded are used to calculate All-under-Heaven. The arts of the Mystery illuminate it.

The Six Beginnings make the male pitchpipes. The Six Intermediaries make the female pitchpipes. Once the pitchpipes, male and female, are tuned to one another, the twelve are used to produce harmonies, and to number the solar conjunctions. The arts of the Mystery illuminate it.

Region, Province, Department, and Family [yield] eighty-one places [i.e., tetragrams]. These are [further] delineated as lower, center, and upper to signify [all within] the four seas. The arts of the Mystery illuminate it.

There are one Ruler, three Dukes, nine Ministers, twenty-seven Councilors, and eighty-one chief Knights. The few as a rule control the many; what lacks visible form [i.e., the Mystery] as a rule controls what has form. The arts of the Mystery illuminate it.

[The following two paragraphs are extremely important. In them Yang Hsiung refutes the classic Taoist utopian vision, which celebrates the golden age of antiquity as a carefree time for the human race prior to the development of the discriminating mind. Yang Hsiung counters this vision by another, in which the ancient sage-king Fu Hsi creates divination so that Man might

finally learn both to discriminate and to see connections. Through the proper use of sacred tools like divination, Man can hope to partake of divinity.]

In antiquity, humans were neither shaken by fear nor worried. They were sluggish in their thinking. They did not divine either by milfoil stalks or by turtle so good luck and ill seeped into one another [i.e., were indistinguishable]. It was then that the sage [Fu Hsi] created milfoil and turtle divination, drilling to get the essence, and relying on the divine in the search to understand favor and blame. The arts of the Mystery illuminate it.

For this reason, those who wish to know the unknowable estimate it by what is in the hexagrams and bone cracks. Those who would come to fathom the profound and probe the distant then tie them to what is in their thoughts. Are not the two [divination and thought] established by single-minded concentration? When one divines with single-minded concentration, the gods prompt the changes [that reveal an answer to the inquiry]. When one deliberates [on this response] with single-minded concentration, one's plans are appropriate. When one establishes what is Right with single-minded concentration, no one can overturn it. When one maintains his principles with single-minded concentration, no one can snatch them away. Therefore, to draw out the infinitude of All-under-Heaven, to dispel the confusion and chaos of All-under Heaven, what else but single-minded concentration can accomplish it?

[In another important paragraph, Yang Hsiung first describes the creative act, whether in the cosmos or in the human mind. Succeeding paragraphs describe the creativity and vitality of the Mystery *text.]*

Now, the act of creation honors its own prototypes and gives physical form to the spontaneously generated [Tao]. When what it follows is great, then its embodiment will be vigorous. When what it follows is petty, then its embodiment will be meager. When what it follows is straight, then its embodiment will be coherent. When what it follows is crooked, then its embodiment will be scattered. Therefore, it neither eliminates what exists nor forces what is not. We may compare it to the physical body, where any increase would be superfluous and any deletion would mean a deficiency. Therefore, the essential structure [of the creative act] rests in the spontaneously generated [Tao], while its external elaboration rests in human affairs. Can it really be diminished or increased?

Now all those in the first position in the nine Appraisals [i.e., Appraisals 1, 4, and 7] are what patterns the beginning and fathoms the depths. All those in third position [Appraisals 3, 6, and 9] are what completes the end and pushes the whole to extremes. All those in the second position [Appraisals 2, 5, and 8] are what combines events and seeks the center. The Way of Man takes its image from it.

[The *Mystery*] focuses on its events but not on its phrasing. It multiplies its changes but not its patterns. If [the *Mystery*] were not economical [in its expressions], then its points would not be detailed. If it were not a summary account, then its responses would not have universal application. If it were not simple yet complete, then the events it describes would not be wide-ranging. If it were not deep, then its ideas would not reveal anything. Because of that, pattern is used to see into the essential; and phrasing, to look into true conditions. If we take a close look at the phrases it lays out, then surely the heart's desire will become apparent.

[From the single Tao, there have evolved four kinds of change. Operating by turns, these four kinds of change provide models for human society. The concluding paragraphs of the essay define key terms for the reader. By means of such definitions, Yang Hsiung seeks to prove the ultimate utility of moral action.]

Therefore the Way has continuity and development. It has [abrupt] change and [gradual] metamorphosis. When continuity and development conform with the Tao, we take them as divine. When change and metamorphosis are in accord with Time, we find them fitting. Therefore, although continuous, [an entity] can still change. Only then is Heaven's way attained. Although changing, [an entity] can still be continuous. Only then is Heaven's way complied with. Now, if things did not continue on [the model of their forebears], they would not be born. And if they did not change, they would not be completed. Therefore, to know continuity but not change is to have things lose their own rules. And to know change but not continuity is to have things lose their uniform aspects. When change is untimely, things lose their foundation. And when continuity goes counter to internal pattern, things lose their regulating principle. Continuity and change lead to more continuity and change. They are the very law and model for the state and family. Action [by this] model is synonymous with efficacy in success and failure.

The warp that establishes Heaven is called "yin and yang." The woof that gives form to Earth is called "vertical and horizontal." The course that reveals Man is called "benighted and enlightened." Of yin and yang we say, "They join their divided [selves to give birth to the myriad things]." Of vertical and horizontal we say, "The woof threads through its warp" [to create significant pattern]. Of the benighted and enlightened we say, "They distinguish their characteristic qualities." Yin and yang hold all the limits. Warp and woof function as meeting places. Benighted and enlightened refer to the substantive nature. If yang had no yin, it would have no partner to join in its operations. If the warp had no woof, there would be no way for it to complete its fitting [pattern]. If the enlightened had no benighted, there would be no way he could distinguish his virtue. Yin and yang are the means to draw out the true conditions. Vertical and horizontal are the means to illuminate internal pattern. Enlightened and benighted are the means to shed light on affairs. When true conditions are drawn out, when patterns are illuminated, when affairs are made brilliant—this is the Way of the noble man.

> Contact, back and forth,
> With fragrant smoke rising,
> This is the gate of gain and ruin.

Now, what is gain and what is ruin? Gain is good fortune and ruin is calamity. In Heaven and Earth, good fortune is conformity [to prevailing trends], and calamity, going against them. In the mountains ard riverways, good fortune is the low, and calamity, the high. In the Way of Man, good fortune is the upright, and calamity, the perverse. Therefore, the noble man is inwardly upright and outwardly compliant, always humbling himself before others. This is why the outcome of his actions is good fortune and not calamity. If in good fortune one does no evil, good fortune cannot give rise to calamity. If in calamity, one does good, calamity cannot become good fortune.

> Evil and good!
> Evil and good!
> Evil and good!

These are what ultimately reveal the noble man. Now, [for others], when the joy of good fortune ends, the worry of calamity begins.

What Heaven and Earth value is called good fortune. What the ghosts and gods bless is called good fortune. What the Way of Man delights in is called good fortune. Whatever is despised and abhorred is called calamity. Therefore, when there is too much vice in good fortune, correspondent calamities rise up. In the daytime, men's calamities are few. At night, men's calamities are many. As day and night are interspersed, the good fortune and calamity associated with them are mixed.

NUMBERS SYSTEM OF THE MYSTERY
Hsüan shu

[This essay is comparable to the "Discussion of the Trigrams" ("Shuo kua") section found in the so-called "Ten Wings" of the Changes. *The essay explains the entire system of correlations to be employed by the diviner when applying the individual texts of the* Mystery *to personal situations. We should remember always that such number correlations alert the reader to the profound order inherent in the universe.*

The autocommentary begins with several paragraphs that have been summarized in the "Introduction" to this book. These sections, therefore, have been omitted here.]

Three and Eight correspond to:
    Wood
    East
    Spring
    the days *chia* and *yi*
    the zodiacal periods *yin* and *mao*
    the note *chüeh*
    the color, green
    the taste, bitter
    the smell, sour
    the form, contracting and expanding
    the Phase produced, fire
    the Phase conquered, Earth
    the time to give birth
    of the viscera, the spleen
    the nature, benevolence
    the emotion, happiness
    the duty, demeanor
    the application, "reverence that makes for solemnity"
    the omen, drought
    the emperor T'ai-hao
    the god Kou-mang
    the stars that attend its [the east's] position
    the category, scaly creatures
    thunder
    drums
    booming sounds
    newness
    bustling activity
    doors
    windows
    heirs
    those who inherit
    leaves
    main threads
    pardons
    expiations
    many sons
    going out

giving
bamboo
grasses
seeds
fruits
fish
drawing tools
compasses
rice fields
carpentry
spears
green prodigies
nose ailments
wildness

Four and Nine correspond to:
Metal
West
autumn
the days *keng* and *hsin*
the zodiacal periods *shen* and *yu*
the note *shang*
the color, white
the taste, acrid
the smell, rank
the form, violent change
the Phase produced, Water
the Phase conquered, Wood
the time to kill
of viscera, the liver
the promotion of the corporeal soul
the nature, righteousness
the emotion, anger
the duty, speech
the application, "compliance that makes for good order"
the omen, rain
the emperor Shao Hao
the god Ju-shou
the stars that attend its [the west's] direction
the category, hairy things
witchdoctors
invocations by shamans
fierce beasts [such as tigers]

    what is old
    metallic rings
    gates
    mountains
    limits
    borders
    [inner] city walls
    bones
    rocks
    bracelets and girdle ornaments
    head ornaments
    heavy jewels
    metal buttons
    pounding of rice
    mortars
    strength
    whatever is suspended
    sparking fire by drilling wood
    weapons [or, "troops"]
    shackles
    teeth
    horns
    scorpions
    poisons
    puppies
    entering
    seizing
    netting
    plundering
    thieving
    ordering
    the carpenter's square
    metalworking
    battle axes
    white prodigies
    muteness
    slander

Two and Seven correspond to:
    Fire
    South
    Summer
    the days *ping* and *ting*

the zodiacal periods *szu* and *wu*
the note *chih*
the color, red
the taste, bitter
the smell, scorched
the form, what is above
the Phase produced, Earth
the Phase conquered, Metal
the time to nourish
of the viscera, the lungs
the promotion of the ethereal soul (*hun*)
the nature, ritual
the emotion, joy
the duty, sight
the application, "clarity that makes for wisdom"
the omen, heat
the emperor Yen ti
the god Chu-jung
the stars that attend its [the south's] direction
the category, feathered things
stoves
silk
nets
rope
pearls
patterns [including writing]
mixtures
seals
ribbons
books
whatever is light
whatever is high
towers
wine
spitting
shooting with an arrow
dagger-axes
armor
thickets
the Commanding General
string
working with fire
knives

red prodigies
blindness
laxity

One and Six correspond to:
Water
North
Winter
the days *jen* and *kuei*
the zodiacal periods *tzu* and *hai*
the note *yü*
the color, black
the taste, salty
the smell, rotted
the form, what is below
the Phase produced, Wood
the Phase conquered, Fire
the time to store
of the viscera, the testicles and kidneys
the promotion of sperm
the nature, wisdom
the emotion, sorrow
the duty, hearing
the application, "perceptiveness that makes for [good] planning"
the omen, [undue] cold
the emperor Chuan Hsü
the god Hsüan-ming
the stars that attend its [the north's] direction
the category, things with shells
ghosts
sacrifices
temples
wells
caves
burrows
mirrors
jade
treading
making long trips
laboring
blood
ointments
coveting
containing

hibernating animals
hunting with fire
shutting
robbing
the Director of Public Works
laws
standards
water works
shields
black prodigies
deafness
urgency

On Five: Five corresponds to
Earth
Center
the four seasons
the days *wu* and *chi*
the zodiacal periods *ch'en, hsü, ch'ou,* and *wei*
the note *kung*
the color, yellow
the taste, sweetness
the smell, fragrant
the forms, verticality
the Phase produced, Metal
the Phase conquered, Water
the time to join together
of the viscera, the heart/mind
the promotion of the divine soul
the nature, trustworthiness
the emotion, fear
the duty, thought
the application, "prescience that makes for sageliness"
the omen, wind
the emperor Huang-ti (Yellow Emperor)
the god Hou-t'u
the stars that attend its [circumpolar] diretion
its category, what is naked [i.e., human]
tumuli
bottles
palaces
residences
the center courtyard rainwell
"internal" affairs

weaving
clothes
furs
cocoons
raw floss
beds
sleeping mats
complying
cherishing
tools or vessels with bellies
oils
lacquer
glue
sacks
pouches
carriages
hubs
sowing
harvesting
foodstuffs
flesh
coffins
calves
thoroughfares
meetings
the capital
measures
weights
earthworks
bows and arrows
yellow prodigies
stupidity
benightedness

Among the five Phases, the one in power is "the king." The one "the king" produces is "the minister." The "old king" is the one deposed. The one that [would] conquer the king is imprisoned. The one that is conquered by the [new] king dies.

Of the Musical Notes,
  Kung is the ruler.
  Chih is affairs.

Shang is the minister.
Chüeh is the people.
Yü is the common people.

Of the Pitch Standards,
Huang-chung (middle C), the "Yellow Bell," produces *lin-chung* (G).
Lin-chung produces *t'ai-ts'ou* (D).
T'ai-ts'ou produces *nan-lü* (A).
Nan-lü produces *ku-hsien* (E).
Ku-hsien produces *ying-chung* (B).
Ying-chung produces *sui-pin* (F sharp).
Sui-pin produces *ta-lü* (D flat).
Ta-lu produces *yi-tse* (A flat).
Yi-tse produces *chia-chung* (E flat).
Chia-chung produces *wu-yi* (B flat).
Wu-she produces *chung-lü* (F).

[Of the Twelve Earthly Branches,]
Tzu and *wu* count as 9.
Ch'ou and *wei* count as 8.
Yin and *shen* count as 7.
Mao and *yü* count as 6.
Ch'en and *hsü* count as 5.
Ssu and *hai* count as 4.

Therefore, the sum of the "male" pitch standards is 42 and the sum of the "female," 36. The sum of the combined male and female pitches, with some "returning" and some "blocking," altogether is 78. The number of the Yellow Bell [which is 81] is set up by it. [In other words, 78 equals 81 once 3 is added to symbolize the triadic realms of Heaven-Earth-Man.] Their use as measures depends upon the fact that all are produced by the Yellow Bell.

[Of the Ten Heavenly Stems,]
Chia and *chi* count as 9.
Yi and *keng* count as 8.
Ping and *hsin* count as 7.
Ting and *jen* count as 6.
Wu and *kuei* count as 5.

The notes are born of the days. The pitch standards are born of the zodiacal periods. The notes are used to express men's essential substance. The pitch standards are used to harmonize the notes. When the notes and pitchpipes are attuned to one other, the eight distinctive timbres [of various instruments] are produced.

Of the Nine Heavens,
> The first is made Center (no. 1 of the tetragrams).
> The second is made Defectiveness (no. 10).
> The third is made Following (no. 19).
> The fourth is made Change (no. 28).
> The fifth is made Purity (no. 37).
> The sixth is made Enlargement (no. 46).
> The seventh is made Diminishment (no. 55).
> The eighth is made Sinking (no. 64).
> The ninth is made Completion (no. 73).

Of the Nine Earths,
> The first is sand and mud.
> The second is marshes and pools.
> The third is small islets and banks.
> The fourth is low fields.
> The fifth is fields at the middle range.
> The sixth is high fields.
> The seventh is low mountains.
> The eighth is mountains of medium height.
> The ninth is high mountains.

Of the Nine [Types] of Men,
> The first is the low man.
> The second is the commoner.
> The third is the man who advances.
> The fourth is low rank.
> The fifth is middle rank.
> The sixth is high rank.
> The seventh is the man of lost ambitions.
> The eighth is the ill or infected.
> The ninth is the man in extremities.

Of the Nine Body Parts,
> No. 1 corresponds to hands and feet.
> No. 2 corresponds to [lower] arms and shin.
> No. 3 corresponds to thighs and upper arms.
> No. 4 is the waist.
> No. 5 is the belly.

No. 6 is the shoulders.

No. 7 is the throat.

No. 8 is the face.

No. 9 is the forehead.

Of the Nine Grades of Relations,

No. 1 corresponds to great-great-grandchildren.

No. 2 corresponds to great-grandchildren.

No. 3 corresponds to grandchildren.

No. 4 corresponds to children.

No. 5 corresponds to the self.

No. 6 corresponds to the father.

No. 7 corresponds to the grandfather.

No. 8 corresponds to the great-grandfather.

No. 9 corresponds to great-great-grandfather.

Of the Nine Apertures,

Nos. 1 and 6 correspond to the urethra and the ear.

Nos. 2 and 7 correspond to the eyes.

Nos. 3 and 8 correspond to the nostrils.

Nos. 4 and 9 correspond to the mouth.

No. 5 corresponds to the anus.

The Nine Orders are ranked from 1 to 9.

Of the Nine Affairs,

The first is careful planning.

The second is hesitation in all directions.

The third is self-assurance.

The fourth is outer-directed activity.

The fifth is inner harmony.

The sixth is abundance.

The seventh is waning.

The eighth is wasting.

The ninth is total destruction.

Of the Nine Decades,

No. 1 corresponds to the first decade.

No. 2 corresponds to the second decade.

No. 3 corresponds to the third decade.

No. 4 corresponds to the fourth decade.

No. 5 corresponds to the fifth decade.

No. 6 corresponds to the sixth decade.

No. 7 corresponds to the seventh decade.
No. 8 corresponds to the eighth decade.
No. 9 corresponds to the ninth decade.

[There follows a section that is summarized in the "Introduction."]

ELABORATION OF THE MYSTERY
Hsüan wen

[This corresponds to the "Wen yen" section of the Changes, *which treats the first two* Changes *hexagrams as a microcosm for the entire* Yi ching *system. The "Elaboration" autocommentary explains Tetragram 1, entitled "The Center," as a microcosm for the world of Heaven-Earth-Man, as well as for the* Mystery *text.]*

In regard to [the five mantic formulae]

Without (*wang*),
Extending (*chih*),
Covering (*meng*),
Completing (*ch'iu*),
Hidden (*ming*):

Without refers to the north and to winter. It is whatever still lacks form. Extending refers to the east and to spring. It is whatever has substance but no pattern as yet. Cover refers to the south, to summer, to things growing tall. It is everything that can be gotten and increased. Completing refers to the west and to autumn. It is things all achieving [the potential implied by] their images and coming to completion. What has form then returns to the formless; therefore, it is called Hidden. Thus the myriad things are Without [form] in the north, are Extending in the east, are Covering in the south, are Completing in the west, and are Hidden in the north. And so,

Without [as primordial chaos] is the house where Being resides.
Extending is the plain background for pattern.
Covering is the master of loss.
Completing is the repository of life.
Hidden is the storehouse for clarity.

Without provides a house for its *ch'i.*
Extending prods its species [into life].
Covering carries its growth to the limit.
Completing finishes its accomplishments.
Hidden returns to its secret places.

Without and Covering push one another to the limit. Extending and Completing restrain one another. Coming out of Hidden, going into Hidden, the new and old exchange places. As yin and yang [*ch'i*] succeed one another, the pure and the sullied depose one another. What is about to come advances, and what has been achieved retreats. What has already been used is generally despised. What is appropriate for the time generally is honored. Heaven is patterned and earth is plain. They do not change their positions. Without, Extending, Covering, Completing, and Hidden!

Speech derives from Without. Conduct derives from Without. Calamity and good fortune derive from Without. The time that corresponds to Without is Mysterious indeed! Conduct as a rule leaves traces. Speech as a rule has sounds. Good fortune as a rule brings gifts of dried meat. Calamity as a rule has what takes form. This we call Extending. And once there is Extending there can be Covering. Once there is Covering there can be Completing. And once there is Completing then it can revert to the Hidden! For this reason, the time that corresponds to Without can generally be controlled [meaning, we can forestall calamity in the early stages.]

The eighty-one tetragrams evolve from Without. Heaven's dazzling light comes out of the infinite; its fiery brilliance comes out of the boundless. Therefore, the time that corresponds to Without is Mysterious indeed! For this reason, Heaven's Way [is to]:

Empty, so as to store them.
Activate, so as to catalyze them.
Exalt, so as to look down on them.
Pare, so as to regulate them.
End, so as to seclude them.

So profound is it that none can fathom it! So glorious is it that none can surpass it!

Therefore, in imitation of the Tao the noble man hiding in the profound is enough to embody the divine. His initiating activity is enough to impress the masses. His lofty character and quality of mind are enough to reflect on those below. His paring and cutting [i.e., his regulations and punishments] are enough to cause [others] to quake with fear and apprehension. His reclusion and hidden depth are enough to cause [him] to withdraw [from the world]. Because the noble man can [emulate] these five [activities of the Mystery], therefore we describe [him also in terms of the phrases] Without, Extending, Covering, Completing, and Hidden.

Someone might ask what is meant by, "Primal oneness encompasses all./ It is profound"? It says, the worthy man is one with Heaven and Earth insofar as his thoughts embrace the many kinds of being. His thoughts unite them at center but they have not yet taken form outside. He lives alone and yet he is happy. He alone thinks and so he worries. Happiness so great cannot be borne. Sorrow so great cannot be overcome. Therefore it is said to be "profound."

What is meant by, "Spiritual forces war in darkness"? It says, the petty man's heart is impure. When it is about to make form outside, yin and yang are arrayed in battle lines to fight over good luck and bad. With yang, [the heart] battles for good luck; with yin, for bad luck. "As with the wind, one knows the tiger. / As with a cloud, one knows the dragon." The worthy man initiates action and the myriad categories are held in common.

What is meant by, "The dragon emerges at the center"? It says, the characteristic virtue of the dragon is apparent for the first time. If yin has not culminated, then yang will not be born. If disorder has not culminated, then virtue will not assume form. The noble man cultivates virtue, thereby awaiting the proper moment. He does not rise up before the proper moment, nor draw back after it has already passed. Whether in action or at rest, whether obscure or eminent, he does not stray from the norm. Can this be said of anyone else but the noble man? Thus "head and tail are fit for use."

What is meant by, "Lowliness, emptiness, nothingness, compliance— despite a full portion of nature and Decree, still he is blocked"? It says, the petty man cannot find it in his heart to embrace emptiness or to dwell in low places. Although he is debased, he cannot be approached. Although he is empty, he cannot be filled. When doing without would be appropriate, he is capable of possessing. When compliance would be appropriate, he is capable of striking out in an untried direction. Therefore, "despite a full portion of nature and Decree," he lacks the humility to avoid inappropriate action. That is why "he is blocked."

What is meant by, "The sun centered in the sky"? It says, the noble man rides on [that is, takes advantage of] his position, making it serve as his carriage and as his horse. The frontboard of the carriage and the braided tail of the horse can be put to use in making a circuit of All-under-Heaven. Therefore, the sun "helps him become master."

What is meant by, "The moon losing its fullness / Is not as good as new light in the west"? It says, the petty man in the fullness of his powers brings needless ruin upon himself. Water increases in the deep abyss [as] trees lose some of their limbs. In the mountains, the emaciated are killed off; in the marshes, the plump grow in number. The worthy man sees, but none among the masses understand.

What is meant by, "Repository of the fully ripe"? It says, the humane are afflicted by the inhumane. The just are afflicted by the unjust. The noble man is magnanimous enough to lead the masses. He is gentle enough to make things secure. Heaven and Earth accommodate every single thing. Only inhumanity and injustice are not accommodated by [one allied with] Heaven and Earth. Therefore, "Water is the repository of rectitude."

What is meant by, "Yellow is not yellow"? It says, the small man fails to model himself on the center. By rule, all of the first positions [in each set of the three Tables] are beginnings, all of the threes are ends. The twos attain the proper center. The noble man residing in obscurity is upright. Residing in good fortune, he keeps himself humble. Residing in calamity, he turns [the blame] back on himself. The petty man residing in obscurity is perverted. Residing in good fortune, he is arrogant. Residing in calamity, he is at his wit's end. Therefore,

> When the noble man attains a position, he flourishes.
> When he loses it, he keeps his equanimity.
> When the petty man attains a position, he is tyrannical.
> When he loses it, he perishes.

At Appraisal 8, even if he attains a position still it "overturns the norms of autumn."

What is meant by, "When souls are overturned, *ch'i* and form revert"? It says, the excessive culminates above. What culminates above then moves on in the cycle. The excessive goes below, where it is then overturned. The soul is overturned already, I daresay. The *ch'i* and form could not possibly remain and not revert. Does it mean that the noble man in his old age has reached the end of his time? Yang culminates above. Yin culminates below. The *ch'i* and form are at odds with each other. The ghosts and gods obstruct one another. The worthy man is apprehensive, while the petty man is presumptuous.

"Primal oneness encompasses all. / It is profound" refers to great receptivity. "Spiritual forces war in darkness" refers to mutual attack. "The dragon emerges at the center" refers to affairs proceeding smoothly. "Blocked to lowliness and emptiness" refers to not being fairminded. "The sun centered in the sky" refers to all-pervasive light. "The moon losing its fullness" refers to depletion of the surplus. "Respository of the fully ripe" refers to taking the tried and true as a model. "Yellow is not yellow" refers to losing the central thread. "Overturned souls reverting" refers to exhausting Heaven's conditions.

[The mantic formulae] Without, Extending, Covering, and Completing appraise the many Hidden situations.

The phrase "Primal oneness encompasses all. / It is profound" describes a situation where "the stuff embraced has no bounds." "Spiritual forces war in darkness" describes "good and evil in two rows." "The dragon emerges at the center" describes "laws and institutions that are civilized." "Blocked to lowliness and emptiness" describes "subjects' ways that are unfit." "The sun centered in the sky" describes "riding on the firmness of *Ch'ien* [Hexagram 1 in the *I ching,* signifying pure masculinity]." "The moon losing its fullness" describes "the way to contemplate waxing and waning." "Repository of the fully ripe" describes "the ability to employ punishment and suasive virtue." "Yellow is not yellow" describes "the inability to proceed further in company with others." "Overturned souls reverting" describes "time by rule having its limits."

Without, Extending, Covering, and Completing—only then at last has one reached the limit of the spirit realm.

What is valued in Heaven and Earth is called "life." What is honored among things is called "human." The great principle of humankind is called "good order." What good order depends upon is the ruler. Nothing else can compare to the ruler in exalting Heaven and broadening Earth, in classifying the many and in pairing things, so that they do not lose their order. Now, Heaven rules in the regions above, and Earth, in the regions below. The ruler rules in the center. Looking up to Heaven, he finds that Heaven is not weary. Looking down to Earth, he finds that Earth is not indolent. The weary are not like Heaven. The indolent are not like Earth. It has never been the case—in the past or in the present—that the weary and indolent exhibit ability in their affairs. For this reason, the sage looks up to Heaven and takes constancy as [his] rule. He plumbs the limits of the divine; he mines the [possibilities for] change. He understands things completely; he exhausts [the potential inherent in] natural conditions. The sage would match his body with Heaven-and-Earth, aim for the numinosity of the ghosts and gods, push his transformations to the limit with yin and yang, and participate in the integrity of the four seasons. Contemplating Heaven, he becomes Heaven. Contemplating Earth, he becomes Earth. Contemplating divinities, he becomes divine. Contemplating Time, he becomes timely. Heaven, Earth, the gods, and Time—with all these he is in accord, so how could he enter into contradiction?

REPRESENTATIONS OF THE MYSTERY
Hsüan yi

[Tradition compares this essay to parts of the "Appended Texts" commentary to the Changes *(also called the Great Commentary). The first two paragraphs list the component parts of the* Mystery *and suggest the conditions necessary to comprehend it.]*

The phrasing in the Appraisals of the *Mystery* sometimes is couched in terms of *ch'i* [according to the Five Phases], sometimes in terms of category, sometimes in terms of the twists and turns of human affairs.

Venture to ask questions about its nature and examine its families [tetragrams]. Carefully observe what one happens upon. Catalog it by event, detail it by number. In meeting the gods, see them as Heavenly. In coming up against Earth, see it as fields to be sown. If all such conditions are met, then the true condition of the Mystery will be attained!

So it is that the Heads refer to the Heaven-given nature. The Polar Oppositions refers to contrasting the right pairs of tetragrams. The Interplay refers to shuffling them together. The Fathomings are the means whereby to know the true circumstances. The Evolution expands it. The Illumination clarifies it. The Numbers serves as a classificatory method. The Elaboration makes for adornment. The Representation refers to likenesses. The Diagram refers to images. The Revelation refers to its origin and end.

[The following paragraph summarizes Yang Hsiung's ideas regarding the relation of human nature to fate.]

Tradition says, "Only Heaven takes the initiative to send down life to the common people." It causes their demeanors to move, mouths to talk, eyes to see, ears to hear, and minds to think. If they have good models, then they are perfected. If they have no proper models, then they are imperfect. With integrity, they have reason not to be in awe of anything. The Representation likens it to a canon.

[The following five paragraphs stress the fundamental "naturalness" of various human institutions, correlating them with the number system of the Mystery. *In a sense, this section plays off part of the "Appended Texts" commentary to the* I ching, *which suggests that certain human activities find their sacred analogue in various trigrams and hexagrams.]*

Draping the lapel cloth makes the upper garments. Pleating lengths of cloth makes the lower garments. The regulations regarding upper and lower garments are used to inform All-under Heaven. The Representation likens it to the numbers three and eight.

Fitting together leather strips makes a breastplate. Capping the lance makes a halberd. Breastplates worn and halberds borne are used to inspire awe in the irreverent. The Representation likens it to the numbers four and nine.

Honored among the honorable is the ruler. Low among the lowly is the subordinate. Distinctions between ruler and subordinate are used to demarcate superior and inferior. The Representation likens it to the numbers two and seven.

The gods and ghosts are formless and scattered. One thinks of them as having no fixed abode. They have no winter or summer; there are no set intervals for sacrificing to them. Therefore, the sage makes them manifest through the ritual canon. The Representation likens it to the numbers one and six.

When the time is Heaven's time and the strength is the strength of Earth, there will be nothing but wine, nothing but food. "There one initiates the sowing and the reaping." The Representation likens it to the number five.

[The following three paragraphs suggest the sacred models for Thought, Good Fortune, and Calamity, the designations given to the three successive sets of three Appraisals that belong to each Head text.]

The ancients treasured the turtle and used cowries as money. In later generations, the noble man exchanged them for metal coins and silk. The states and royal houses circulated them. The masses gained by it. The Representation likens it to Thought.

Principalities were established and kingdoms founded; emoluments were dispersed and ranks distributed, in order to guide the Hundred Salaried [of the bureaucratic establishment]. The Representation likens it to Good Fortune.

When the wicked are brought down only by the Five Mutilating Punishments, the Representation likens it to Calamity.

Grasping the jade table, crowned with the jade circlet, he ranks in perfect order the many [feudal] rulers. The Representation likens it to the eighty-one Head texts.

[The final section explicates the Mystery *in terms of the intertwined musical and astronomical systems.]*

Jujube wood makes a shuttle. Split wood makes a weaving frame. Once the shuttle and the frame are provided, people can keep warm with their help. The Representation likens it to the warp and woof.

Carve and cut calabash, bamboo, leather, wood, earth, and metal to make musical instruments. "Strike the music stone, pluck the silk strings" to harmonize All-under-Heaven. The Representation likens it to the Eight Airs.

Yin and yang are interspersed. Male and female do not grow weary of one another. Human after human, thing after thing, each develops according to its category. The Representation likens it to the Deficit and the Surplus [intercalary Appraisals found after Tetragram 81].

Sun and moon succeed one another. Stars and planets do not crash into one another. The timbres and pitchpipes are calibrated. Odd and even vary in *ch'i*. Father and sons have different faces. Elder and younger brothers are not twins. Lords and kings, none are the same. The Representation likens it to the yearly cycle.

Whatever roars and bares its teeth has immature horns. Whatever flaps about by wings has only two feet. What has neither horns nor wings [i.e., humankind] has the capacity to use the Way and its Power. The Representation likens it to the fair apportionment of the nine-day period [among sets of two successive Appraisals].

Dwelling in the seen, one comes to know the hidden. Deducing from the near, one estimates the far. The sage infers the outermost reaches of yin and yang. He examines the hidden aspects of divine light. The Representation likens it to the gnomon and the quarter-hour marks.

At one time it is bright. At one time it is dark. The firm and the weak continually alternate. To know yin is to go against the flow. To know yang is to follow with it. The Representation likens it to day and night.

Searching above, searching below, he honors the Heavenly norms. Transmitting the past, carrying the future forward, he honors the arts of Heaven; without any erratic change or innovation, he honors Heaven's categories. The Representation likens it to the Heavenly Origin.

Heaven-and-Earth acts as a divine womb to everything. Cosmic laws, being easy to follow, continue forever, without end. The end is whatever is about to go away. The beginning is whatever is about to come. The Representation likens it to [the five mantic formulae] Without, Extending, Covering, Completing and Hidden.

Therefore, if we make water like a stream, then the water can flow freely. If we make our conduct like Virtue, then our conduct attains its Mean. If we make our speech like a model, then our speech attains a rightness. When speech is right, then it has no equal. When conduct attains the Mean, then it has no faults. When water flows freely, then it has no breaks. Because there is no break, it lasts long. Because there is no fault, it is fit to contemplate. Because it is the only possible choice, it is fit to hear. What is fit to hear is the absolute perfection of the sage. What is fit to contemplate is the virtue of the sage. What is fit to last forever is the Way of Heaven and Earth. For this reason, the various sages long ago in initiating the affairs of civilization above likened them to Heaven, and below likened them to Earth, and at center likened them to Man.

Heaven and Earth form the container. Sun and moon are fixed sources of light. The Five Phases hold together the categories. The Five Sacred Mountains act as masters to the other mountains. The Four Great Rivers act as elders to the other waterways. The Five Classics encompass all the normative patterns in the cosmos. If Heaven, Earth, and Man all oppose a proposed action, the great affairs of All-under-Heaven are bound to go awry!

DIAGRAM OF THE MYSTERY
Hsüan t'u

[This compares with part of the "Appended Texts" commentary (also called the Great Commentary) to the Changes. *The first paragraph of the essay interweaves references to the structure of the* Mystery *text with references to the main structural features of the universe. The next three paragraphs speak of the order of the tetragrams as it relates to the yearly cycle of the seasons.]*

The one *Mystery* like a capital dominates the three Regions (of Heaven, Earth, and Man). The Regions fit together the Nine Provinces. Branching out, they are conveyed to the various Departments, which are in turn subdivided and apportioned into the multitude of Families. Affairs are managed in their midst. The dark has the Northern Dipper as its precise center [in the night sky]. Sun and moon establish boundaries for their camps. Yin and yang in deep secrecy make contact. The four seasons by stealth take their place. The Five Phases conceal their actions. Once the Six Directions [up, down, north, south, east, and west] flow together [into one another with no visible separation], the Seven Mansions [assigned to each quarter of the sky] revolve in succession [around the Dipper]. One follows the obscure to produce the calendar. Then the six *chia* [a sequential order of the Heavenly Stems and Earthly Branches used to mark time in ancient China] within obey, and the eighty-one tetragrams are in full measure. The male and female pitchpipes are extremely subtle tools. The calendrical calculations hide the regular cycles. The Diagram makes an image of the Mystery's form. The Appraisals convey its accomplishments.

The Beginnings are located in [the tetragrams] Center (no. 1 of the tetragrams), Defectiveness (no. 10), and Following (no. 19) [corresponding to a period of four months, from the eleventh to the second months of the Han dynasty calendar]. As the Hundred Plants begin to sprout, only then does report of it stimulate Heaven. Thunder hammers the deepest recesses [of Earth] so that many things on all sides are roused. In the first month, aid goes to the weak and undeveloped so that their roots are drawn out from the Origin. In the east the Green Dragon [a constellation in the eastern sky that symbolizes yang *ch'i*] stirs. The rays of light are diffused even unto the deep abyss below earth, prompting the myriad things to rise up. Heaven and Earth are all renewed.

The Centers are located in [the tetragrams] Change (no. 28), Purity (no. 37), and Enlargement (no. 46). They symbolize Heaven's twice-bright nature [which has both sun and moon], and the brilliant flash of thunder and windstorms. All things proceed in timely fashion. Yin comes to completion in the northwest. Yang rises up in the southeast. Despite the response inside, outside the response is lofty and auspicious. The dragon soars to Heaven. And growing species knows no bounds. A march south is not advantageous, for it will encounter the dying light.

The Ends are located in [the tetragrams] Diminishment (no. 55), Sinking (no. 64), and Completion (no. 73) [corresponding to the last four months of the lunar year, months 7–10 in Han times]. Heaven's Root reverts to face [the north]; the mature *ch'i* gathers in its essences. It bores into the myriad things, so that all begin to cry out in their difficulties. Deeply uniting with the Yellow Purity, it broadly encompasses the seeds of the many living things. The Great Handle [of the Polestar] "like the clouds, dispenses blessings along its path," overseeing each earthly region at the proper time. The deviant plans, [however] high-flying, it pulls back. Only then will [all creation] conform to the divine spirits [of Heaven-and-Earth]. On all sides encompassing the end and the beginning, the works of Heaven, Earth, and Man are all completed and good.

Diagram of the Mystery

[The following paragraph opens with a contrast between Heaven and Earth, yang and yin. It goes on to relate these two powers to human society. The next two paragraphs return to the Mystery *text. In dividing the text into nine equal parts, they suggest that the text is comparable to the nine great divisions of Heaven or of Earth.]*

Heaven governs its Way. Earth disposes its tasks. Yin and yang are interspersed so that there are male and female. The Way of Heaven is a perfect compass. The Way of Earth is a perfect carpenter's square. The compass in motion describes a complete circle through the sites. The square, unmoving, secures things in their proper place. Describing a complete circle makes divine light possible. Securing things makes congregation by species possible. Congregating in species makes riches possible, while divine light makes the highest honor possible. Now the "Mystery" is the Way of Heaven, the Way of Earth, and the Way of Man. Taken together these three ways are called Heavenly. They are synonymous with the way of ruler to subject, father to son, husband to wife.

The *Mystery* has one single Way. Being one, it gives rise to things in threes. Being one, it gives birth to things in threes. Those that have arisen by threes are the Region, the Province, the Department, and the Family. As for those born by threes, yang *ch'i* divided by threes makes up the Three Layers of Thought, Good Fortune, and Calamity. Squared [the three] make up the Nine Sites of the Appraisals. That is a case of having a common root but separate growth. It is the warp of Heaven and Earth. On all sides it pervades high and low; it is what joins the myriad things. With a complete circuit of the Nine Sites, the end of the cycle to the beginning is correctly oriented. The calendar begins in the eleventh month; it ends in the tenth month. The layers in the net of Heaven amount to Nine Courses, with each Course forty days long.

Whatever truly has inner force is preserved in the Center (no. 1 of the tetragrams). Whatever propagates and issues forth is preserved in Defectiveness (no. 10). Clouds coursing and rain falling are preserved in Following (no. 19). Shifting rhythms and altered measures are preserved in Change (no. 28). Precious light bathing the whole is preserved in Purity (no. 37). Whatever is empty within but great without is preserved in Enlargement (no. 46). Paring and retreating, waning and apportioning are preserved in Diminishment (no. 55). Descending, falling, obscuring, and hiding in darkness are preserved in Sinking (no. 64). Coming to a good end in regard to nature and the Decree is preserved in Completion (no. 73). For this reason, [Courses] 1–9 [replicate] the Calculations for the waxing and waning of yin and yang.

[The concluding paragraphs explain the numerical system underlying the Mystery. *First, reference is made to the Chinese system of Heavenly Stems*

and Earthly Branches as it relates to the ancient Chinese lunar calendar. Then some of the more obvious correlations for Appraisals 1–9 are given. Finally, the divination method used in the Mystery *is related to calendrical theories in vogue in Yang Hsiung's time.]*

Explaining it another way, if we are at *tzu* [the first of the Twelve Earthly Branches, correlated with north], it is evident that yang is born in the eleventh month while yin ends in the tenth month. If we are at *wu* [the seventh of the Twelve Earthly Branches, correlated with south], it is evident that yin is born in the fifth month while yang ends in the fourth month. For giving birth to yang, nothing is as good as *tzu*. For giving birth to yin, nothing is as good as *wu*. The excellence of *tzu* is perfection, in the northwest, then, just as *wu* is at its highest point in the southwest.

Therefore, the thinking heart/mind is assigned to 1. Turning it over [in one's mind] is assigned to 2. Completion of the idea is assigned to 3. Branching out is assigned to 4. What is light is assigned to 5. Extreme greatness is assigned to 6. Defeat and diminishment are assigned to 7. Falling off is assigned to 8. Absolute destruction is assigned to 9. In regard to the birth of the divine, nothing takes priority over 1. Nothing is more abundant than 5 in regard to centering and harmonizing. Nothing is hampered more than 9 in regard to being stuck in difficulties. Now, the number 1 corresponds to the first intimations in thought. The number 4 corresponds to the stuff of good fortune. The number 7 corresponds to the steps to calamity. The number 3 corresponds to completed thought. The number 6 is the height of good fortune. The number 9 is the extreme of calamity. Appraisals 2, 5, and 8 are the centers of the three sets of three Appraisals.

Good fortune by rule departs, calamity by rule succeeds it. Once the Nine Positions are out, they become the residences of the noble and petty man. A person in Positions 1–3 is poor, lowly, and exercised in mind; in 4–6, he is wealthy, honored, and in high position; in 7–9, he suffers blame and calamity. Positions 1 to 5 cause waxing. Positions 5 to 9 cause waning. The higher numbers may appear honored, but in fact they are depleted. The smaller numbers may appear lowly, but in fact they are prospering. Waxing and waning are bound together. Honor and dishonor are joined. As good fortune arrives, calamity departs. As calamity arrives, good fortune flees. Hidden and immersed, the Way seems debased. High and culminating, the Way seems lofty.

Night and day succeed one another. Husband and wife are tied to one another. Beginning and end produce one another. Father and son succeed one another. Sun and moon join or separate. Such is the duty of ruler and subject. For the eldest to the youngest, there is an order. This is the boundary between old and young. Two by two they go, like leaves of the gate. This is the meeting between friends. One day and one night make a single day. One yin and one yang give birth to the myriad things. More numbers correspond to day; fewer correspond to night. [In the 729 Appraisals assigned 81 tetragrams there are 365 yang lines and 364 yin lines.] This reflects the moon's waning and the sun's bulging fullness. The ruler's course shines while the light of the subject's course is extinguished. The noble man's way is whole, while the petty man's way is defective.

> 1 and 6 share the same ancestor.
> 2 and 7 share the same light.
> 3 and 8 become friends.
> 4 and 9 are a common way.
> 5 and 5 protect each other.

The *Mystery* has one compass and one square, one line and one level. These make the vertical and horizontal divisions to the Way of Heaven and Earth. They bring into conformity the numbers of yin and yang. If we liken them to the divine light, they elucidate the obscure and dark places. Then the level and upright way of the Eight Directions can be ascertained. The *Mystery* uses 6 × 9 (= 54) numbers. For the divining stalks, multiples of 3 × 6 (= 18) are used. The principles of Heaven-and-Earth use 2 × 9 (also = 18). The *Mystery* certainly then uses 18 [as a base]! The sum of the Grand Accumulation begins with 18 divining stalks and ends at 54. If we combine the numbers of sticks that mark the beginning and the end [= 72], we halve it to make the Grand Center [= 36]. The 36 divining stalks of the Grand Center are used to regulate the 729 Appraisals. Altogether 26,244 stalks make up the Grand Accumulation, [with] 72 stalks per day for the 364 and $\frac{1}{2}$ days of the year. A "Surplus" Appraisal fills it out, in order to accord with the days of the year and have the pitchpipes and calendar go in their course.

Therefore, [the Mystery] from *tzu* [the first of the Twelve Earthly Branches] goes to *ch'en* [fifth in the same system], and from *ch'en* to *shen* [ninth in the same system]. It then goes from *shen* back to *tzu*, capping it with a return to *chia* [the first sign in the Ten Heavenly Stems system, marking the beginning of another cycle]. And so the concordance cycles of 19 years, of 1,539 years, and of 4,617 years coincide with the beginnings of the cycles. Then unexplained lunar eclipses will all decline in number. Such is the Way of the Mystery.

REVELATION OF THE MYSTERY
Hsüan kao

[This essay compares with parts of the "Discussion of the Trigrams" (Shuo kua) *commentary to the* Changes. *As in earlier autocommentaries by Yang Hsiung, the term "Mystery" refers at points both to the cosmic Tao and to Yang's own neoclassic of that name.*

The first paragraph suggests the absolute perfection of the Mystery, *whose pages perfectly mirror all the component parts of the universe.]*

The Mystery gives birth to two divine images. The two divine images give birth to the spherical universe. The cosmic sphere gives birth to Three Models of Heaven-Earth-Man [represented by the unbroken, once-broken, and twice-broken lines respectively]. The Three Models give birth to the Nine Positions [i.e., the nine Appraisals attached to each tetragram]. The *Mystery* in having the model "One" reaches unto Heaven. Therefore, we speak of it as "having Heaven" in its contents. The *Mystery* in having the model "Two" reaches unto Earth. Therefore, we speak of it as "having Earth." The *Mystery* in having the model "Three" reaches unto Man. Therefore, we speak of it as "having Man."

Heaven is complete only after it has three bases. Therefore, we call them Beginning, Middle, and End. Earth takes form only after it has three bases. Therefore, we call them Below, Center, and Above. Man is revealed only after he has three bases. Therefore, we call them Thought, Good Fortune, and Calamity. What is united above and united below go in and out of the Nine Sites [another name for the nine Appraisals]. The lesser rules and the greater rules make the full circuit of the Nine Dwellings.

What we call the Mystery is the storehouse of the gods. In regard to Heaven, we take the unseen as the Mystery. In regard to Earth, we take the Formless as the Mystery. In regard to Man, we take the heart and belly [the inmost reactions] as the Mystery. Heaven hiding away in the northwest [the direction of pure yin *ch'i*] pens up the transforming essences. Earth hiding away in the Yellow Springs secretes the flowering of the corporeal soul. Man hiding away in thought contains the quintessential power. Heaven is arched and vaulted, but everywhere it reaches to the lower parts. Earth in all directions thins out at the edges [See THC 1/A1], but it faces the upper regions. Man in teeming multitudes takes his place at the center. Heaven turns in a circle so its cycles are unending. Earth is stable and quiet so its growth is not delayed. Man complies with Heaven and Earth so his operations never come to an end.

[Beginning with three rhyming couplets, the following two paragraphs demonstrate that the cosmos is filled with examples of complementary, yet opposing entities. They conclude from this that various distinctions in human society are not only necessary but fully natural.]

Heaven and Earth face each other.
Sun and moon are in conjunction.
Mountain and valley flow into one another.
Light and heavy float on one another.
Yin and yang succeed one another.
High and low rank do not defile one another.

For this reason, Earth is a pit while Heaven is high. The moon hurries while the sun tarries. The Five Phases each in turn become king. The four seasons are not all strong [at the same time]. The sun gives light to the day, while the moon gives light to the night. The Mane constellation as a rule rises up in winter, while the Fire Star [Antares] declines in summer. North to south are fixed positions set by the poles, while east to west flow the *ch'i* currents. The myriad things are interspersed in their midst.

The Mystery in a single act of virtue creates the Five Productions. In a single act of punishment it creates the Five Conquests. The Five Productions do not cut each other down. The Five Conquests go contrary to each other. That they do not cut each other down is the only reason that they succeed one another. That they do not go contrary to each other is the only reason that they can regulate one another. Succeeding one another provides a model for the way of father to son. Regulating one another provides a model for the treasured relation between ruler and subject.

[The following two paragraphs suggest that the true classic (like the true sage) investigates only the constants, since no useful conclusions can be drawn from anomalies in nature or in human society.]

The *Mystery* records the sun and the direction of the Dipper, but it does not record the moon. It is by the constant and the full that the irregular is ordered. When the Jupiter year [equal to twelve lunar years] is completed, the solar year is off unless for every nineteen years there are seven intercalary months. This is Heaven's Compensation.

Yang is active and exhaling. Yin is quiet and inhaling. The way of yang is constant abundance. The way of yin is constant deficiency. Such is the way of yin and yang. Heaven, being strong and virile, is active and creative. In one night and one day, it makes one complete revolution, with some left over. The sun has [its trip] south and [its trip] north. The moon has its going and coming. If the sun did not move south and north, then there would be no winter and summer. If the moon did not go and come, then the lunar cycle would not be complete. The sage investigates changes in the moon's appearance and location, as well as departures from its orbit. He only finds a norm in the constant sequence of sun and moon, and in the order of male and female. He makes them the canonical model for all eternity. Therefore, the *Mystery* in grand fashion comprises Heaven's Origin, binding and securing it to what is to come.

[The following two paragraphs summarize the mysterious power inherent in the text of the Mystery. *Although the* Mystery *focuses on the constant patterns in the universe, it should not be thought of as prosaic, but divine,*

for the Mystery *teaches us how to extrapolate from the known to the unknown aspects operating in universe.]*

When the great has no borders and change has no set time, only then does it become the gods and ghosts. The gods wander in the Six Exalted Ones (i.e., Heaven, Earth, and the Four Seasons]. Infinite in number are the myriad things; as they move, so are they always pouring out. Hence, we have the phrasing of the *Mystery,* which sinks down to plumb the depths in the lower regions and floats up to reach the highest limits, by turns appearing crooked or straight, dispersed or gathered. So excellent is it that its flavors are never exhausted. So great is it that its types are never exhausted. Joining above, joining below, it does not move in a single direction. Far or near, without a constant rule, it proceeds by categories. Sometimes many and sometimes few, affairs are fitted to what is relatively clear.

Therefore, those who are good at talking about Heaven and Earth use human affairs by way of comparison. As clarity and obscurity push against one other, "sun and moon succeed one another." As year after year jostles one against the other, Heaven and Earth continue to fashion more things. Of it we say, "The gods and spirits go on forever."

Those who seek the origin find it difficult to trace. Those who follow out the branches find it easy to follow. Therefore, those having clans and ancestors are evaluated in terms of filial piety as a rule. And those who would order ruler and minister are evaluated in terms of loyalty as a rule. This is a true revelation and a great teaching.

Index

Index

Index

Kou-mang, 352
ku magic. *See* magic
k'un bird. *See* magical birds
kung ("equitable treatment"/"fairness"), 36,
   115, 152, 242, 244, 321, 338, 344, 365

Laboring (THC80), 339, 340
laissez-faire. See non-purposive activity
language, 186, 251, 353, 363, 369; pattern
   in, 15, 270–72. *See also* rhetoric
Lao tzu, 2–3, 5, 213; cited, 2–3, 44, 47, 49,
   79, 117, 132, 152, 174–75, 233, 247, 255,
   280, 288, 309, 319
law, 76, 114, 124, 182, 188, 248, 260, 291,
   308, 365. *See also* cosmic laws; Legalists;
   punishments
Law (THC40), 339, 341
learning, 83, 183, 226. *See also* education;
   study; teacher
Legalists, 234. *See also* Confucians;
   individual authors by name; just state;
   law; ruler; Yang Hsiung
Legion (THC32), 339, 342
"lessen desires," 254
Lesser Cold solar period, 43, 56
life, defined, 366
"likening to oneself" (*shu*), 2, 18. *See also*
   consideration; reciprocity
Liu ruling clan. *See* Han court
logic. *See* categorical thinking
Logicians, 14, 138, 237
longevity. *See* immortality
Lu, 10
luan. See Magical birds
luck, 129. *See also ming*
lunar lodge (constellation), 55

magic, 314; geomancy, 264; *ku* magic, 303.
   See also exorcism; numerology
magical animals. *See ssu*
magical birds, 168; *k'un* bird, 149–50; *luan*
   and *feng*, 277–78; phoenix, 168, 278;
   wan-ch'u, 280–81
magicians, 196
male/female relations. *See* gender roles
Man (as triadic realm), 24, 182, 185, 216,
   246, 344; partaking of divine, 349; Way
   of, 38, 47, 89, 126, 251, 349, 351, 371.
   See also human nature; Heaven-Earth-
   Man, as triadic realms; Men, Nine Types
   of; noble man; gentleman

Man-ch'eng, 38
Mandate of Heaven. Heaven's Mandate
Mane constellation, 375
mantic formulae, of *Changes*, 362–63, 365,
   366, 369
marriage. *See* family; rites, betrothal/
   marriage
Massing (THC59), 338, 342
Master. *See* Confucius
Mean, 34, 37, 55, 72, 87, 106–7, 126, 131,
   162, 182, 206, 234, 271, 321, 333, 369.
   See also Doctrine of the Mean
Measure (THC52), 338, 341
medicine/medical theory, 51, 88, 105, 111,
   135, 139, 202, 233, 251, 282, 316, 334
Men, Nine Types of, 360
Mencius, 12, 17; cited, 69, 81, 104, 293. *See
   also* just state
merchants, 36, 150, 165, 244, 271, 333. *See
   also* profit
Metal, correlations of, 115, 119, 143, 169,
   354–55; cosmic phase for Appraisals, 48,
   55, 114, 137, 146; cosmic phase for
   Heads, 114, 221, 306. *See also* Five
   Phases, enumeration orders of
metamorphosis, defined, 350
milfoil. *See* divination; yarrow stalks
Milky Way, 320
mind. *See* heart/mind; "unmoved mind";
   Void, as metaphor for mind
ming (Decree), and Virtue, 323; defined,
   323. *See also chih ming*; Confucius; fate
ministers, 17, 231–32; chief, 200, 202, 300.
   See also officials; remonstrance; ruler
Mired (THC3), 337, 341
miser, 251–53
misfortune. *See* good fortune/calamity
Model Sayings (*Fa yen*), 10; cited, 74, 182
Modesty (HEX15), 47
moon, 318; as changeable, 375; movements
   of, 232, 368, 370, 375; symbolism of, 33,
   102, 231, 291
moral choice, 102–3, 249. *See also*
   goodness; Virtue
moral integrity. *See* integrity
mourning rites. *See* rites, mourning
Mt. T'ai, 170
music, 10, 16, 120–22, 187, 271, 321;
   ancient masters of, 348. *See also* pitch
   standards
Musical Notes, 358

Musicmaster Ling-lun, 348
Mutual Conquest Cycle. *See* Five Conquests
Mutual Production Cycle. *See* Five
  Productions
Mysterious Power, 174–75, 302
Mystery, active mode of, 346; approaching
  the, 346; arts of, 347–48; characteristic
  activities of, 342–47, 373; distancing the,
  346; *hsüan* defined, 2–3, 343–44; primal
  state of, 30, 342–43; quiescent mode of,
  346; Way of the, 344, 346, 373. *See also*
  Canon of Supreme Mystery; cosmogonic
  stages; Tao; utility, Mystery as ultimate
  in; Way
Mystery Palace, 279
Mystery Springs, 335. *See also* Yellow
  Springs

names. *See* "rectification of names"
nature and Decree (*hsing ming*), 32, 343,
  364. *See also* human nature; *ming*
neo-Confucianism, 12
Nine Affairs, 361
Nine Apertures, 361
Nine Arrows, 219
Nine Barbarians, 205–6
Nine Body Parts, 360
Nine Cauldrons, 199, 201
Nine Conferrals, 219
Nine Courses, 371
Nine Decades, 361
Nine Districts, 345
Nine Dwellings, 374
Nine Earths, 360
Nine Empty Positions, 347, 372, 374
Nine Grades of Relations, 361
Nine Heavens, 360
Nine Orders, 361
Nine Positions. *See* Nine Empty Positions
Nine Provinces of China, 308, 369
Nine Sites, 371, 374
Nine Tripods. *See* Nine Cauldrons
Nine Types of Men, 360
"no gap," 156–57, 328, 339. *See also*
  harmony
nobility, defined, 16–17, 87, 178, 295
noble man, 243, 276; as godlike, 363;
  imitating Tao, 175, 309, 363; vs. petty
  man, 113, 120, 125, 145–46, 166, 169,
  190, 212–13, 226, 266, 271, 277, 280,
  296, 339, 345, 365, 373. *See also*

gentleman; nobility
non-purposive activity (*wu wei*), 37, 110,
  132
Numbers of the Mystery (*Hsüan shu*), 8, 9,
  14, 23, 367
Numen Pool, 286–87
numerology, 50, 137, 186, 347, 367, 372;
  correlations of, 351–58

Odd (intercalary App.),335
Odes, 10, 17; cited, 57–58, 62, 120, 127,
  142, 160, 161, 163, 211
officials, 17, 58, 259, 288, 316; assigned to
  App. 4, 57, 65, 142, 146, 175, 183, 205;
  in/near retirement, 119. *See also* bureaucratic selection; career advancement;
  ministers; patronage; remonstrance; ruler
  old age/aging, 17, 65–66, 75, 123, 180, 190,
  257, 262, 277, 284, 285, 318, 330, 339;
  App. 7 symbolizes, 65, 285; virtue in, 66,
  119, 365
omens. *See* portents
On the Verge (THC78), 339, 340
oneness, 51, 82–83, 342; primal, 230, 363,
  365. *See also chih yi*; cosmogonic stages;
  duality
onesidedness, 82, 84, 243, 245. *See also*
  goodness, as impartial
Opposition (THC8), 337, 340
order, 366; divine cosmic, 23, 51, 55, 195,
  283, 351; integrated, 212; social, 44, 51–
  52, 128, 172, 212, 244–45, 248, 251

Packing (THC31), 195, 339, 342
Pandora's box, 105
Pao Hsi (Fu Hsi), 172, 348–49
parent. *See* family
patrilineal line of descent, 178, 181, 231,
  238, 279–80, 283–85, 321. *See also*
  family; gender
patronage, 107, 214
pattern (*wen*), 55, 181–82, 349–51, 355; as
  eternal constant, 55, 187, 189; cosmic/in
  Nature, 13, 29, 36, 38, 88, 104, 172, 185,
  187, 195, 203, 212, 230, 238, 244, 305,
  369; cultural, 211–12, 214; divine
  derivation of, 110, 214, 236, 305; Heaven
  as constant, 38, 212, 258, 327, 363, 369;
  moral, 104, 211; opposed to plain, 211–
  12, 214, 270, 337, 362; seasonal, 230;
  societal, 104, 108, 185, 211, 345, 351.